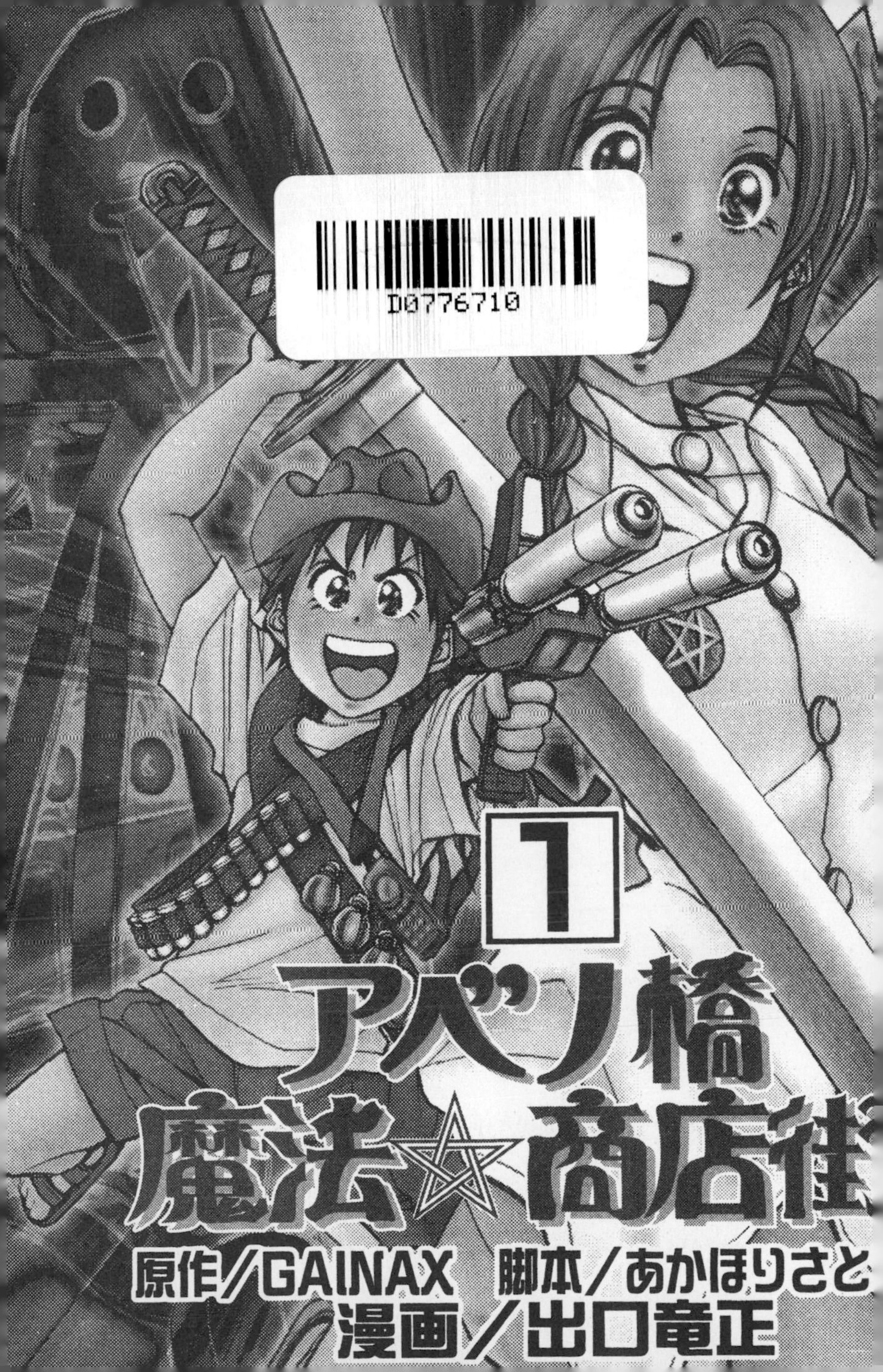
1
アベノ橋
魔法☆商店街
原作／GAINAX　脚本／あかほりさとる
漫画／出口竜正

ABENOBASHI
MAGICAL SHOPPING ARCADE

VOLUME ONE

CREATED BY
GAINAX

WRITTEN BY
SATORU AKAHORI

ILLUSTRATED BY
RYUSEI DEGUCHI

TOKYOPOP®

HAMBURG // LONDON // LOS ANGELES // TOKYO

Abenobashi: Magical Shopping Arcade Vol. 1
Created by GAINAX
Written by Satoru Akahori
Illustrated by Ryusei Deguchi

Translation - Beni Axia Hirayama
English Adaptation - Jamie S. Rich
Copy Editor - Hope Donovan
Retouch and Lettering - Abelardo Bigting,
Yoohae Yang and Haruko Furukawa
Production Artists - John Lo and James Dashiell
Cover Design - Raymond Makowski

Editor - Paul Morrissey
Digital Imaging Manager - Chris Buford
Pre-Press Manager - Antonio DePietro
Production Managers - Jennifer Miller and Mutsumi Miyazaki
Art Director - Matt Alford
Managing Editor - Jill Freshney
VP of Production - Ron Klamert
President and C.O.O. - John Parker
Publisher and C.E.O. - Stuart Levy

A  Manga

TOKYOPOP Inc.
5900 Wilshire Blvd. Suite 2000
Los Angeles, CA 90036

E-mail: info@TOKYOPOP.com
Come visit us online at www.TOKYOPOP.com

ISBN: 1-59182-790-6

First TOKYOPOP printing: August 2004
10 9 8 7 6 5 4 3 2 1
Printed in the USA

CONTENTS

ABEN★BASHI
MAGICAL SHOPPING ARCADE

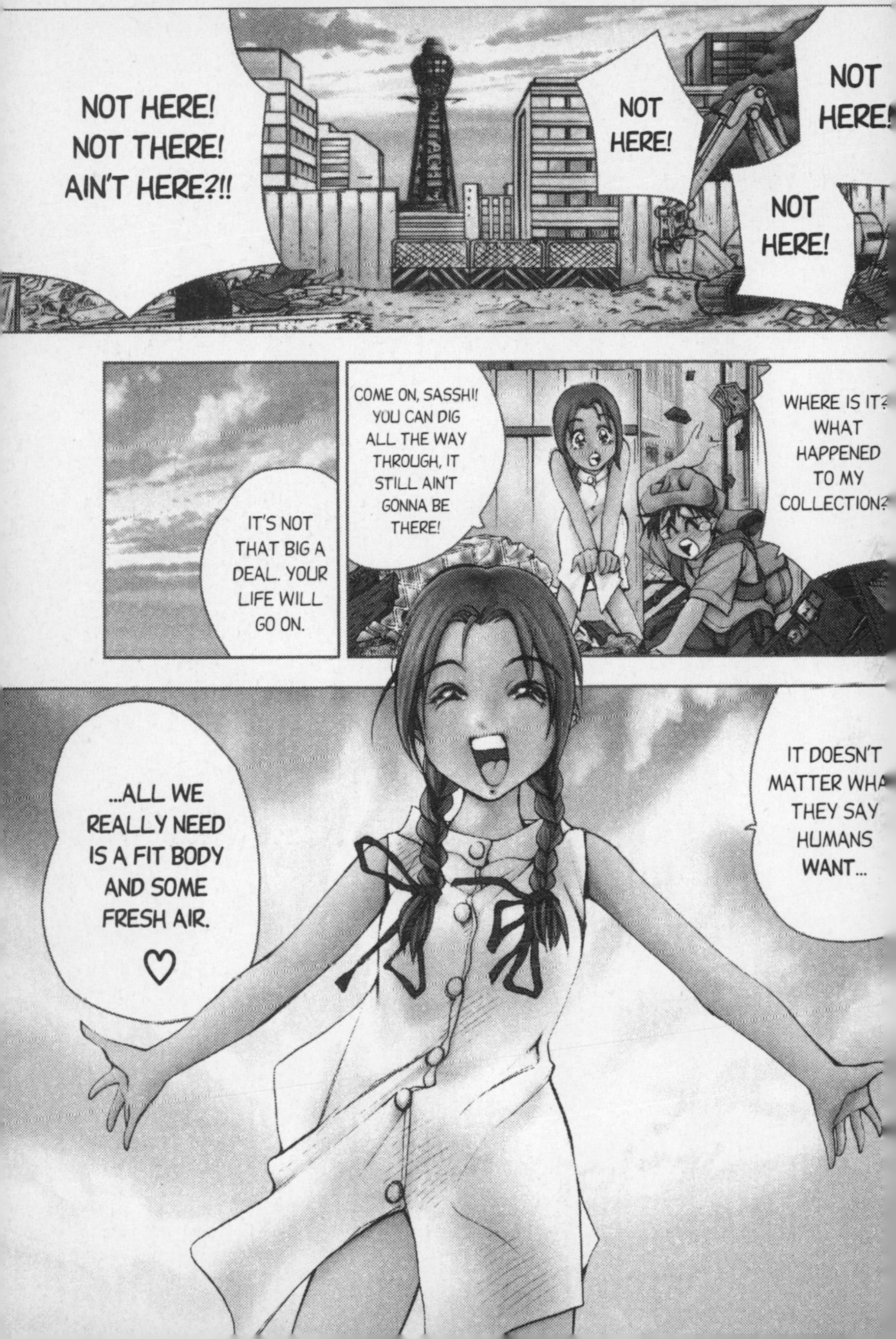
NOT HERE
NOT HERE!
NOT HERE!
NOT HERE! NOT THERE! AIN'T HERE?!!
WHERE IS IT? WHAT HAPPENED TO MY COLLECTION?
COME ON, SASSHI! YOU CAN DIG ALL THE WAY THROUGH, IT STILL AIN'T GONNA BE THERE!
IT'S NOT THAT BIG A DEAL. YOUR LIFE WILL GO ON.
IT DOESN'T MATTER WHA THEY SAY HUMANS WANT...
...ALL WE REALLY NEED IS A FIT BODY AND SOME FRESH AIR. ♡

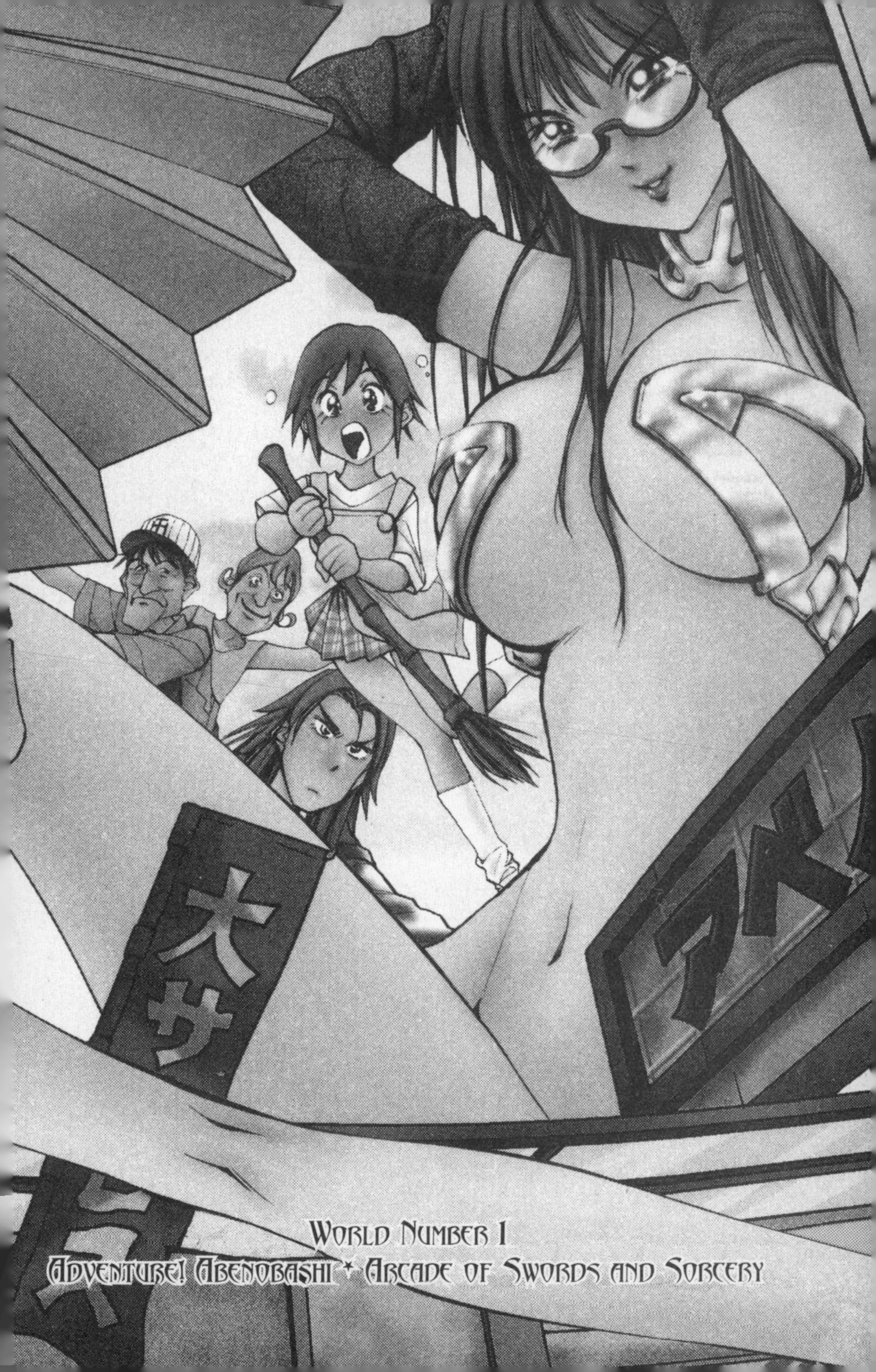

World Number 1
Adventure! Abenobashi ✦ Arcade of Swords and Sorcery

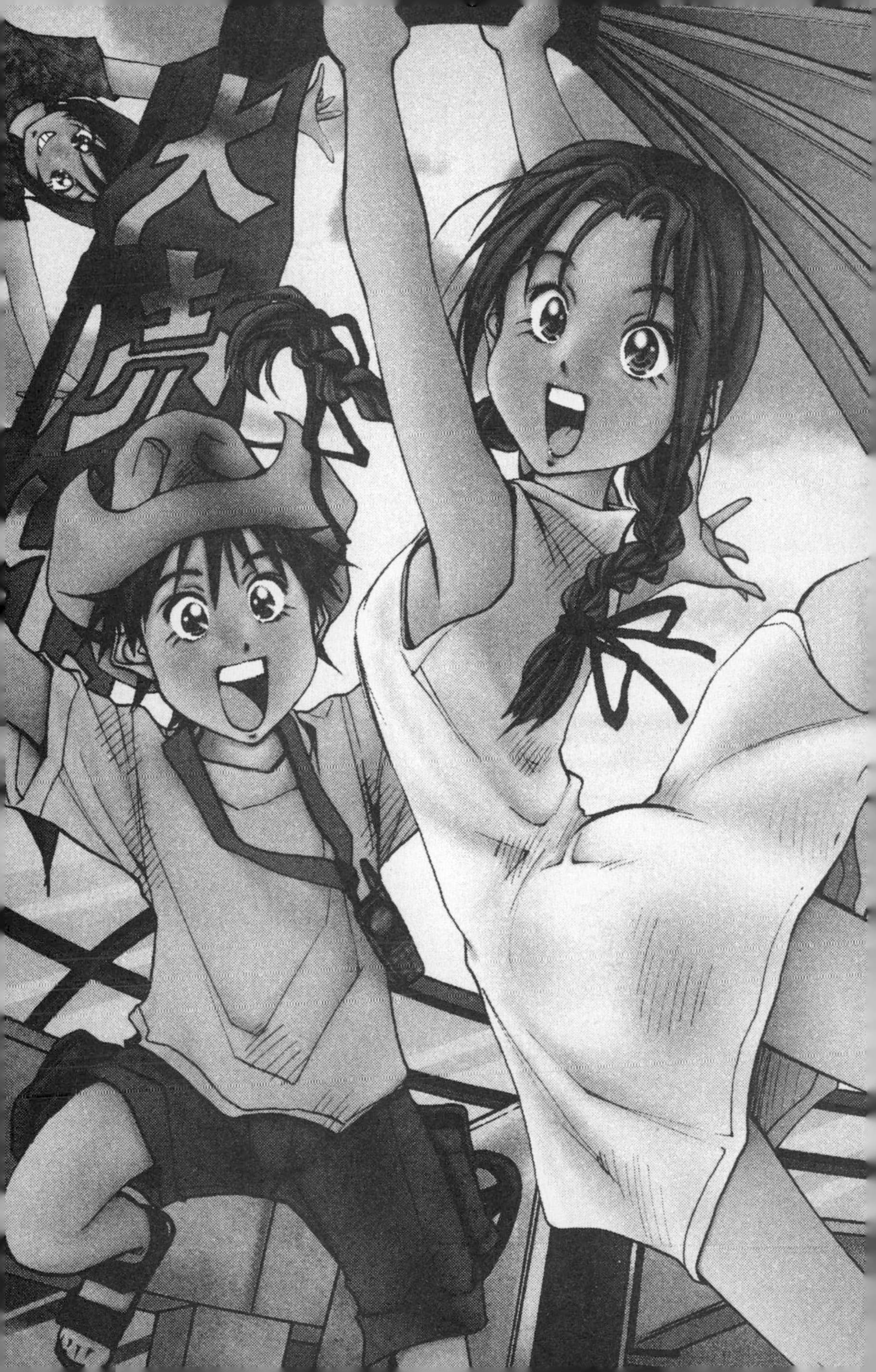

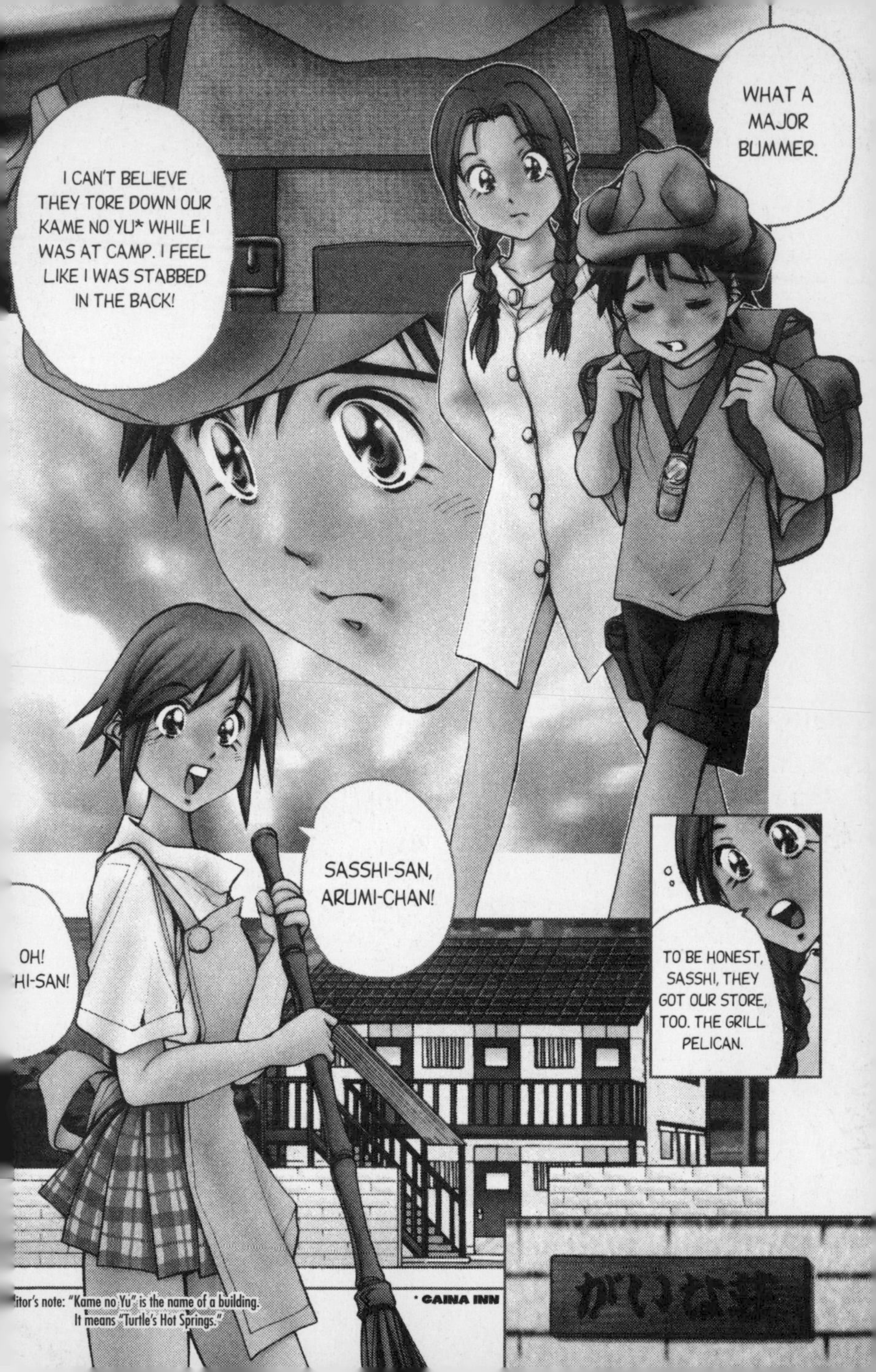
WHAT A MAJOR BUMMER.
I CAN'T BELIEVE THEY TORE DOWN OUR KAME NO YU* WHILE I WAS AT CAMP. I FEEL LIKE I WAS STABBED IN THE BACK!
TO BE HONEST, SASSHI, THEY GOT OUR STORE, TOO. THE GRILL PELICAN.
SASSHI-SAN, ARUMI-CHAN!
OH! HI-SAN!
* GAINA INN
itor's note: "Kame no Yu" is the name of a building. It means "Turtle's Hot Springs."

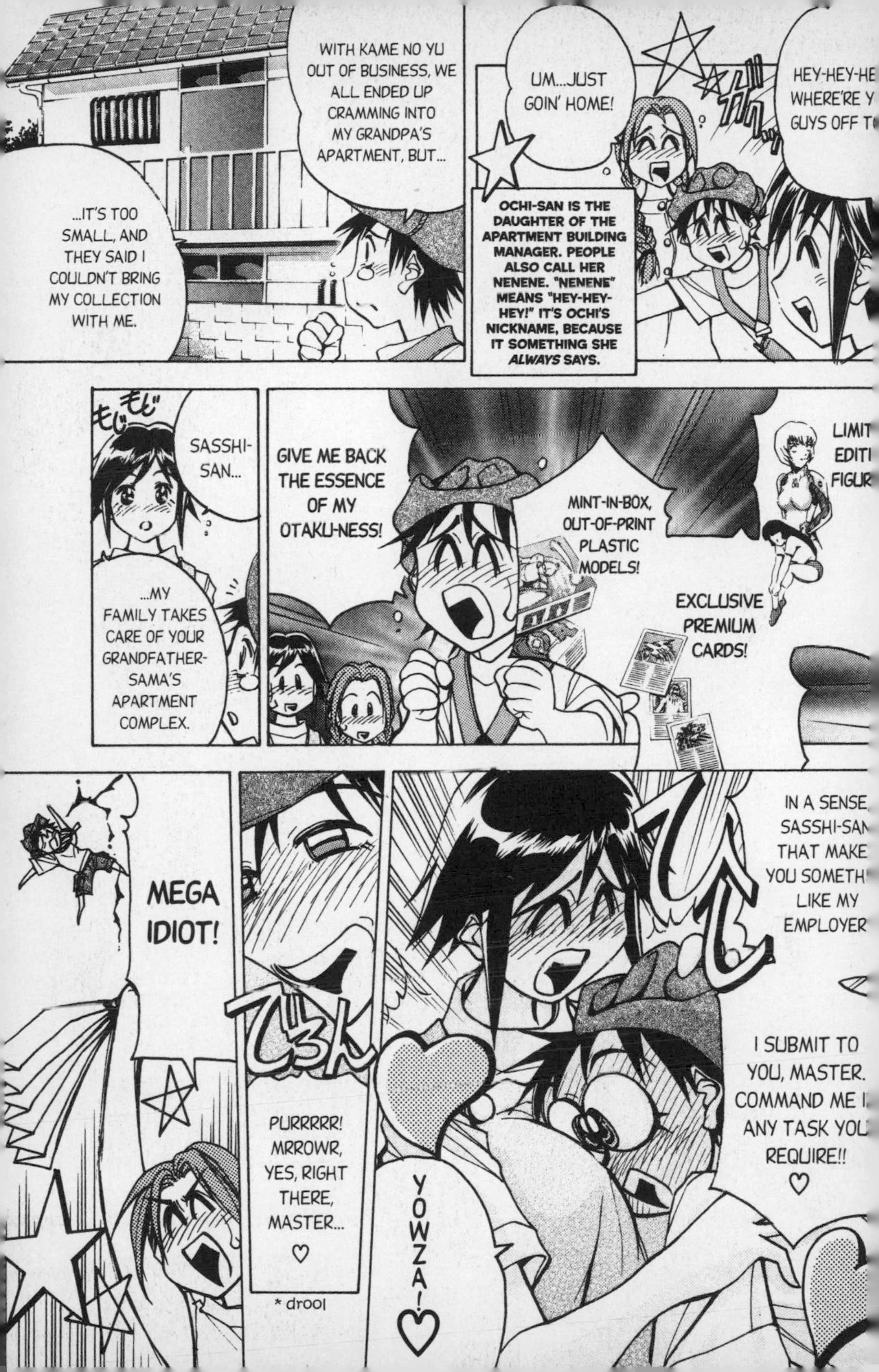
HEY-HEY-HE WHERE'RE Y GUYS OFF T
UM...JUST GOIN' HOME!
OCHI-SAN IS THE DAUGHTER OF THE APARTMENT BUILDING MANAGER. PEOPLE ALSO CALL HER NENENE. "NENENE" MEANS "HEY-HEY-HEY!" IT'S OCHI'S NICKNAME, BECAUSE IT SOMETHING SHE *ALWAYS* SAYS.
WITH KAME NO YU OUT OF BUSINESS, WE ALL ENDED UP CRAMMING INTO MY GRANDPA'S APARTMENT, BUT...
...IT'S TOO SMALL, AND THEY SAID I COULDN'T BRING MY COLLECTION WITH ME.
LIMIT EDITI FIGUR
MINT-IN-BOX, OUT-OF-PRINT PLASTIC MODELS!
GIVE ME BACK THE ESSENCE OF MY OTAKU-NESS!
EXCLUSIVE PREMIUM CARDS!
SASSHI-SAN...
...MY FAMILY TAKES CARE OF YOUR GRANDFATHER-SAMA'S APARTMENT COMPLEX.
IN A SENSE, SASSHI-SAN THAT MAKE YOU SOMETH LIKE MY EMPLOYER
I SUBMIT TO YOU, MASTER. COMMAND ME I ANY TASK YOU REQUIRE!! ♡
YOWZA! ♡
PURRRRR! MRROWR, YES, RIGHT THERE, MASTER... ♡
* drool
MEGA IDIOT!

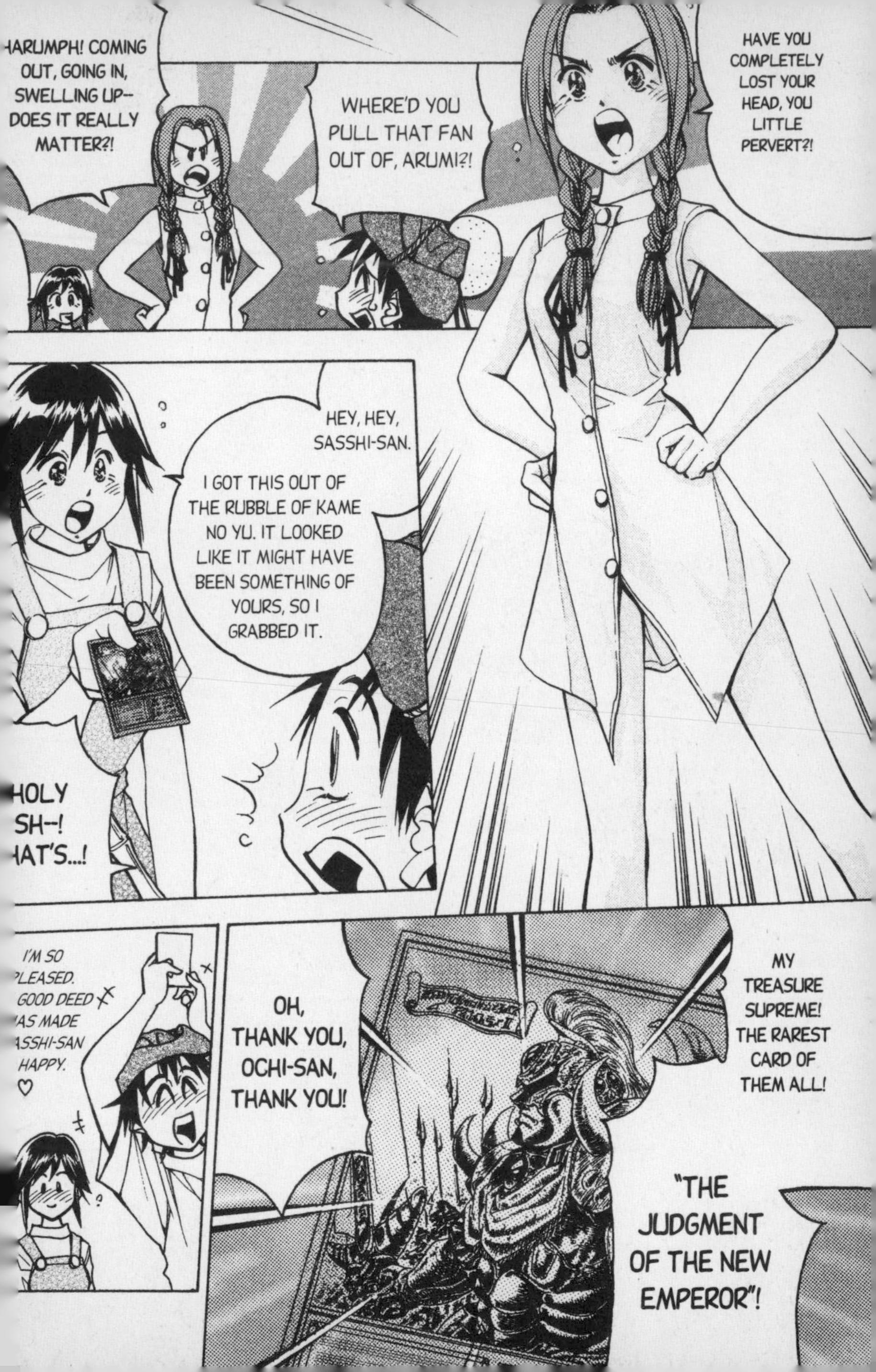
HAVE YOU COMPLETELY LOST YOUR HEAD, YOU LITTLE PERVERT?!
WHERE'D YOU PULL THAT FAN OUT OF, ARUMI?!
HARUMPH! COMING OUT, GOING IN, SWELLING UP-- DOES IT REALLY MATTER?!
HEY, HEY, SASSHI-SAN.
I GOT THIS OUT OF THE RUBBLE OF KAME NO YU. IT LOOKED LIKE IT MIGHT HAVE BEEN SOMETHING OF YOURS, SO I GRABBED IT.
HOLY SH--! HAT'S...!
MY TREASURE SUPREME! THE RAREST CARD OF THEM ALL!
OH, THANK YOU, OCHI-SAN, THANK YOU!
"THE JUDGMENT OF THE NEW EMPEROR"!
I'M SO PLEASED. GOOD DEED HAS MADE ASSHI-SAN HAPPY. ♡

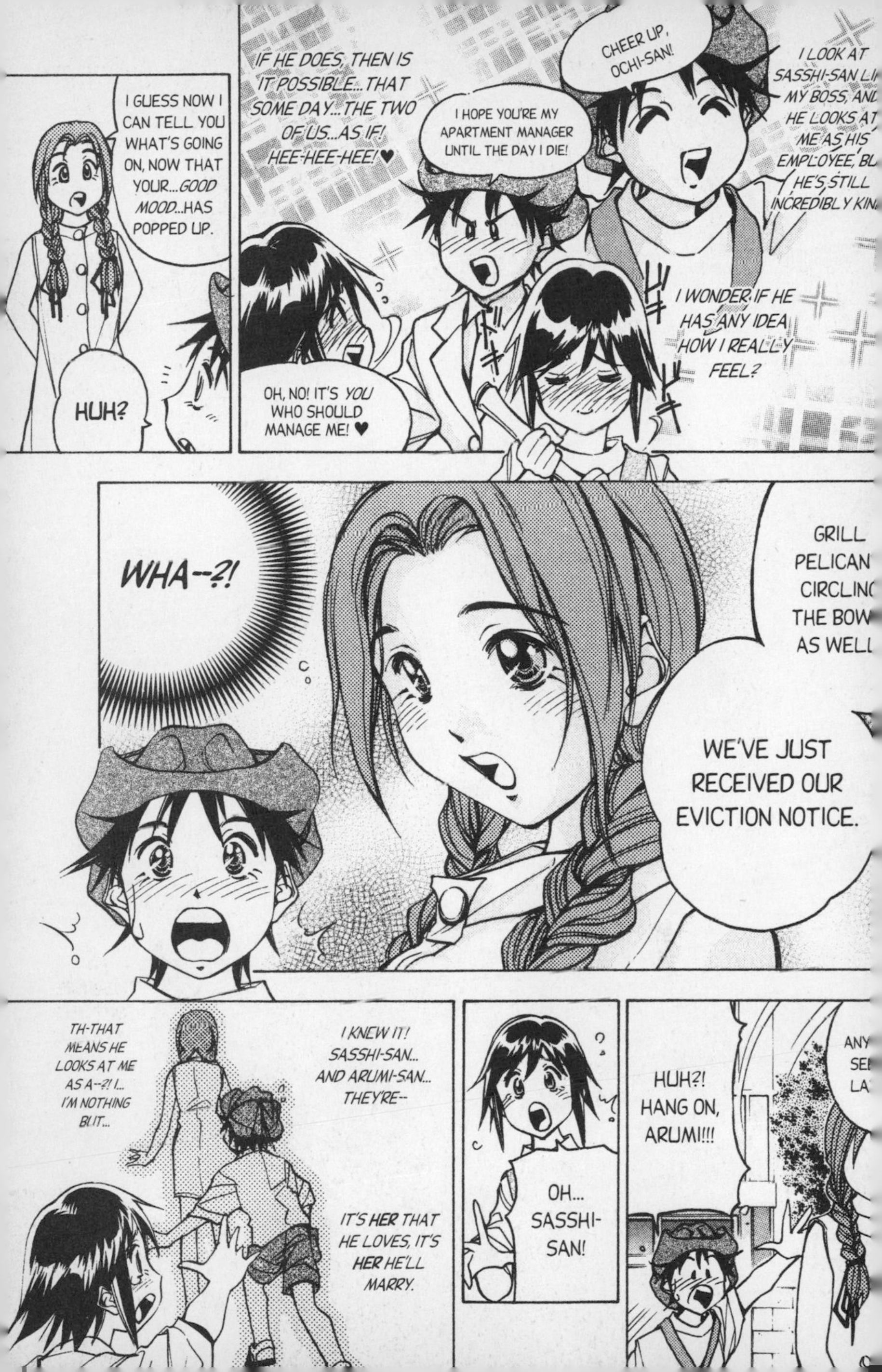
I LOOK AT SASSHI-SAN LI MY BOSS, AND HE LOOKS AT ME AS HIS EMPLOYEE, BU HE'S STILL INCREDIBLY KIN
CHEER UP, OCHI-SAN!
I HOPE YOU'RE MY APARTMENT MANAGER UNTIL THE DAY I DIE!
IF HE DOES, THEN IS IT POSSIBLE... THAT SOME DAY... THE TWO OF US... AS IF! HEE-HEE-HEE! ♥
I WONDER IF HE HAS ANY IDEA HOW I REALLY FEEL?
OH, NO! IT'S YOU WHO SHOULD MANAGE ME! ♥
I GUESS NOW I CAN TELL YOU WHAT'S GOING ON, NOW THAT YOUR... GOOD MOOD... HAS POPPED UP.
HUH?
GRILL PELICAN CIRCLIN THE BOW AS WELL
WE'VE JUST RECEIVED OUR EVICTION NOTICE.
WHA--?!
ANY SE LA
HUH?! HANG ON, ARUMI!!!
OH... SASSHI-SAN!
I KNEW IT! SASSHI-SAN... AND ARUMI-SAN... THEY'RE--
TH-THAT MEANS HE LOOKS AT ME AS A--?! I... I'M NOTHING BUT...
IT'S HER THAT HE LOVES, IT'S HER HE'LL MARRY.

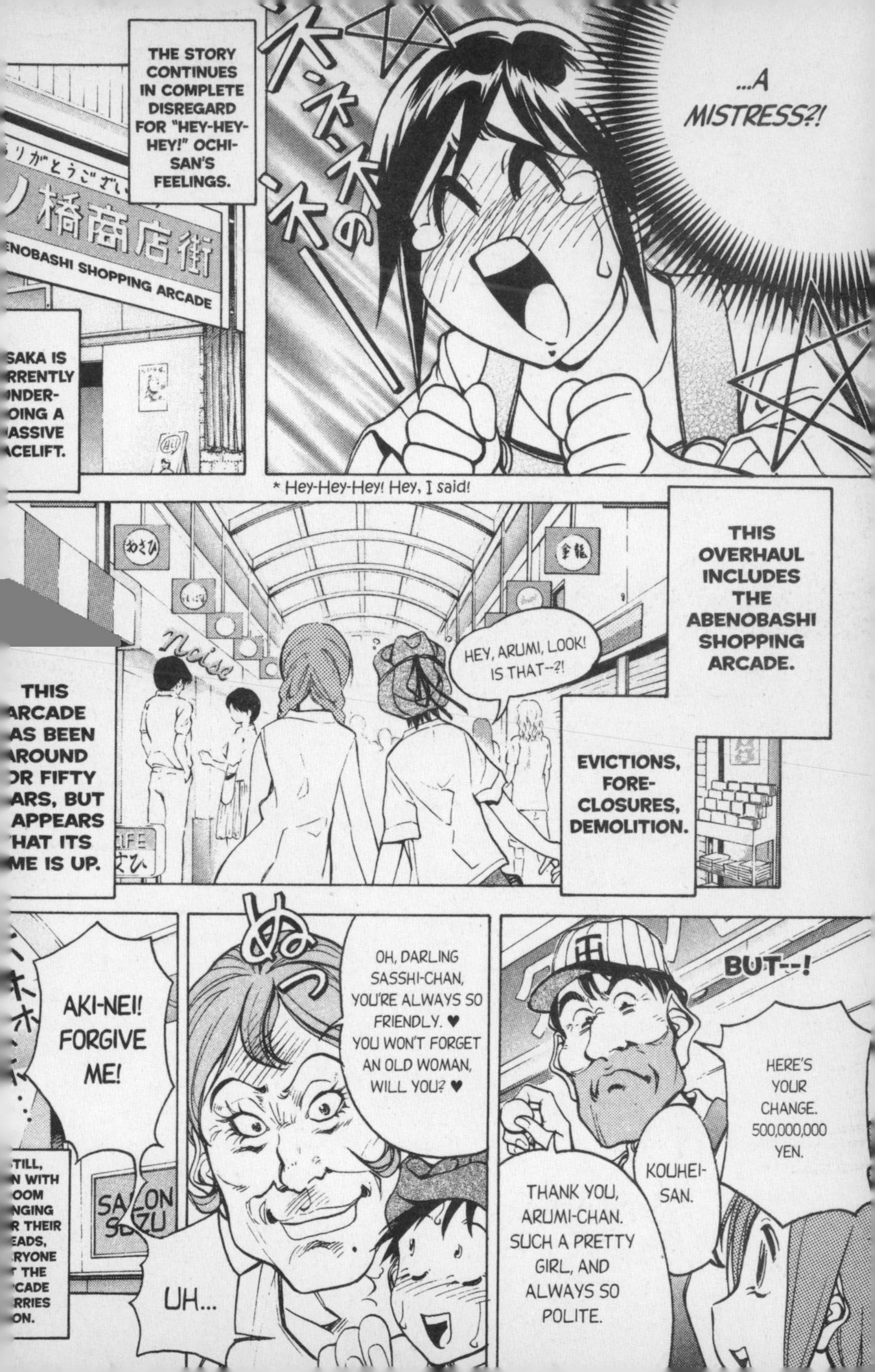
...A MISTRESS?!
THE STORY CONTINUES IN COMPLETE DISREGARD FOR "HEY-HEY-HEY!" OCHI-SAN'S FEELINGS.
ENOBASHI SHOPPING ARCADE
SAKA IS RRENTLY UNDER-OING A ASSIVE ACELIFT.
THIS OVERHAUL INCLUDES THE ABENOBASHI SHOPPING ARCADE.
EVICTIONS, FORE-CLOSURES, DEMOLITION.
HEY, ARUMI, LOOK! IS THAT--?!
THIS ARCADE AS BEEN AROUND OR FIFTY ARS, BUT APPEARS THAT ITS ME IS UP.
BUT--!
HERE'S YOUR CHANGE. 500,000,000 YEN.
KOUHEI-SAN.
THANK YOU, ARUMI-CHAN. SUCH A PRETTY GIRL, AND ALWAYS SO POLITE.
OH, DARLING SASSHI-CHAN, YOU'RE ALWAYS SO FRIENDLY. ♥ YOU WON'T FORGET AN OLD WOMAN, WILL YOU? ♥
UH...
AKI-NEI! FORGIVE ME!
STILL, N WITH OOM NGING R THEIR EADS, RYONE T THE CADE RRIES ON.

* Hey-Hey-Hey! Hey, I said!

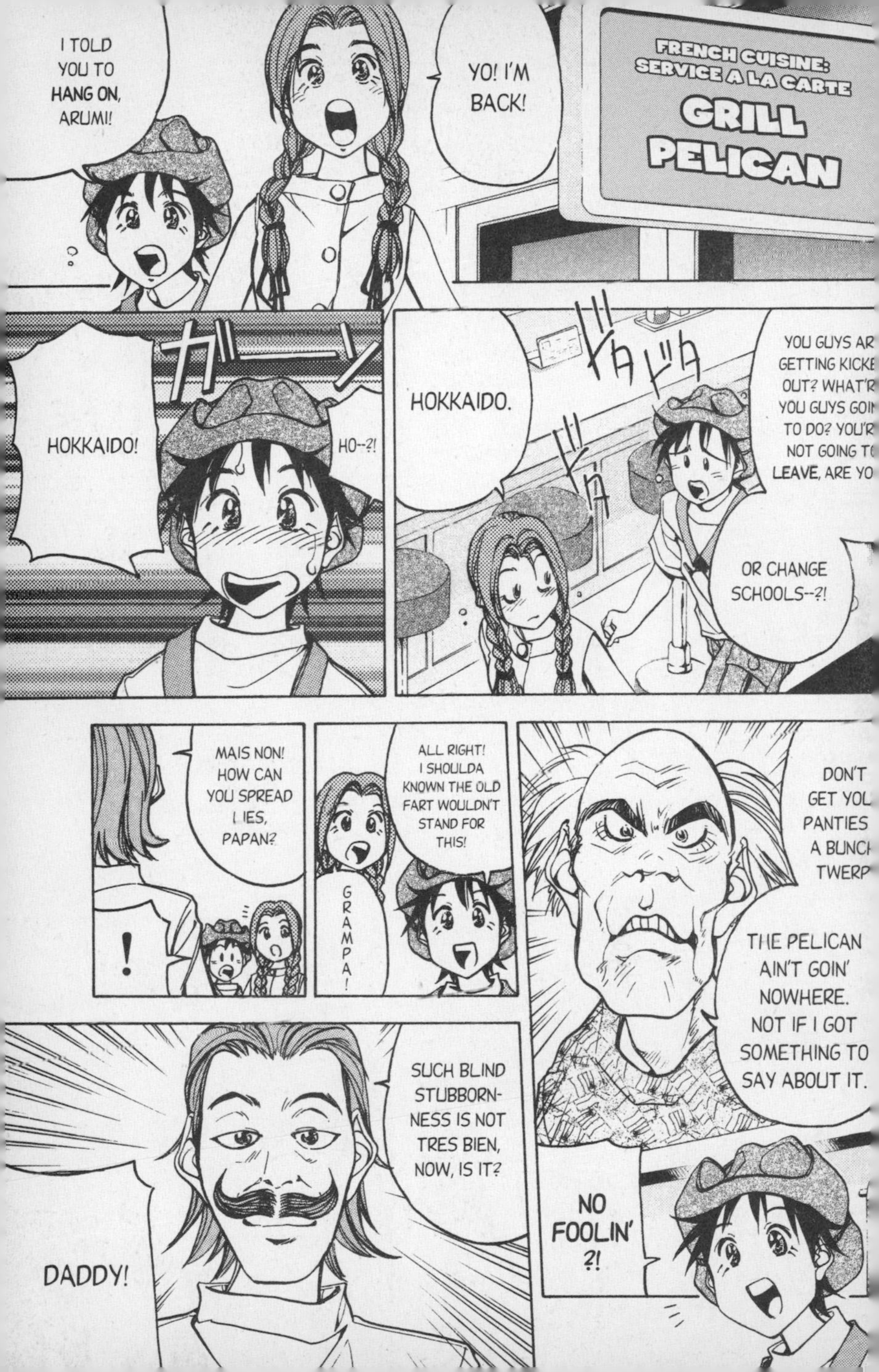
FRENCH CUISINE: SERVICE A LA CARTE
GRILL PELICAN
YO! I'M BACK!
I TOLD YOU TO HANG ON, ARUMI!
ドタドタ
YOU GUYS AR GETTING KICKE OUT? WHAT'R YOU GUYS GOIN TO DO? YOU'R NOT GOING T LEAVE, ARE YO
OR CHANGE SCHOOLS--?!
HOKKAIDO.
ガーン
HO--?!
HOKKAIDO!
DON'T GET YOU PANTIES A BUNCH TWERP
THE PELICAN AIN'T GOIN' NOWHERE. NOT IF I GOT SOMETHING TO SAY ABOUT IT.
ALL RIGHT! I SHOULDA KNOWN THE OLD FART WOULDN'T STAND FOR THIS!
GRAMPA!
MAIS NON! HOW CAN YOU SPREAD LIES, PAPAN?
!
NO FOOLIN' ?!
SUCH BLIND STUBBORN-NESS IS NOT TRES BIEN, NOW, IS IT?
DADDY!

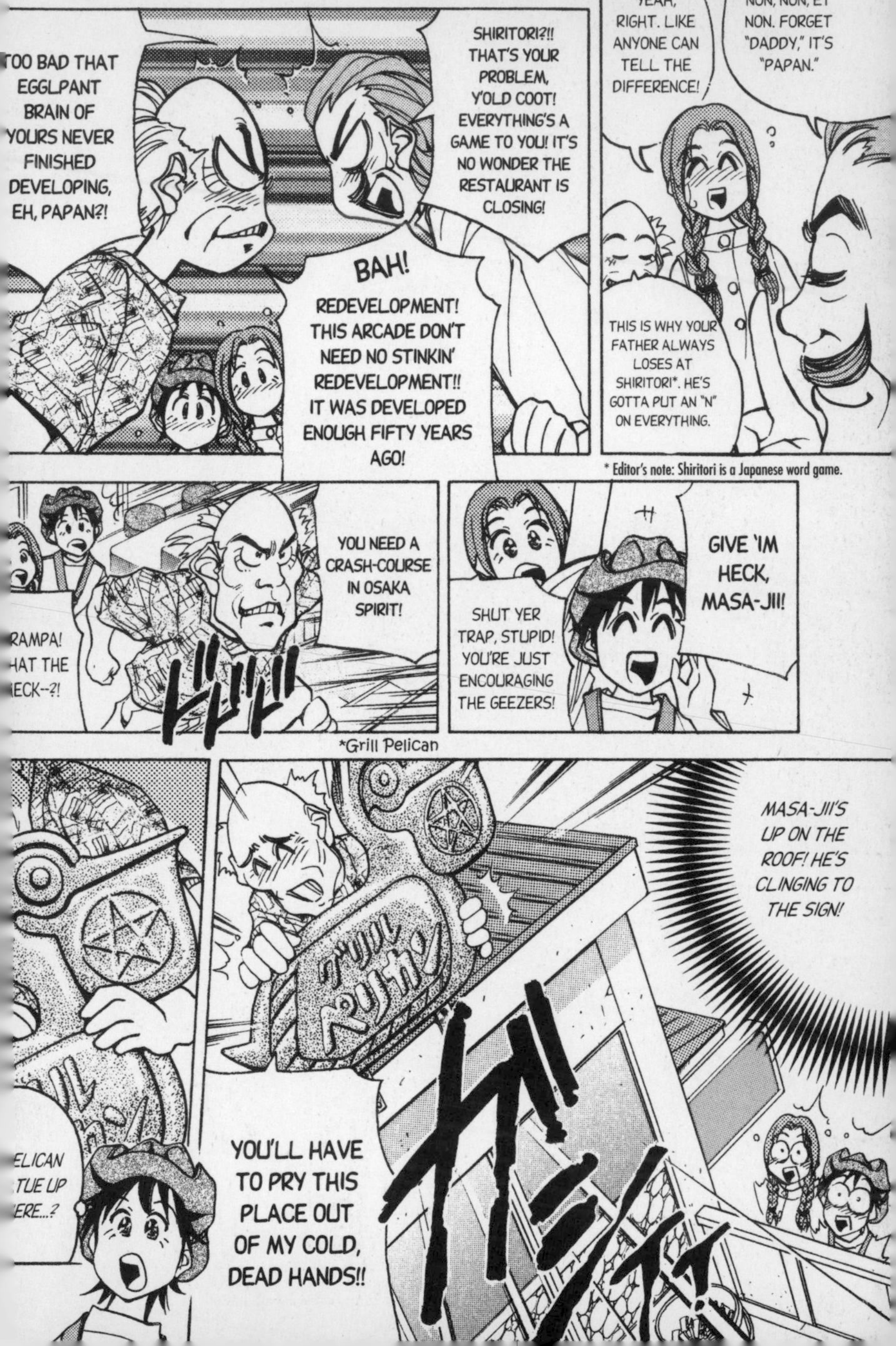
NON, NON, ET NON. FORGET "DADDY," IT'S "PAPAN."
YEAH, RIGHT. LIKE ANYONE CAN TELL THE DIFFERENCE!
THIS IS WHY YOUR FATHER ALWAYS LOSES AT SHIRITORI*. HE'S GOTTA PUT AN "N" ON EVERYTHING.
SHIRITORI?!! THAT'S YOUR PROBLEM, Y'OLD COOT! EVERYTHING'S A GAME TO YOU! IT'S NO WONDER THE RESTAURANT IS CLOSING!
BAH! REDEVELOPMENT! THIS ARCADE DON'T NEED NO STINKIN' REDEVELOPMENT!! IT WAS DEVELOPED ENOUGH FIFTY YEARS AGO!
TOO BAD THAT EGGLPANT BRAIN OF YOURS NEVER FINISHED DEVELOPING, EH, PAPAN?!
GIVE 'IM HECK, MASA-JII!
SHUT YER TRAP, STUPID! YOU'RE JUST ENCOURAGING THE GEEZERS!
YOU NEED A CRASH-COURSE IN OSAKA SPIRIT!
RAMPA! HAT THE ECK--?!
MASA-JII'S UP ON THE ROOF! HE'S CLINGING TO THE SIGN!
YOU'LL HAVE TO PRY THIS PLACE OUT OF MY COLD, DEAD HANDS!!
ELICAN TUE UP ERE...?

* Editor's note: Shiritori is a Japanese word game.

*Grill Pelican

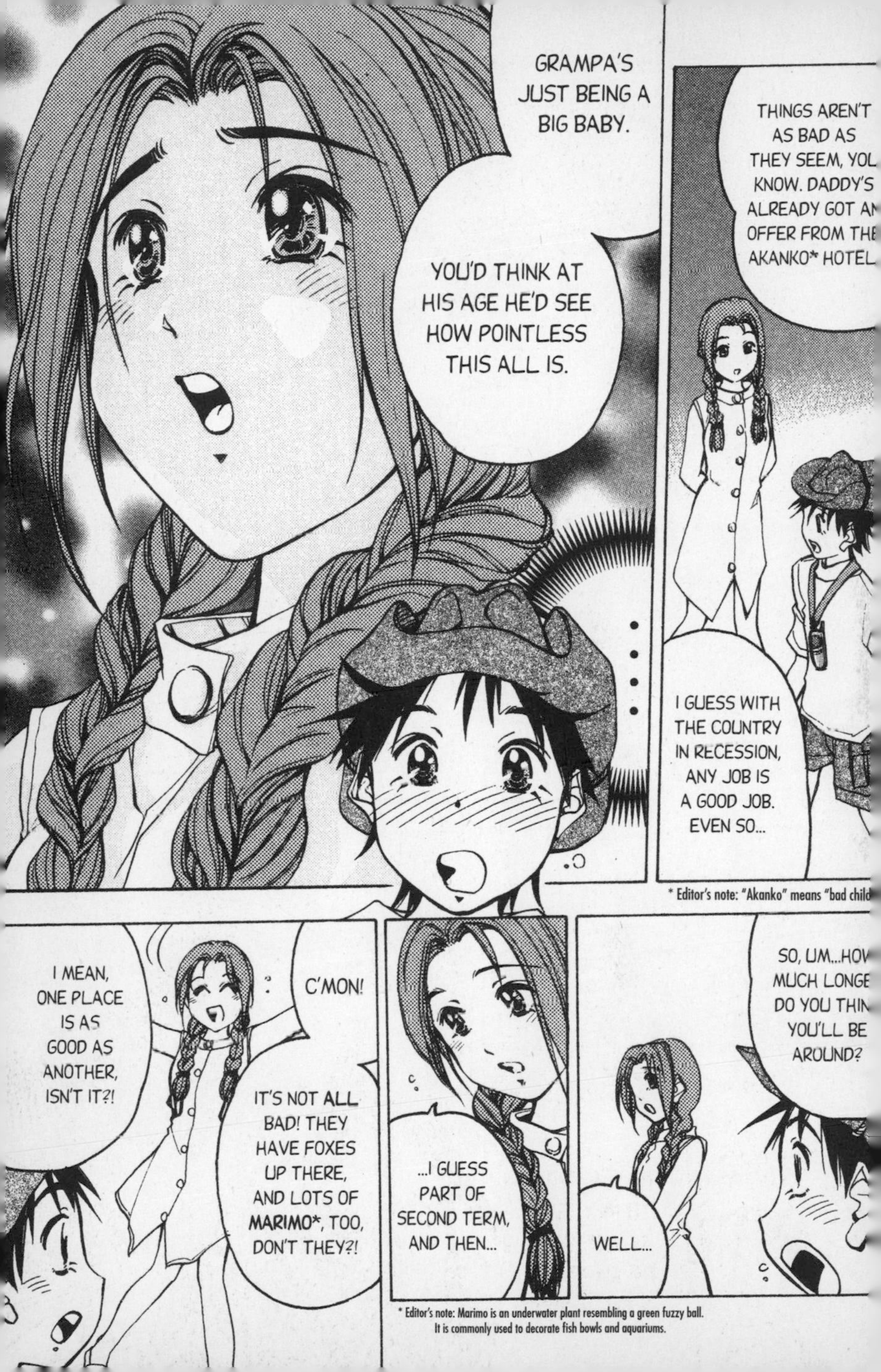
THINGS AREN'T AS BAD AS THEY SEEM, YO KNOW. DADDY'S ALREADY GOT A OFFER FROM TH AKANKO* HOTEL.
I GUESS WITH THE COUNTRY IN RECESSION, ANY JOB IS A GOOD JOB. EVEN SO...
GRAMPA'S JUST BEING A BIG BABY.
YOU'D THINK AT HIS AGE HE'D SEE HOW POINTLESS THIS ALL IS.
SO, UM...HO MUCH LONGE DO YOU THIN YOU'LL BE AROUND?
WELL...
...I GUESS PART OF SECOND TERM, AND THEN...
C'MON!
I MEAN, ONE PLACE IS AS GOOD AS ANOTHER, ISN'T IT?!
IT'S NOT ALL BAD! THEY HAVE FOXES UP THERE, AND LOTS OF MARIMO*, TOO, DON'T THEY?!

* Editor's note: "Akanko" means "bad child

* Editor's note: Marimo is an underwater plant resembling a green fuzzy ball. It is commonly used to decorate fish bowls and aquariums.

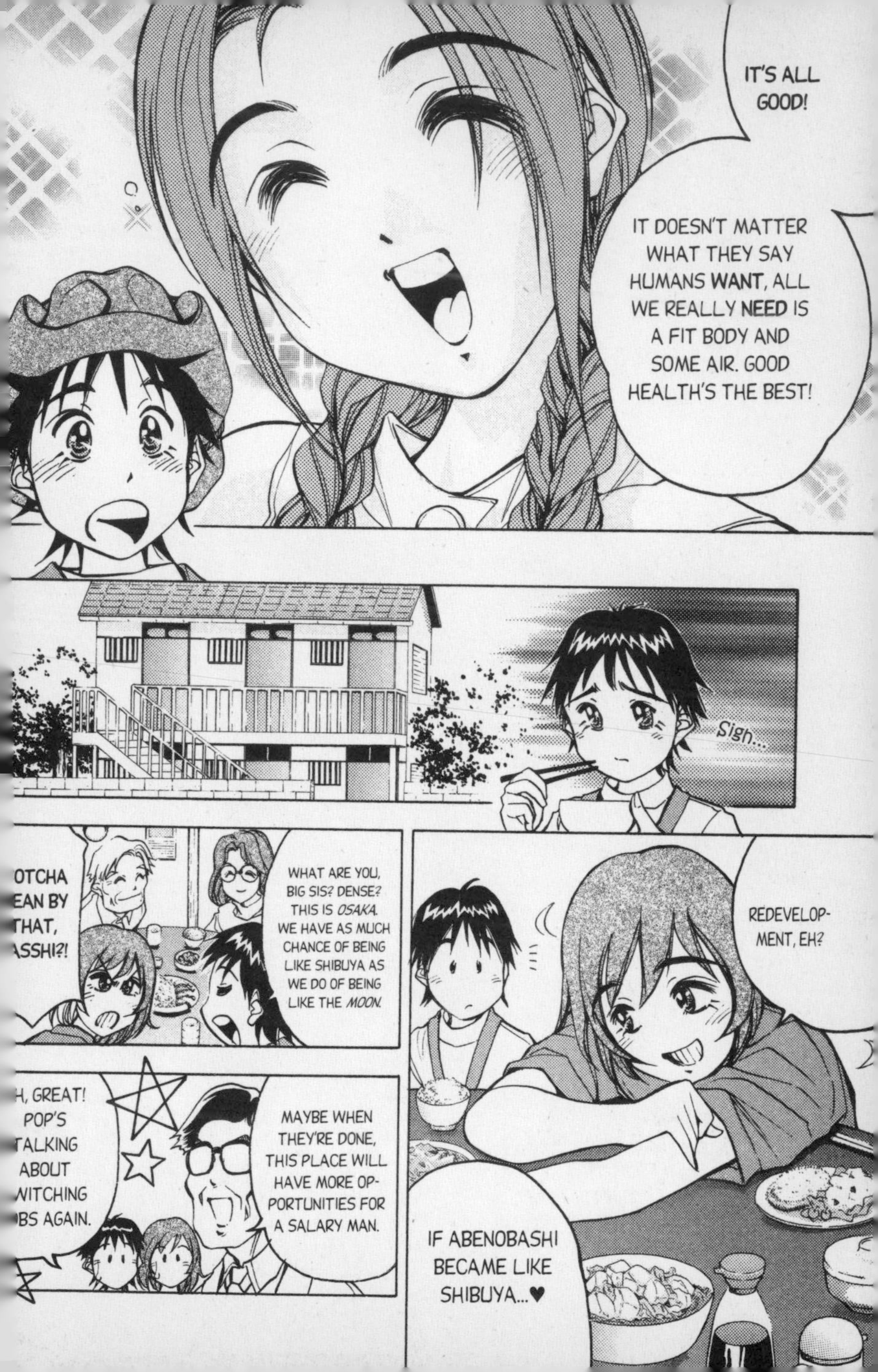
IT'S ALL GOOD!
IT DOESN'T MATTER WHAT THEY SAY HUMANS WANT, ALL WE REALLY NEED IS A FIT BODY AND SOME AIR. GOOD HEALTH'S THE BEST!
Sigh...
REDEVELOP-MENT, EH?
IF ABENOBASHI BECAME LIKE SHIBUYA...♥
WHAT ARE YOU, BIG SIS? DENSE? THIS IS OSAKA. WE HAVE AS MUCH CHANCE OF BEING LIKE SHIBUYA AS WE DO OF BEING LIKE THE MOON.
OTCHA EAN BY THAT, ASSHI?!
MAYBE WHEN THEY'RE DONE, THIS PLACE WILL HAVE MORE OP-PORTUNITIES FOR A SALARY MAN.
H, GREAT! POP'S TALKING ABOUT WITCHING OBS AGAIN.

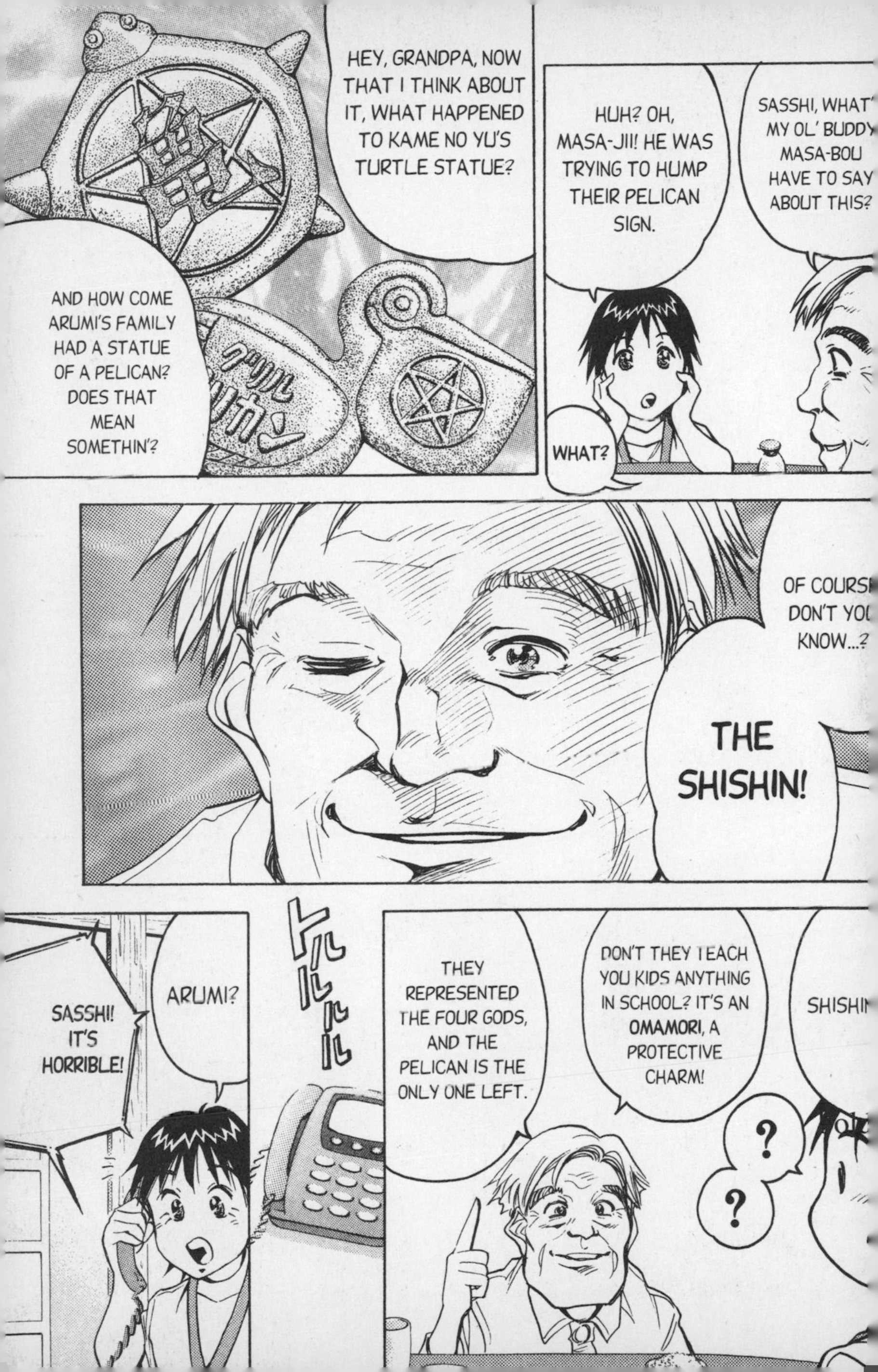
SASSHI, WHAT' MY OL' BUDDY MASA-BOU HAVE TO SAY ABOUT THIS?
HUH? OH, MASA-JII! HE WAS TRYING TO HUMP THEIR PELICAN SIGN.
WHAT?
HEY, GRANDPA, NOW THAT I THINK ABOUT IT, WHAT HAPPENED TO KAME NO YU'S TURTLE STATUE?
AND HOW COME ARUMI'S FAMILY HAD A STATUE OF A PELICAN? DOES THAT MEAN SOMETHIN'?
OF COURS DON'T YO KNOW...?
THE SHISHIN!
SHISHI
?
?
DON'T THEY TEACH YOU KIDS ANYTHING IN SCHOOL? IT'S AN **OMAMORI**, A PROTECTIVE CHARM!
THEY REPRESENTED THE FOUR GODS, AND THE PELICAN IS THE ONLY ONE LEFT.
トルルルル
ARUMI?
SASSHI! IT'S HORRIBLE!

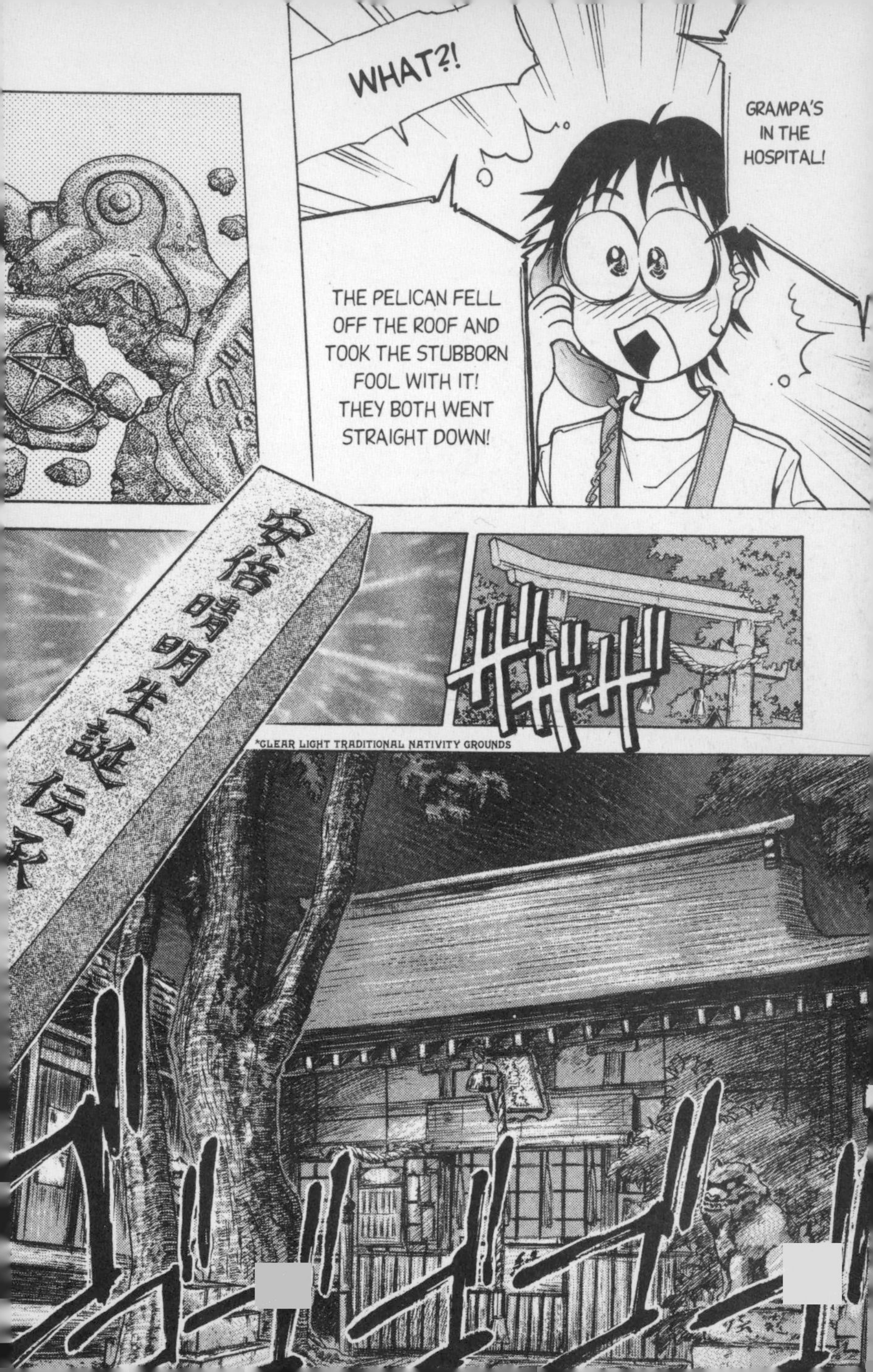
GRAMPA'S IN THE HOSPITAL!
WHAT?!
THE PELICAN FELL OFF THE ROOF AND TOOK THE STUBBORN FOOL WITH IT! THEY BOTH WENT STRAIGHT DOWN!
安倍晴明生誕伝
*CLEAR LIGHT TRADITIONAL NATIVITY GROUNDS

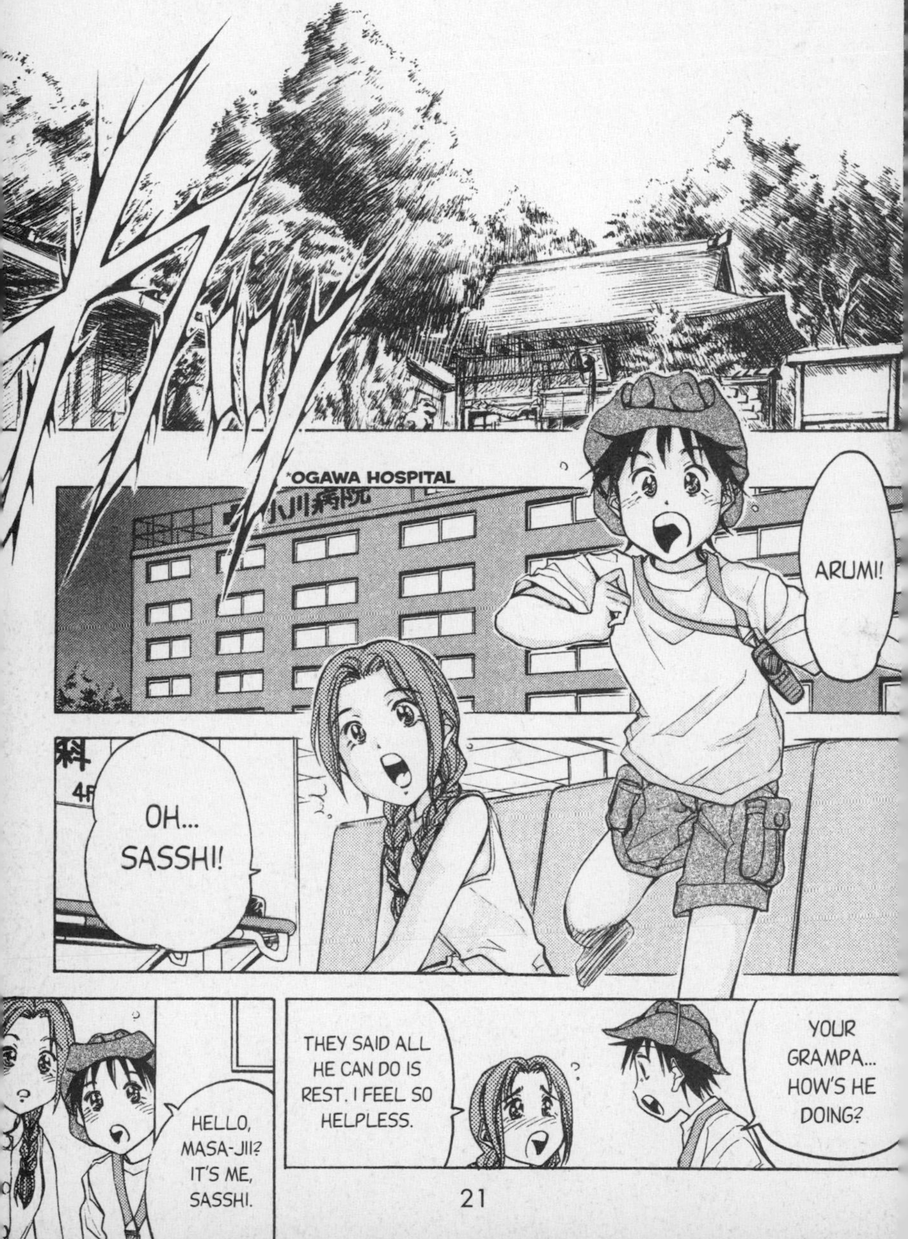
*OGAWA HOSPITAL
ARUMI!
OH... SASSHI!
YOUR GRAMPA... HOW'S HE DOING?
THEY SAID ALL HE CAN DO IS REST. I FEEL SO HELPLESS.
HELLO, MASA-JII? IT'S ME, SASSHI.

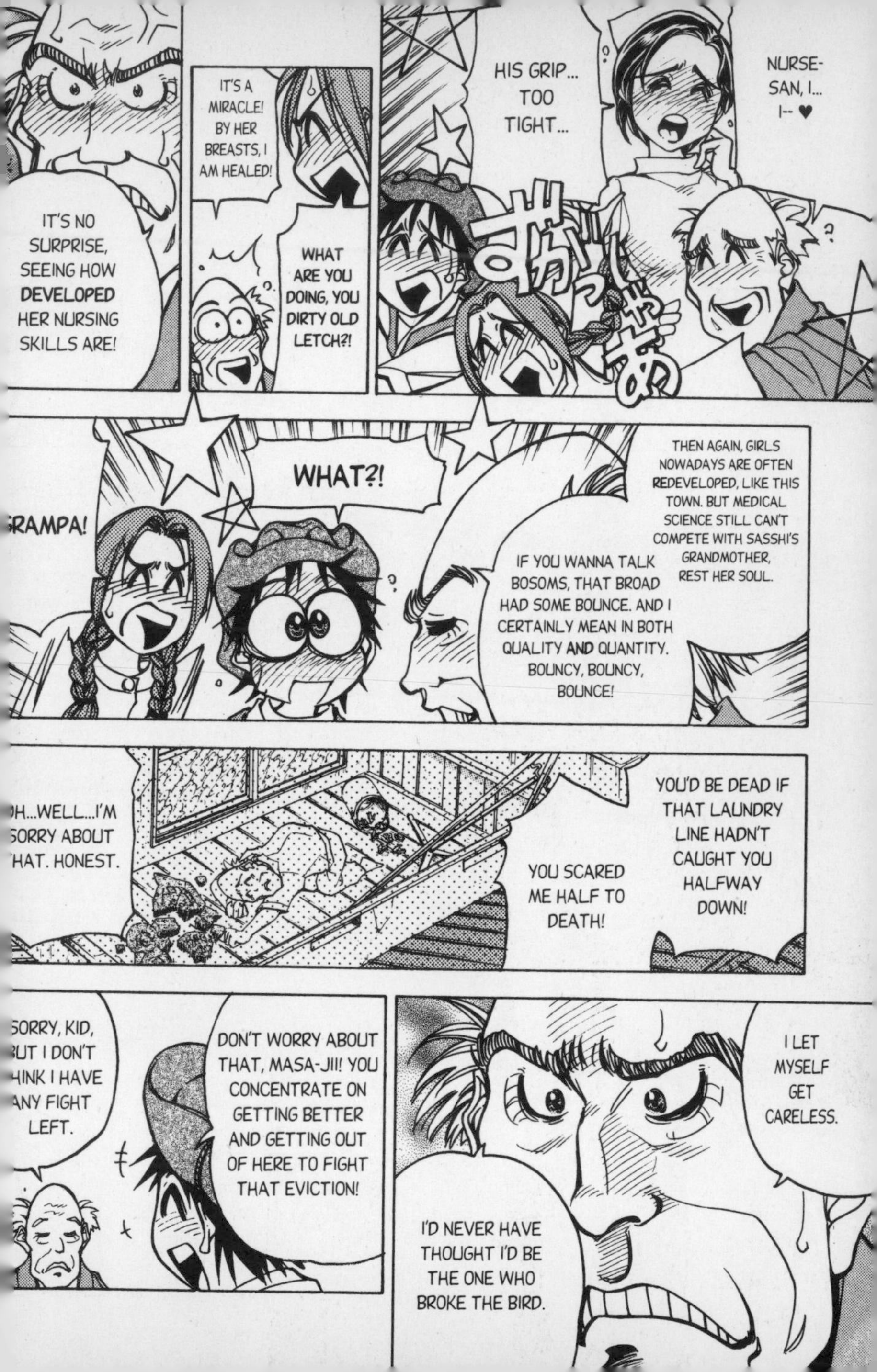
NURSE-SAN, I... I-- ♥
HIS GRIP... TOO TIGHT...
IT'S A MIRACLE! BY HER BREASTS, I AM HEALED!
WHAT ARE YOU DOING, YOU DIRTY OLD LETCH?!
IT'S NO SURPRISE, SEEING HOW **DEVELOPED** HER NURSING SKILLS ARE!
THEN AGAIN, GIRLS NOWADAYS ARE OFTEN **RE**DEVELOPED, LIKE THIS TOWN. BUT MEDICAL SCIENCE STILL CAN'T COMPETE WITH SASSHI'S GRANDMOTHER, REST HER SOUL.
IF YOU WANNA TALK BOSOMS, THAT BROAD HAD SOME BOUNCE. AND I CERTAINLY MEAN IN BOTH QUALITY **AND** QUANTITY. BOUNCY, BOUNCY, BOUNCE!
WHAT?!
GRAMPA!
YOU'D BE DEAD IF THAT LAUNDRY LINE HADN'T CAUGHT YOU HALFWAY DOWN!
YOU SCARED ME HALF TO DEATH!
OH...WELL...I'M SORRY ABOUT THAT. HONEST.
I LET MYSELF GET CARELESS.
I'D NEVER HAVE THOUGHT I'D BE THE ONE WHO BROKE THE BIRD.
DON'T WORRY ABOUT THAT, MASA-JII! YOU CONCENTRATE ON GETTING BETTER AND GETTING OUT OF HERE TO FIGHT THAT EVICTION!
SORRY, KID, BUT I DON'T THINK I HAVE ANY FIGHT LEFT.

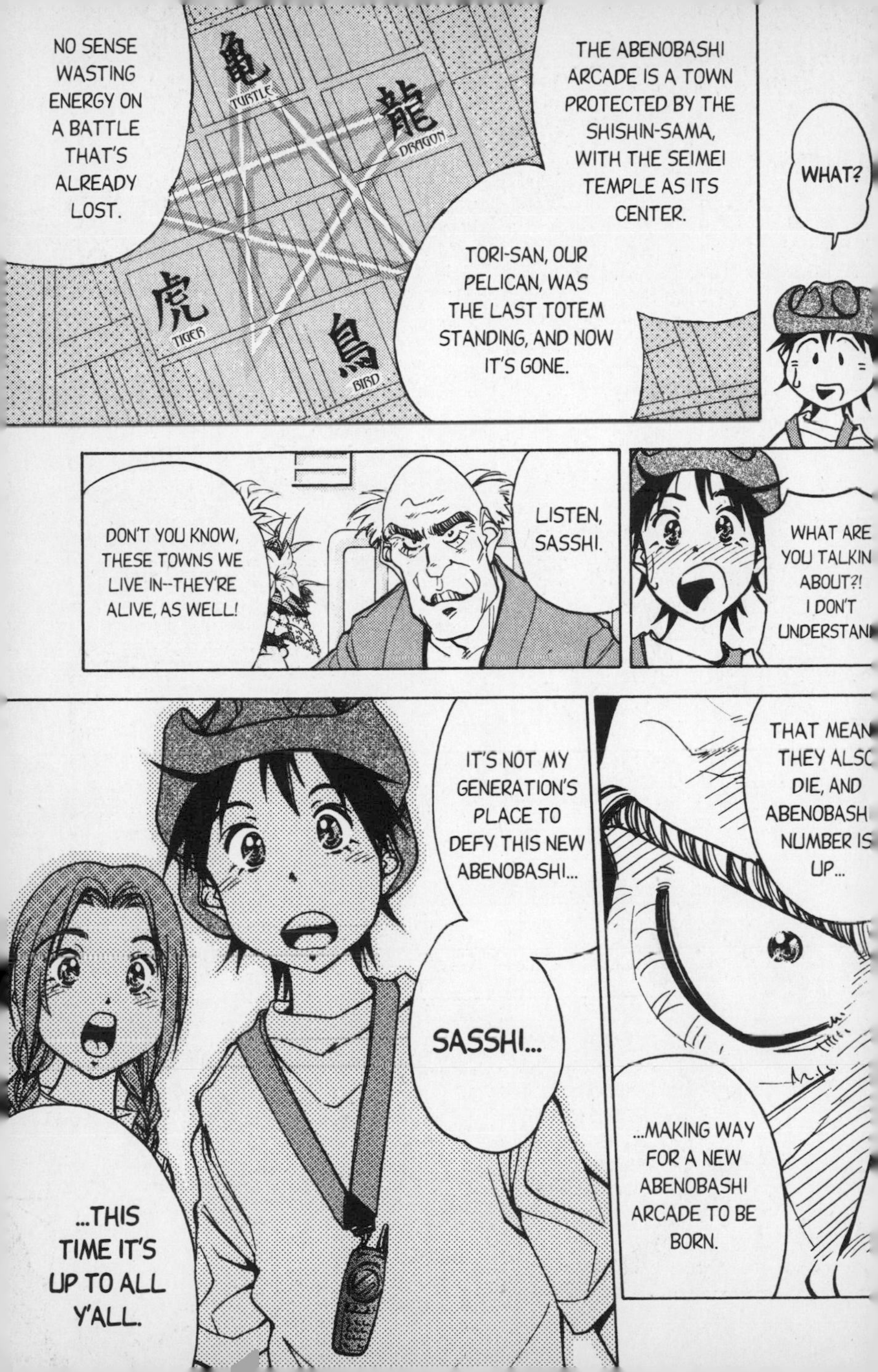
WHAT?
THE ABENOBASHI ARCADE IS A TOWN PROTECTED BY THE SHISHIN-SAMA, WITH THE SEIMEI TEMPLE AS ITS CENTER.
TORI-SAN, OUR PELICAN, WAS THE LAST TOTEM STANDING, AND NOW IT'S GONE.
NO SENSE WASTING ENERGY ON A BATTLE THAT'S ALREADY LOST.
亀
TURTLE
龍
DRAGON
虎
TIGER
鳥
BIRD
WHAT ARE YOU TALKIN ABOUT?! I DON'T UNDERSTAN
LISTEN, SASSHI.
DON'T YOU KNOW, THESE TOWNS WE LIVE IN--THEY'RE ALIVE, AS WELL!
THAT MEAN THEY ALS DIE, AND ABENOBASH NUMBER IS UP...
...MAKING WAY FOR A NEW ABENOBASHI ARCADE TO BE BORN.
IT'S NOT MY GENERATION'S PLACE TO DEFY THIS NEW ABENOBASHI...
SASSHI...
...THIS TIME IT'S UP TO ALL Y'ALL.

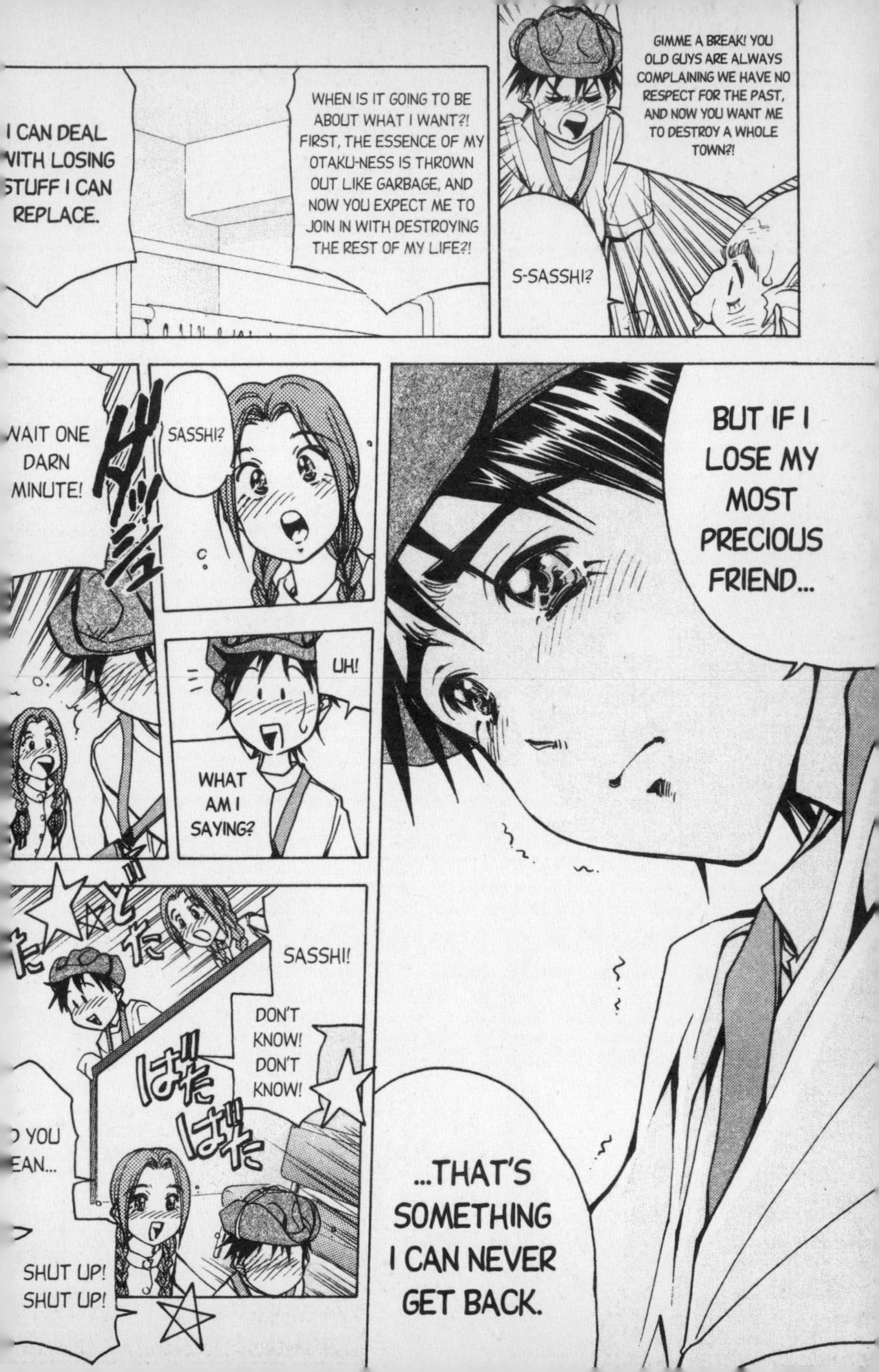
GIMME A BREAK! YOU OLD GUYS ARE ALWAYS COMPLAINING WE HAVE NO RESPECT FOR THE PAST, AND NOW YOU WANT ME TO DESTROY A WHOLE TOWN?!
S-SASSHI!?
WHEN IS IT GOING TO BE ABOUT WHAT I WANT?! FIRST, THE ESSENCE OF MY OTAKU-NESS IS THROWN OUT LIKE GARBAGE, AND NOW YOU EXPECT ME TO JOIN IN WITH DESTROYING THE REST OF MY LIFE?!
I CAN DEAL WITH LOSING STUFF I CAN REPLACE.
BUT IF I LOSE MY MOST PRECIOUS FRIEND...
...THAT'S SOMETHING I CAN NEVER GET BACK.
SASSHI!?
UH!
WHAT AM I SAYING?
WAIT ONE DARN MINUTE!
SASSHI!
DON'T KNOW! DON'T KNOW!
ばた ばた
D YOU EAN...
SHUT UP! SHUT UP!

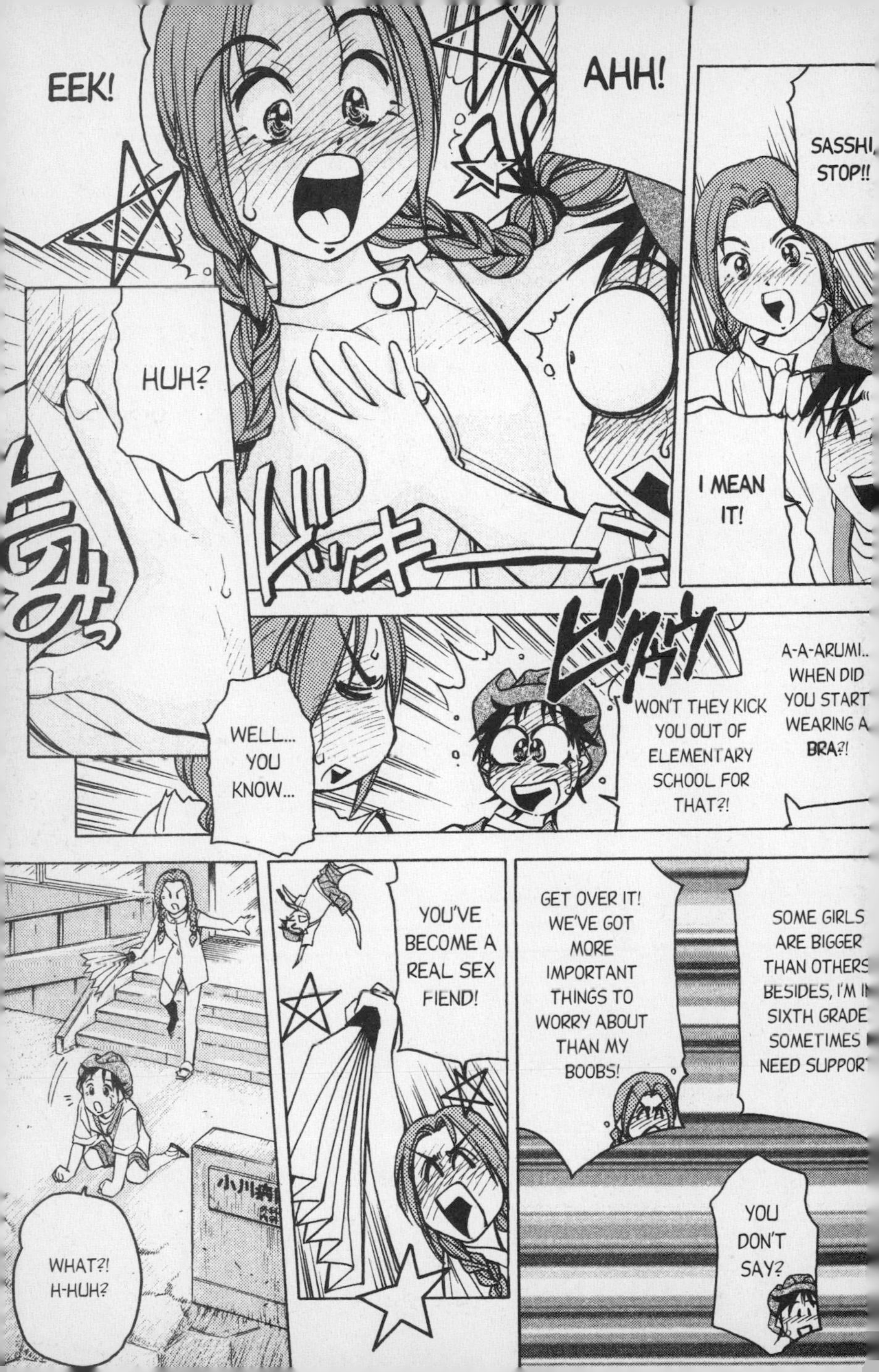
SASSHI, STOP!!
I MEAN IT!
AHH!
EEK!
HUH?
ドッキー
A-A-ARUMI... WHEN DID YOU START WEARING A BRA?!
WON'T THEY KICK YOU OUT OF ELEMENTARY SCHOOL FOR THAT?!
WELL... YOU KNOW...
SOME GIRLS ARE BIGGER THAN OTHERS BESIDES, I'M IN SIXTH GRADE SOMETIMES NEED SUPPORT
GET OVER IT! WE'VE GOT MORE IMPORTANT THINGS TO WORRY ABOUT THAN MY BOOBS!
YOU DON'T SAY?
YOU'VE BECOME A REAL SEX FIEND!
WHAT?! H-HUH?

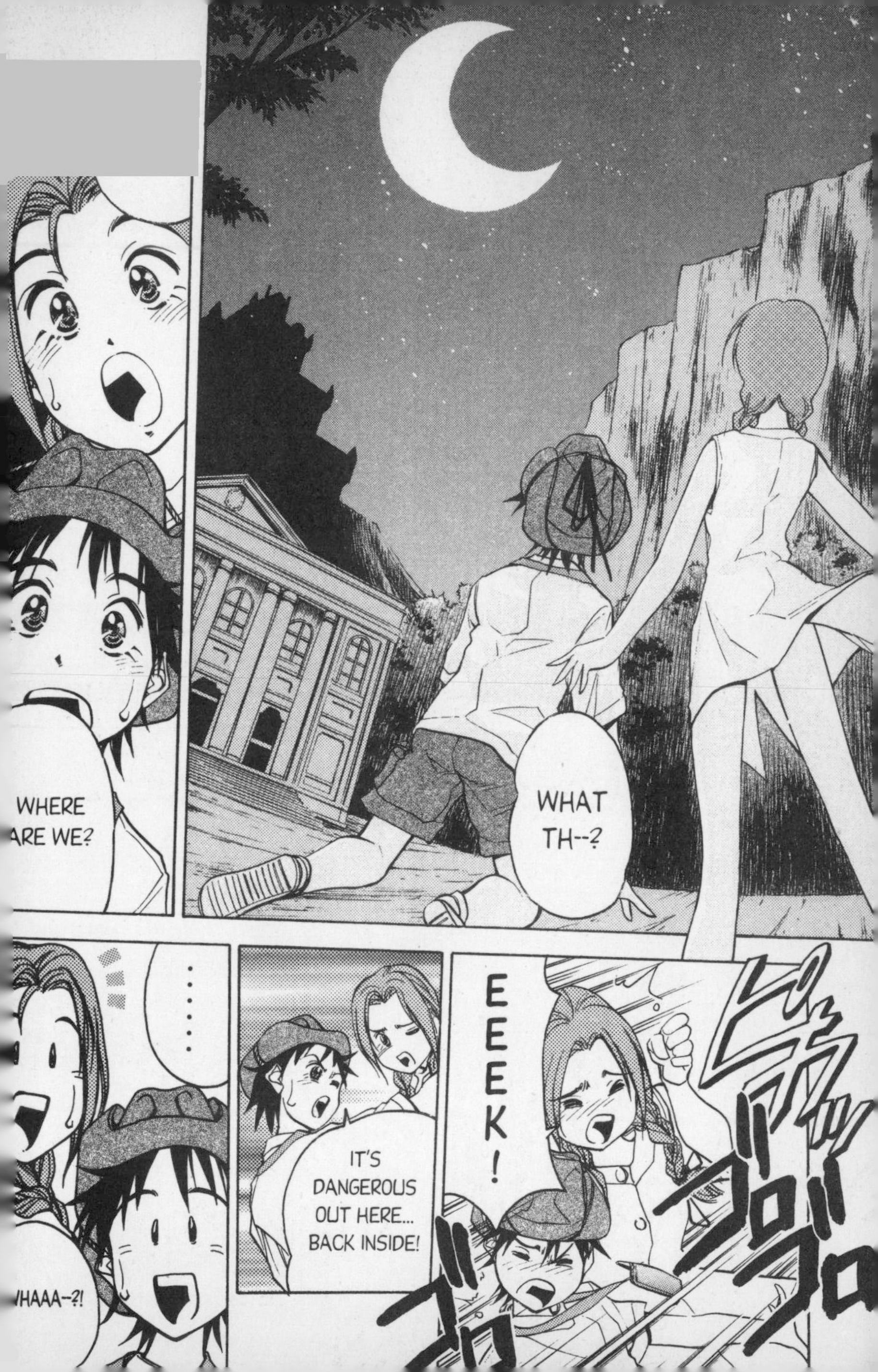
WHAT TH--?
WHERE ARE WE?
EEEK!
IT'S DANGEROUS OUT HERE... BACK INSIDE!
......
WHAAA--?!

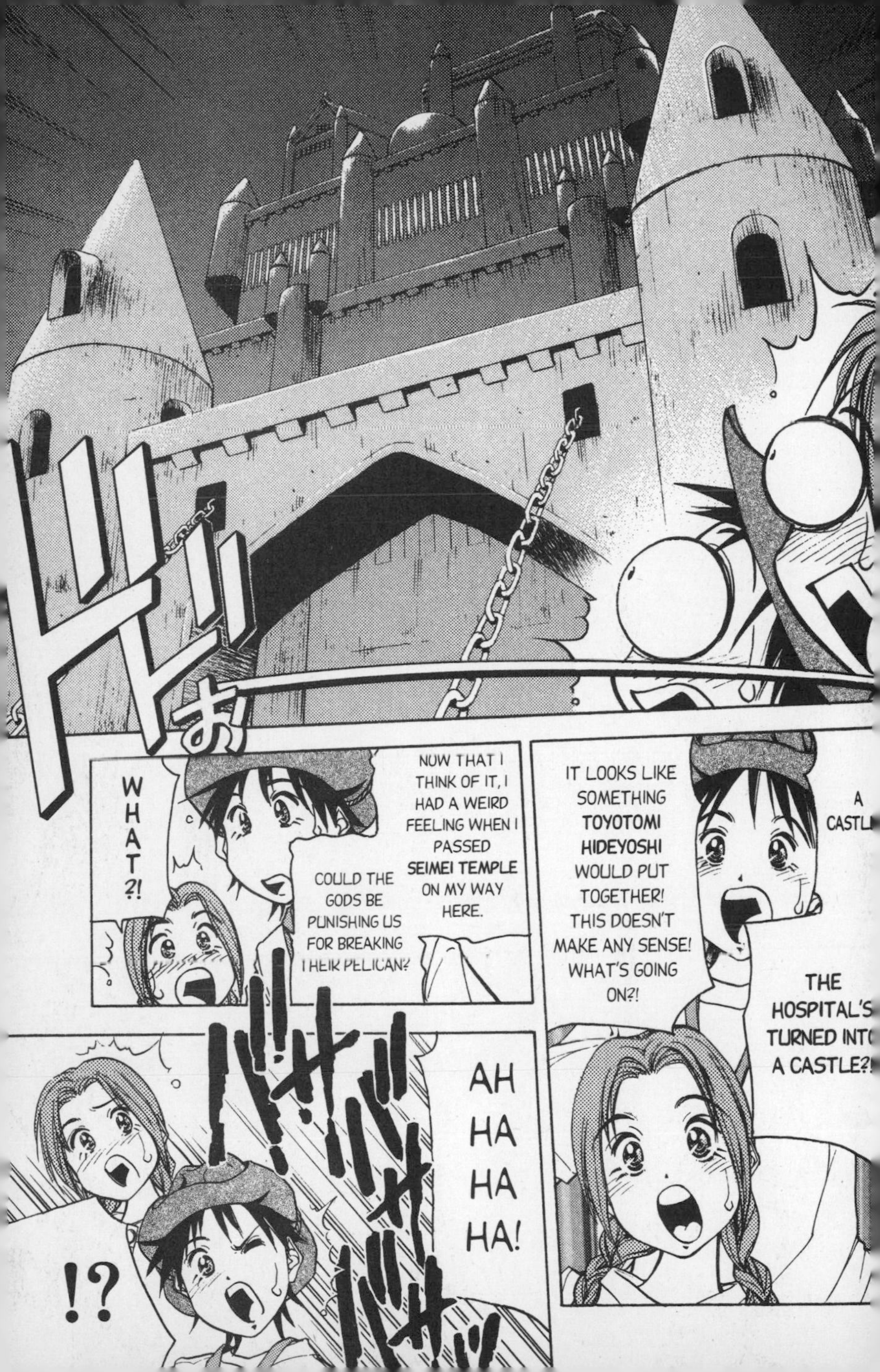
A CASTL
IT LOOKS LIKE SOMETHING **TOYOTOMI HIDEYOSHI** WOULD PUT TOGETHER! THIS DOESN'T MAKE ANY SENSE! WHAT'S GOING ON?!
NOW THAT I THINK OF IT, I HAD A WEIRD FEELING WHEN I PASSED **SEIMEI TEMPLE** ON MY WAY HERE.
COULD THE GODS BE PUNISHING US FOR BREAKING THEIR PELICAN?
WHAT?!
THE HOSPITAL'S TURNED INTO A CASTLE?!
AH HA HA HA!
!?

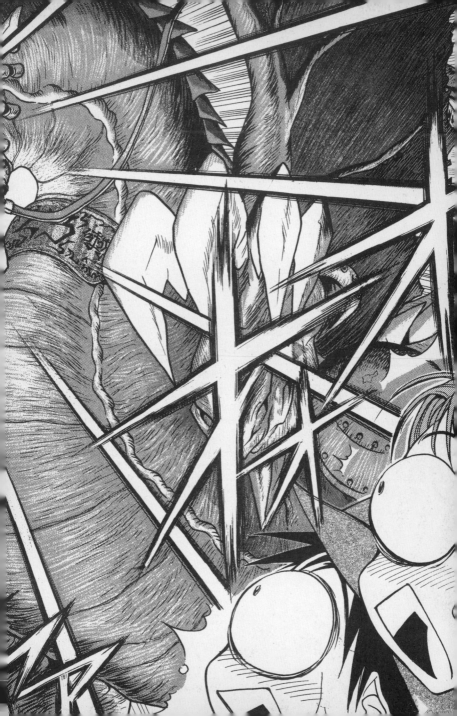

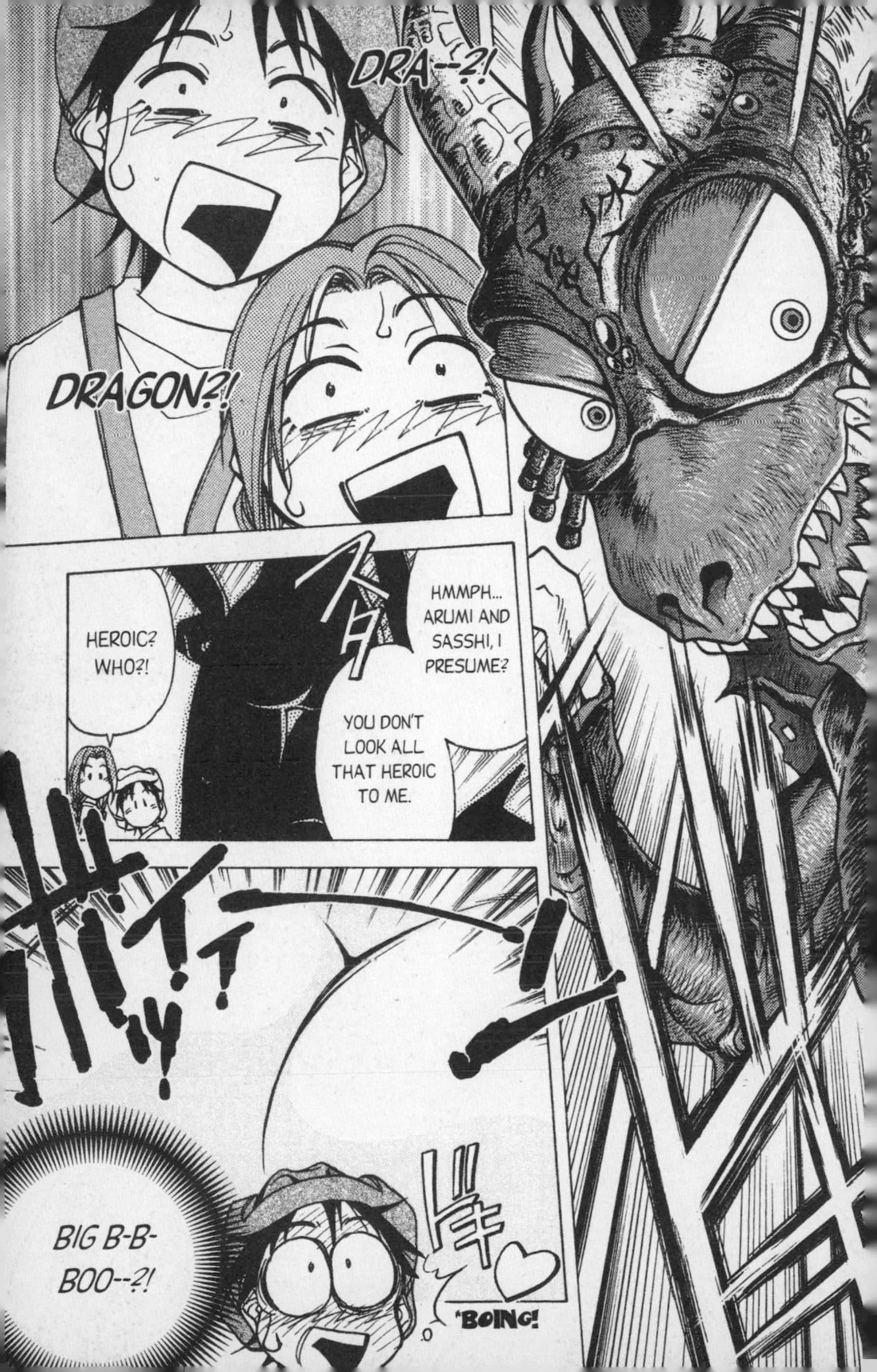
DRA--?!
DRAGON?!
HMMPH... ARUMI AND SASSHI, I PRESUME?
YOU DON'T LOOK ALL THAT HEROIC TO ME.
HEROIC? WHO?!
BIG B-B-BOO--?!
*BOING!

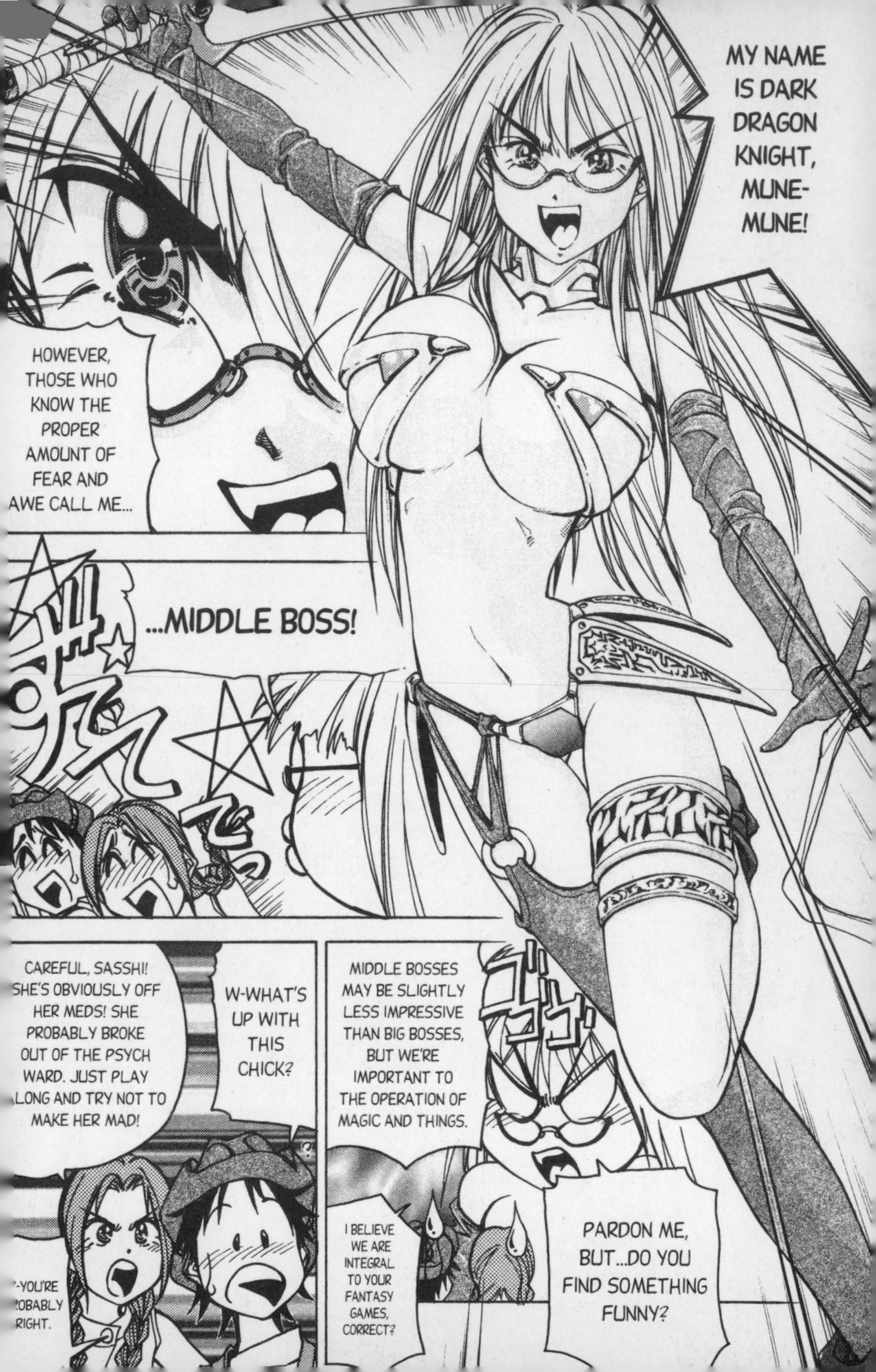
MY NAME IS DARK DRAGON KNIGHT, MUNE-MUNE!
HOWEVER, THOSE WHO KNOW THE PROPER AMOUNT OF FEAR AND AWE CALL ME...
...MIDDLE BOSS!
MIDDLE BOSSES MAY BE SLIGHTLY LESS IMPRESSIVE THAN BIG BOSSES, BUT WE'RE IMPORTANT TO THE OPERATION OF MAGIC AND THINGS.
PARDON ME, BUT...DO YOU FIND SOMETHING FUNNY?
I BELIEVE WE ARE INTEGRAL TO YOUR FANTASY GAMES, CORRECT?
W-WHAT'S UP WITH THIS CHICK?
CAREFUL, SASSHI! SHE'S OBVIOUSLY OFF HER MEDS! SHE PROBABLY BROKE OUT OF THE PSYCH WARD. JUST PLAY ALONG AND TRY NOT TO MAKE HER MAD!
-YOU'RE ROBABLY RIGHT.

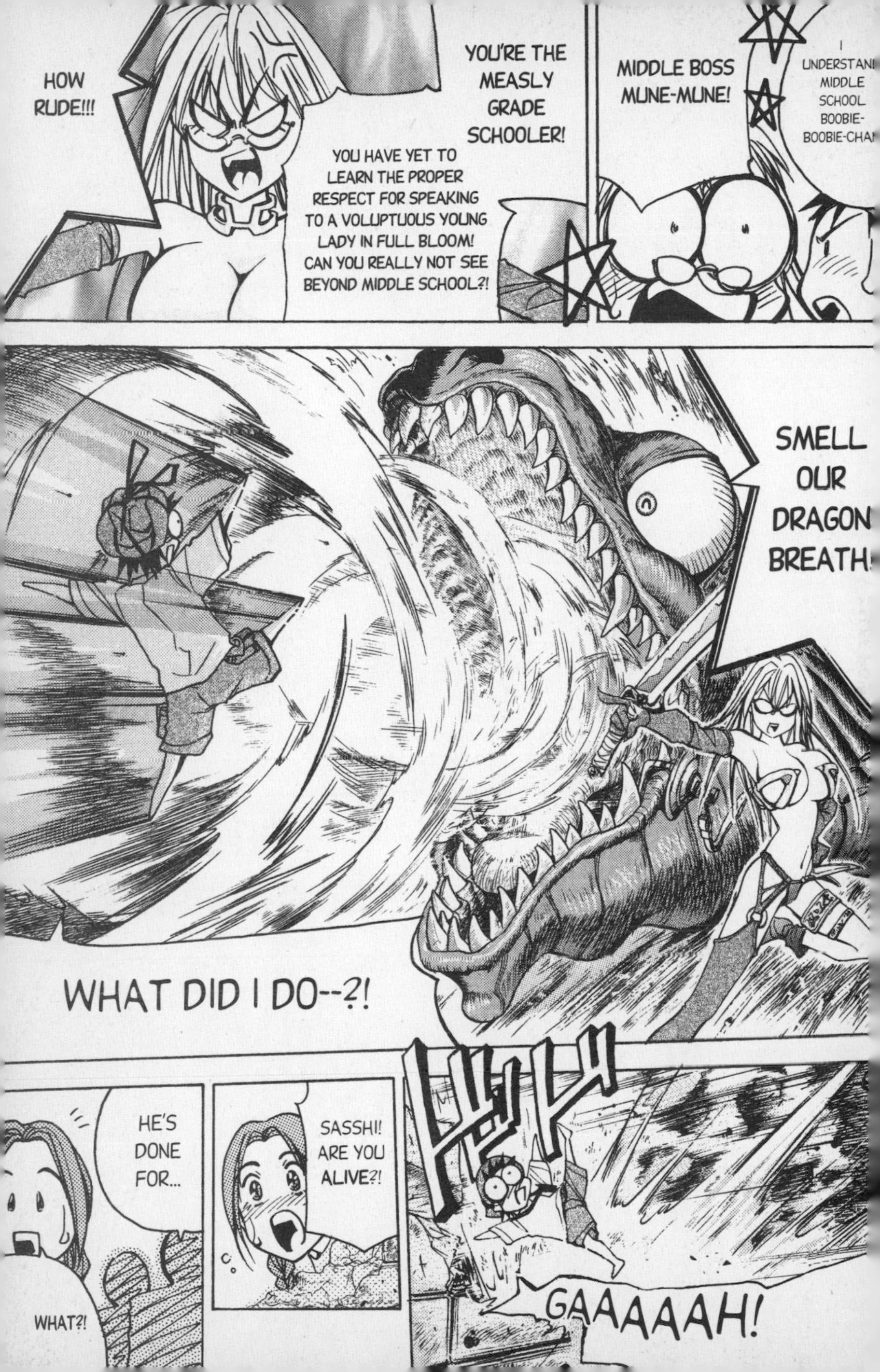
I UNDERSTAN MIDDLE SCHOOL BOOBIE-BOOBIE-CHA
MIDDLE BOSS MUNE-MUNE!
YOU'RE THE MEASLY GRADE SCHOOLER!
HOW RUDE!!!
YOU HAVE YET TO LEARN THE PROPER RESPECT FOR SPEAKING TO A VOLUPTUOUS YOUNG LADY IN FULL BLOOM! CAN YOU REALLY NOT SEE BEYOND MIDDLE SCHOOL?!
SMELL OUR DRAGON BREATH!
WHAT DID I DO--?!
GAAAAAH!
SASSHI! ARE YOU ALIVE?!
HE'S DONE FOR...
WHAT?!

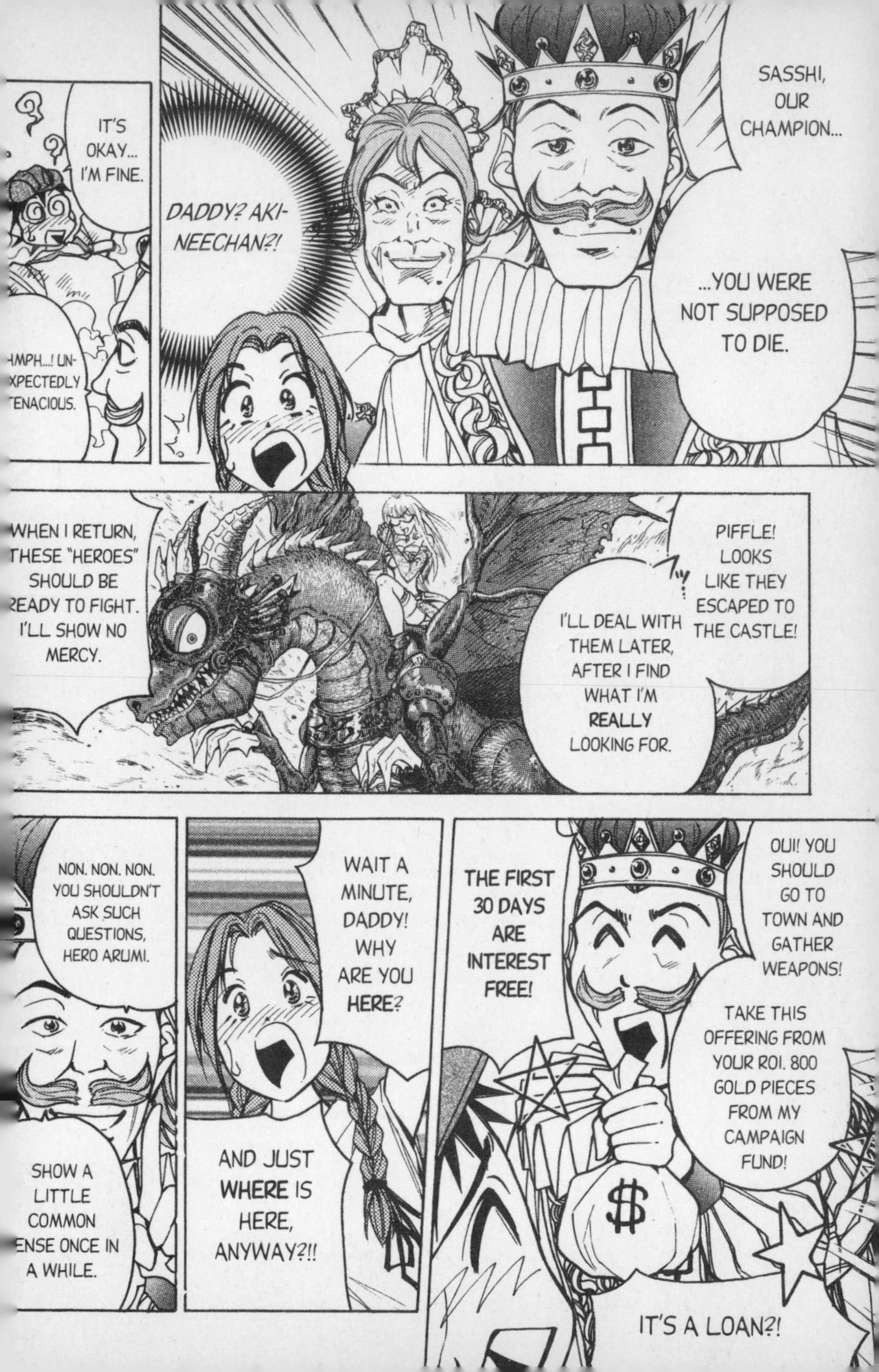
SASSHI, OUR CHAMPION...
...YOU WERE NOT SUPPOSED TO DIE.
DADDY? AKI-NEECHAN?!
IT'S OKAY... I'M FINE.
HMPH...! UN-XPECTEDLY TENACIOUS.
PIFFLE! LOOKS LIKE THEY ESCAPED TO THE CASTLE!
I'LL DEAL WITH THEM LATER, AFTER I FIND WHAT I'M **REALLY** LOOKING FOR.
WHEN I RETURN, THESE "HEROES" SHOULD BE READY TO FIGHT. I'LL SHOW NO MERCY.
OUI! YOU SHOULD GO TO TOWN AND GATHER WEAPONS!
TAKE THIS OFFERING FROM YOUR ROI. 800 GOLD PIECES FROM MY CAMPAIGN FUND!
THE FIRST 30 DAYS ARE INTEREST FREE!
IT'S A LOAN?!
WAIT A MINUTE, DADDY! WHY ARE YOU **HERE?**
AND JUST **WHERE** IS HERE, ANYWAY?!!
NON. NON. NON. YOU SHOULDN'T ASK SUCH QUESTIONS, HERO ARUMI.
SHOW A LITTLE COMMON SENSE ONCE IN A WHILE.

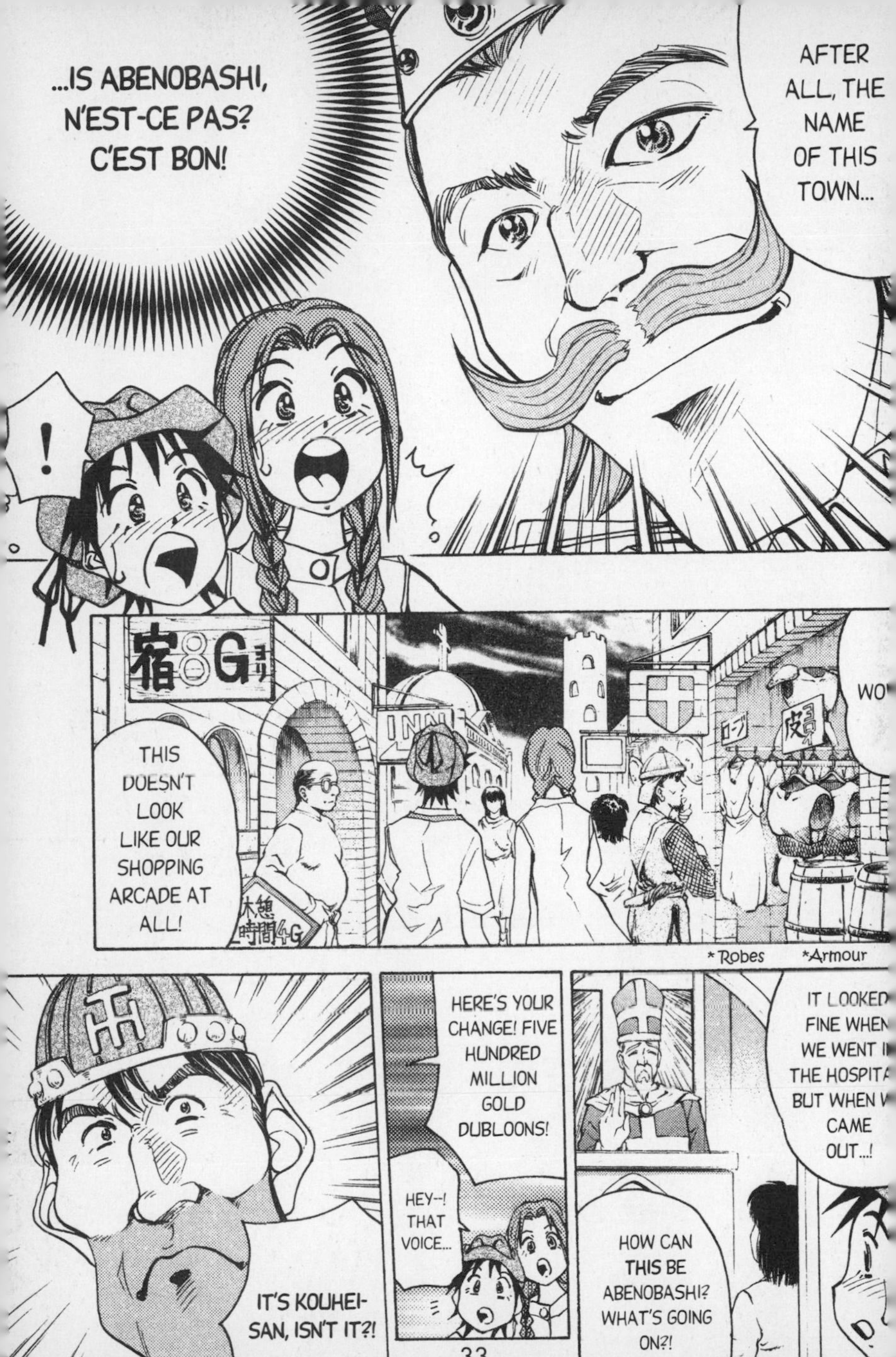
AFTER ALL, THE NAME OF THIS TOWN...
...IS ABENOBASHI, N'EST-CE PAS? C'EST BON!
!
WO
宿 8G ヨリ
INN
THIS DOESN'T LOOK LIKE OUR SHOPPING ARCADE AT ALL!
休憩時間4G
ローブ
皮ヨロイ
*Robes
*Armour
IT LOOKED FINE WHEN WE WENT I THE HOSPITA BUT WHEN W CAME OUT...!
HOW CAN THIS BE ABENOBASHI!? WHAT'S GOING ON?!
HERE'S YOUR CHANGE! FIVE HUNDRED MILLION GOLD DUBLOONS!
HEY--! THAT VOICE...
IT'S KOUHEI-SAN, ISN'T IT?!

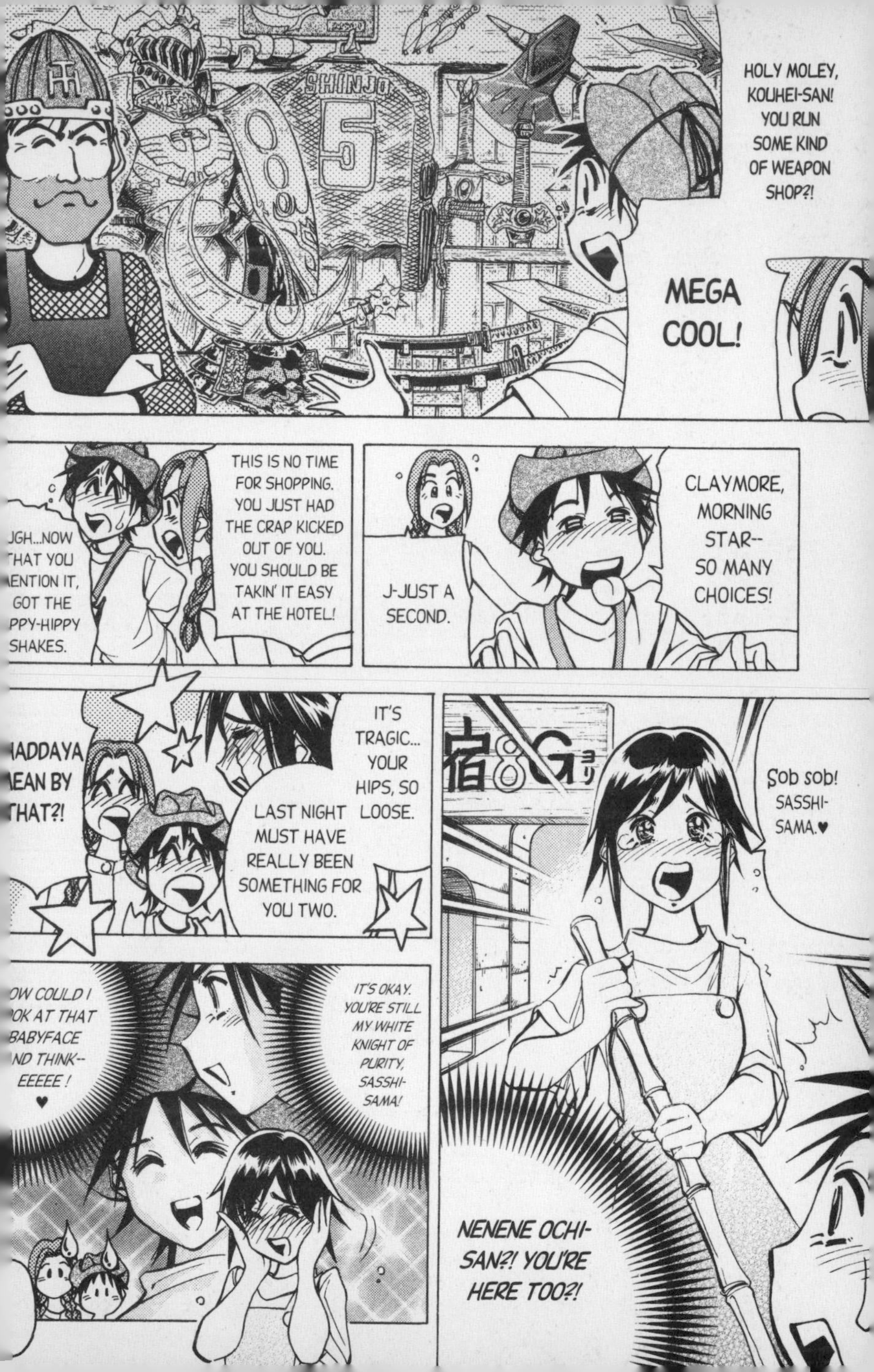
HOLY MOLEY, KOUHEI-SAN! YOU RUN SOME KIND OF WEAPON SHOP?!
MEGA COOL!
CLAYMORE, MORNING STAR-- SO MANY CHOICES!
J-JUST A SECOND.
THIS IS NO TIME FOR SHOPPING. YOU JUST HAD THE CRAP KICKED OUT OF YOU. YOU SHOULD BE TAKIN' IT EASY AT THE HOTEL!
GH...NOW THAT YOU ENTION IT, GOT THE PPY-HIPPY SHAKES.
Sob sob! SASSHI-SAMA.♥
NENENE OCHI-SAN?! YOU'RE HERE TOO?!
IT'S TRAGIC... YOUR HIPS, SO LOOSE.
LAST NIGHT MUST HAVE REALLY BEEN SOMETHING FOR YOU TWO.
ADDAYA EAN BY THAT?!
IT'S OKAY. YOU'RE STILL MY WHITE KNIGHT OF PURITY, SASSHI-SAMA!
OW COULD I OK AT THAT BABYFACE ND THINK-- EEEEE! ♥

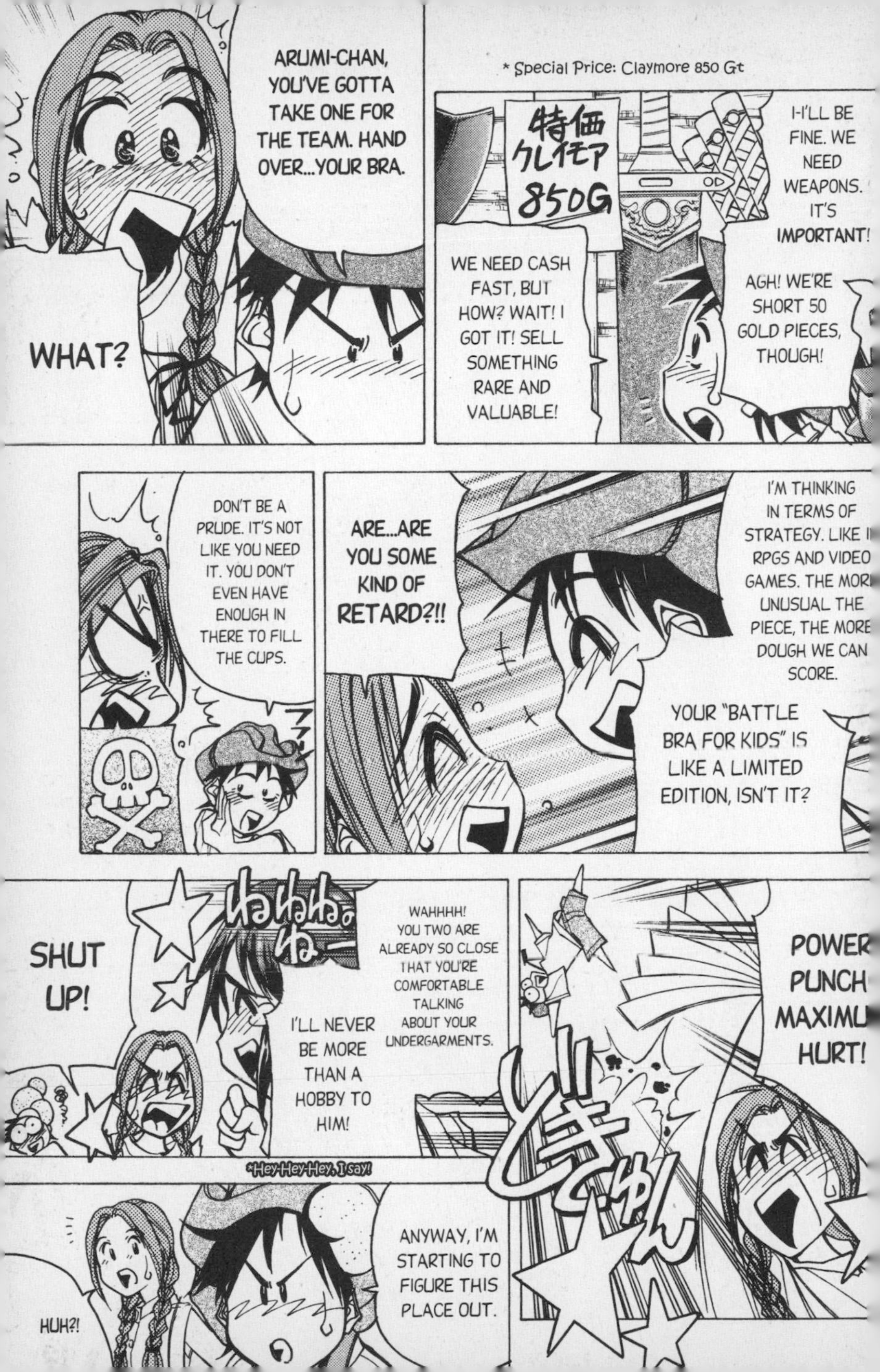

* Special Price: Claymore 850 Gt
特価
クレイモア
850G
I-I'LL BE FINE. WE NEED WEAPONS. IT'S IMPORTANT!
AGH! WE'RE SHORT 50 GOLD PIECES, THOUGH!
WE NEED CASH FAST, BUT HOW? WAIT! I GOT IT! SELL SOMETHING RARE AND VALUABLE!
ARUMI-CHAN, YOU'VE GOTTA TAKE ONE FOR THE TEAM. HAND OVER...YOUR BRA.
WHAT?
I'M THINKING IN TERMS OF STRATEGY. LIKE I RPGS AND VIDEO GAMES. THE MORE UNUSUAL THE PIECE, THE MORE DOUGH WE CAN SCORE.
YOUR "BATTLE BRA FOR KIDS" IS LIKE A LIMITED EDITION, ISN'T IT?
ARE...ARE YOU SOME KIND OF RETARD?!!
DON'T BE A PRUDE. IT'S NOT LIKE YOU NEED IT. YOU DON'T EVEN HAVE ENOUGH IN THERE TO FILL THE CUPS.
POWER PUNCH MAXIMU HURT!
ときゅん
WAHHHH! YOU TWO ARE ALREADY SO CLOSE THAT YOU'RE COMFORTABLE TALKING ABOUT YOUR UNDERGARMENTS.
I'LL NEVER BE MORE THAN A HOBBY TO HIM!
ぬぬぬぬ。ぬー
SHUT UP!
*Hey-Hey-Hey, I say!
ANYWAY, I'M STARTING TO FIGURE THIS PLACE OUT.
HUH?!

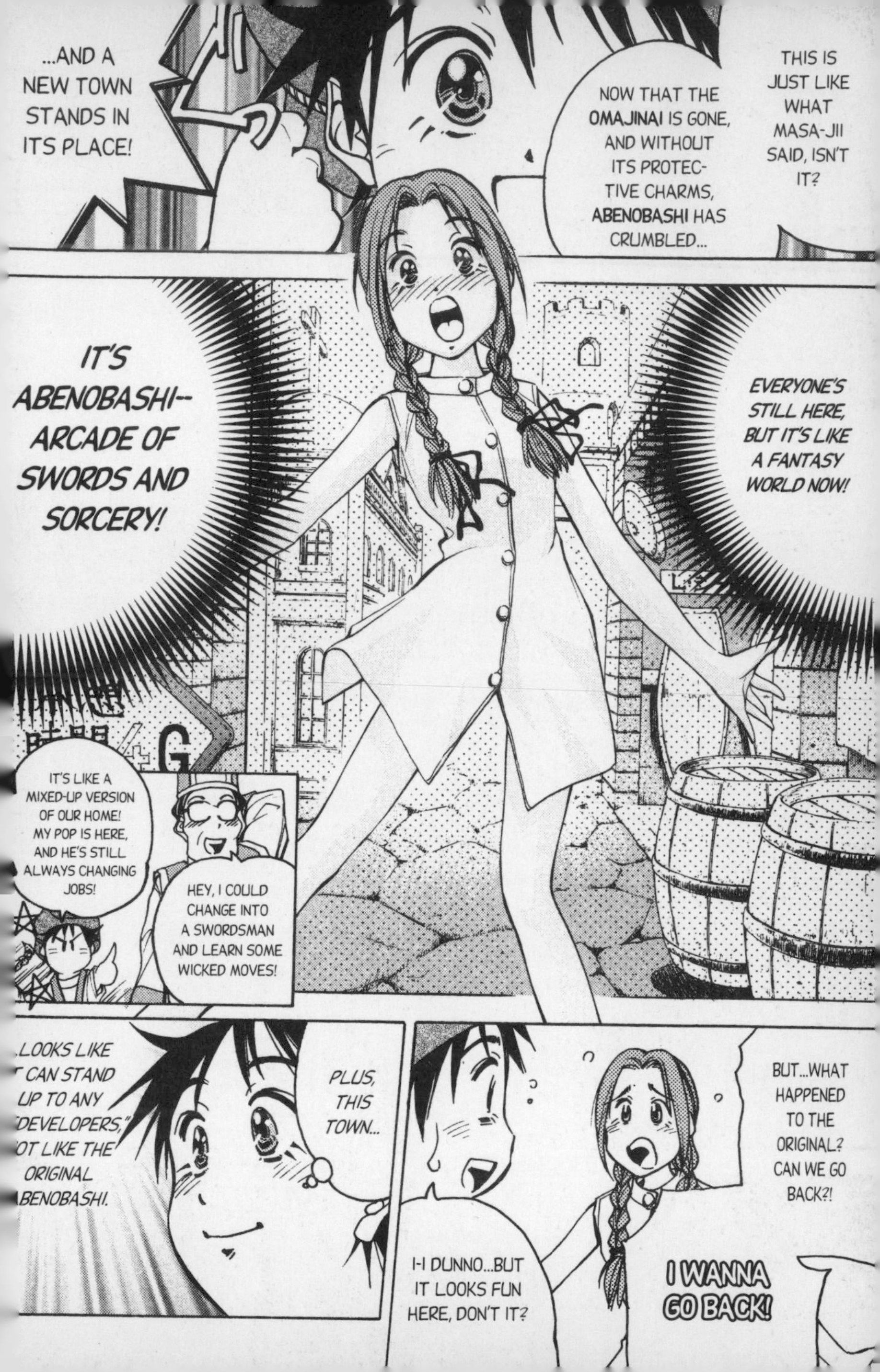
THIS IS JUST LIKE WHAT MASA-JII SAID, ISN'T IT?
NOW THAT THE **OMAJINAI** IS GONE, AND WITHOUT ITS PROTEC- TIVE CHARMS, **ABENOBASHI** HAS CRUMBLED...
...AND A NEW TOWN STANDS IN ITS PLACE!
EVERYONE'S STILL HERE, BUT IT'S LIKE A FANTASY WORLD NOW!
IT'S ABENOBASHI-- ARCADE OF SWORDS AND SORCERY!
IT'S LIKE A MIXED-UP VERSION OF OUR HOME! MY POP IS HERE, AND HE'S STILL ALWAYS CHANGING JOBS!
HEY, I COULD CHANGE INTO A SWORDSMAN AND LEARN SOME WICKED MOVES!
BUT...WHAT HAPPENED TO THE ORIGINAL? CAN WE GO BACK?!
I-I DUNNO...BUT IT LOOKS FUN HERE, DON'T IT?
I WANNA GO BACK!
PLUS, THIS TOWN...
.LOOKS LIKE T CAN STAND UP TO ANY "DEVELOPERS," OT LIKE THE ORIGINAL BENOBASHI.

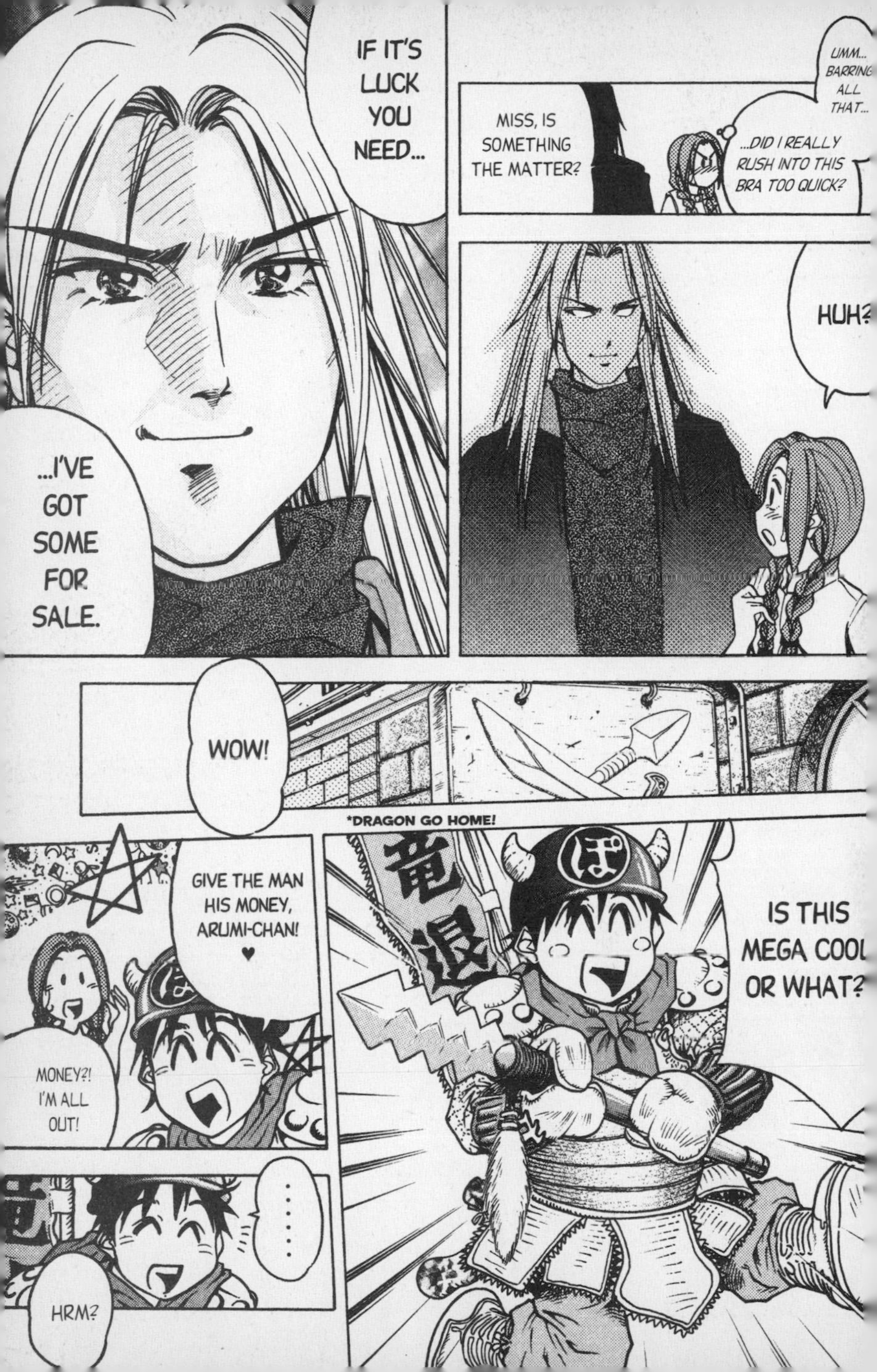
UMM... BARRING ALL THAT...
...DID I REALLY RUSH INTO THIS BRA TOO QUICK?
MISS, IS SOMETHING THE MATTER?
HUH?
IF IT'S LUCK YOU NEED...
...I'VE GOT SOME FOR SALE.
WOW!
*DRAGON GO HOME!
竜退
IS THIS MEGA COOL OR WHAT?
GIVE THE MAN HIS MONEY, ARUMI-CHAN! ♥
MONEY?! I'M ALL OUT!
......
HRM?

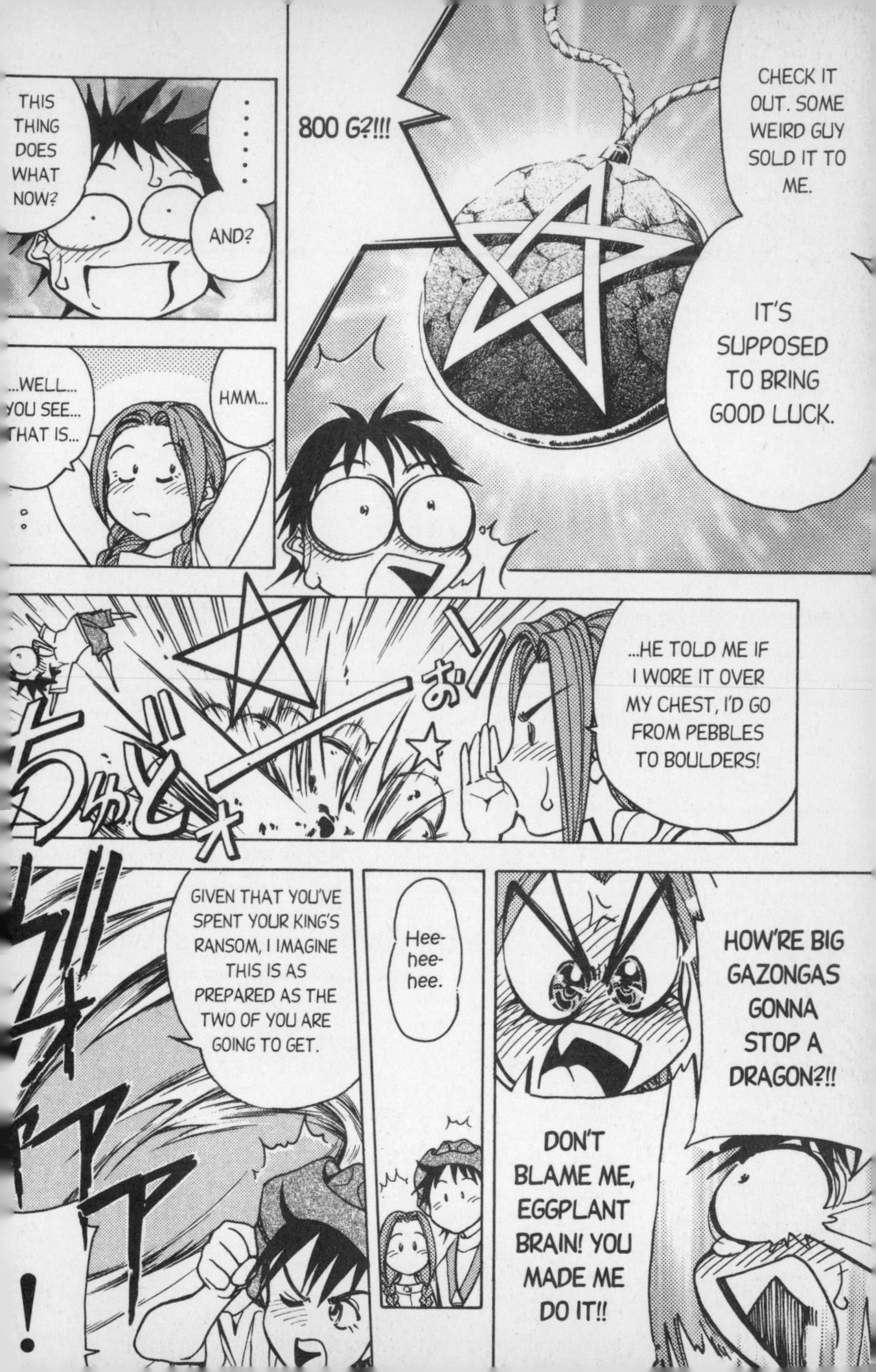
CHECK IT OUT. SOME WEIRD GUY SOLD IT TO ME.
IT'S SUPPOSED TO BRING GOOD LUCK.
800 G?!!!
......
AND?
THIS THING DOES WHAT NOW?
HMM...
...WELL... YOU SEE... THAT IS...
...HE TOLD ME IF I WORE IT OVER MY CHEST, I'D GO FROM PEBBLES TO BOULDERS!
HOW'RE BIG GAZONGAS GONNA STOP A DRAGON?!!
DON'T BLAME ME, EGGPLANT BRAIN! YOU MADE ME DO IT!!
Hee-hee-hee.
GIVEN THAT YOU'VE SPENT YOUR KING'S RANSOM, I IMAGINE THIS IS AS PREPARED AS THE TWO OF YOU ARE GOING TO GET.
!

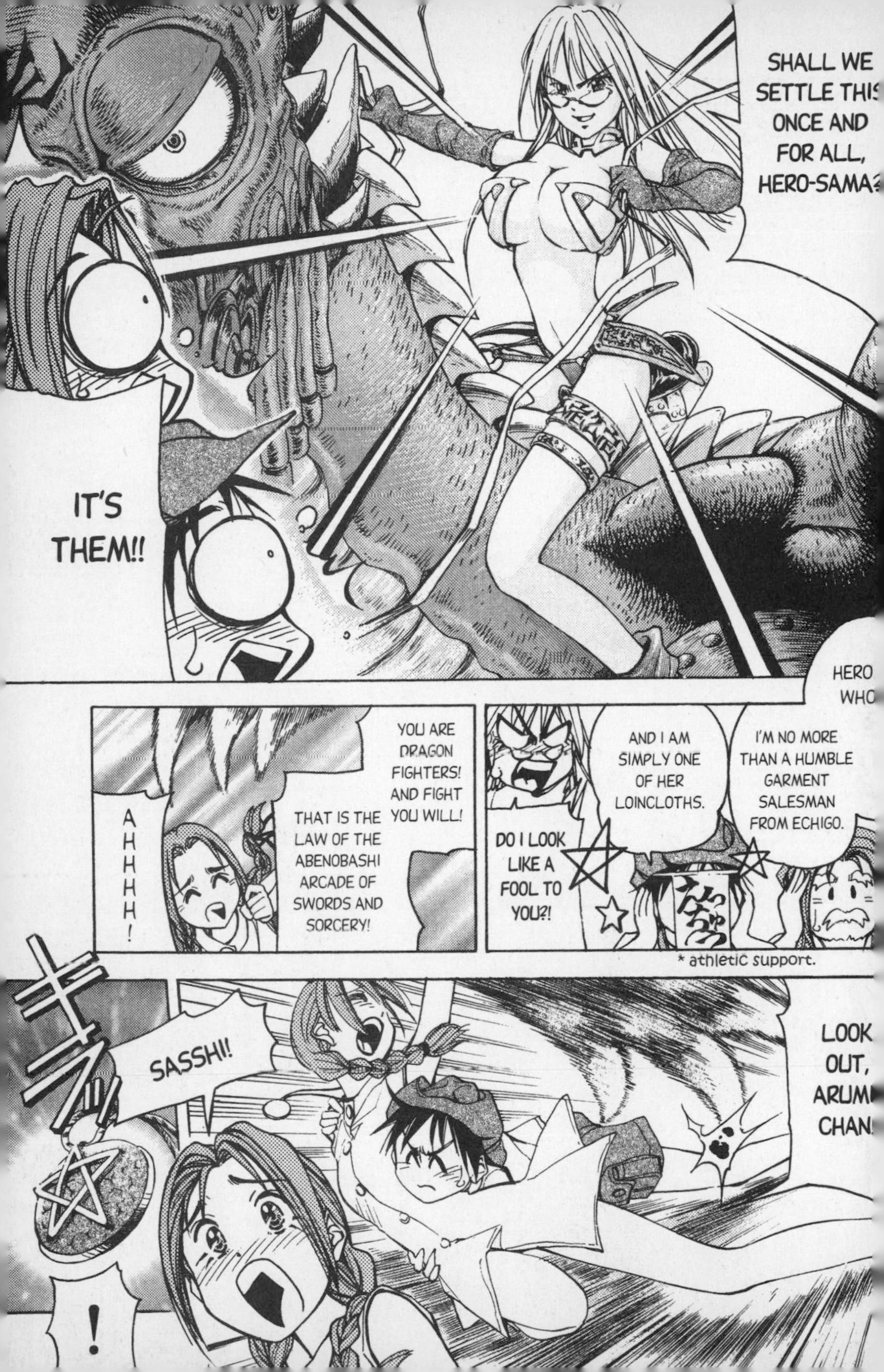
SHALL WE SETTLE THIS ONCE AND FOR ALL, HERO-SAMA?
IT'S THEM!!
HERO WHO
I'M NO MORE THAN A HUMBLE GARMENT SALESMAN FROM ECHIGO.
AND I AM SIMPLY ONE OF HER LOINCLOTHS.
DO I LOOK LIKE A FOOL TO YOU?!
* athletic support.
YOU ARE DRAGON FIGHTERS! AND FIGHT YOU WILL!
THAT IS THE LAW OF THE ABENOBASHI ARCADE OF SWORDS AND SORCERY!
AHHHHH!
LOOK OUT, ARUM CHAN
SASSHI!
!

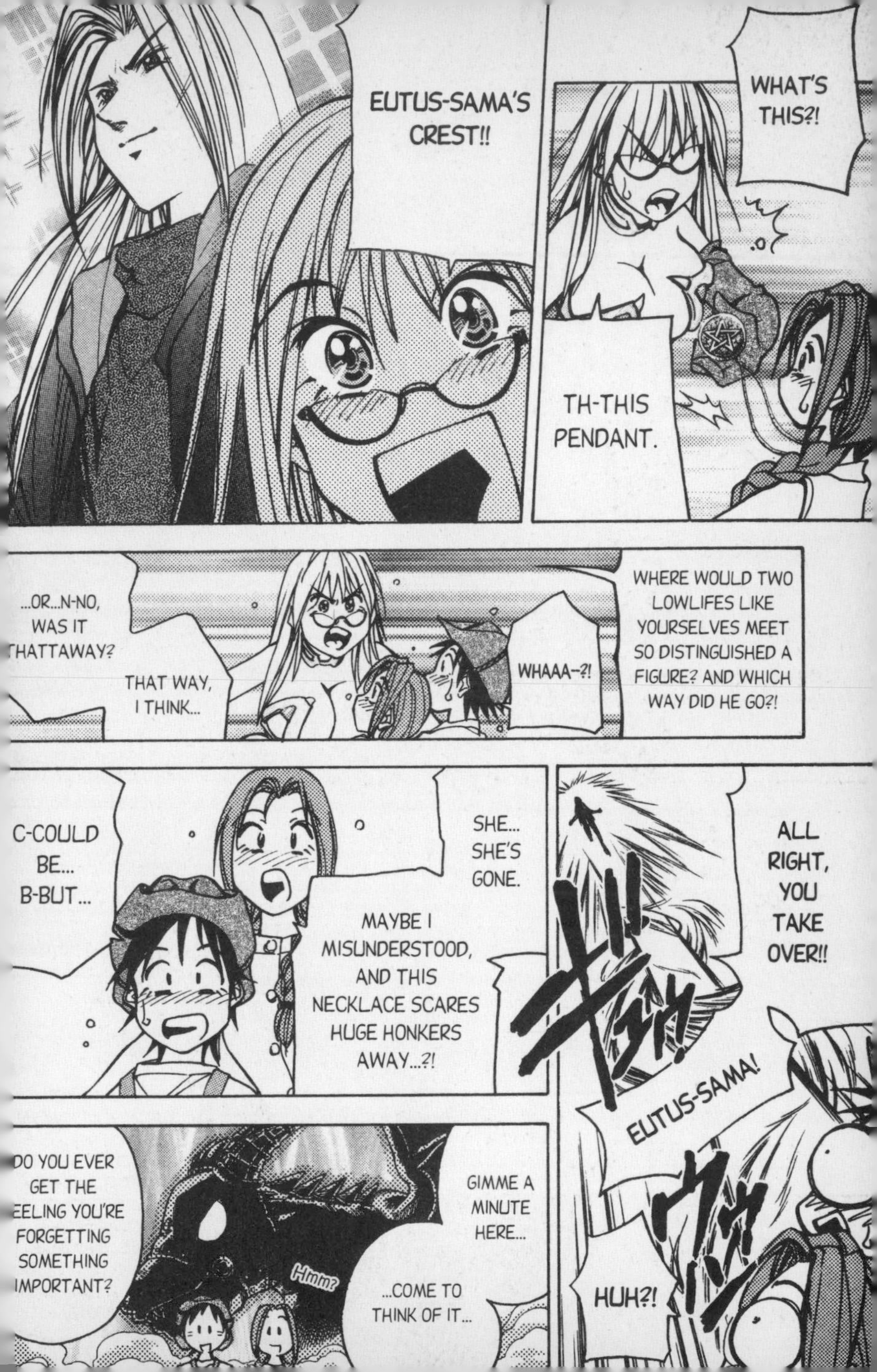
WHAT'S THIS?!
TH-THIS PENDANT.
EUTUS-SAMA'S CREST!!
WHERE WOULD TWO LOWLIFES LIKE YOURSELVES MEET SO DISTINGUISHED A FIGURE? AND WHICH WAY DID HE GO?!
WHAAA-?!
THAT WAY, I THINK...
...OR...N-NO, WAS IT THATTAWAY?
ALL RIGHT, YOU TAKE OVER!!
EUTUS-SAMA!
HUH?!
SHE... SHE'S GONE.
C-COULD BE... B-BUT...
MAYBE I MISUNDERSTOOD, AND THIS NECKLACE SCARES HUGE HONKERS AWAY...?!
GIMME A MINUTE HERE...
...COME TO THINK OF IT...
Hmm?
DO YOU EVER GET THE FEELING YOU'RE FORGETTING SOMETHING IMPORTANT?

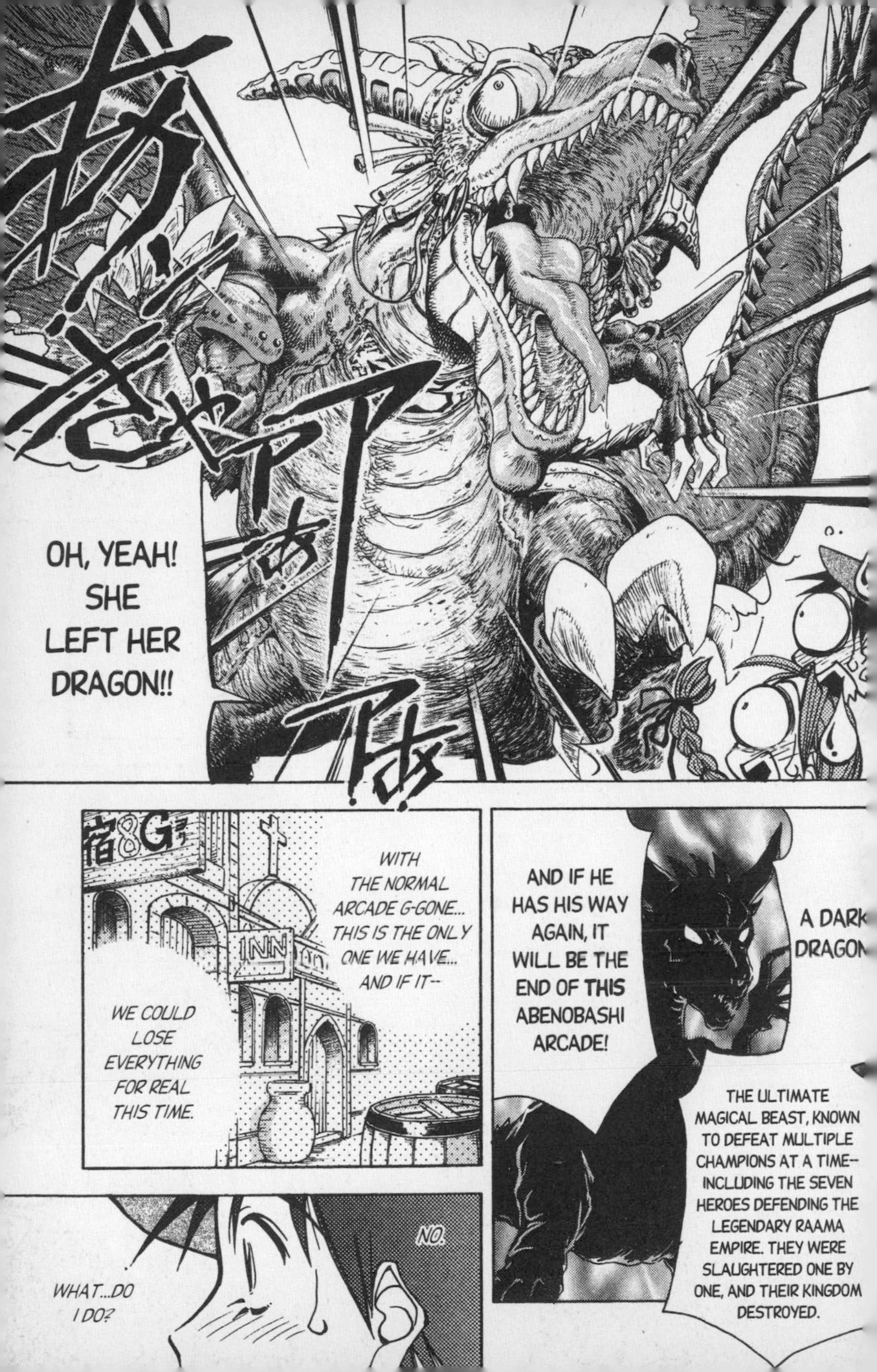
OH, YEAH! SHE LEFT HER DRAGON!!
A DARK DRAGON
THE ULTIMATE MAGICAL BEAST, KNOWN TO DEFEAT MULTIPLE CHAMPIONS AT A TIME-- INCLUDING THE SEVEN HEROES DEFENDING THE LEGENDARY RAAMA EMPIRE. THEY WERE SLAUGHTERED ONE BY ONE, AND THEIR KINGDOM DESTROYED.
AND IF HE HAS HIS WAY AGAIN, IT WILL BE THE END OF THIS ABENOBASHI ARCADE!
宿8G
INN
WITH THE NORMAL ARCADE G-GONE... THIS IS THE ONLY ONE WE HAVE... AND IF IT--
WE COULD LOSE EVERYTHING FOR REAL THIS TIME.
NO.
WHAT...DO I DO?

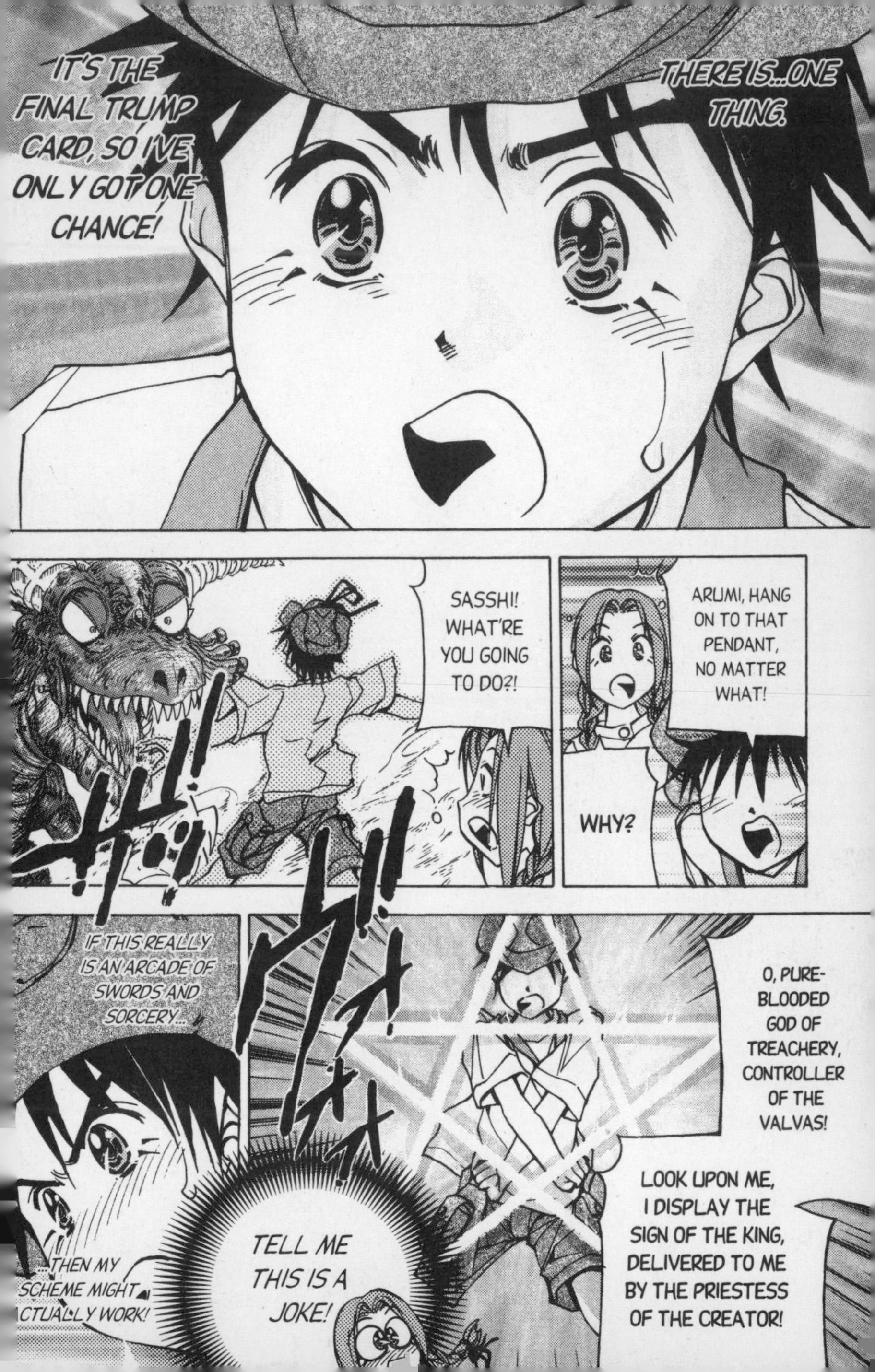
THERE IS...ONE THING.
IT'S THE FINAL TRUMP CARD, SO I'VE ONLY GOT ONE CHANCE!
ARUMI, HANG ON TO THAT PENDANT, NO MATTER WHAT!
WHY?
SASSHI! WHAT'RE YOU GOING TO DO?!
O, PURE-BLOODED GOD OF TREACHERY, CONTROLLER OF THE VALVAS!
LOOK UPON ME, I DISPLAY THE SIGN OF THE KING, DELIVERED TO ME BY THE PRIESTESS OF THE CREATOR!
TELL ME THIS IS A JOKE!
IF THIS REALLY IS AN ARCADE OF SWORDS AND SORCERY...
...THEN MY SCHEME MIGHT ACTUALLY WORK!

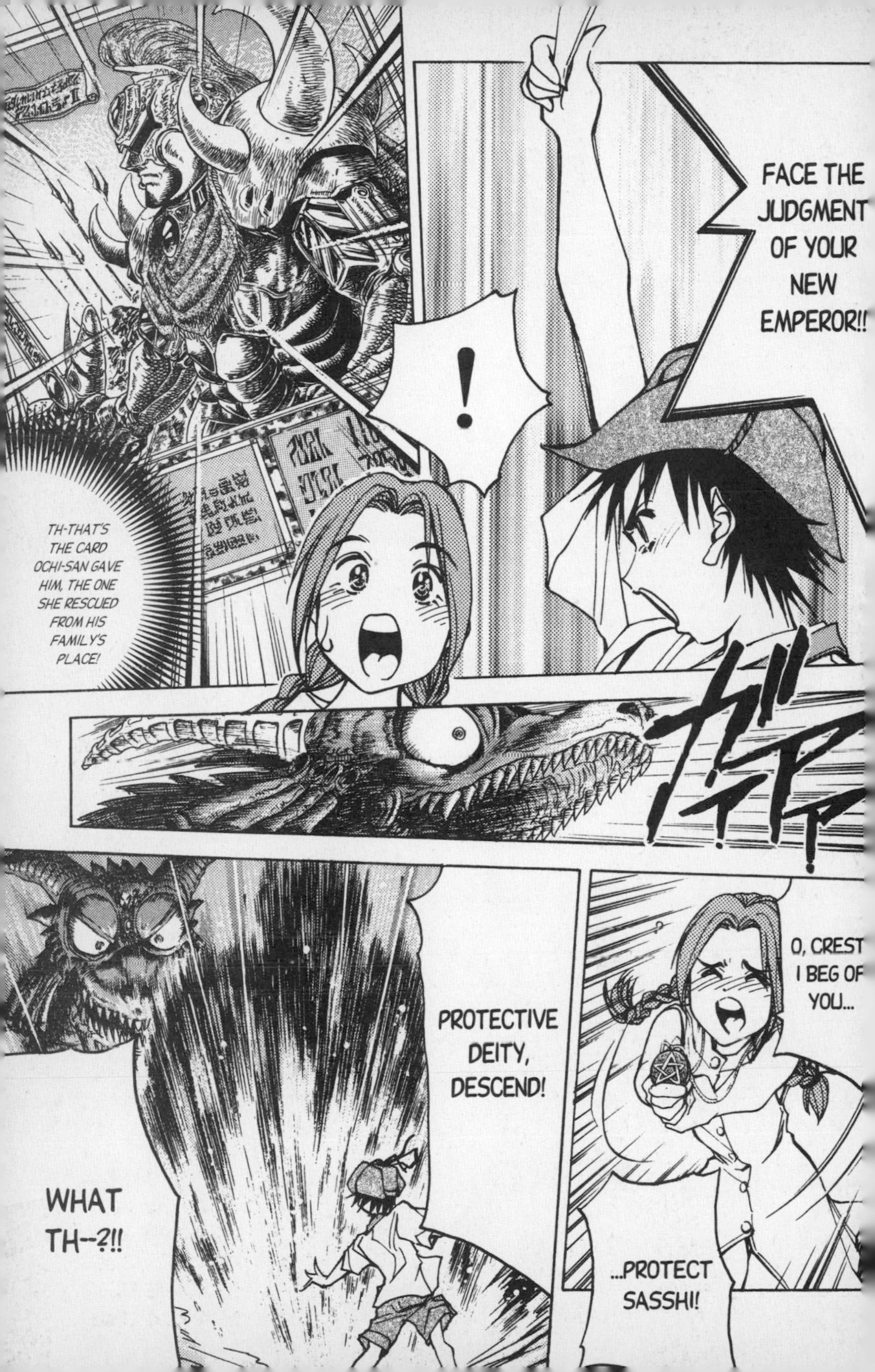
FACE THE JUDGMENT OF YOUR NEW EMPEROR!!
!
TH-THAT'S THE CARD OCHI-SAN GAVE HIM, THE ONE SHE RESCUED FROM HIS FAMILY'S PLACE!
O, CREST I BEG OF YOU...
...PROTECT SASSHI!
PROTECTIVE DEITY, DESCEND!
WHAT TH--?!!

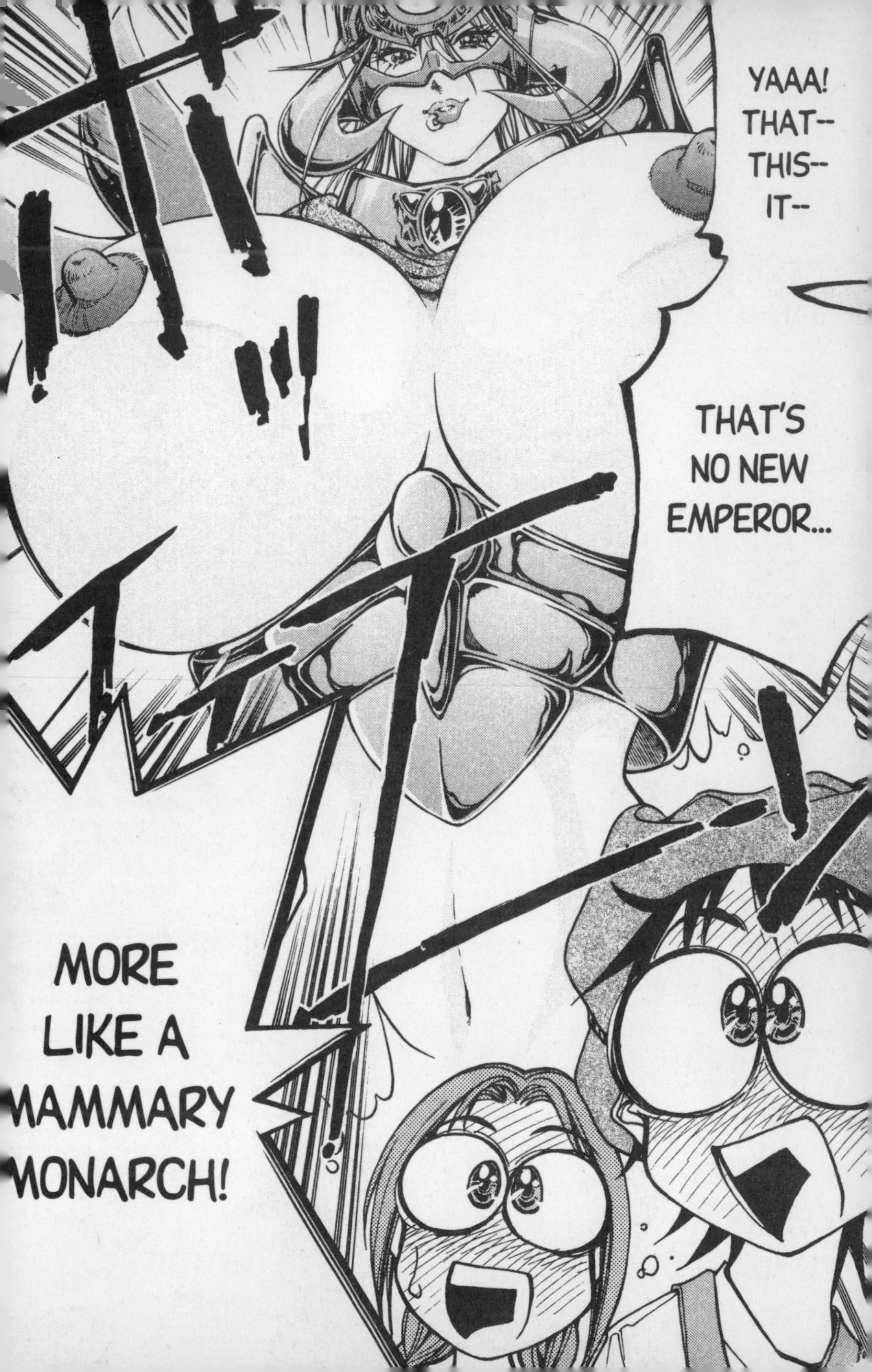
YAAA! THAT-- THIS-- IT--
THAT'S NO NEW EMPEROR...
MORE LIKE A MAMMARY MONARCH!

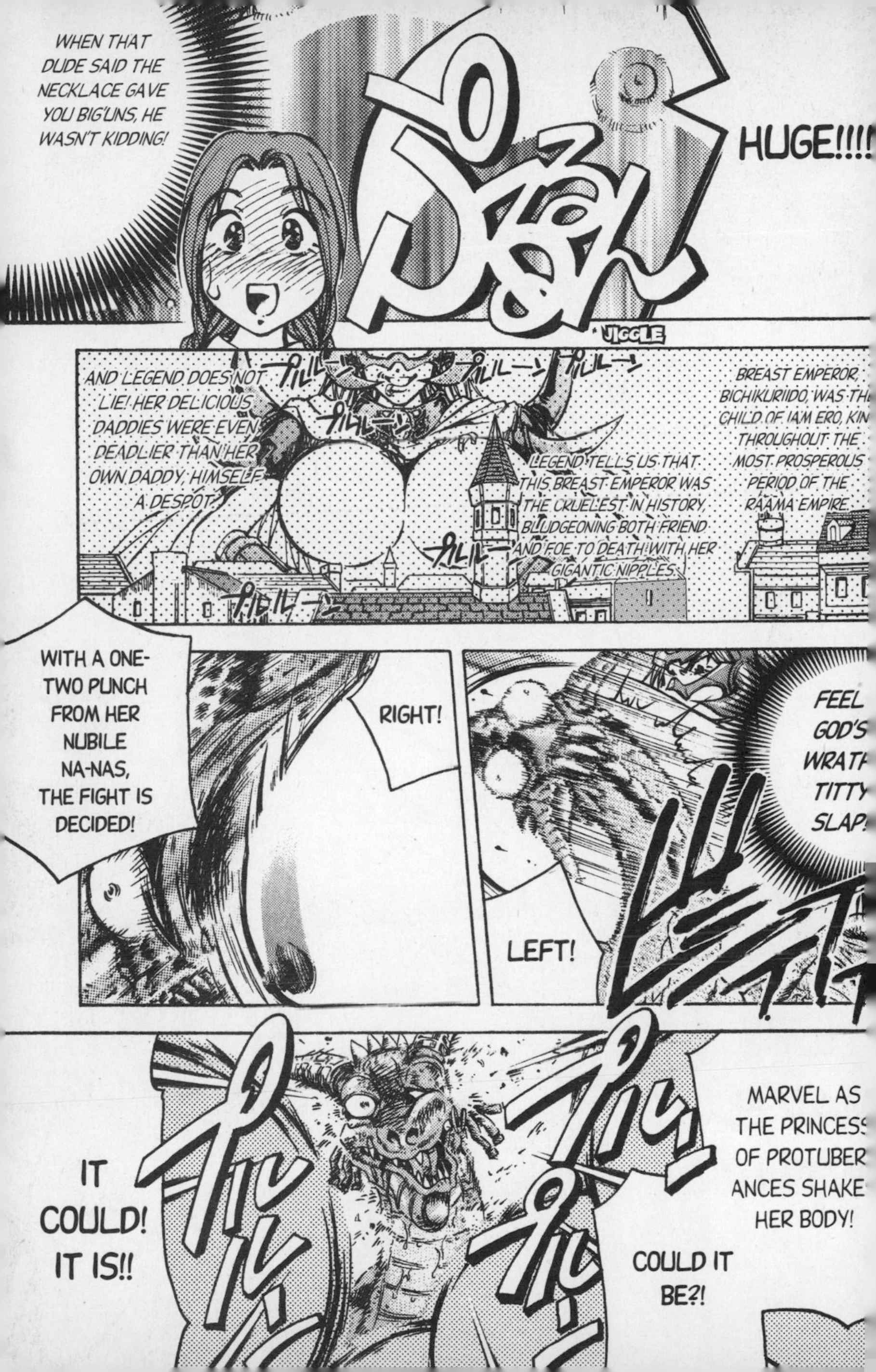
HUGE!!!!
JIGGLE
WHEN THAT DUDE SAID THE NECKLACE GAVE YOU BIG'UNS, HE WASN'T KIDDING!
BREAST EMPEROR, BICHIKURIIDO, WAS TH CHILD OF IAM ERO, KIN THROUGHOUT THE MOST PROSPEROUS PERIOD OF THE RAAMA EMPIRE.
LEGEND TELLS US THAT THIS BREAST EMPEROR WAS THE CRUELEST IN HISTORY, BLUDGEONING BOTH FRIEND AND FOE TO DEATH WITH HER GIGANTIC NIPPLES.
AND LEGEND DOES NOT LIE! HER DELICIOUS DADDIES WERE EVEN DEADLIER THAN HER OWN DADDY, HIMSELF A DESPOT.
FEEL GOD'S WRATH TITTY SLAP!
LEFT!
RIGHT!
WITH A ONE-TWO PUNCH FROM HER NUBILE NA-NAS, THE FIGHT IS DECIDED!
MARVEL AS THE PRINCESS OF PROTUBER ANCES SHAKE HER BODY!
COULD IT BE?!
IT COULD! IT IS!!

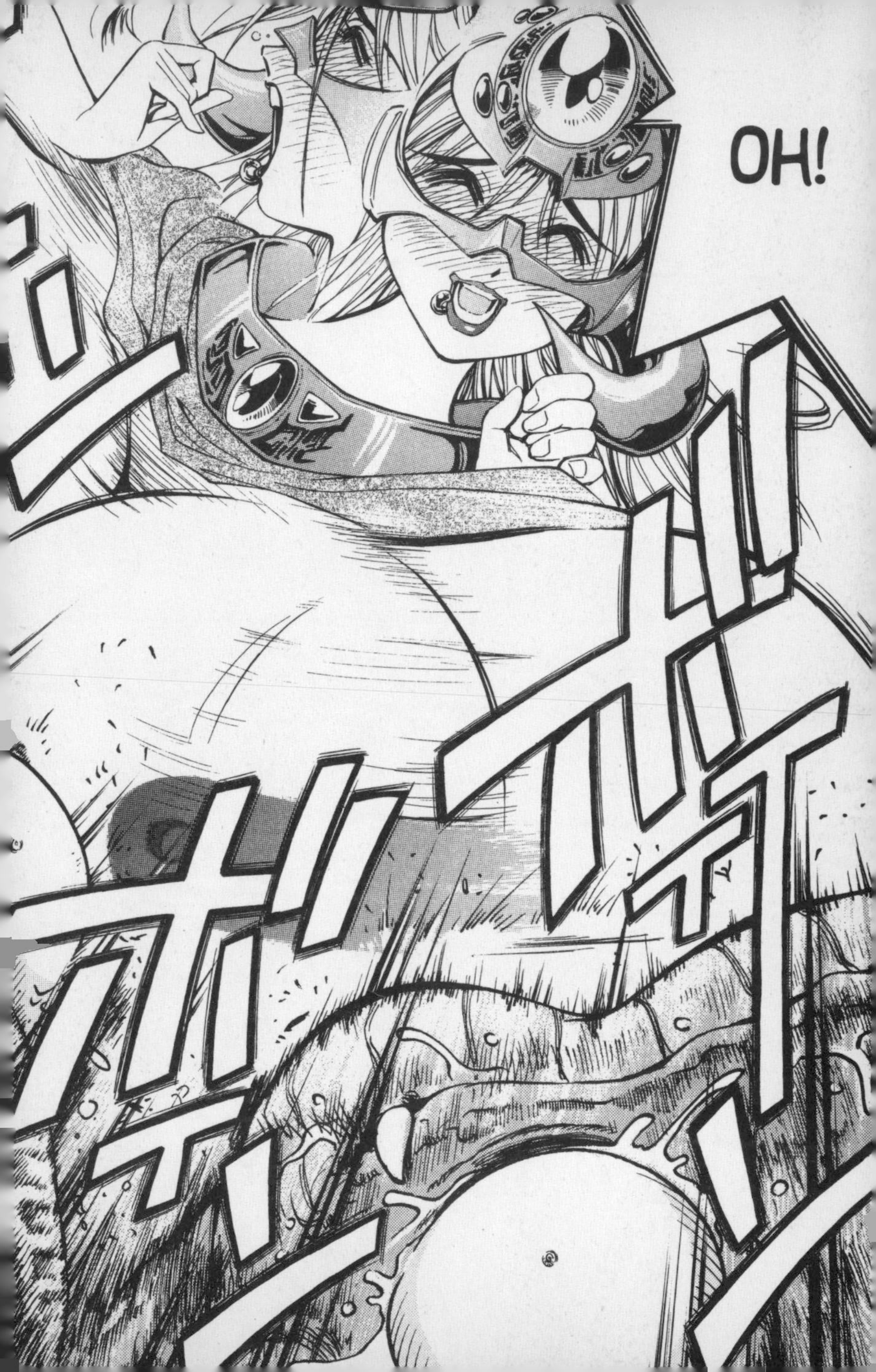
OH!

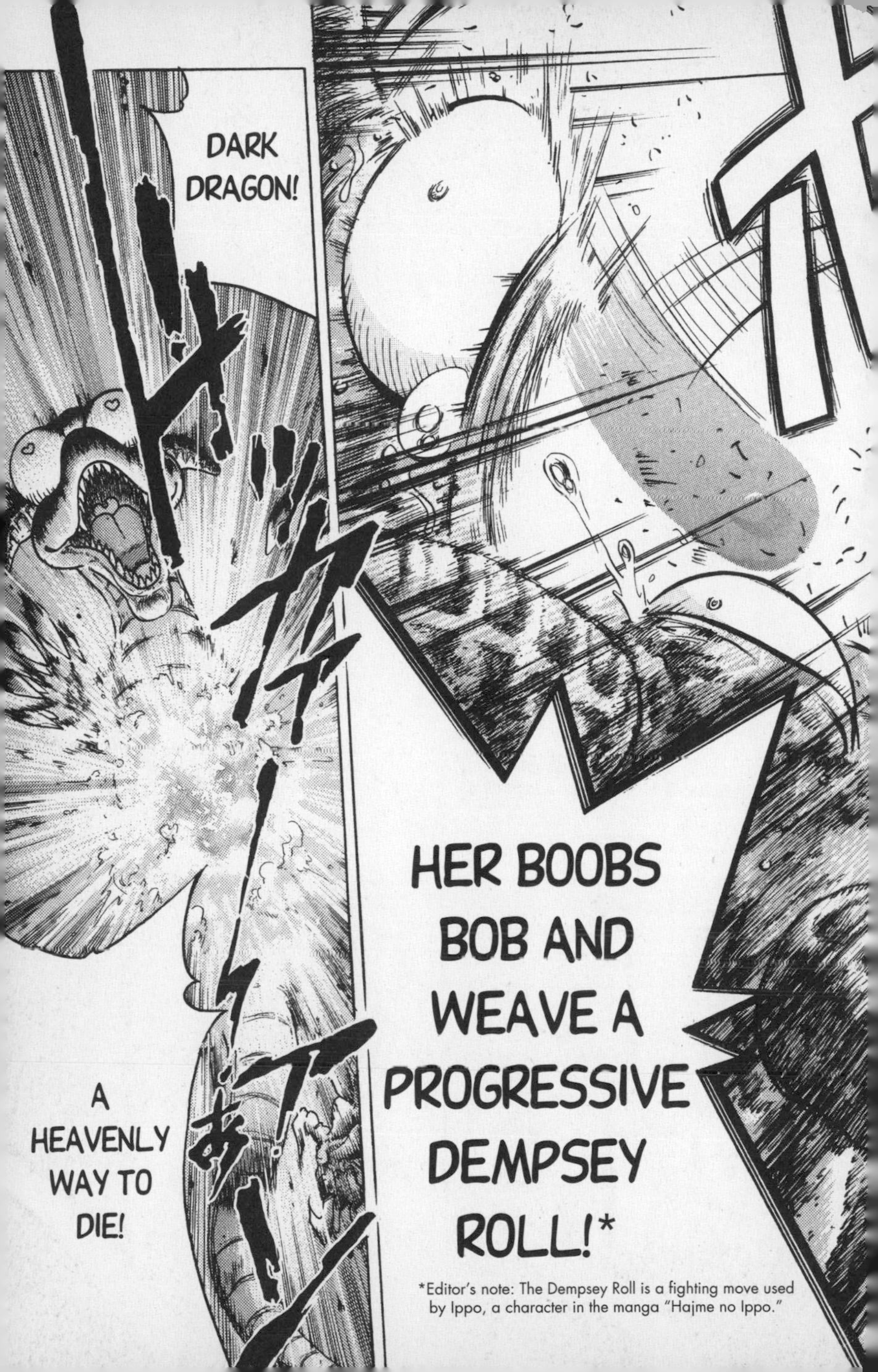
HER BOOBS BOB AND WEAVE A PROGRESSIVE DEMPSEY ROLL!*
DARK DRAGON!
A HEAVENLY WAY TO DIE!

*Editor's note: The Dempsey Roll is a fighting move used by Ippo, a character in the manga "Hajme no Ippo."

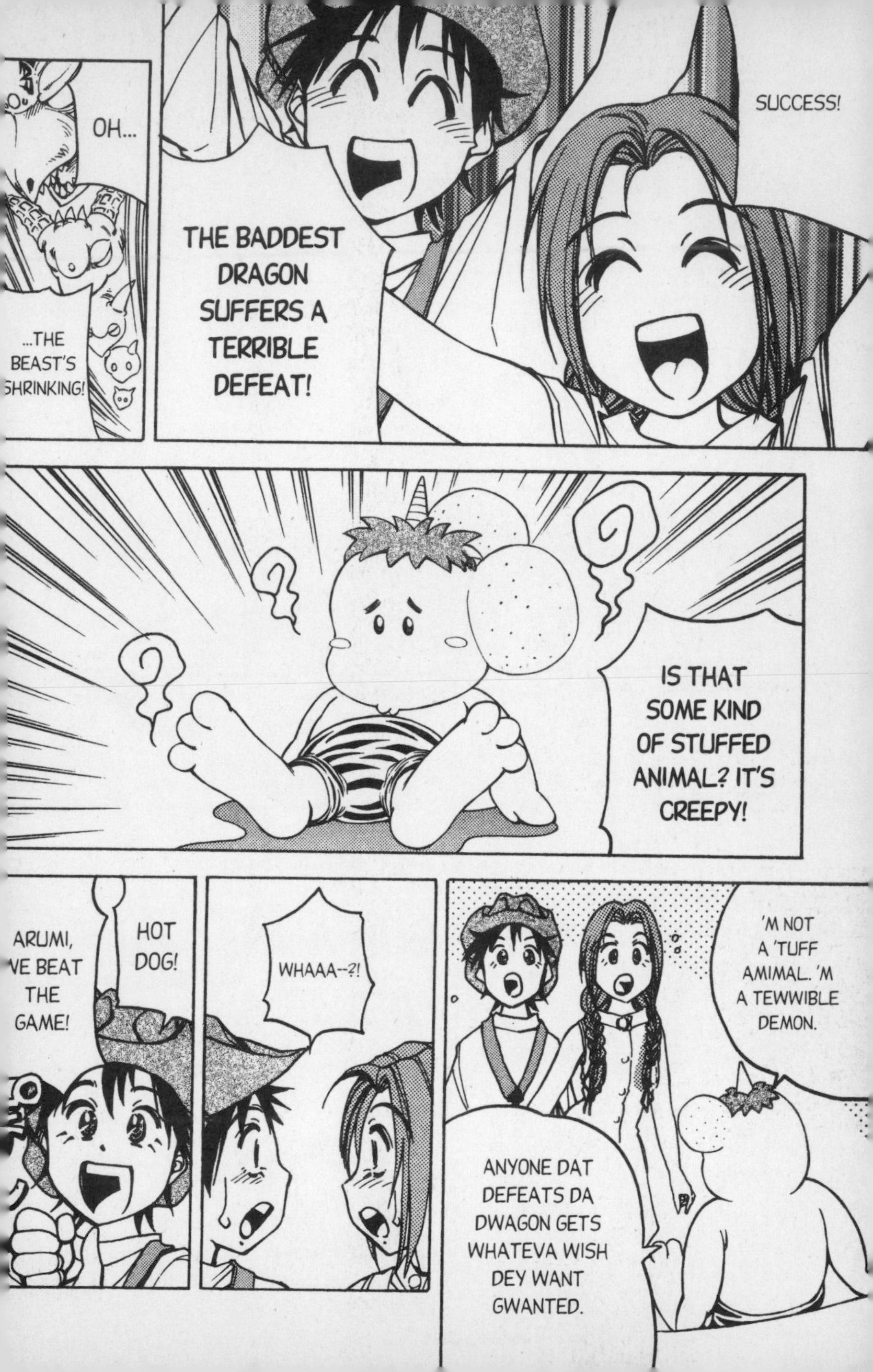
SUCCESS!
THE BADDEST DRAGON SUFFERS A TERRIBLE DEFEAT!
OH...
...THE BEAST'S SHRINKING!
IS THAT SOME KIND OF STUFFED ANIMAL? IT'S CREEPY!
'M NOT A 'TUFF AMIMAL. 'M A TEWWIBLE DEMON.
ANYONE DAT DEFEATS DA DWAGON GETS WHATEVA WISH DEY WANT GWANTED.
WHAAA--?!
HOT DOG!
ARUMI, WE BEAT THE GAME!

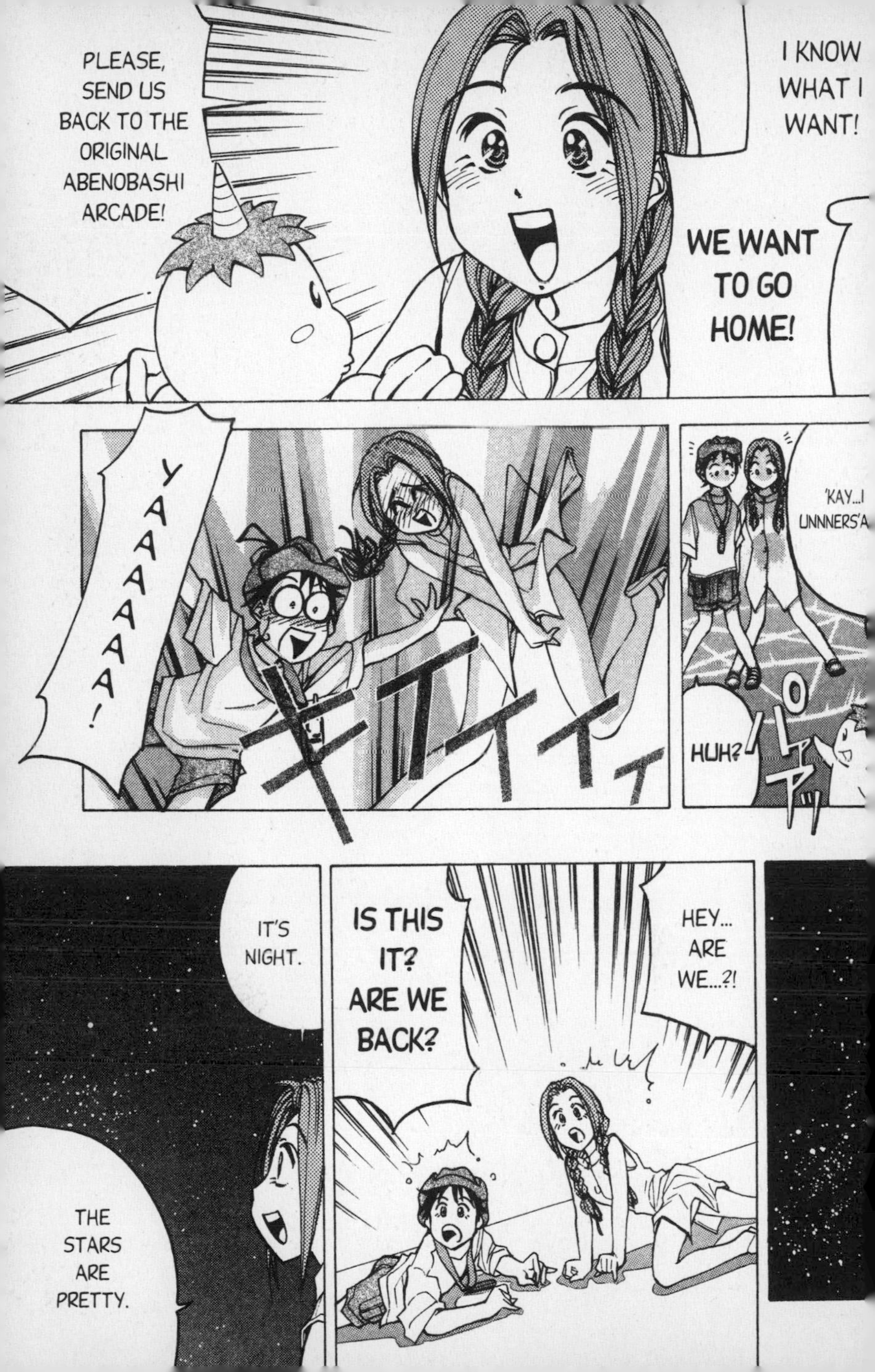
I KNOW WHAT I WANT!
WE WANT TO GO HOME!
PLEASE, SEND US BACK TO THE ORIGINAL ABENOBASHI ARCADE!
'KAY...I UNNNERS'A
HUH?
YAAAAAAA!
HEY... ARE WE...?!
IS THIS IT? ARE WE BACK?
IT'S NIGHT.
THE STARS ARE PRETTY.

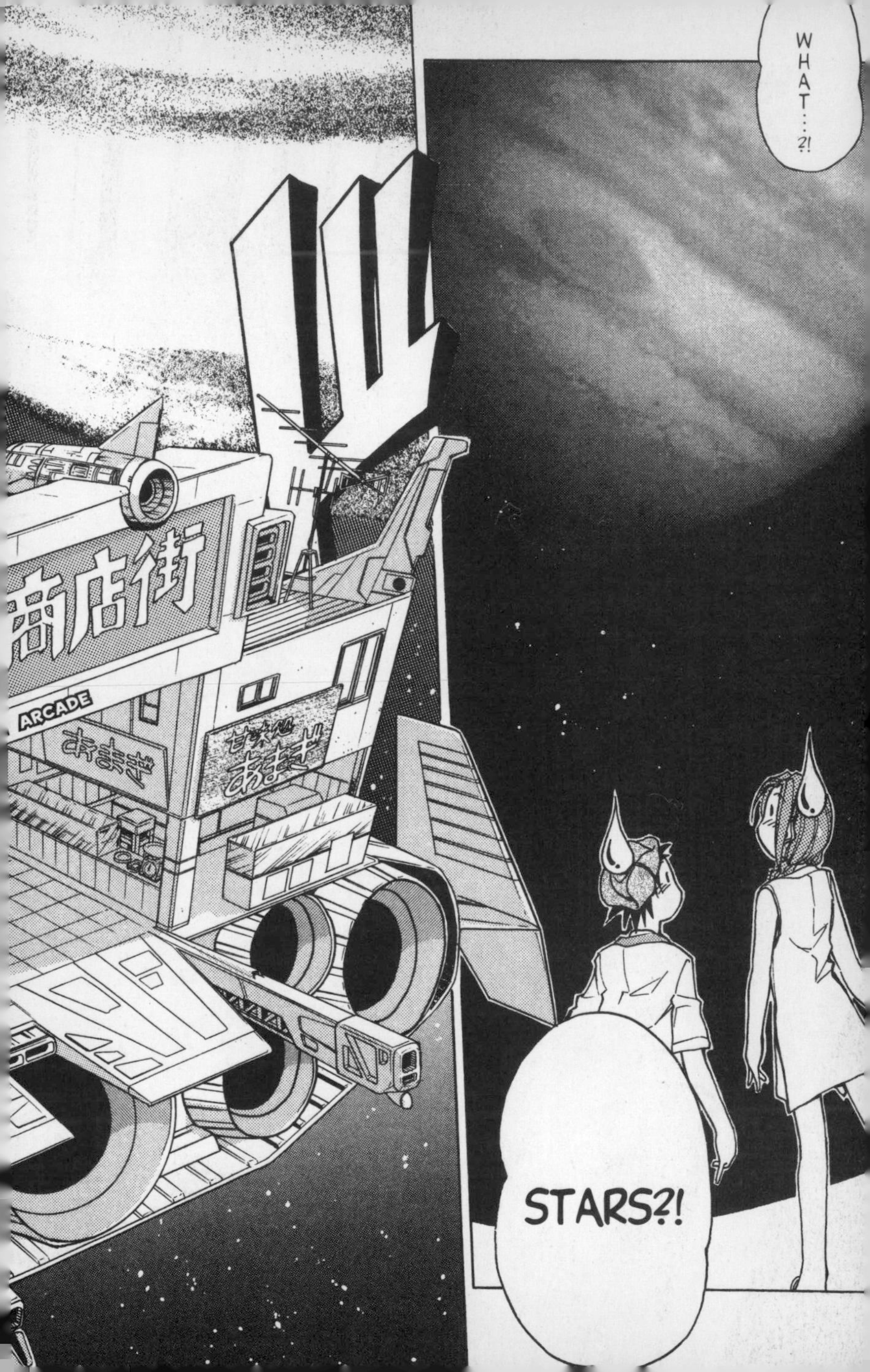
WHAT...?!
STARS?!
商店街
ARCADE
あまぎ
あまぎ

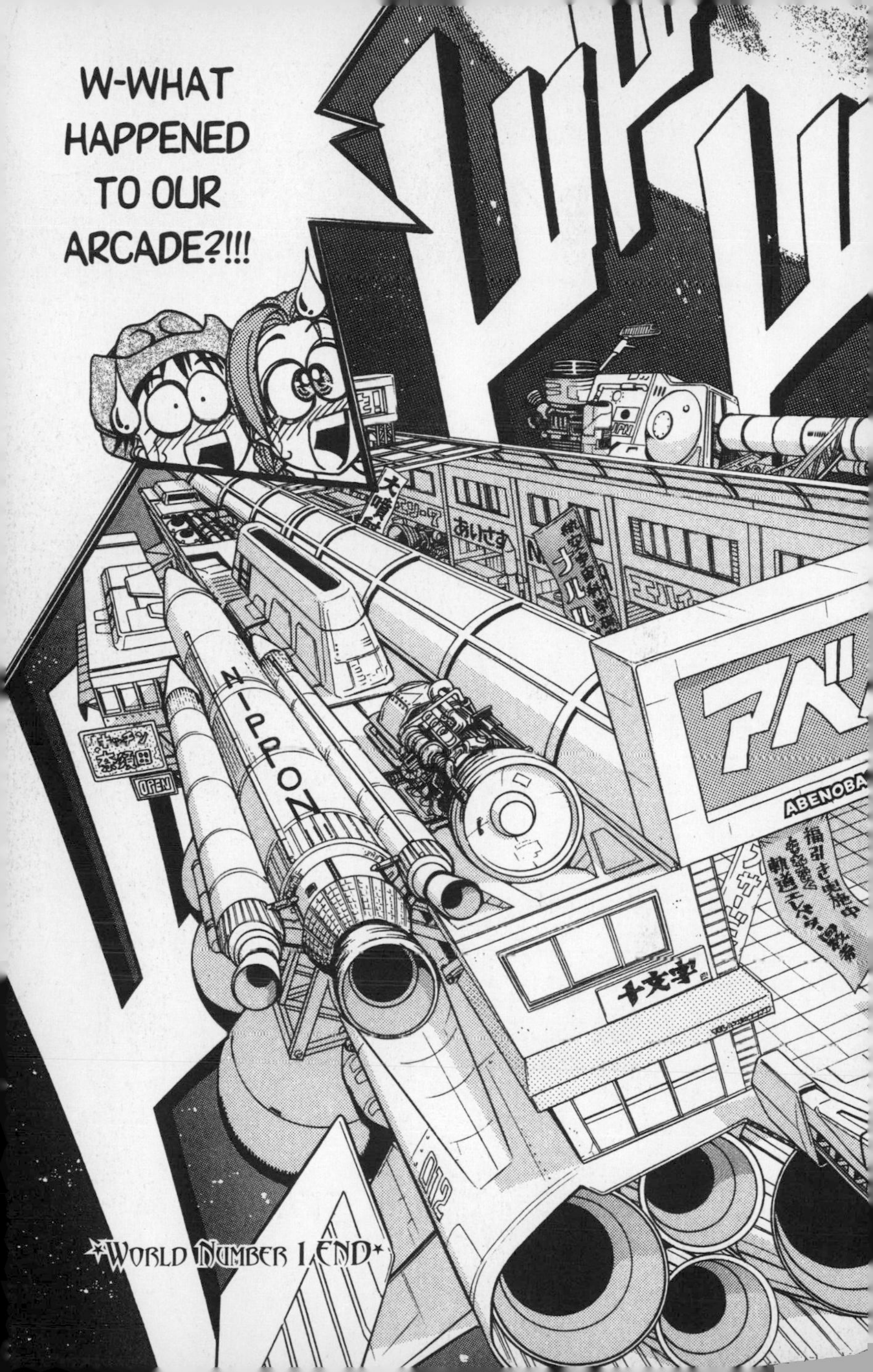
W-WHAT HAPPENED TO OUR ARCADE?!!!
NIPPON
OPEN
ABENOBA
WORLD NUMBER 1, END

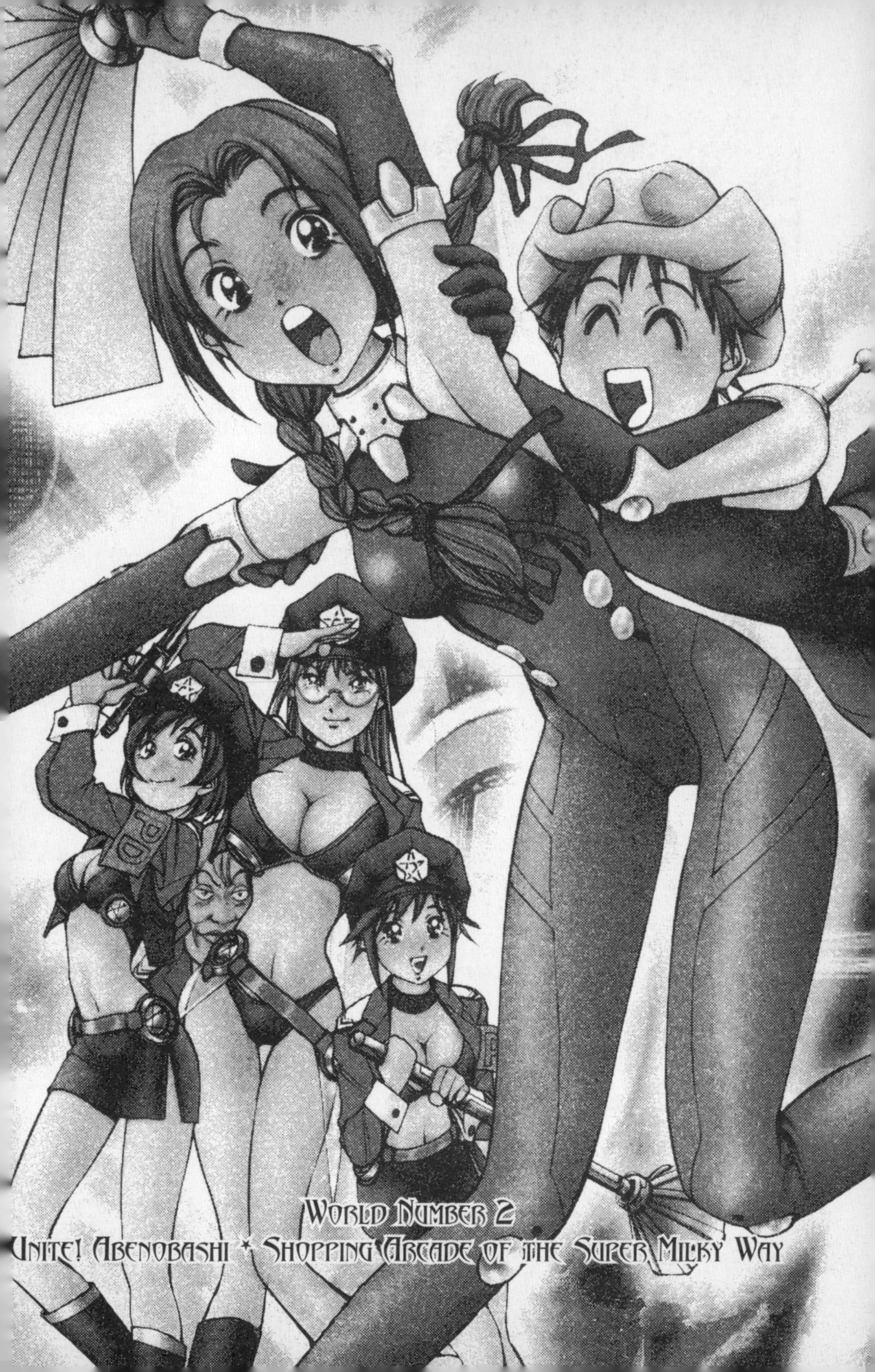
World Number 2
Unite! Abenobashi ☆ Shopping Arcade of the Super Milky Way

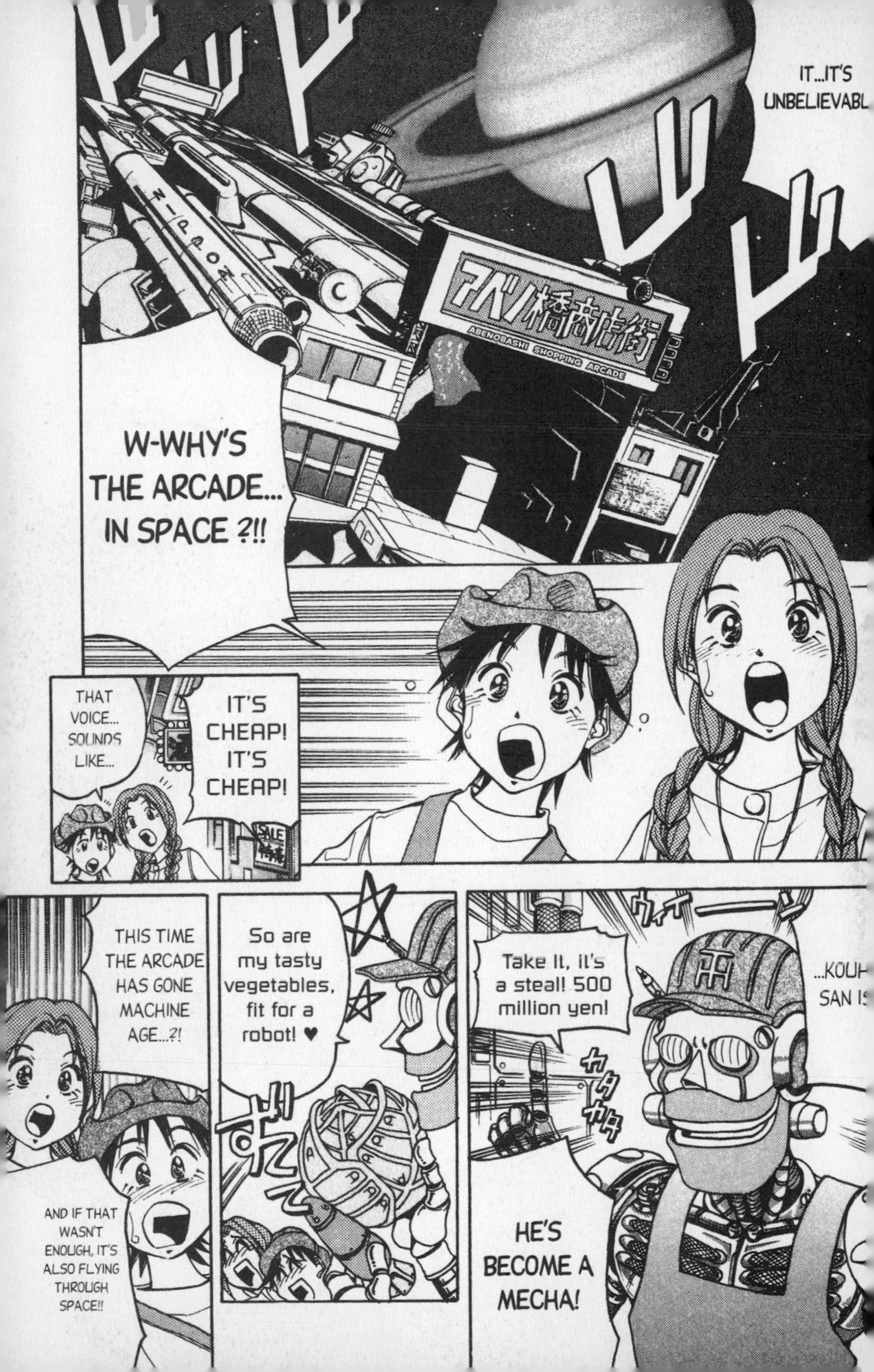
IT...IT'S UNBELIEVABL
NIPPON
アベノ橋商店街
ABENOBASHI SHOPPING ARCADE
W-WHY'S THE ARCADE... IN SPACE ?!!
IT'S CHEAP! IT'S CHEAP!
THAT VOICE... SOUNDS LIKE...
SALE
...KOUH SAN IS
Take it, it's a steal! 500 million yen!
HE'S BECOME A MECHA!
So are my tasty vegetables, fit for a robot! ♥
THIS TIME THE ARCADE HAS GONE MACHINE AGE...?!
AND IF THAT WASN'T ENOUGH, IT'S ALSO FLYING THROUGH SPACE!!

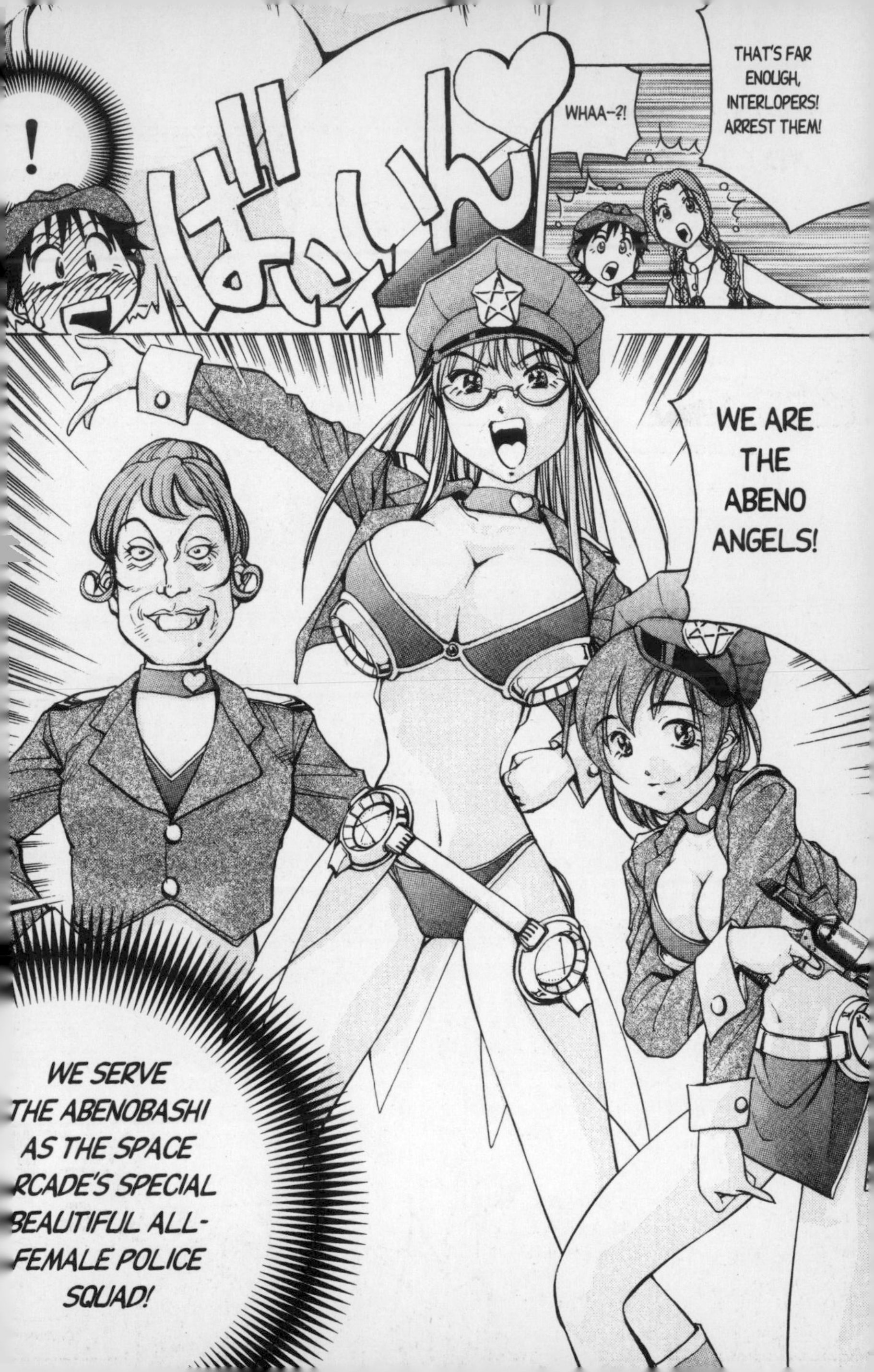
THAT'S FAR ENOUGH, INTERLOPERS! ARREST THEM!
WHAA--?!
!
WE ARE THE ABENO ANGELS!
WE SERVE THE ABENOBASHI AS THE SPACE RCADE'S SPECIAL BEAUTIFUL ALL-FEMALE POLICE SQUAD!

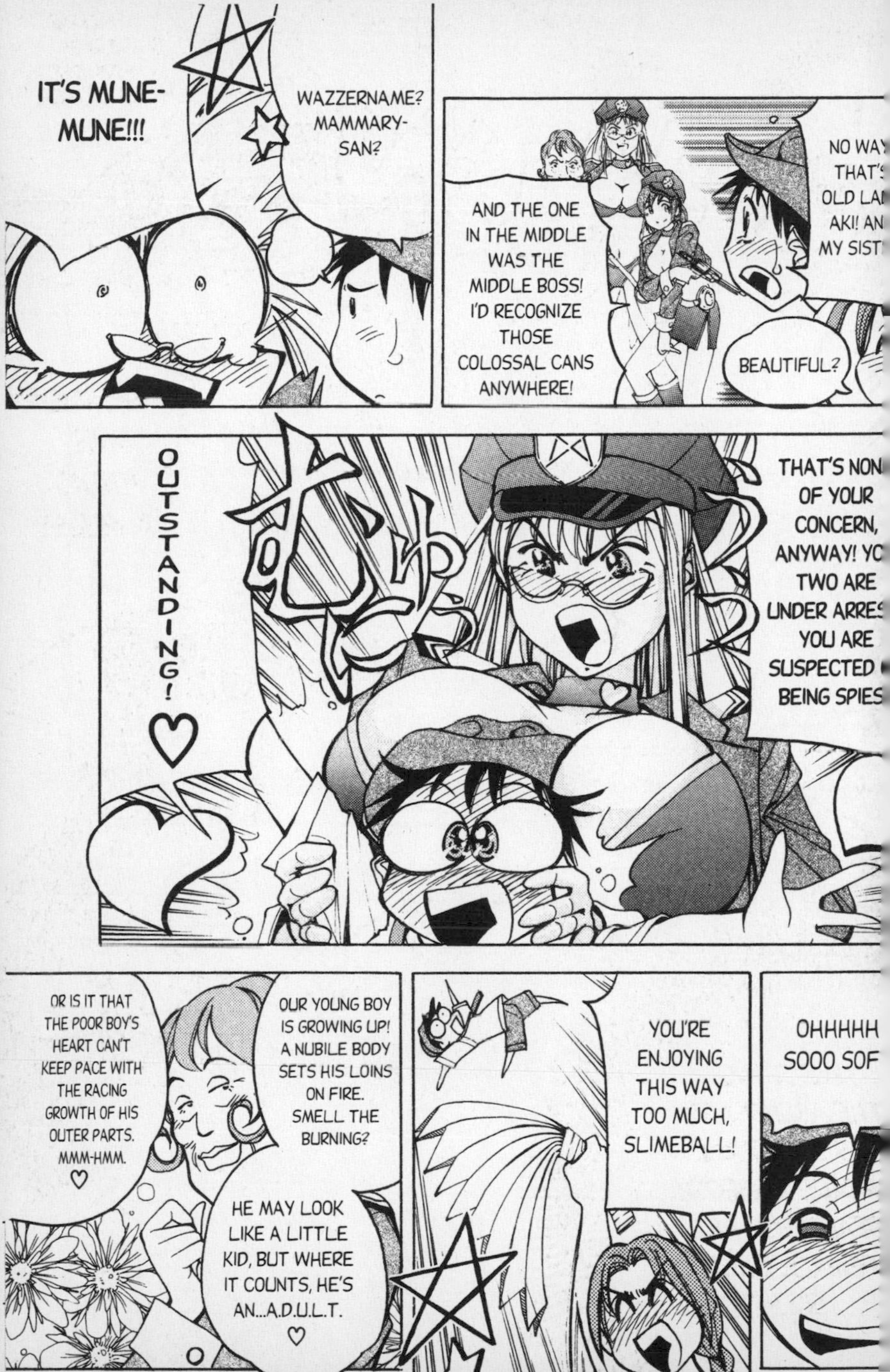
NO WAY THAT'S OLD LA AKI! AN MY SIST
BEAUTIFUL?
AND THE ONE IN THE MIDDLE WAS THE MIDDLE BOSS! I'D RECOGNIZE THOSE COLOSSAL CANS ANYWHERE!
WAZZERNAME? MAMMARY-SAN?
IT'S MUNE-MUNE!!!
THAT'S NON OF YOUR CONCERN, ANYWAY! YO TWO ARE UNDER ARRES YOU ARE SUSPECTED BEING SPIES
OUTSTANDING! ♥
OHHHHH SOOO SOF
YOU'RE ENJOYING THIS WAY TOO MUCH, SLIMEBALL!
OUR YOUNG BOY IS GROWING UP! A NUBILE BODY SETS HIS LOINS ON FIRE. SMELL THE BURNING?
OR IS IT THAT THE POOR BOY'S HEART CAN'T KEEP PACE WITH THE RACING GROWTH OF HIS OUTER PARTS. MMM-HMM. ♥
HE MAY LOOK LIKE A LITTLE KID, BUT WHERE IT COUNTS, HE'S AN...A.D.U.L.T. ♥

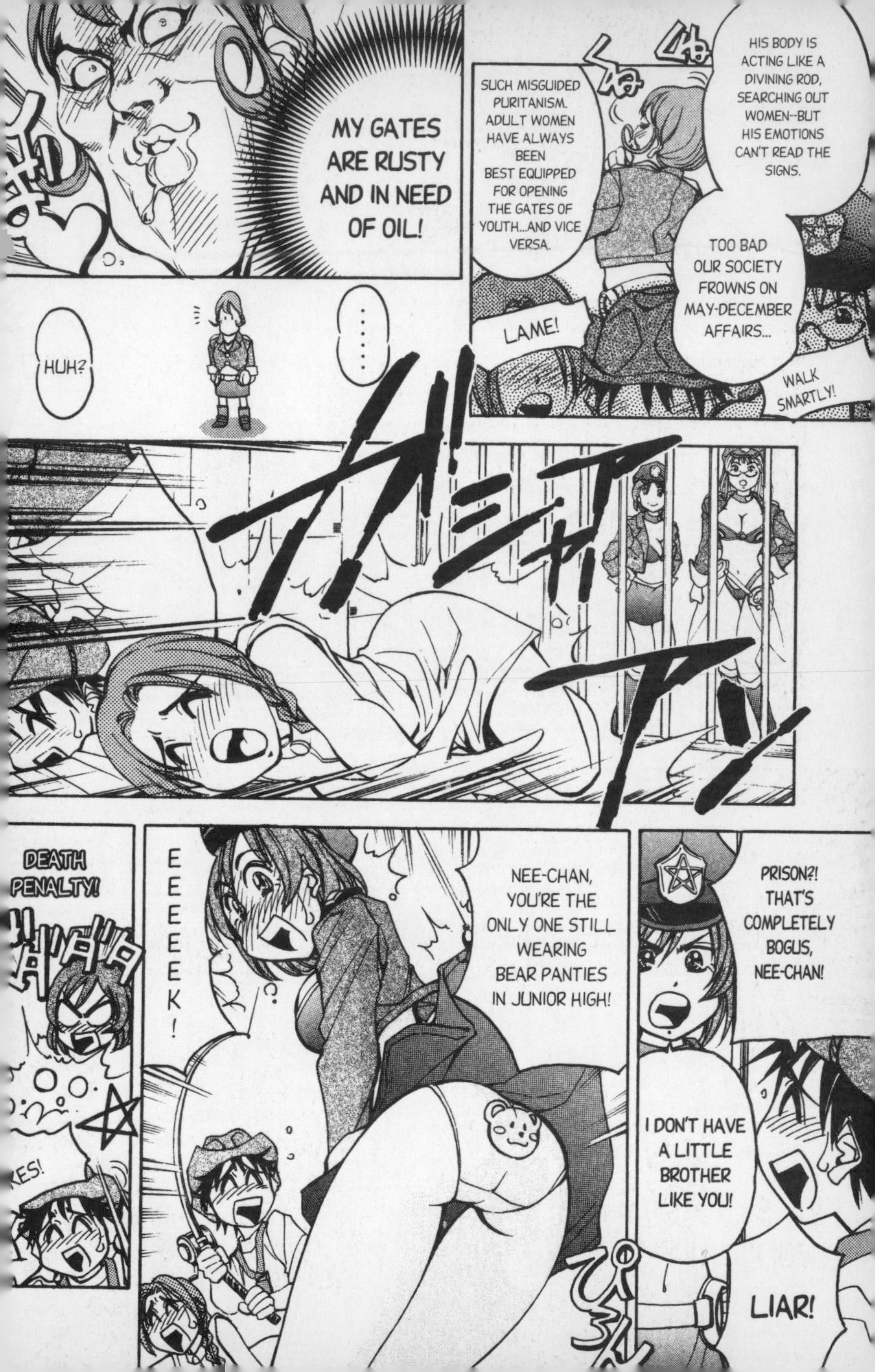

HIS BODY IS ACTING LIKE A DIVINING ROD, SEARCHING OUT WOMEN--BUT HIS EMOTIONS CAN'T READ THE SIGNS.
SUCH MISGUIDED PURITANISM. ADULT WOMEN HAVE ALWAYS BEEN BEST EQUIPPED FOR OPENING THE GATES OF YOUTH...AND VICE VERSA.
TOO BAD OUR SOCIETY FROWNS ON MAY-DECEMBER AFFAIRS...
LAME!
WALK SMARTLY!
MY GATES ARE RUSTY AND IN NEED OF OIL!
......
HUH?
ガシャアン
PRISON?! THAT'S COMPLETELY BOGUS, NEE-CHAN!
I DON'T HAVE A LITTLE BROTHER LIKE YOU!
LIAR!
NEE-CHAN, YOU'RE THE ONLY ONE STILL WEARING BEAR PANTIES IN JUNIOR HIGH!
EEEEEK!
DEATH PENALTY!

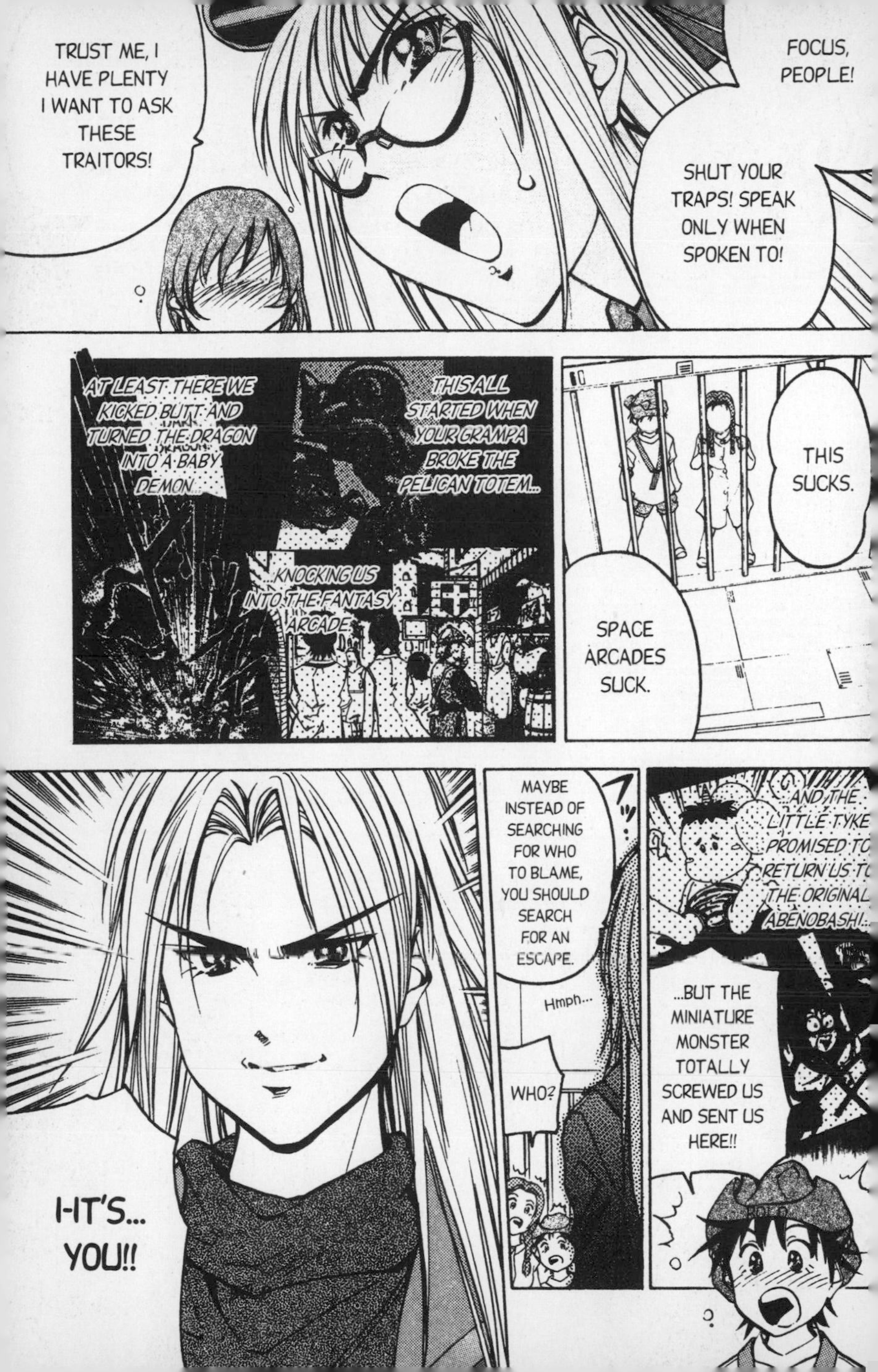
FOCUS, PEOPLE!
SHUT YOUR TRAPS! SPEAK ONLY WHEN SPOKEN TO!
TRUST ME, I HAVE PLENTY I WANT TO ASK THESE TRAITORS!
THIS SUCKS.
SPACE ARCADES SUCK.
THIS ALL STARTED WHEN YOUR GRAMPA BROKE THE PELICAN TOTEM...
KNOCKING US INTO THE FANTASY ARCADE.
AT LEAST THERE WE KICKED BUTT AND TURNED THE DRAGON INTO A BABY DEMON...
...AND THE LITTLE TYKE PROMISED TO RETURN US TO THE ORIGINAL ABENOBASHI...
...BUT THE MINIATURE MONSTER TOTALLY SCREWED US AND SENT US HERE!!
MAYBE INSTEAD OF SEARCHING FOR WHO TO BLAME, YOU SHOULD SEARCH FOR AN ESCAPE.
Hmph...
WHO?
I-IT'S... YOU!!

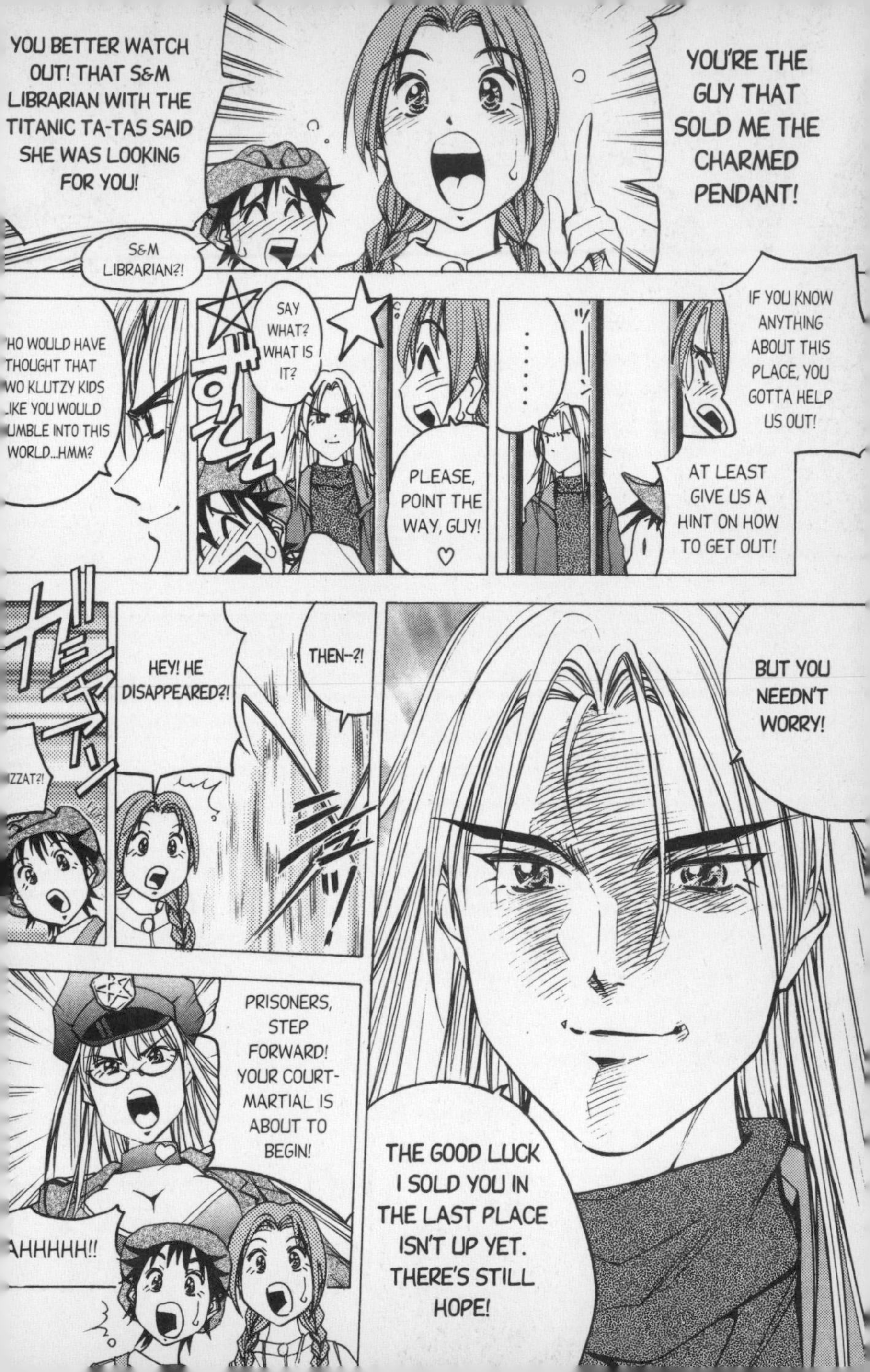
YOU'RE THE GUY THAT SOLD ME THE CHARMED PENDANT!
YOU BETTER WATCH OUT! THAT S&M LIBRARIAN WITH THE TITANIC TA-TAS SAID SHE WAS LOOKING FOR YOU!
S&M LIBRARIAN?!
IF YOU KNOW ANYTHING ABOUT THIS PLACE, YOU GOTTA HELP US OUT!
AT LEAST GIVE US A HINT ON HOW TO GET OUT!
......
!!
PLEASE, POINT THE WAY, GUY! ♡
SAY WHAT? WHAT IS IT?
HO WOULD HAVE THOUGHT THAT WO KLUTZY KIDS IKE YOU WOULD UMBLE INTO THIS WORLD...HMM?
BUT YOU NEEDN'T WORRY!
THE GOOD LUCK I SOLD YOU IN THE LAST PLACE ISN'T UP YET. THERE'S STILL HOPE!
THEN--?!
HEY! HE DISAPPEARED?!
IZZAT?!
PRISONERS, STEP FORWARD! YOUR COURT-MARTIAL IS ABOUT TO BEGIN!
AHHHHH!!

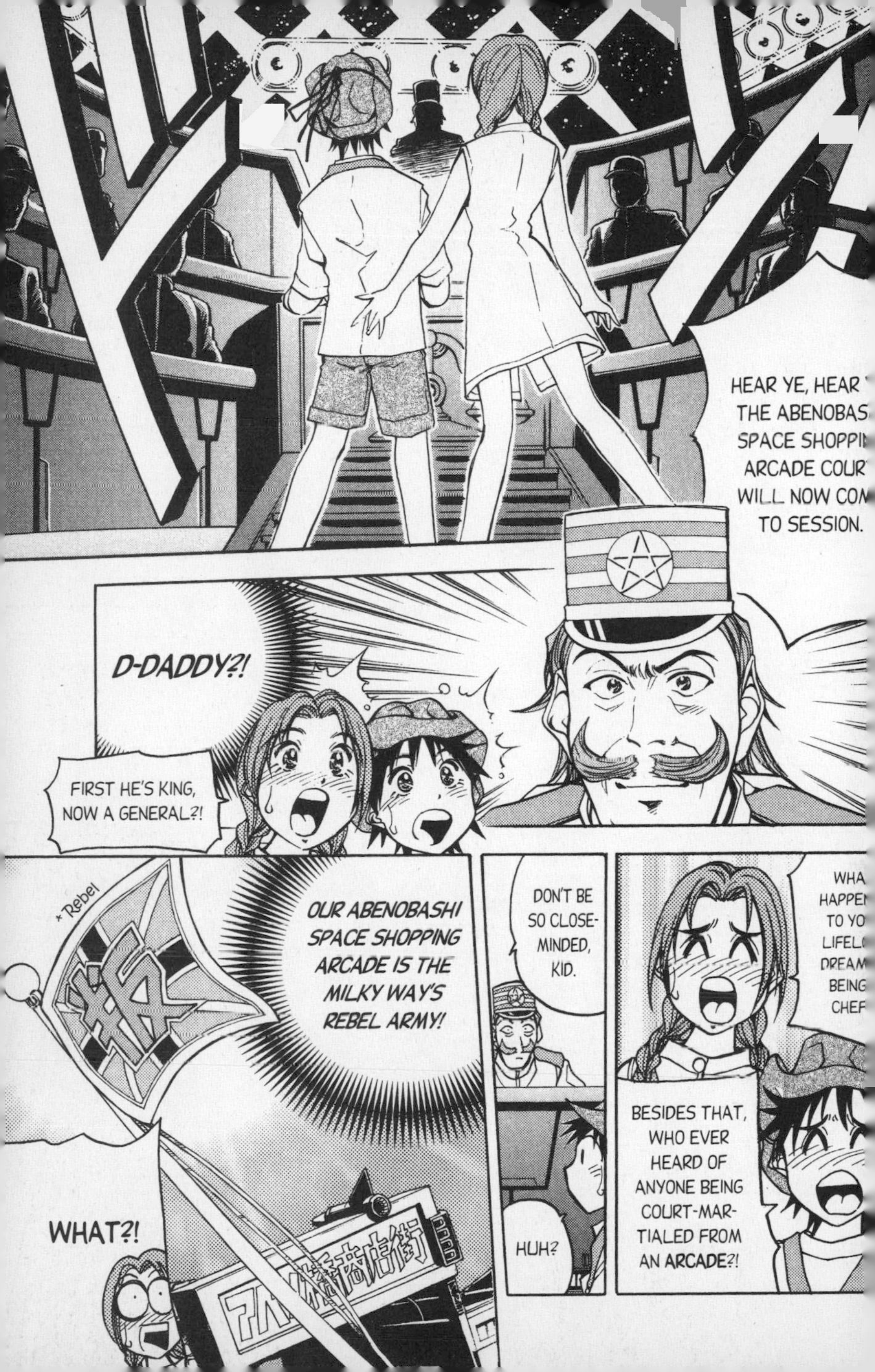
HEAR YE, HEAR
THE ABENOBAS
SPACE SHOPPI
ARCADE COUR
WILL NOW CO
TO SESSION.
D-DADDY?!
FIRST HE'S KING, NOW A GENERAL?!
WHA
HAPPEN
TO YO
LIFEL
DREAM
BEING
CHEF
BESIDES THAT, WHO EVER HEARD OF ANYONE BEING COURT-MARTIALED FROM AN ARCADE?!
DON'T BE SO CLOSE-MINDED, KID.
HUH?
OUR ABENOBASHI SPACE SHOPPING ARCADE IS THE MILKY WAY'S REBEL ARMY!
* Rebel
WHAT?!

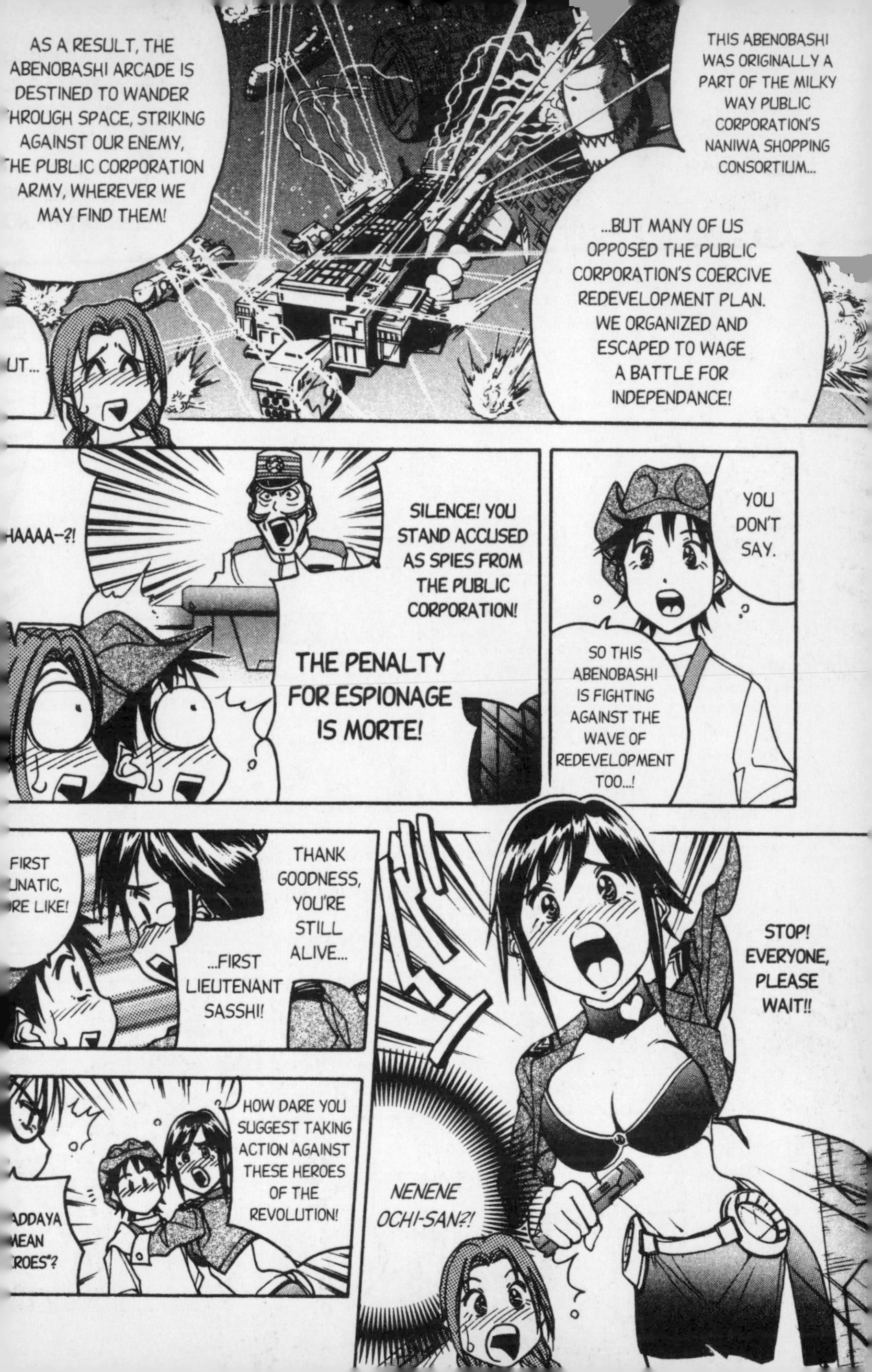
THIS ABENOBASHI WAS ORIGINALLY A PART OF THE MILKY WAY PUBLIC CORPORATION'S NANIWA SHOPPING CONSORTIUM...
...BUT MANY OF US OPPOSED THE PUBLIC CORPORATION'S COERCIVE REDEVELOPMENT PLAN. WE ORGANIZED AND ESCAPED TO WAGE A BATTLE FOR INDEPENDANCE!
AS A RESULT, THE ABENOBASHI ARCADE IS DESTINED TO WANDER THROUGH SPACE, STRIKING AGAINST OUR ENEMY, THE PUBLIC CORPORATION ARMY, WHEREVER WE MAY FIND THEM!
UT...
YOU DON'T SAY.
SO THIS ABENOBASHI IS FIGHTING AGAINST THE WAVE OF REDEVELOPMENT TOO...!
SILENCE! YOU STAND ACCUSED AS SPIES FROM THE PUBLIC CORPORATION!
THE PENALTY FOR ESPIONAGE IS MORTE!
HAAAA--?!
STOP! EVERYONE, PLEASE WAIT!!
NENENE OCHI-SAN?!
THANK GOODNESS, YOU'RE STILL ALIVE...
...FIRST LIEUTENANT SASSHI!
FIRST UNATIC, RE LIKE!
HOW DARE YOU SUGGEST TAKING ACTION AGAINST THESE HEROES OF THE REVOLUTION!
ADDAYA MEAN ROES"?

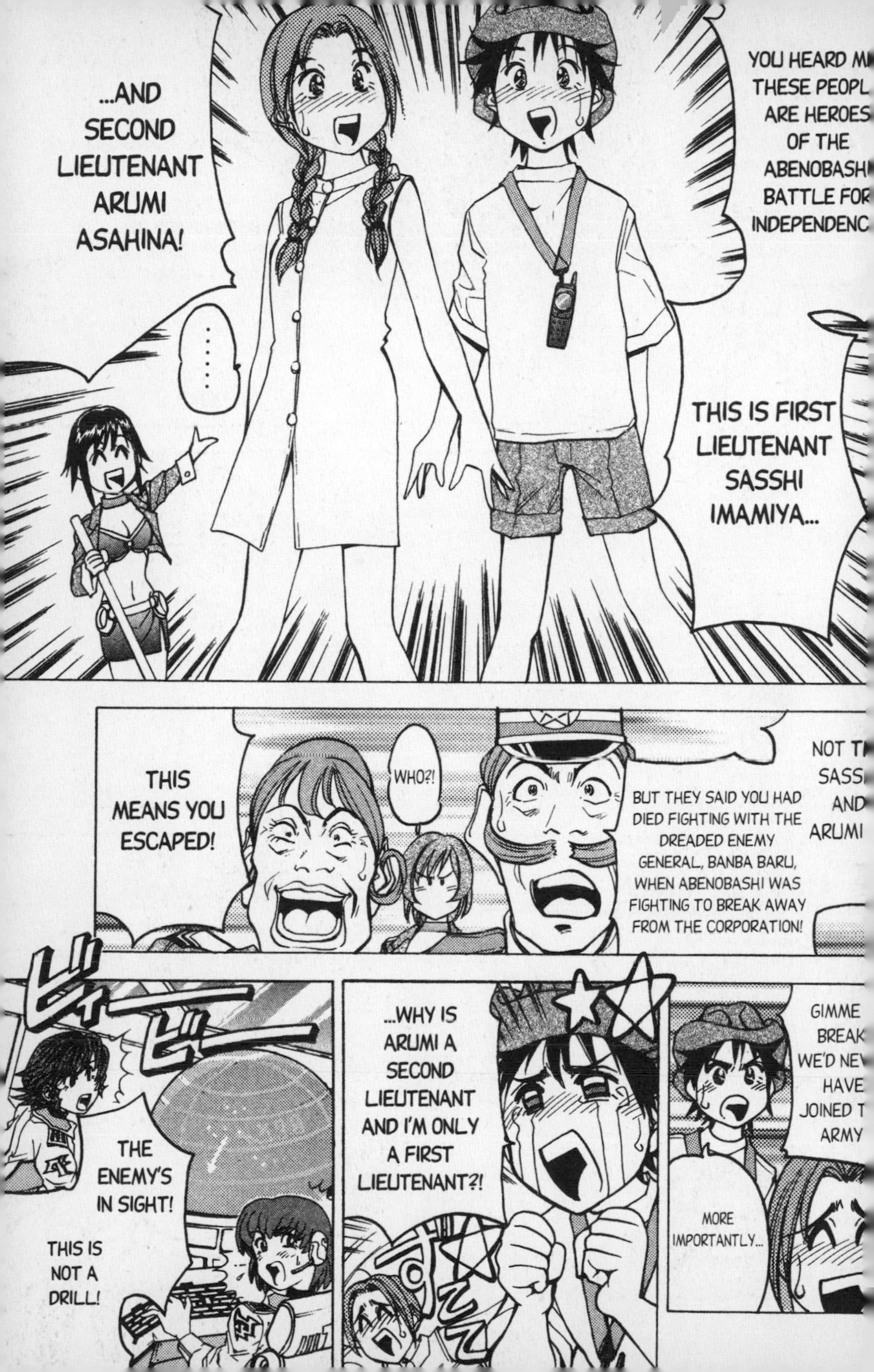

YOU HEARD M THESE PEOPL ARE HEROES OF THE ABENOBASH BATTLE FOR INDEPENDENC
THIS IS FIRST LIEUTENANT SASSHI IMAMIYA...
...AND SECOND LIEUTENANT ARUMI ASAHINA!
......
NOT T SASS AND ARUMI
BUT THEY SAID YOU HAD DIED FIGHTING WITH THE DREADED ENEMY GENERAL, BANBA BARU, WHEN ABENOBASHI WAS FIGHTING TO BREAK AWAY FROM THE CORPORATION!
WHO?!
THIS MEANS YOU ESCAPED!
GIMME BREAK WE'D NE HAVE JOINED T ARMY
MORE IMPORTANTLY...
...WHY IS ARUMI A SECOND LIEUTENANT AND I'M ONLY A FIRST LIEUTENANT?!
ビィー ビー
THE ENEMY'S IN SIGHT!
THIS IS NOT A DRILL!

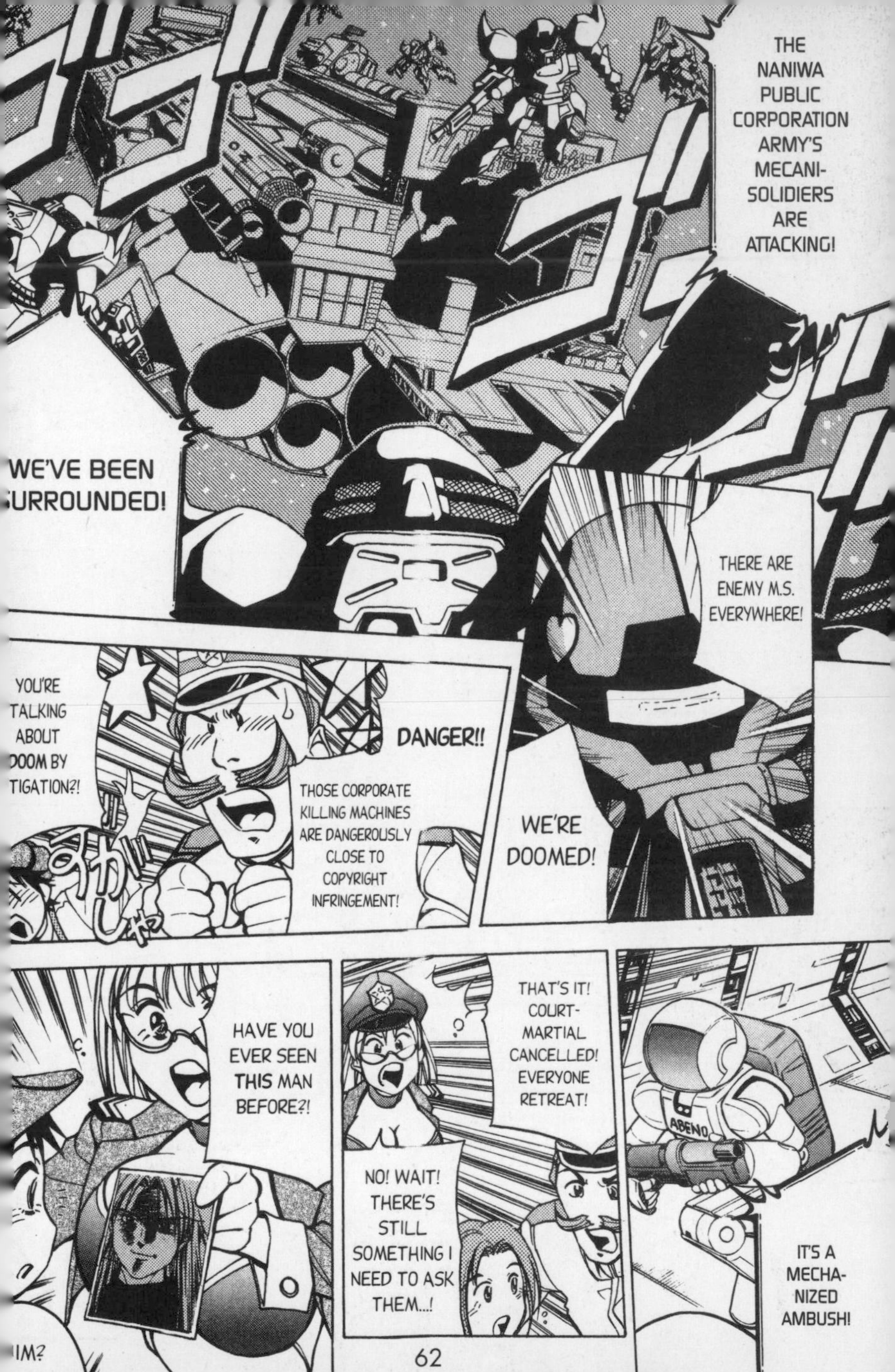
THE NANIWA PUBLIC CORPORATION ARMY'S MECANI-SOLIDIERS ARE ATTACKING!
WE'VE BEEN SURROUNDED!
THERE ARE ENEMY M.S. EVERYWHERE!
WE'RE DOOMED!
DANGER!!
THOSE CORPORATE KILLING MACHINES ARE DANGEROUSLY CLOSE TO COPYRIGHT INFRINGEMENT!
YOU'RE TALKING ABOUT DOOM BY TIGATION?!
IT'S A MECHANIZED AMBUSH!
ABENO
THAT'S IT! COURT-MARTIAL CANCELLED! EVERYONE RETREAT!
NO! WAIT! THERE'S STILL SOMETHING I NEED TO ASK THEM...!
HAVE YOU EVER SEEN **THIS** MAN BEFORE?!
IM?

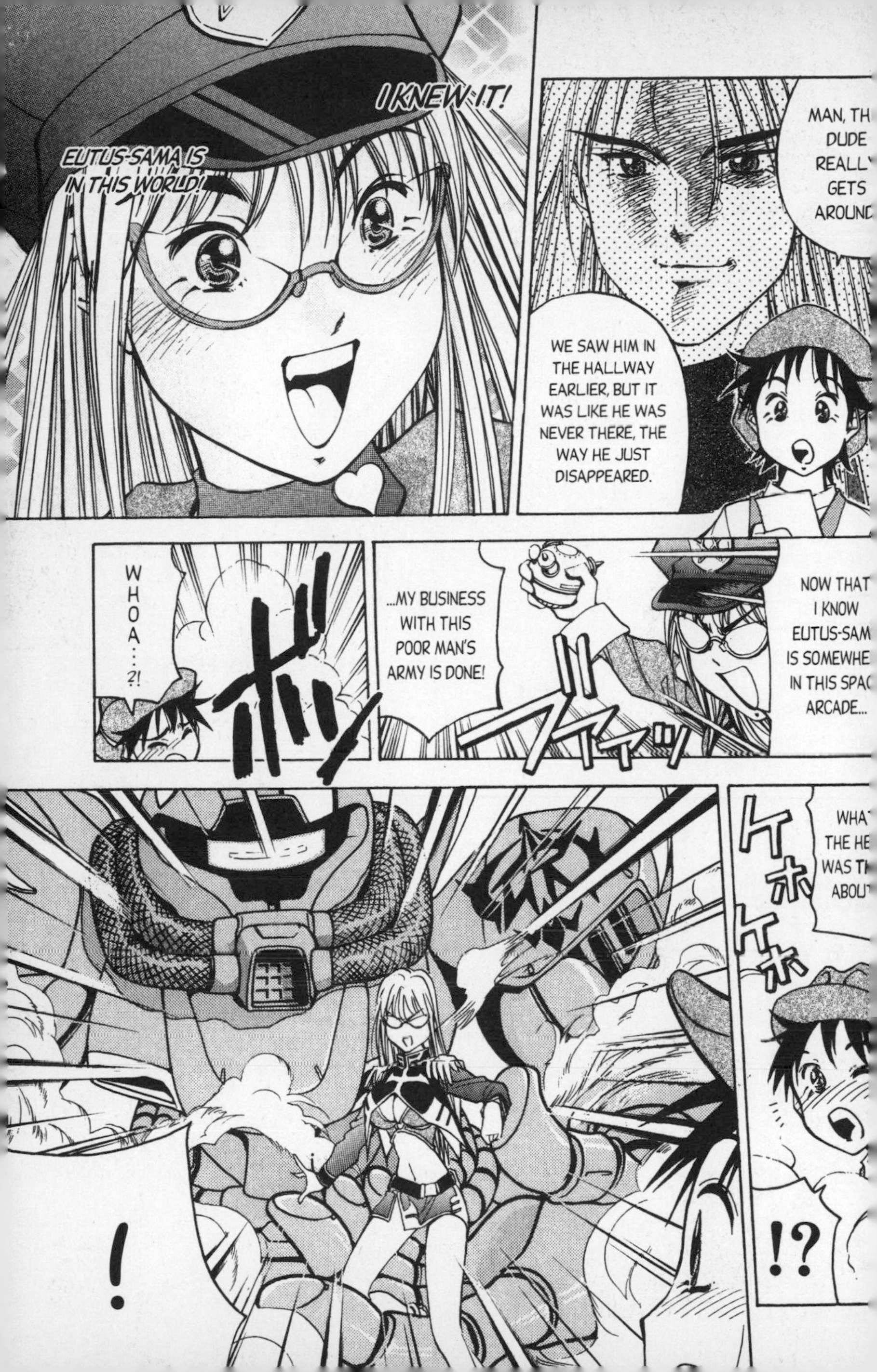
MAN, TH DUDE REALLY GETS AROUND
WE SAW HIM IN THE HALLWAY EARLIER, BUT IT WAS LIKE HE WAS NEVER THERE, THE WAY HE JUST DISAPPEARED.
I KNEW IT!
EUTUS-SAMA IS IN THIS WORLD!
NOW THAT I KNOW EUTUS-SAM IS SOMEWHE IN THIS SPAC ARCADE...
...MY BUSINESS WITH THIS POOR MAN'S ARMY IS DONE!
WHOA...?!
WHA THE HE WAS TH ABOU
ケホケホ
!?
!

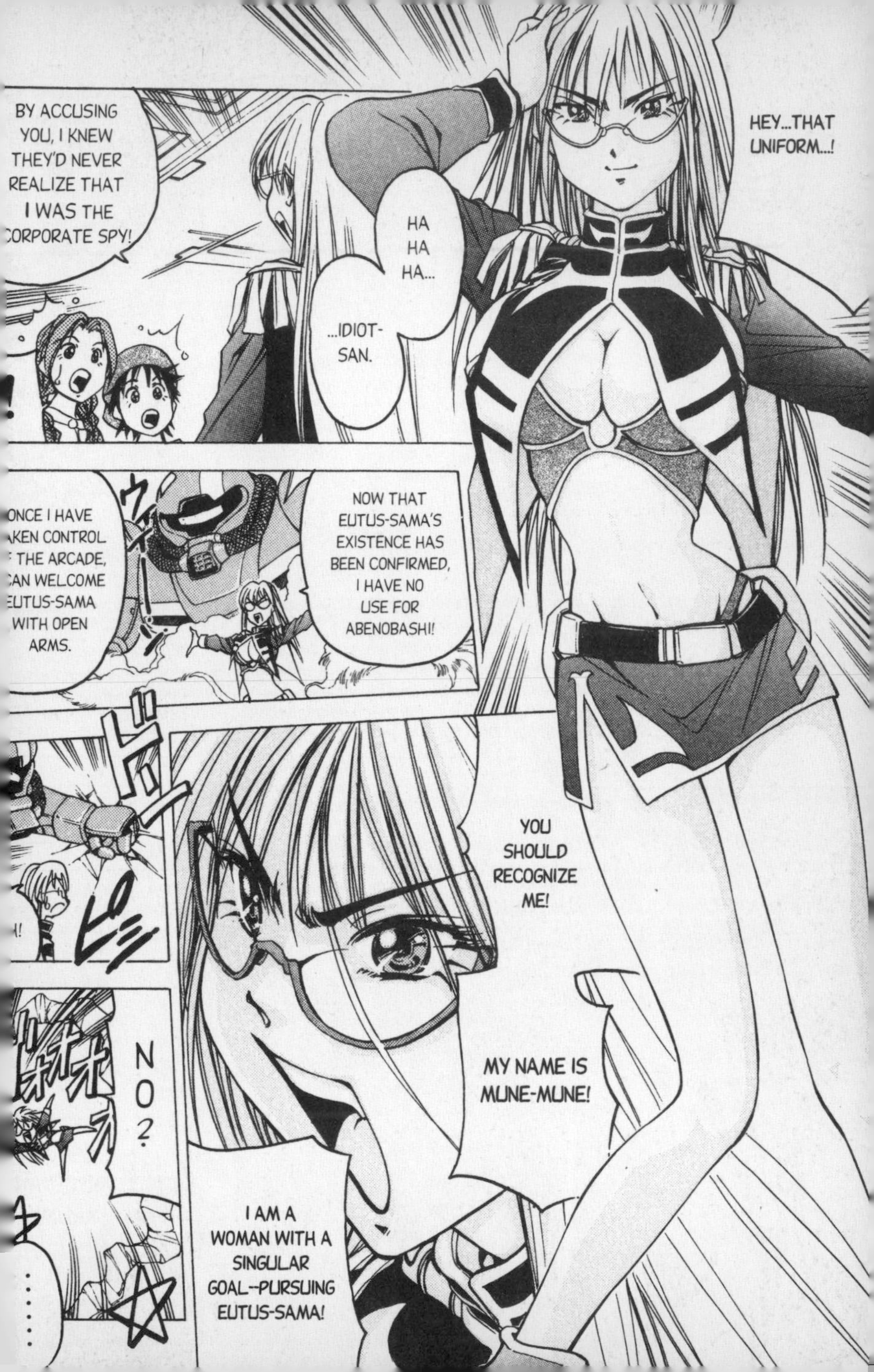
HEY...THAT UNIFORM...!
YOU SHOULD RECOGNIZE ME!
MY NAME IS MUNE-MUNE!
I AM A WOMAN WITH A SINGULAR GOAL--PURSUING EUTUS-SAMA!
HA HA HA...
...IDIOT-SAN.
BY ACCUSING YOU, I KNEW THEY'D NEVER REALIZE THAT I WAS THE CORPORATE SPY!
NOW THAT EUTUS-SAMA'S EXISTENCE HAS BEEN CONFIRMED, I HAVE NO USE FOR ABENOBASHI!
ONCE I HAVE AKEN CONTROL F THE ARCADE, CAN WELCOME EUTUS-SAMA WITH OPEN ARMS.
NO?

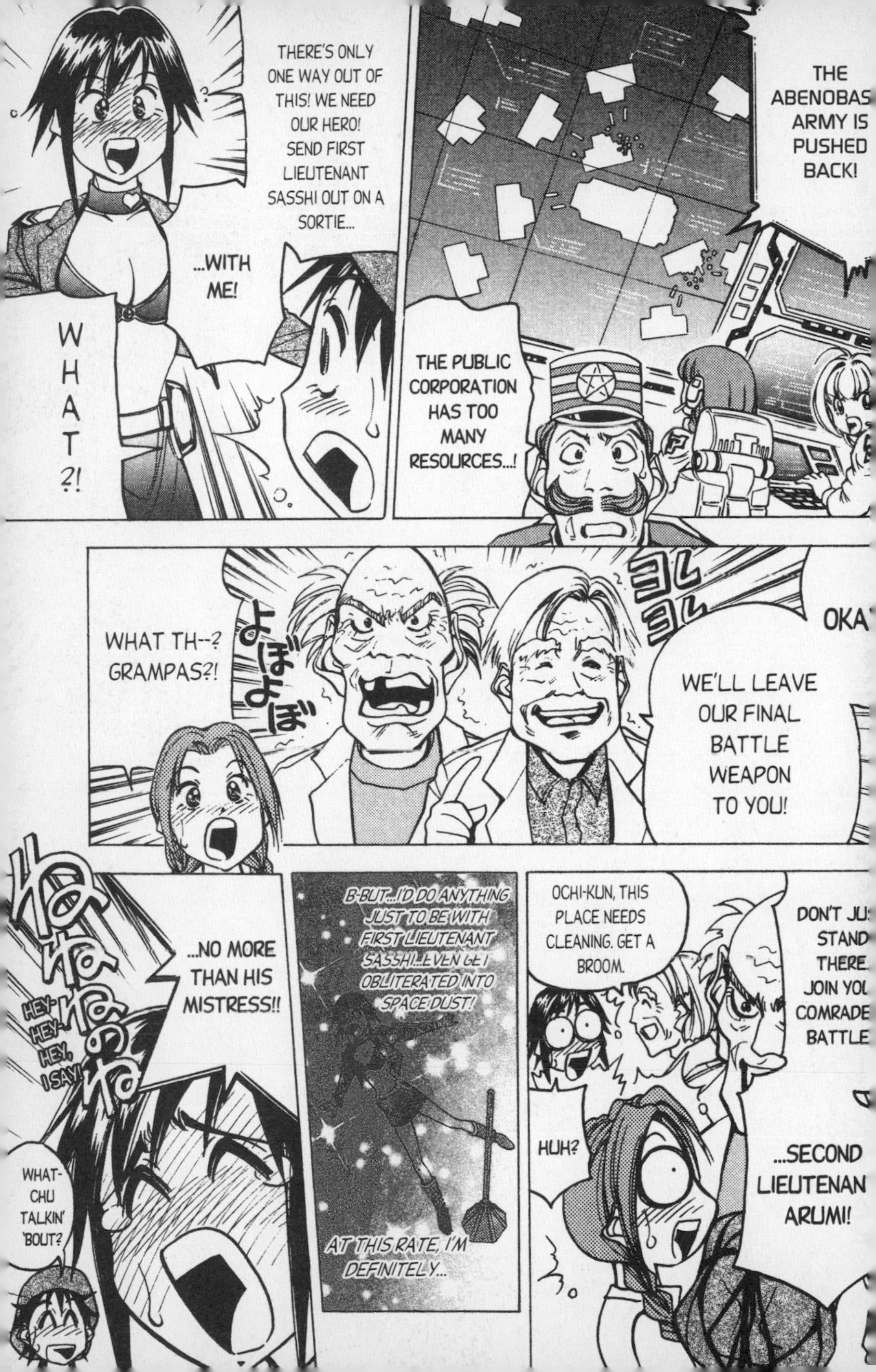
THE ABENOBAS ARMY IS PUSHED BACK!
THE PUBLIC CORPORATION HAS TOO MANY RESOURCES...!
THERE'S ONLY ONE WAY OUT OF THIS! WE NEED OUR HERO! SEND FIRST LIEUTENANT SASSHI OUT ON A SORTIE...
...WITH ME!
WHAT?!
OKA
WE'LL LEAVE OUR FINAL BATTLE WEAPON TO YOU!
ヨレヨレ
よぼよぼ
WHAT TH--? GRAMPAS?!
DON'T JU STAND THERE. JOIN YOU COMRADE BATTLE
OCHI-KUN, THIS PLACE NEEDS CLEANING. GET A BROOM.
HUH?
...SECOND LIEUTENAN ARUMI!
B-BUT...I'D DO ANYTHING JUST TO BE WITH FIRST LIEUTENANT SASSHI...EVEN GET OBLITERATED INTO SPACE DUST!
AT THIS RATE, I'M DEFINITELY...
...NO MORE THAN HIS MISTRESS!!
ねねねのね
HEY-HEY-HEY, I SAY!
WHAT-CHU TALKIN' 'BOUT?

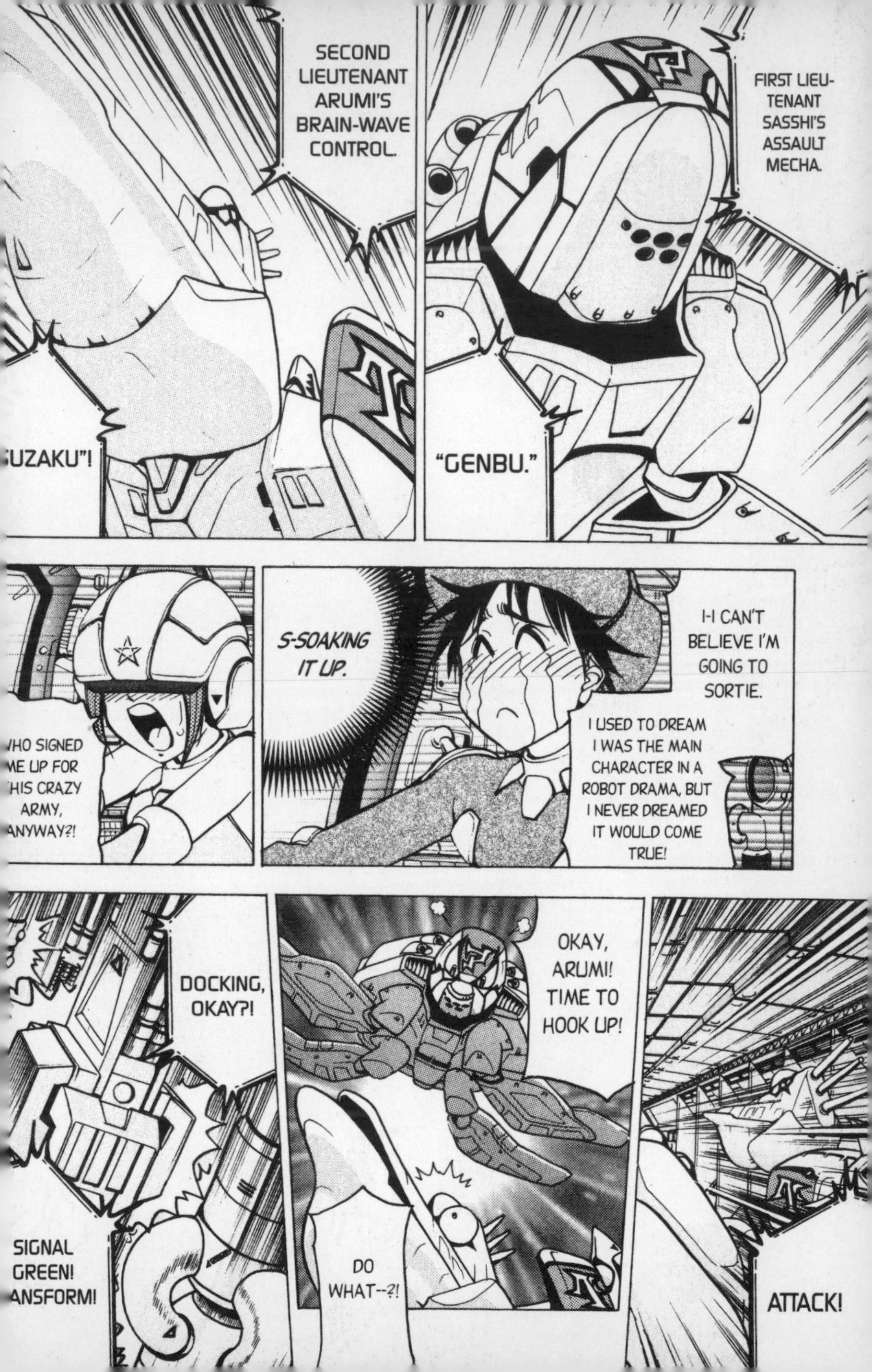
FIRST LIEU-TENANT SASSHI'S ASSAULT MECHA.
"GENBU."
SECOND LIEUTENANT ARUMI'S BRAIN-WAVE CONTROL.
UZAKU"!
I-I CAN'T BELIEVE I'M GOING TO SORTIE.
I USED TO DREAM I WAS THE MAIN CHARACTER IN A ROBOT DRAMA, BUT I NEVER DREAMED IT WOULD COME TRUE!
S-SOAKING IT UP.
WHO SIGNED ME UP FOR THIS CRAZY ARMY, ANYWAY?!
ATTACK!
OKAY, ARUMI! TIME TO HOOK UP!
DO WHAT--?!
DOCKING, OKAY?!
SIGNAL GREEN! ANSFORM!

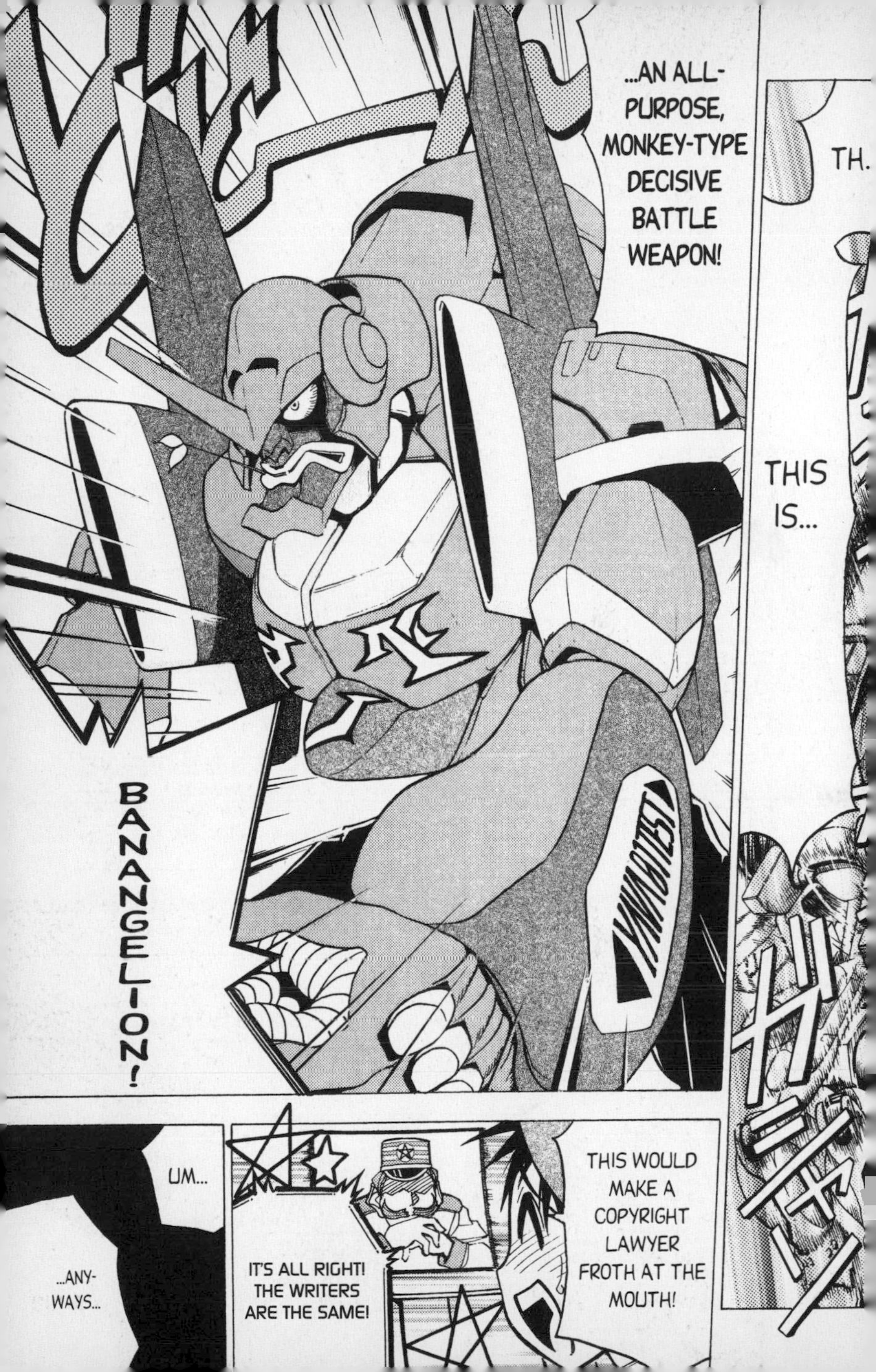

TH.
THIS IS...
...AN ALL-PURPOSE, MONKEY-TYPE DECISIVE BATTLE WEAPON!
BANANGELION!
THIS WOULD MAKE A COPYRIGHT LAWYER FROTH AT THE MOUTH!
IT'S ALL RIGHT! THE WRITERS ARE THE SAME!
UM...
...ANY-WAYS...

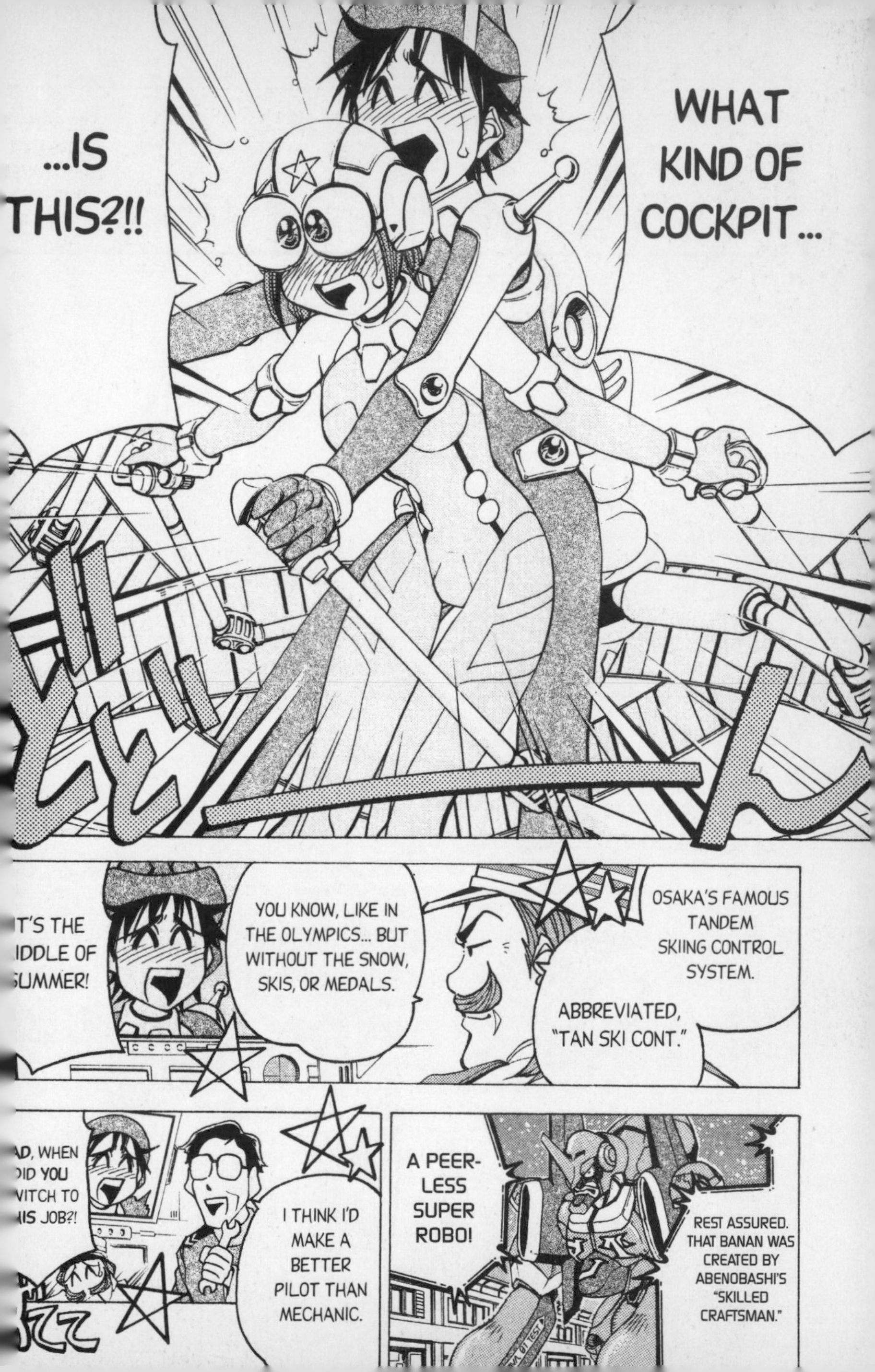
WHAT KIND OF COCKPIT...
...IS THIS?!!
OSAKA'S FAMOUS TANDEM SKIING CONTROL SYSTEM.
ABBREVIATED, "TAN SKI CONT."
YOU KNOW, LIKE IN THE OLYMPICS... BUT WITHOUT THE SNOW, SKIS, OR MEDALS.
T'S THE IDDLE OF SUMMER!
REST ASSURED. THAT BANAN WAS CREATED BY ABENOBASHI'S "SKILLED CRAFTSMAN."
A PEER-LESS SUPER ROBO!
AD, WHEN ID YOU WITCH TO HIS JOB?!
I THINK I'D MAKE A BETTER PILOT THAN MECHANIC.

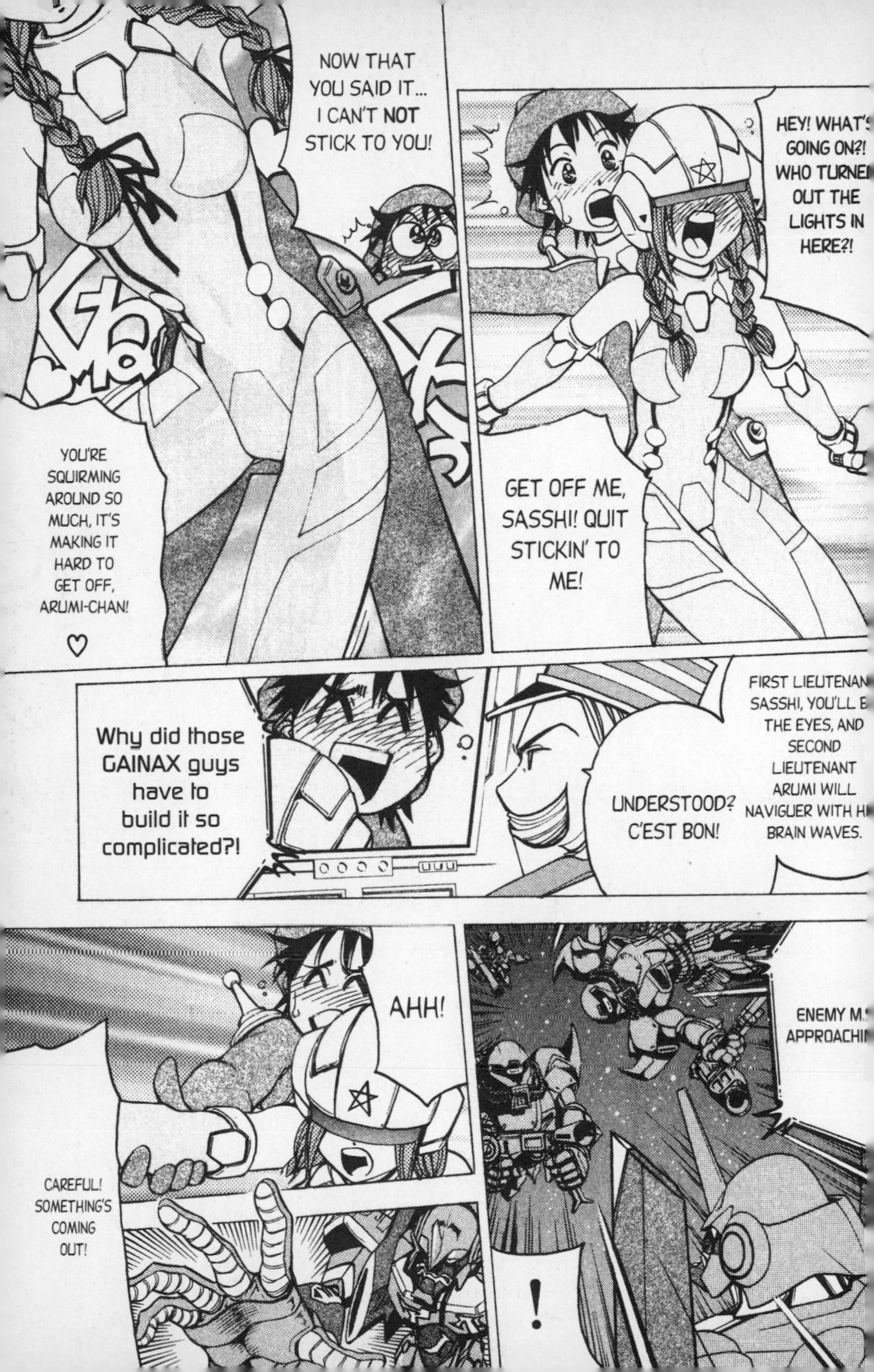

HEY! WHAT'S GOING ON?! WHO TURNED OUT THE LIGHTS IN HERE?!
GET OFF ME, SASSHI! QUIT STICKIN' TO ME!
NOW THAT YOU SAID IT... I CAN'T **NOT** STICK TO YOU!
YOU'RE SQUIRMING AROUND SO MUCH, IT'S MAKING IT HARD TO GET OFF, ARUMI-CHAN! ♡
FIRST LIEUTENAN SASSHI, YOU'LL B THE EYES, AND SECOND LIEUTENANT ARUMI WILL NAVIGUER WITH H BRAIN WAVES.
UNDERSTOOD? C'EST BON!
Why did those GAINAX guys have to build it so complicated?!
ENEMY M.S APPROACHIN
!
AHH!
CAREFUL! SOMETHING'S COMING OUT!

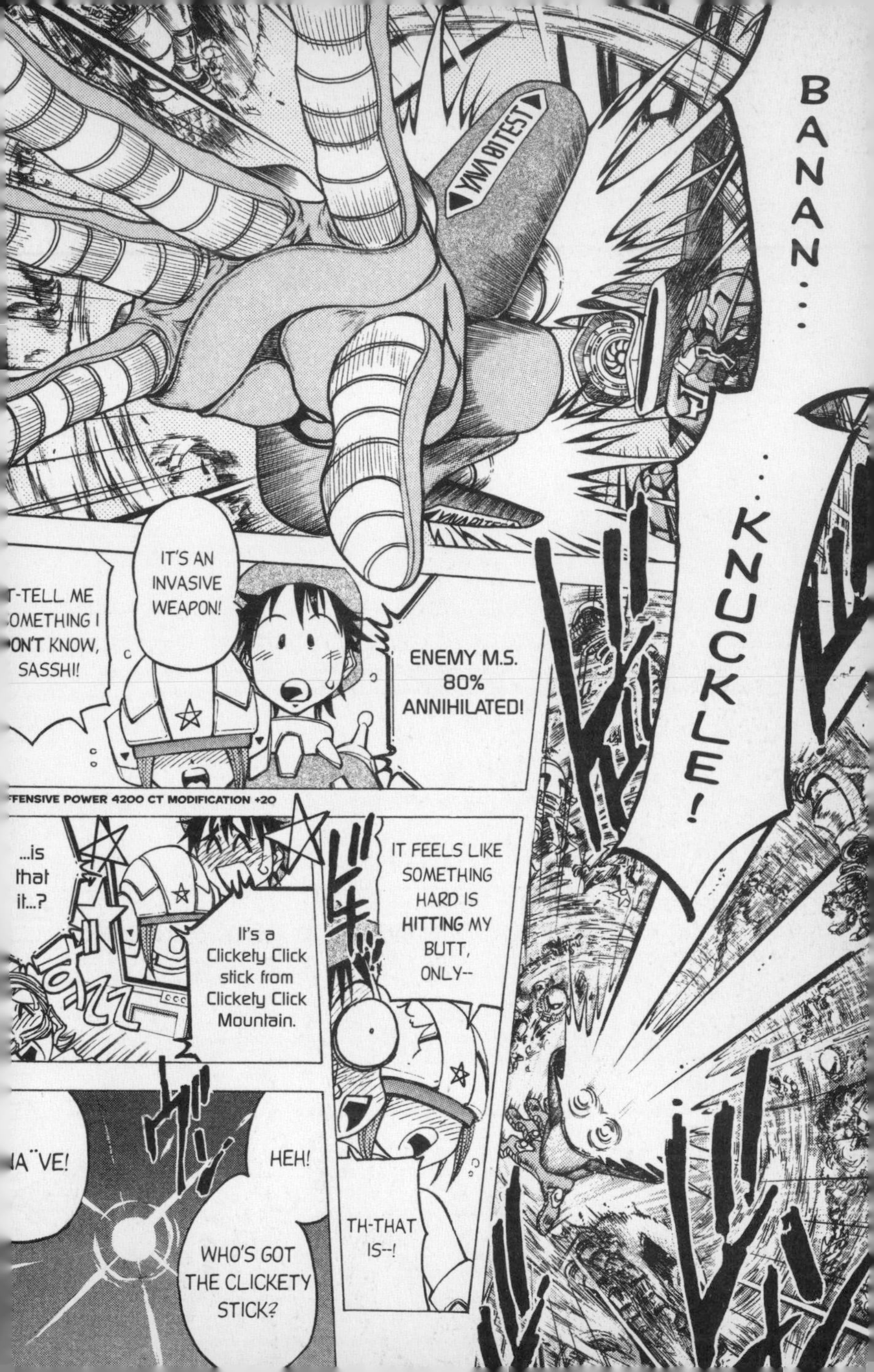
YNVA BITEST
BANAN...
...KNUCKLE!
ENEMY M.S. 80% ANNIHILATED!
IT'S AN INVASIVE WEAPON!
T-TELL ME SOMETHING I DON'T KNOW, SASSHI!
FFENSIVE POWER 4200 CT MODIFICATION +20
IT FEELS LIKE SOMETHING HARD IS HITTING MY BUTT, ONLY--
It's a Clickety Click stick from Clickety Click Mountain.
...is that it...?
TH-THAT IS--!
HEH!
WHO'S GOT THE CLICKETY STICK?
NA¨VE!

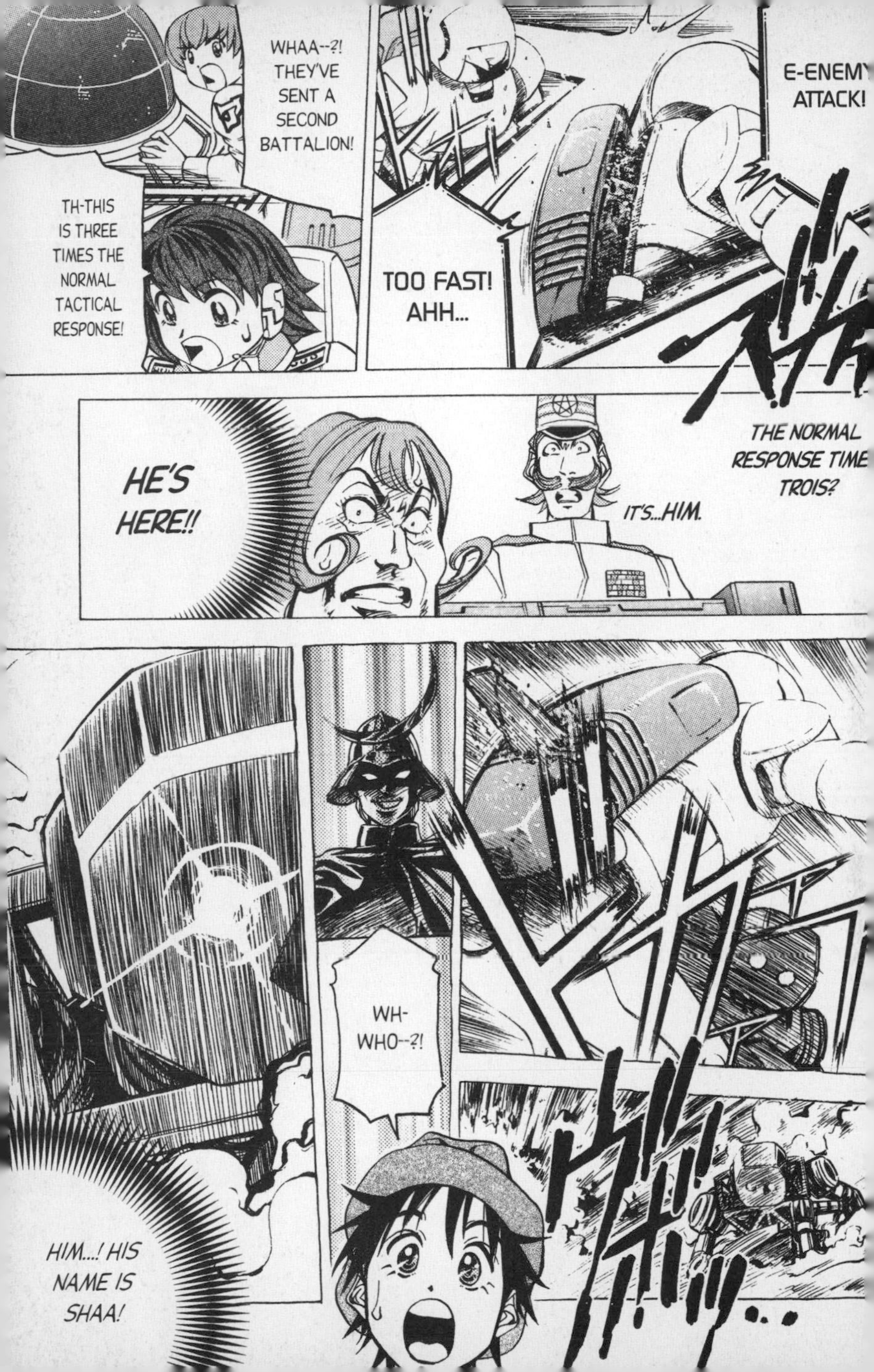
E-ENEMY ATTACK!
TOO FAST! AHH...
WHAA--?! THEY'VE SENT A SECOND BATTALION!
TH-THIS IS THREE TIMES THE NORMAL TACTICAL RESPONSE!
THE NORMAL RESPONSE TIME TROIS?
IT'S...HIM.
HE'S HERE!!
WH-WHO--?!
HIM...! HIS NAME IS SHAA!

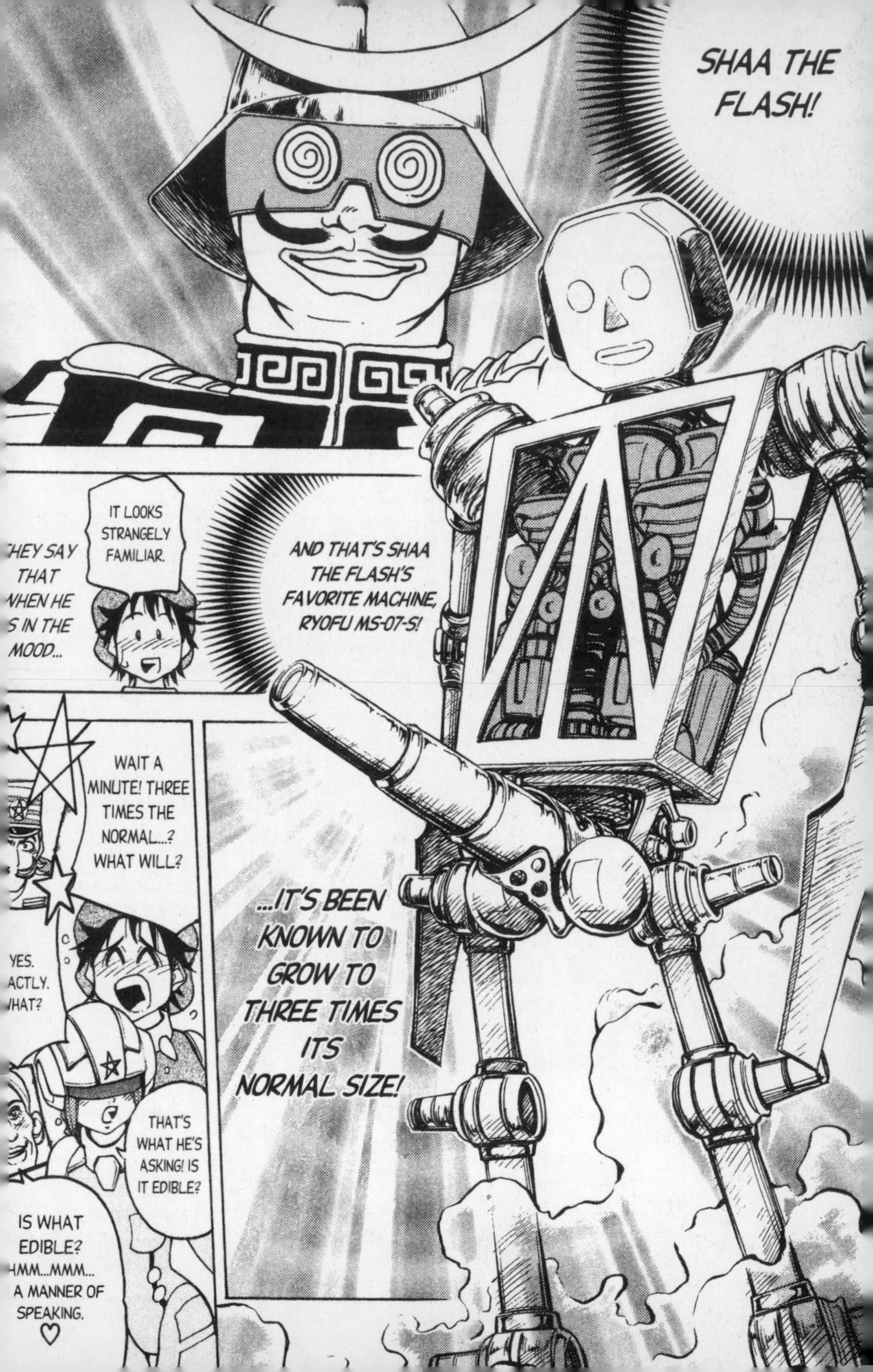
SHAA THE FLASH!
AND THAT'S SHAA THE FLASH'S FAVORITE MACHINE, RYOFU MS-07-S!
IT LOOKS STRANGELY FAMILIAR.
HEY SAY THAT HEN HE S IN THE MOOD...
...IT'S BEEN KNOWN TO GROW TO THREE TIMES ITS NORMAL SIZE!
WAIT A MINUTE! THREE TIMES THE NORMAL...? WHAT WILL?
YES. ACTLY. HAT?
THAT'S WHAT HE'S ASKING! IS IT EDIBLE?
IS WHAT EDIBLE? HMM...MMM... A MANNER OF SPEAKING. ♡

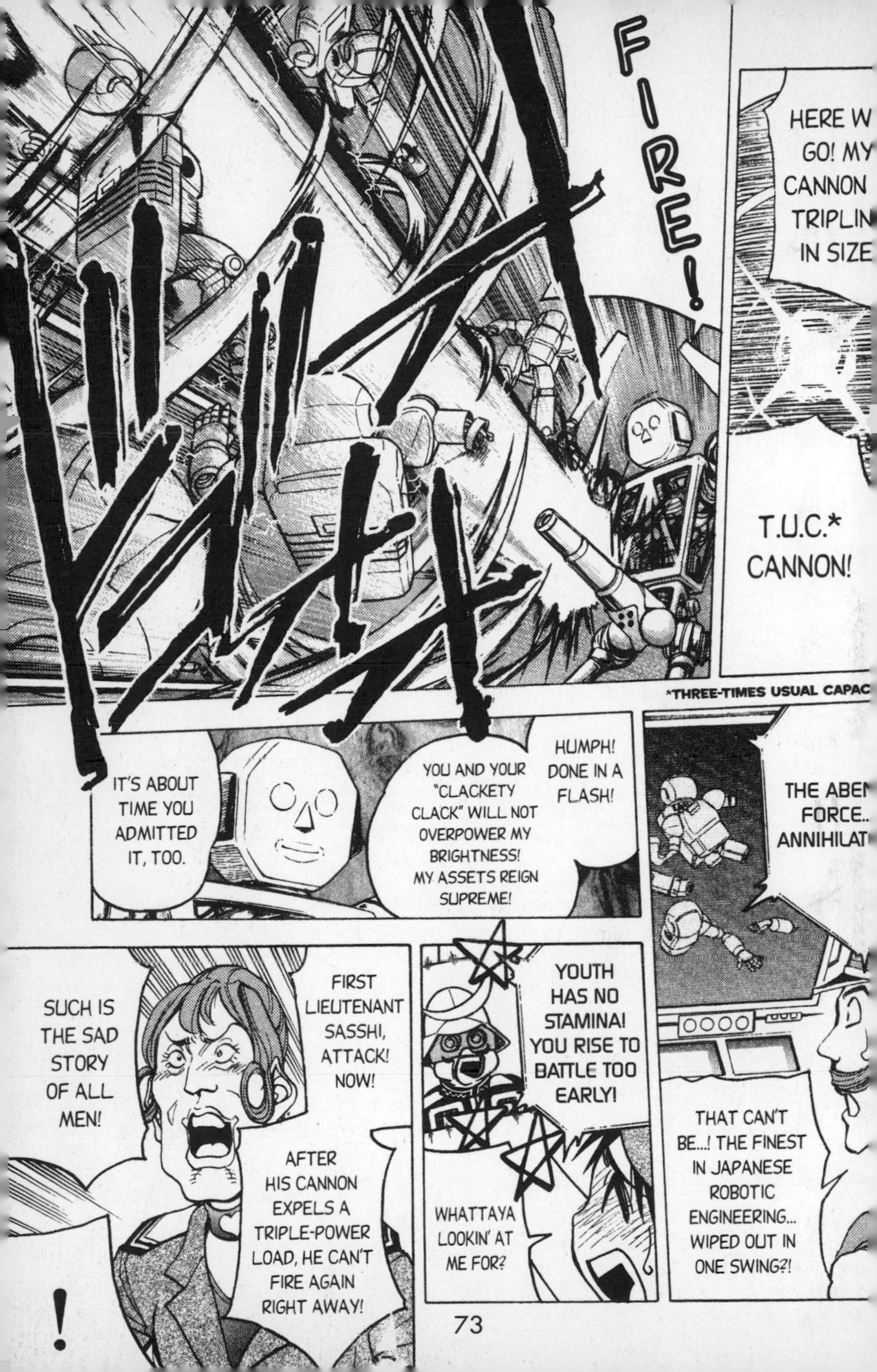
HERE W GO! MY CANNON TRIPLIN IN SIZE
T.U.C.* CANNON!
FIRE!
*THREE-TIMES USUAL CAPAC
THE ABEN FORCE.. ANNIHILAT
THAT CAN'T BE...! THE FINEST IN JAPANESE ROBOTIC ENGINEERING... WIPED OUT IN ONE SWING?!
HUMPH! DONE IN A FLASH!
YOU AND YOUR "CLACKETY CLACK" WILL NOT OVERPOWER MY BRIGHTNESS! MY ASSETS REIGN SUPREME!
IT'S ABOUT TIME YOU ADMITTED IT, TOO.
YOUTH HAS NO STAMINA! YOU RISE TO BATTLE TOO EARLY!
WHATTAYA LOOKIN' AT ME FOR?
FIRST LIEUTENANT SASSHI, ATTACK! NOW!
SUCH IS THE SAD STORY OF ALL MEN!
AFTER HIS CANNON EXPELS A TRIPLE-POWER LOAD, HE CAN'T FIRE AGAIN RIGHT AWAY!
!

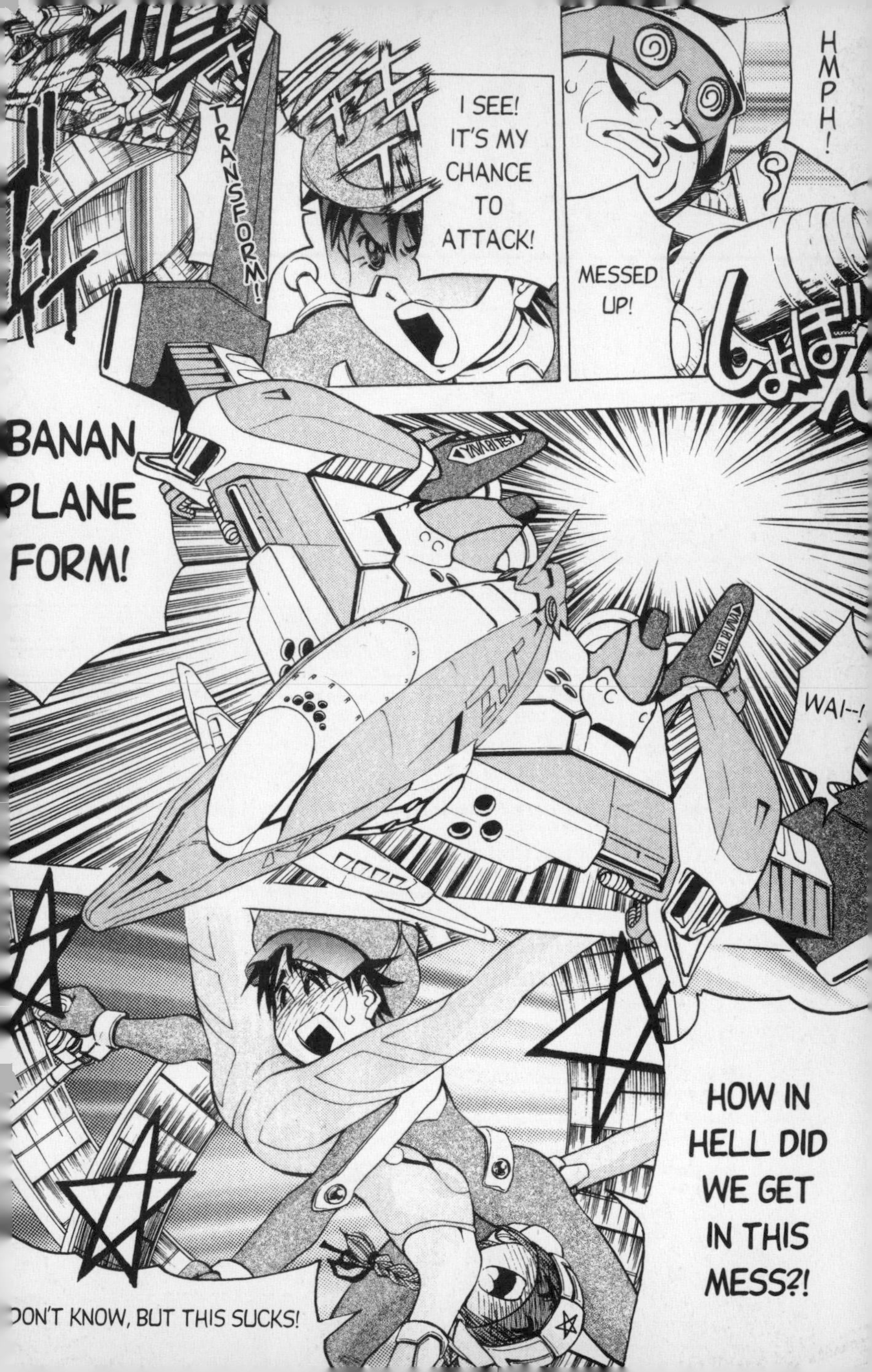
HMPH!
MESSED UP!
しょぼん
I SEE! IT'S MY CHANCE TO ATTACK!
TRANSFORM!
BANAN PLANE FORM!
WAI--!
HOW IN HELL DID WE GET IN THIS MESS?!
DON'T KNOW, BUT THIS SUCKS!

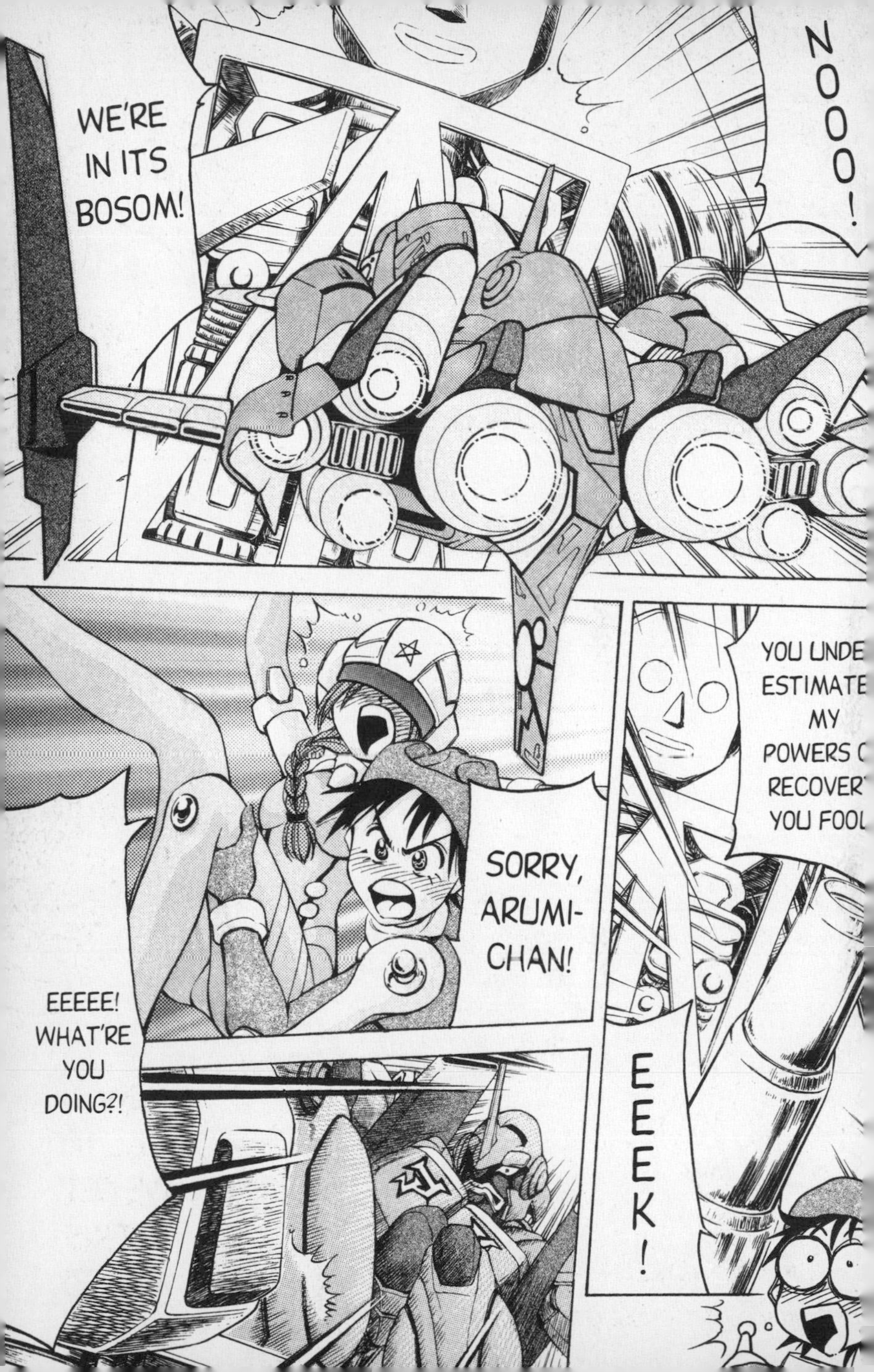
NOOO!
WE'RE IN ITS BOSOM!
YOU UNDE ESTIMATE MY POWERS C RECOVER YOU FOOL
SORRY, ARUMI-CHAN!
EEEK!
EEEEE! WHAT'RE YOU DOING?!

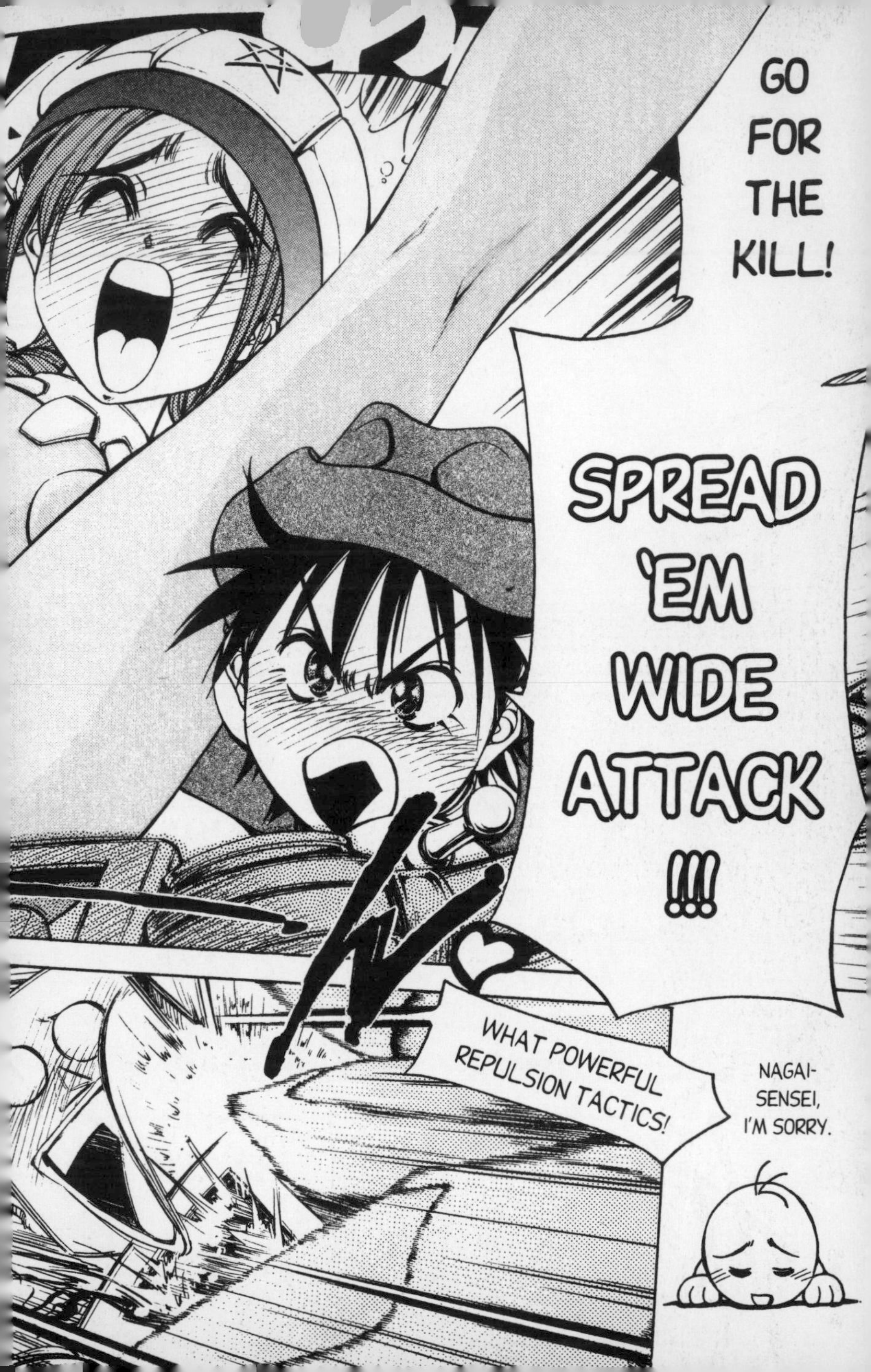
GO FOR THE KILL!
SPREAD 'EM WIDE ATTACK !!!
WHAT POWERFUL REPULSION TACTICS!
NAGAI-SENSEI, I'M SORRY.

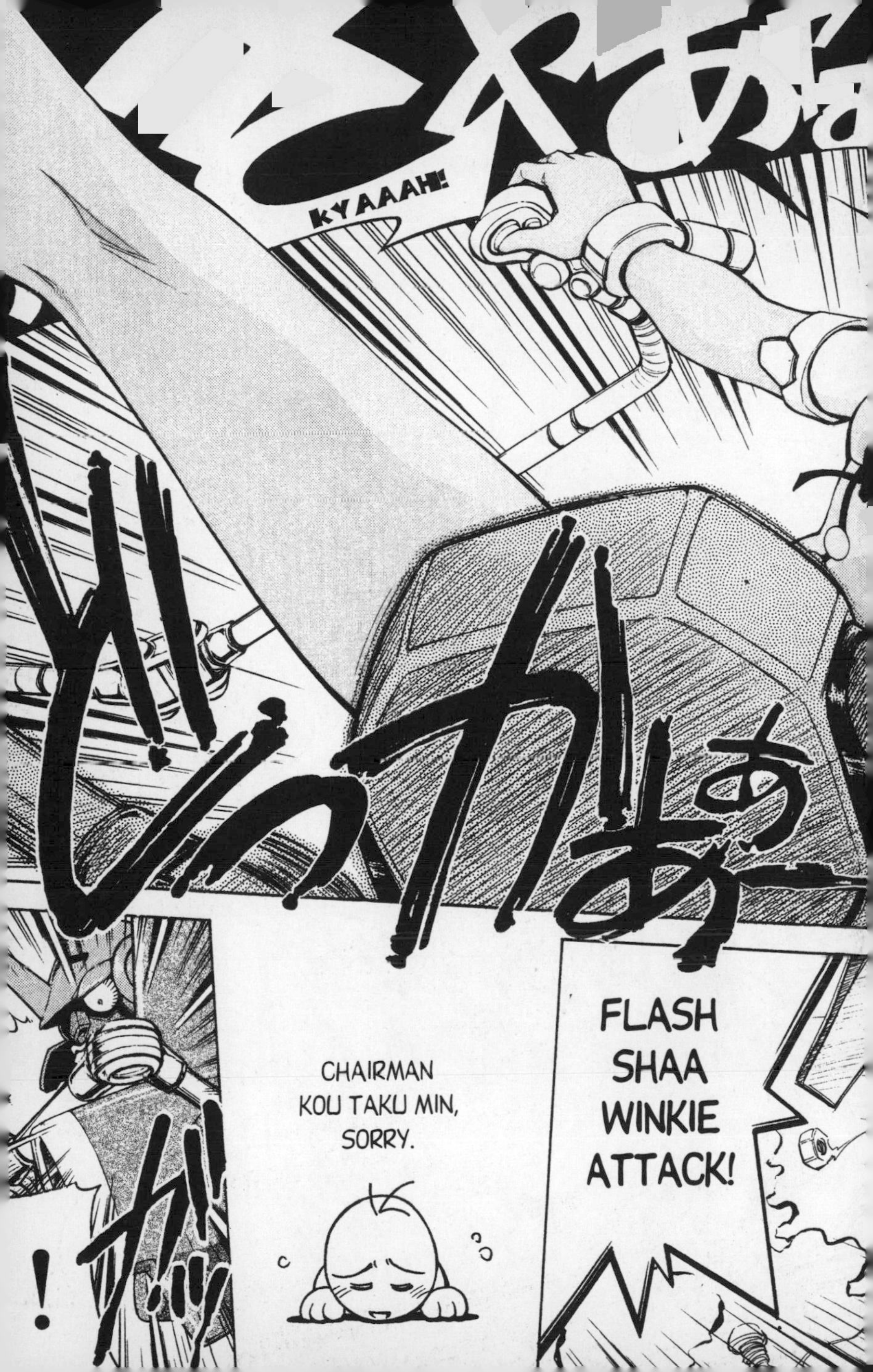
KYAAAH!
FLASH SHAA WINKIE ATTACK!
CHAIRMAN KOU TAKU MIN, SORRY.
!

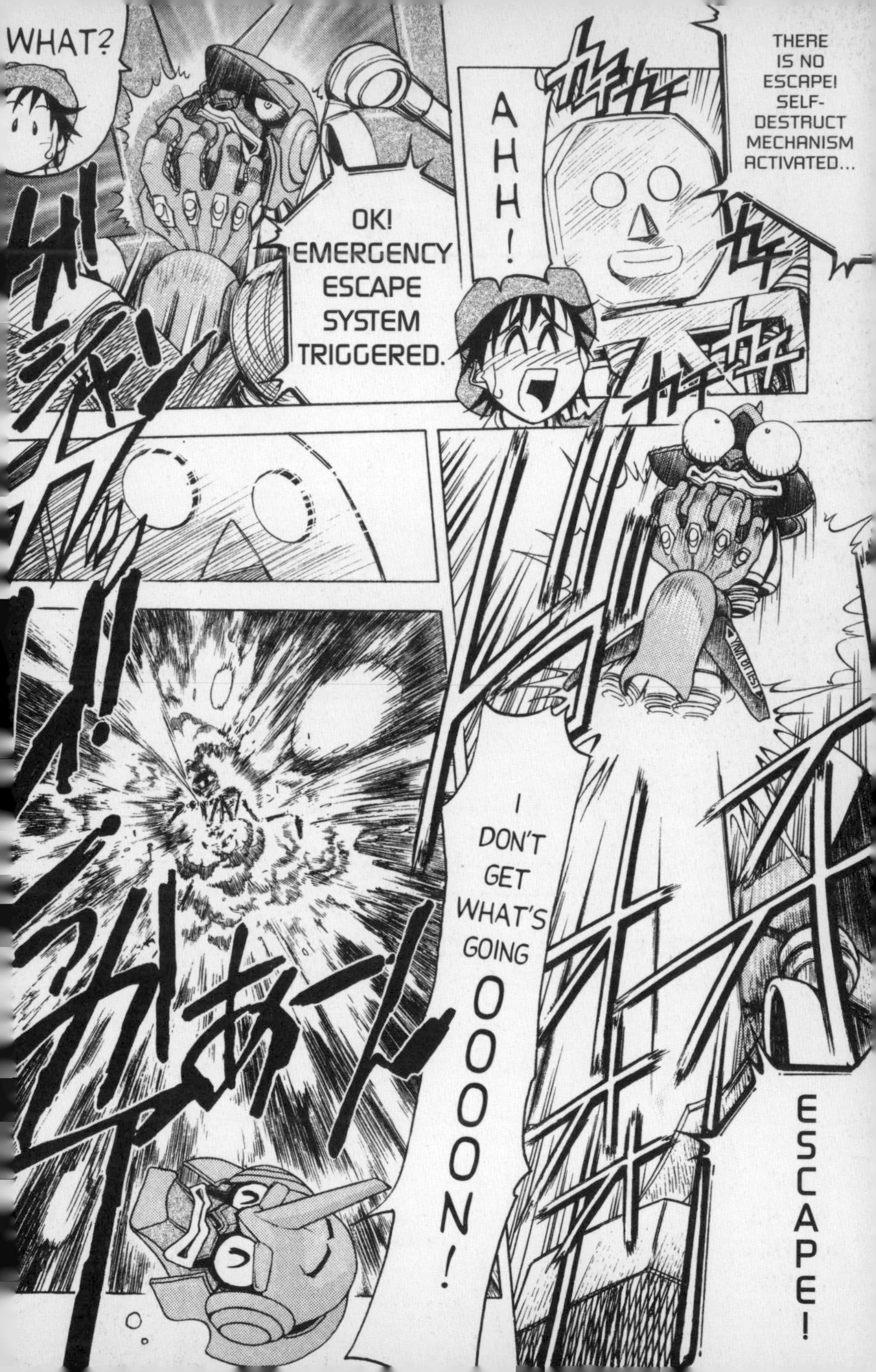
THERE IS NO ESCAPE! SELF-DESTRUCT MECHANISM ACTIVATED...
AHH!
WHAT?
OK! EMERGENCY ESCAPE SYSTEM TRIGGERED.
ESCAPE!
I DON'T GET WHAT'S GOING OOOOON!

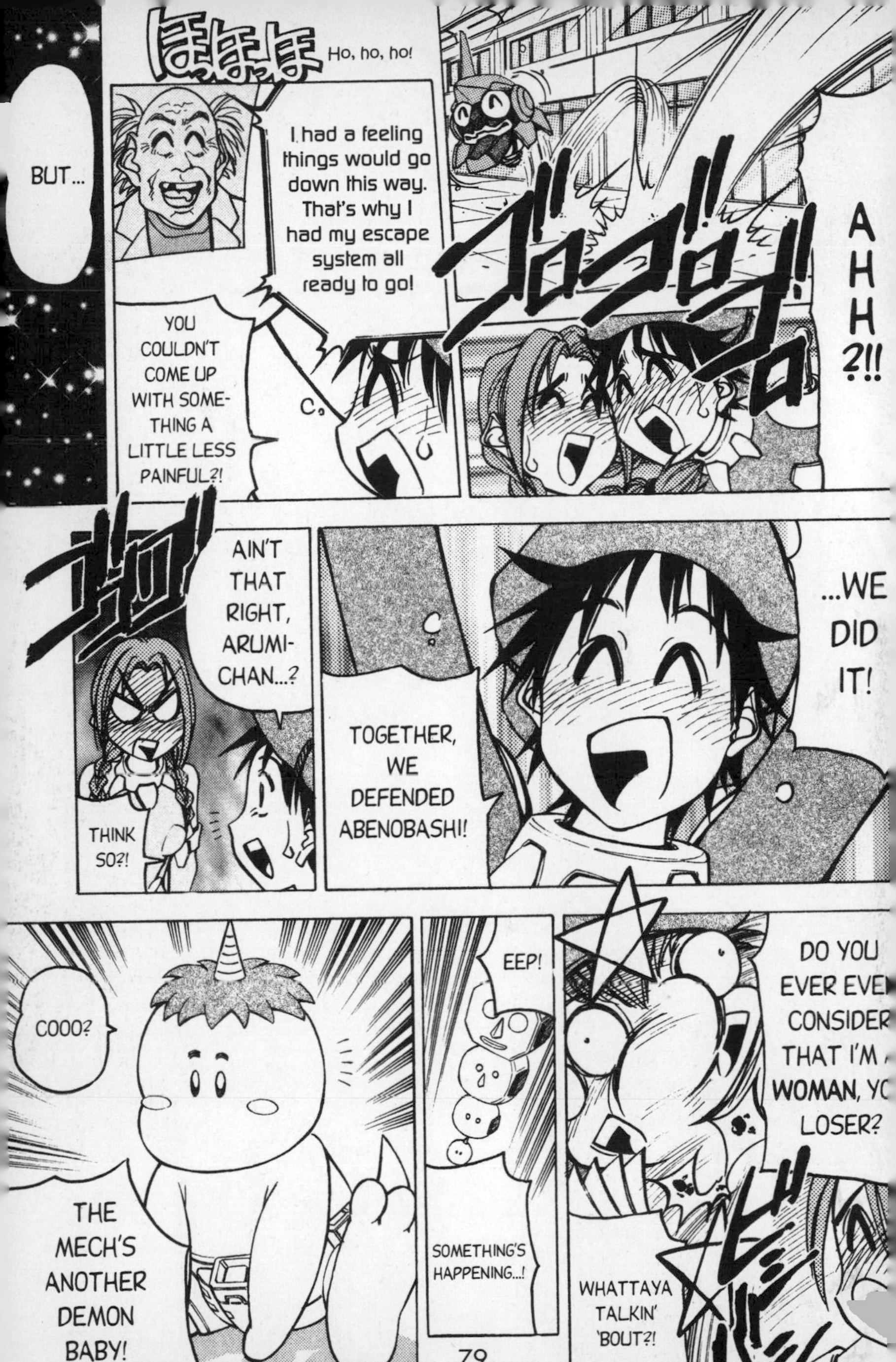
AHH?!!
Ho, ho, ho!
I had a feeling things would go down this way. That's why I had my escape system all ready to go!
YOU COULDN'T COME UP WITH SOMETHING A LITTLE LESS PAINFUL?!
BUT...
...WE DID IT!
TOGETHER, WE DEFENDED ABENOBASHI!
AIN'T THAT RIGHT, ARUMI-CHAN...?
THINK SO?!
DO YOU EVER EVE CONSIDER THAT I'M WOMAN, YO LOSER?
WHATTAYA TALKIN' 'BOUT?!
EEP!
SOMETHING'S HAPPENING...!
COOO?
THE MECH'S ANOTHER DEMON BABY!

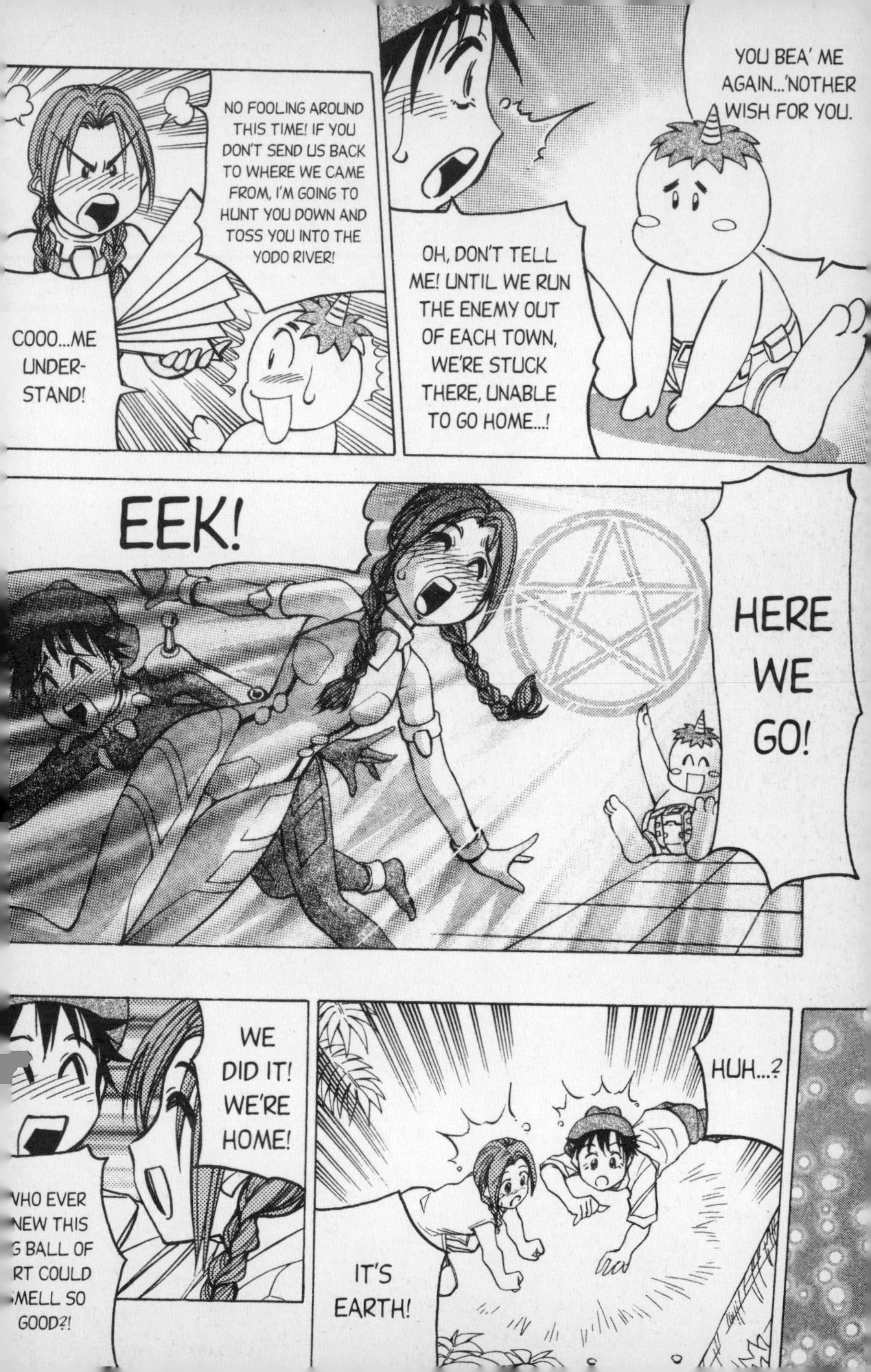
YOU BEA' ME AGAIN...'NOTHER WISH FOR YOU.
OH, DON'T TELL ME! UNTIL WE RUN THE ENEMY OUT OF EACH TOWN, WE'RE STUCK THERE, UNABLE TO GO HOME...!
NO FOOLING AROUND THIS TIME! IF YOU DON'T SEND US BACK TO WHERE WE CAME FROM, I'M GOING TO HUNT YOU DOWN AND TOSS YOU INTO THE YODO RIVER!
COOO...ME UNDER-STAND!
HERE WE GO!
EEK!
HUH...?
IT'S EARTH!
WE DID IT! WE'RE HOME!
VHO EVER NEW THIS G BALL OF RT COULD MELL SO GOOD?!

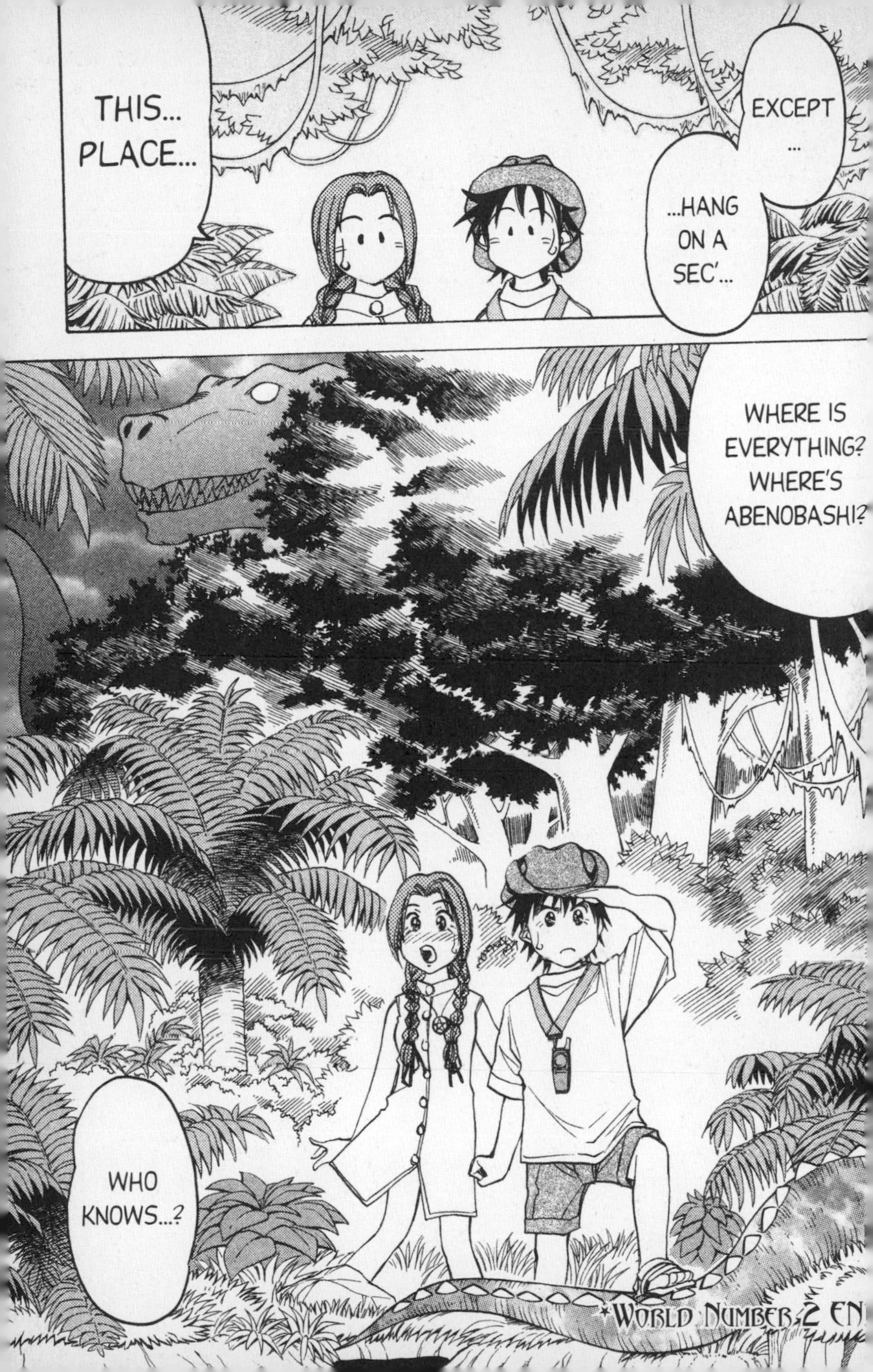
THIS... PLACE...
EXCEPT ...
...HANG ON A SEC'...
WHERE IS EVERYTHING? WHERE'S ABENOBASHI!?
WHO KNOWS...?
WORLD NUMBER 2 EN

ABENOBASHI
MAGICAL SHOPPING ARCADE

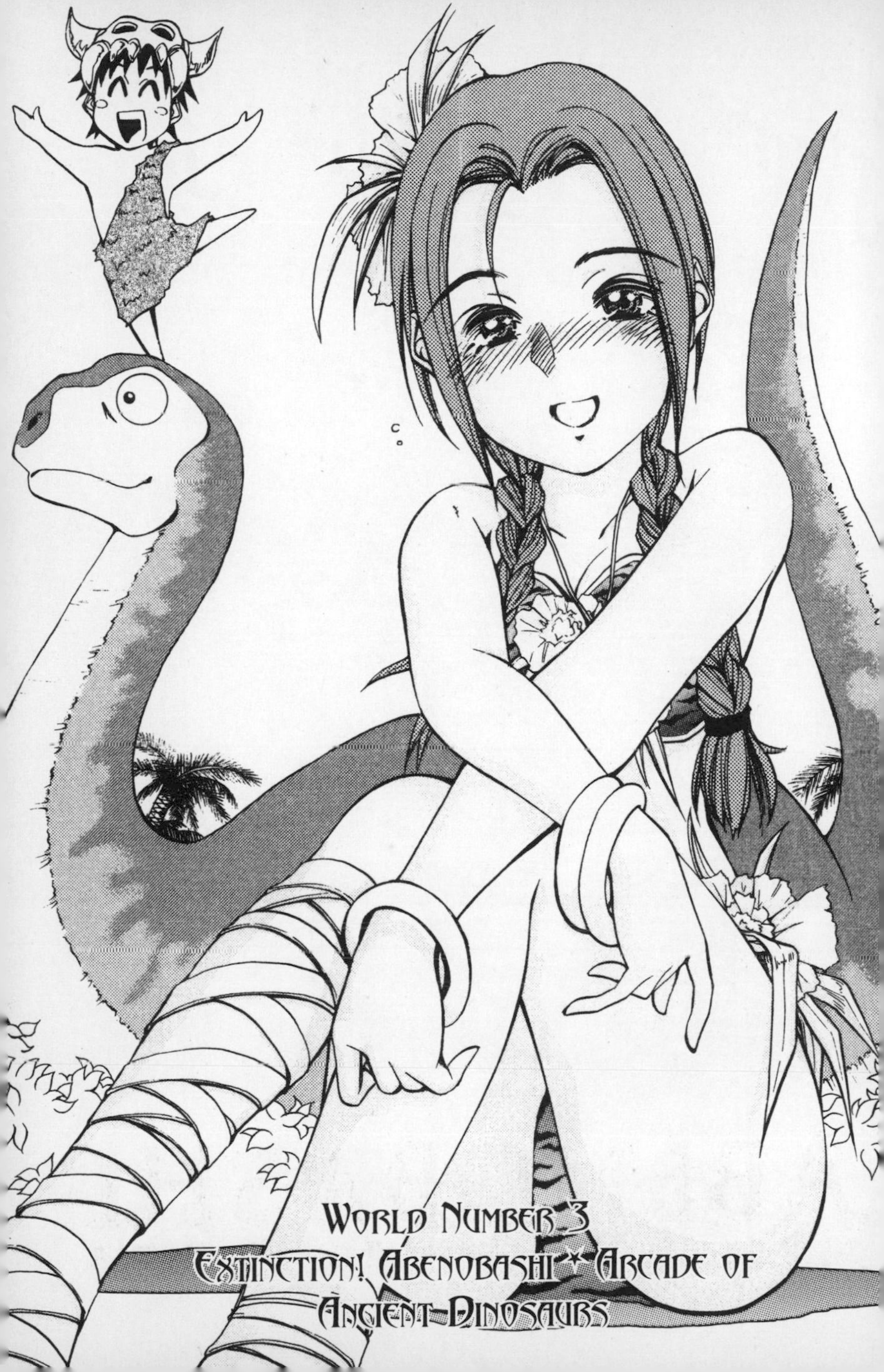
World Number 3
Extinction! Abenobashi ✶ Arcade of Ancient Dinosaurs

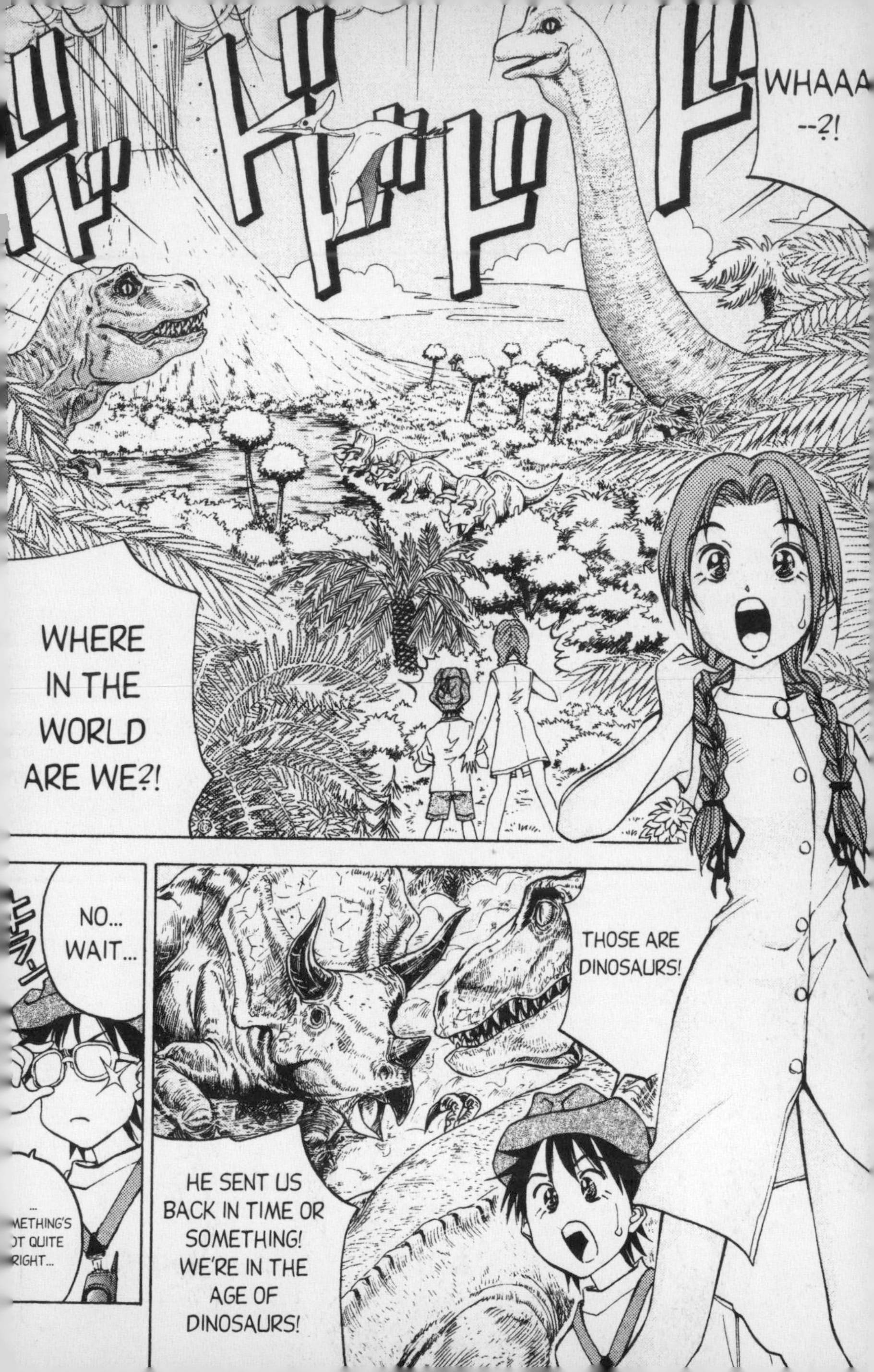
WHAAA --?!
WHERE IN THE WORLD ARE WE?!
THOSE ARE DINOSAURS!
HE SENT US BACK IN TIME OR SOMETHING! WE'RE IN THE AGE OF DINOSAURS!
NO... WAIT...
... METHING'S OT QUITE RIGHT...

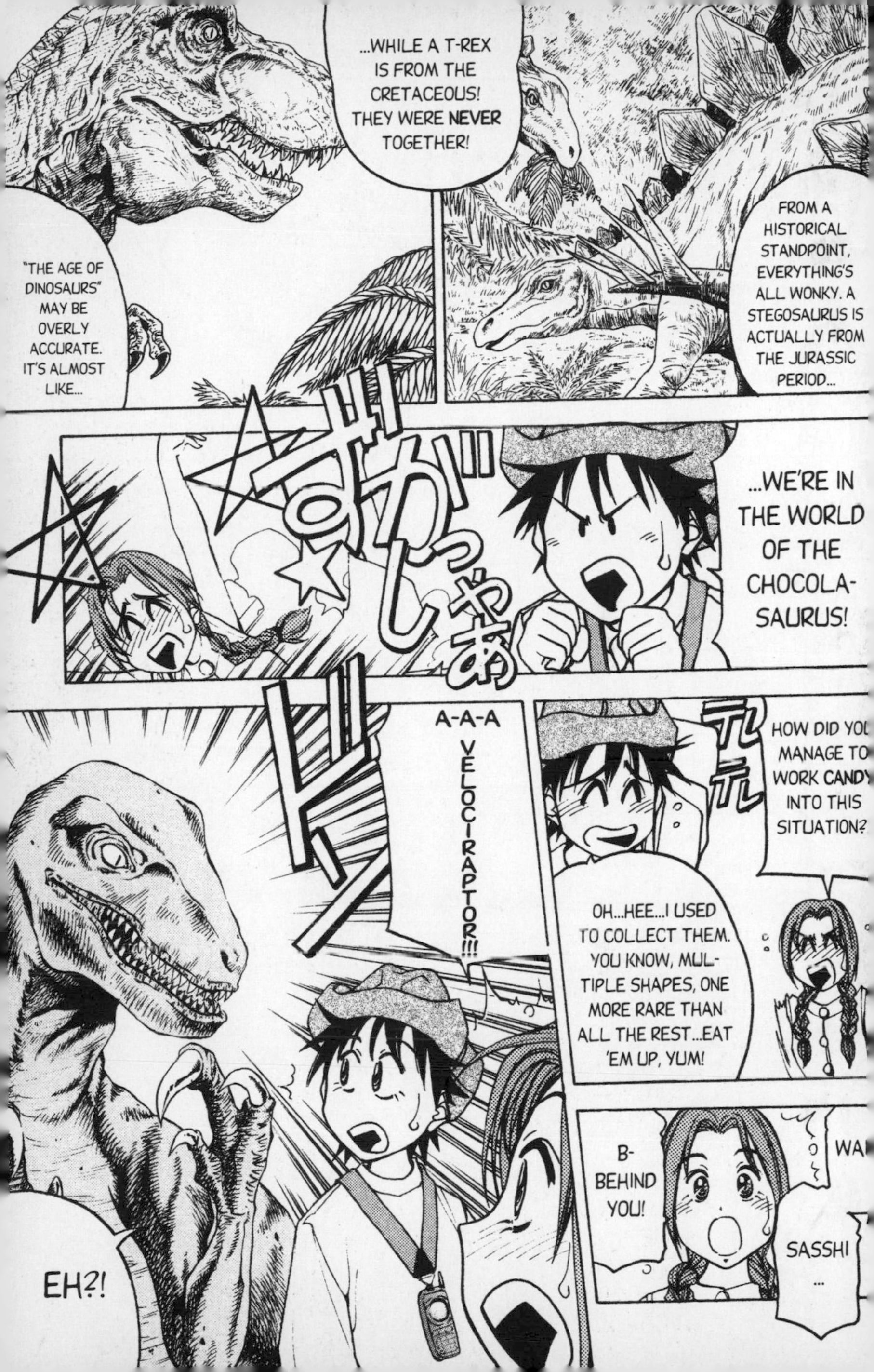
FROM A HISTORICAL STANDPOINT, EVERYTHING'S ALL WONKY. A STEGOSAURUS IS ACTUALLY FROM THE JURASSIC PERIOD...
...WHILE A T-REX IS FROM THE CRETACEOUS! THEY WERE **NEVER** TOGETHER!
"THE AGE OF DINOSAURS" MAY BE OVERLY ACCURATE. IT'S ALMOST LIKE...
...WE'RE IN THE WORLD OF THE CHOCOLA-SAURUS!
HOW DID YOU MANAGE TO WORK **CANDY** INTO THIS SITUATION?
OH...HEE...I USED TO COLLECT THEM. YOU KNOW, MUL-TIPLE SHAPES, ONE MORE RARE THAN ALL THE REST...EAT 'EM UP, YUM!
SASSHI ...
WA
B- BEHIND YOU!
A-A-A VELOCIRAPTOR!!!
EH?!

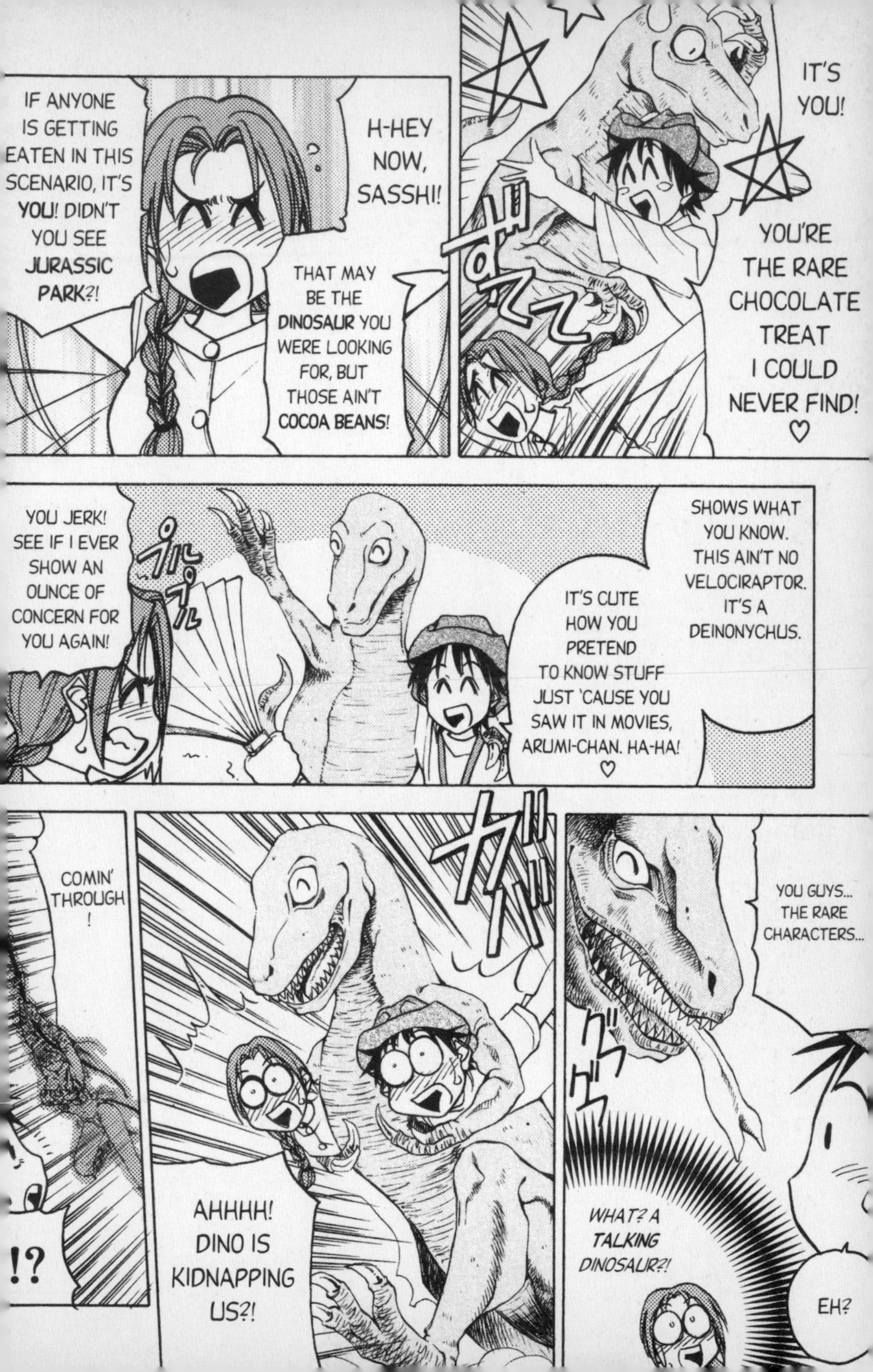
IT'S YOU!
YOU'RE THE RARE CHOCOLATE TREAT I COULD NEVER FIND! ♡
H-HEY NOW, SASSHI!
THAT MAY BE THE **DINOSAUR** YOU WERE LOOKING FOR, BUT THOSE AIN'T **COCOA BEANS**!
IF ANYONE IS GETTING EATEN IN THIS SCENARIO, IT'S **YOU**! DIDN'T YOU SEE **JURASSIC PARK**?!
SHOWS WHAT YOU KNOW. THIS AIN'T NO VELOCIRAPTOR. IT'S A DEINONYCHUS.
IT'S CUTE HOW YOU PRETEND TO KNOW STUFF JUST 'CAUSE YOU SAW IT IN MOVIES, ARUMI-CHAN. HA-HA! ♡
YOU JERK! SEE IF I EVER SHOW AN OUNCE OF CONCERN FOR YOU AGAIN!
YOU GUYS... THE RARE CHARACTERS...
EH?
WHAT?! A ***TALKING*** *DINOSAUR?!*
AHHHH! DINO IS KIDNAPPING US?!
COMIN' THROUGH!
!?

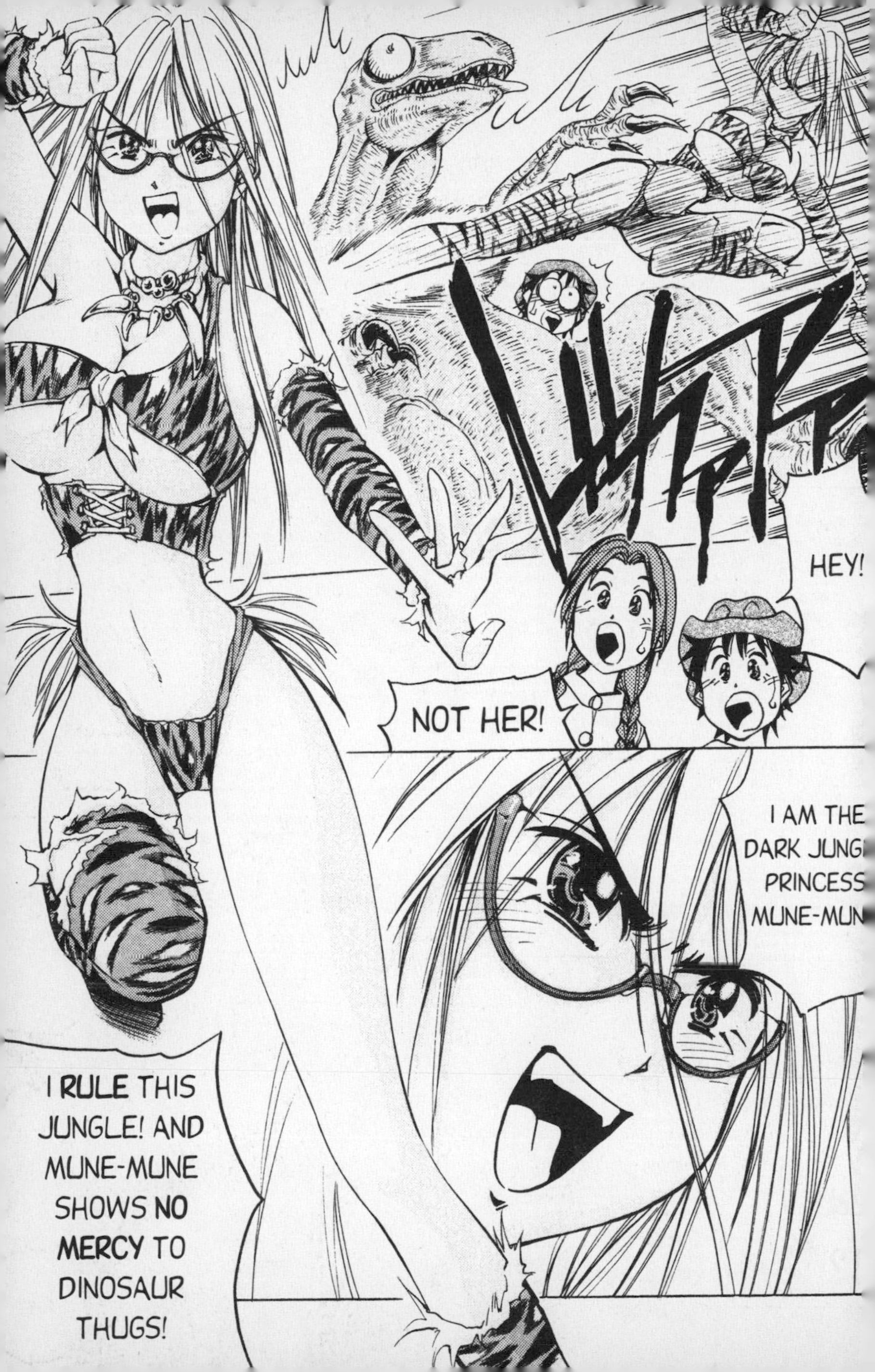
HEY!
NOT HER!
I AM THE DARK JUNG PRINCESS MUNE-MUN
I RULE THIS JUNGLE! AND MUNE-MUNE SHOWS NO MERCY TO DINOSAUR THUGS!

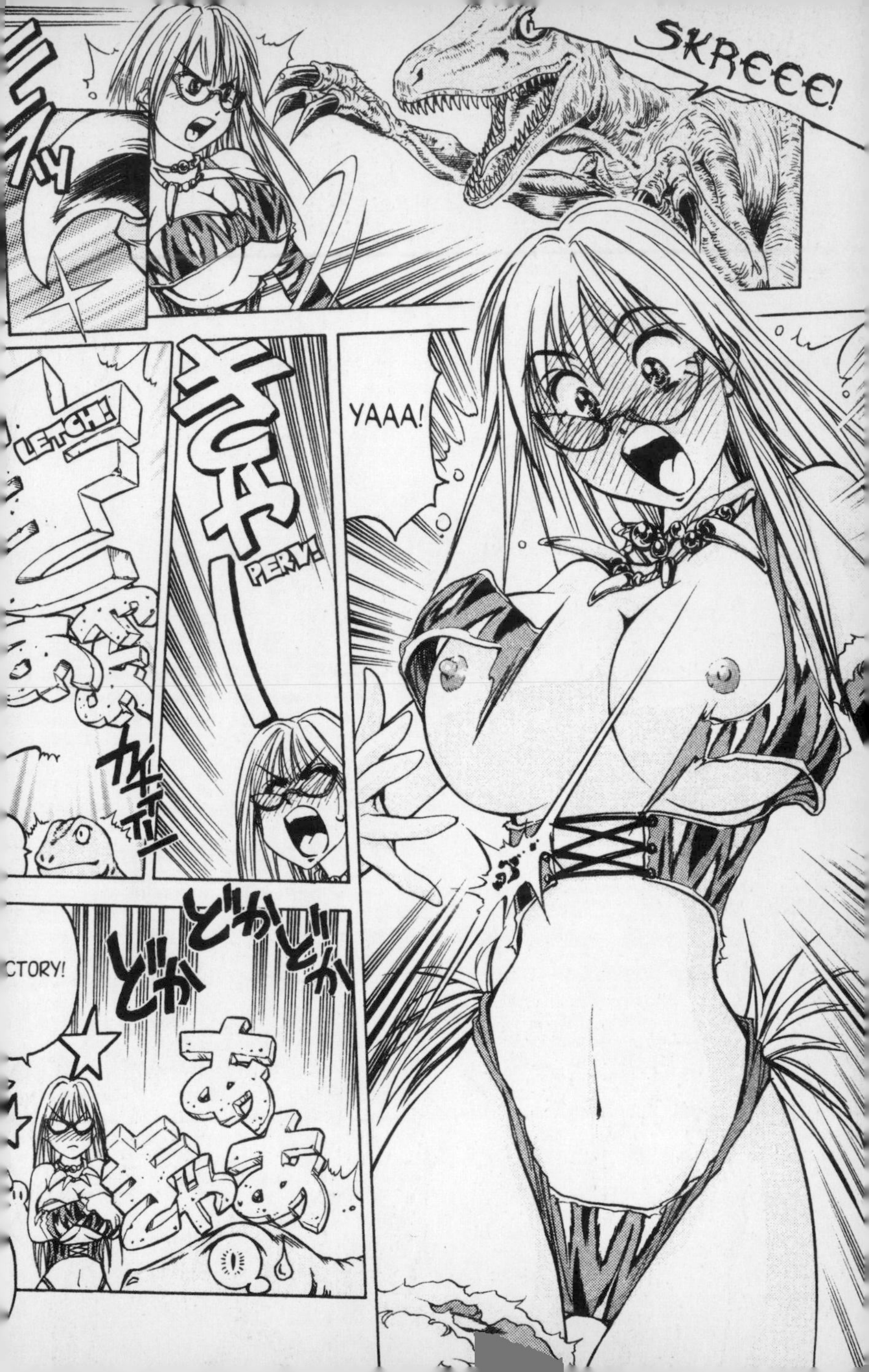
SKREEEE!
YAAA!
きゃー
PERV!
LETCH!
CTORY!

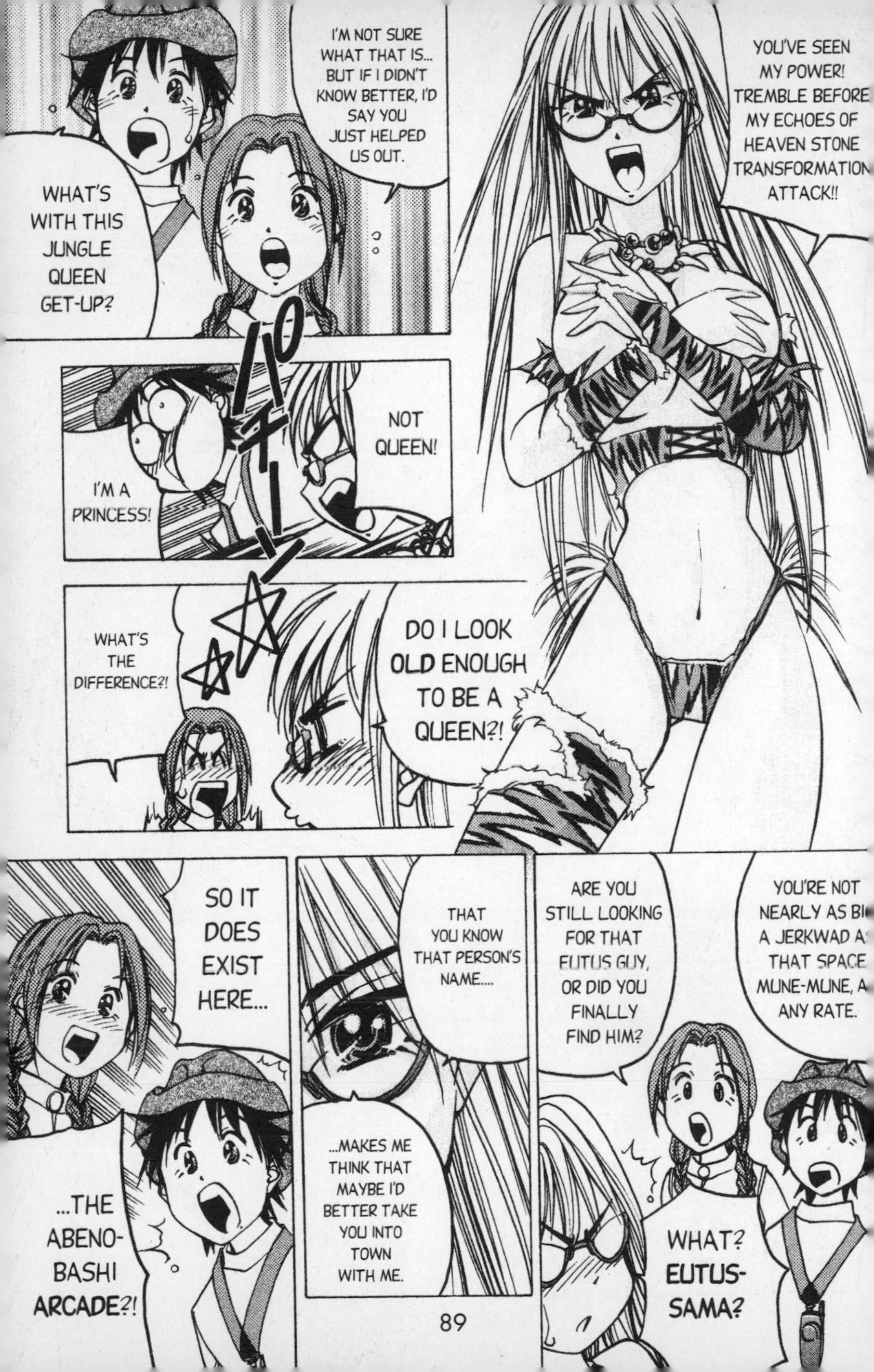
YOU'VE SEEN MY POWER! TREMBLE BEFORE MY ECHOES OF HEAVEN STONE TRANSFORMATION ATTACK!!
I'M NOT SURE WHAT THAT IS... BUT IF I DIDN'T KNOW BETTER, I'D SAY YOU JUST HELPED US OUT.
WHAT'S WITH THIS JUNGLE QUEEN GET-UP?
NOT QUEEN!
I'M A PRINCESS!
DO I LOOK OLD ENOUGH TO BE A QUEEN?!
WHAT'S THE DIFFERENCE?!
YOU'RE NOT NEARLY AS BI A JERKWAD A THAT SPACE MUNE-MUNE, A ANY RATE.
ARE YOU STILL LOOKING FOR THAT EUTUS GUY, OR DID YOU FINALLY FIND HIM?
WHAT? EUTUS-SAMA?
THAT YOU KNOW THAT PERSON'S NAME....
...MAKES ME THINK THAT MAYBE I'D BETTER TAKE YOU INTO TOWN WITH ME.
SO IT DOES EXIST HERE...
...THE ABENO-BASHI ARCADE?!

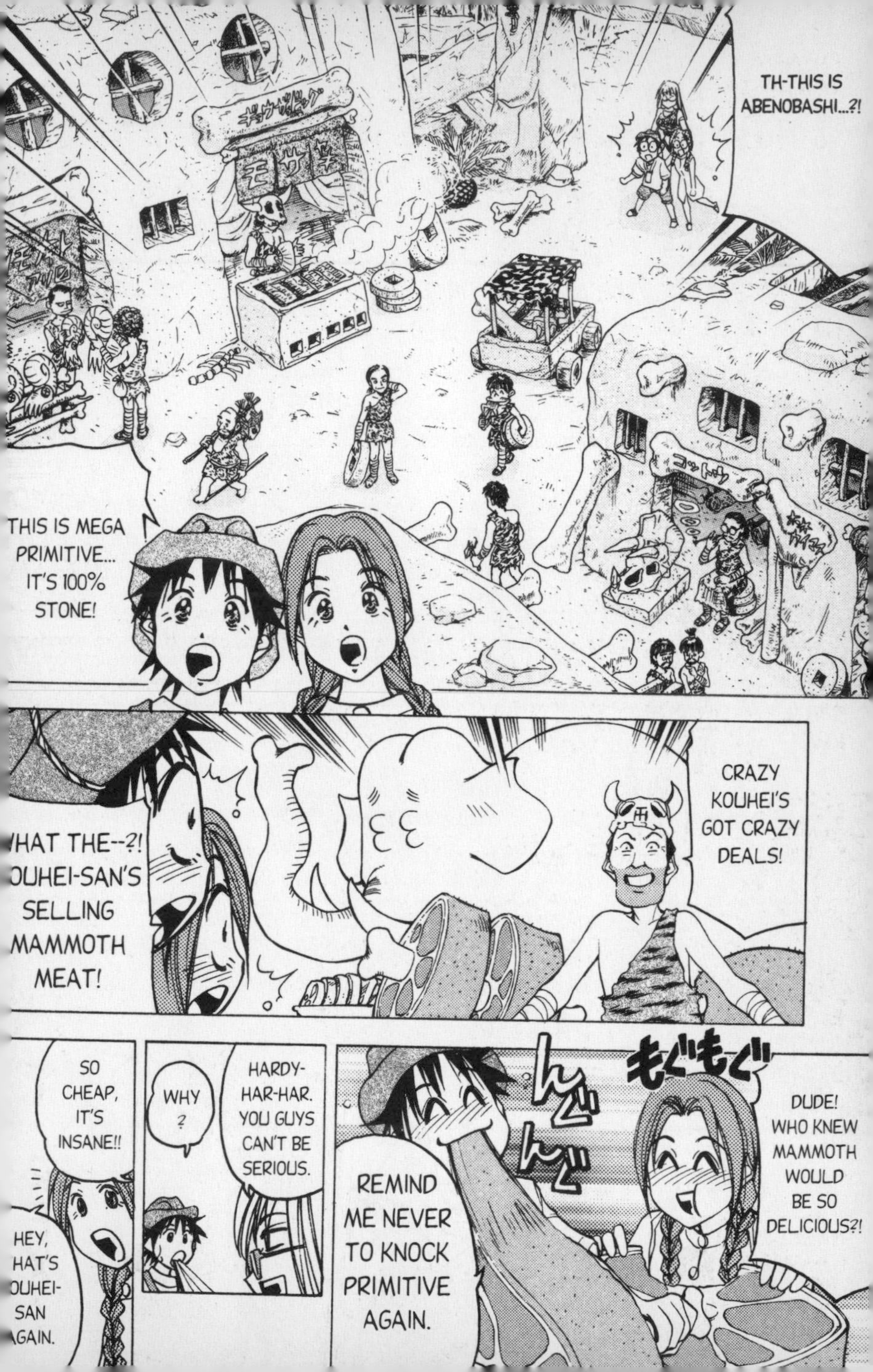
TH-THIS IS ABENOBASHI...?!
THIS IS MEGA PRIMITIVE... IT'S 100% STONE!
CRAZY KOUHEI'S GOT CRAZY DEALS!
WHAT THE--?! OUHEI-SAN'S SELLING MAMMOTH MEAT!
もぐもぐ
DUDE! WHO KNEW MAMMOTH WOULD BE SO DELICIOUS?!
んぐんぐ
REMIND ME NEVER TO KNOCK PRIMITIVE AGAIN.
HARDY-HAR-HAR. YOU GUYS CAN'T BE SERIOUS.
WHY?
SO CHEAP, IT'S INSANE!!
HEY, HAT'S OUHEI-SAN AGAIN.

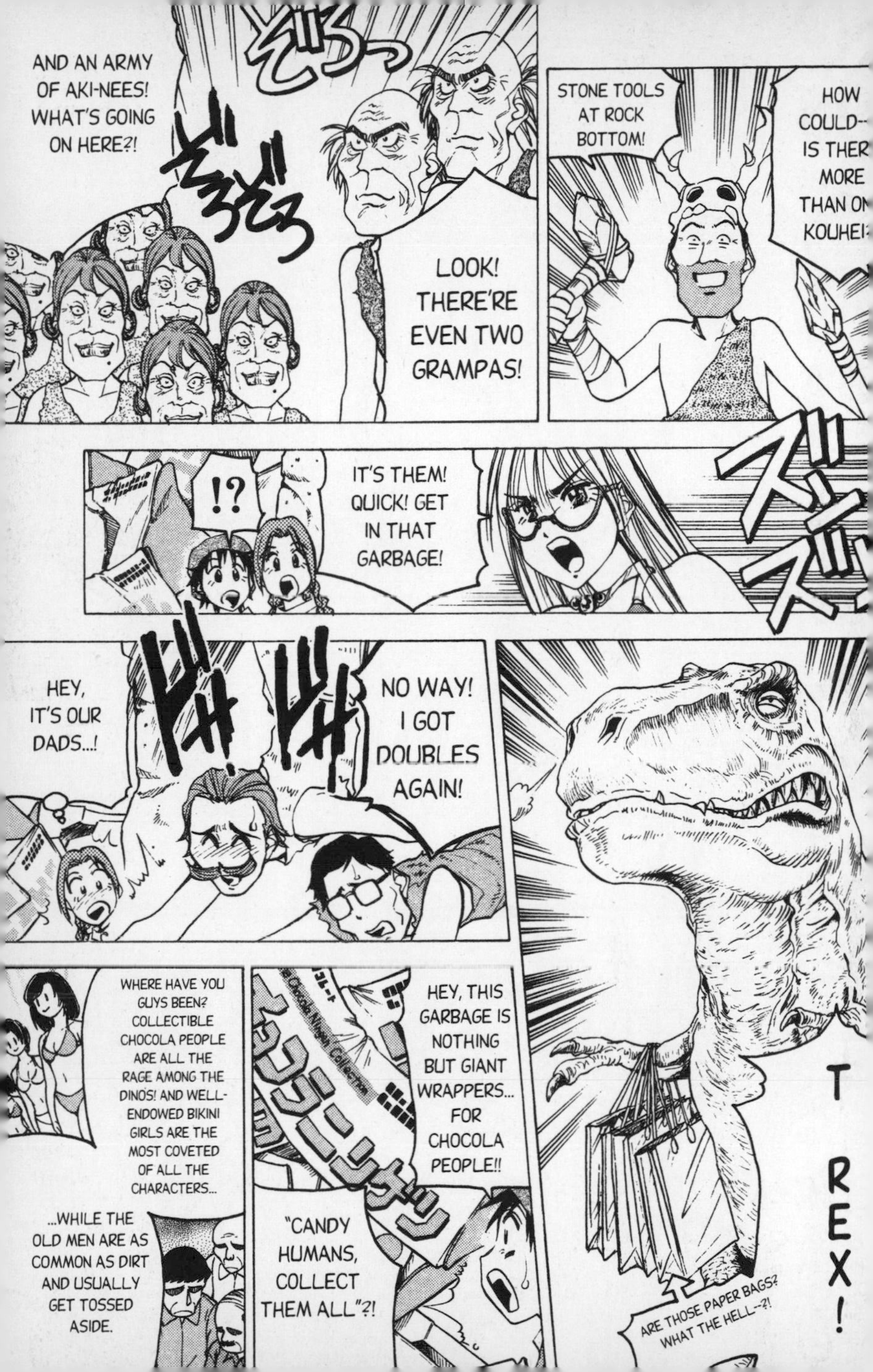
HOW COULD-- IS THER MORE THAN ON KOUHEI!
STONE TOOLS AT ROCK BOTTOM!
ぞろっ
ぞろぞろ
LOOK! THERE'RE EVEN TWO GRAMPAS!
AND AN ARMY OF AKI-NEES! WHAT'S GOING ON HERE?!
IT'S THEM! QUICK! GET IN THAT GARBAGE!
!?
T REX!
ARE THOSE PAPER BAGS? WHAT THE HELL--?!
NO WAY! I GOT DOUBLES AGAIN!
HEY, IT'S OUR DADS...!
HEY, THIS GARBAGE IS NOTHING BUT GIANT WRAPPERS... FOR CHOCOLA PEOPLE!!
"CANDY HUMANS, COLLECT THEM ALL"?!
WHERE HAVE YOU GUYS BEEN? COLLECTIBLE CHOCOLA PEOPLE ARE ALL THE RAGE AMONG THE DINOS! AND WELL-ENDOWED BIKINI GIRLS ARE THE MOST COVETED OF ALL THE CHARACTERS...
...WHILE THE OLD MEN ARE AS COMMON AS DIRT AND USUALLY GET TOSSED ASIDE.

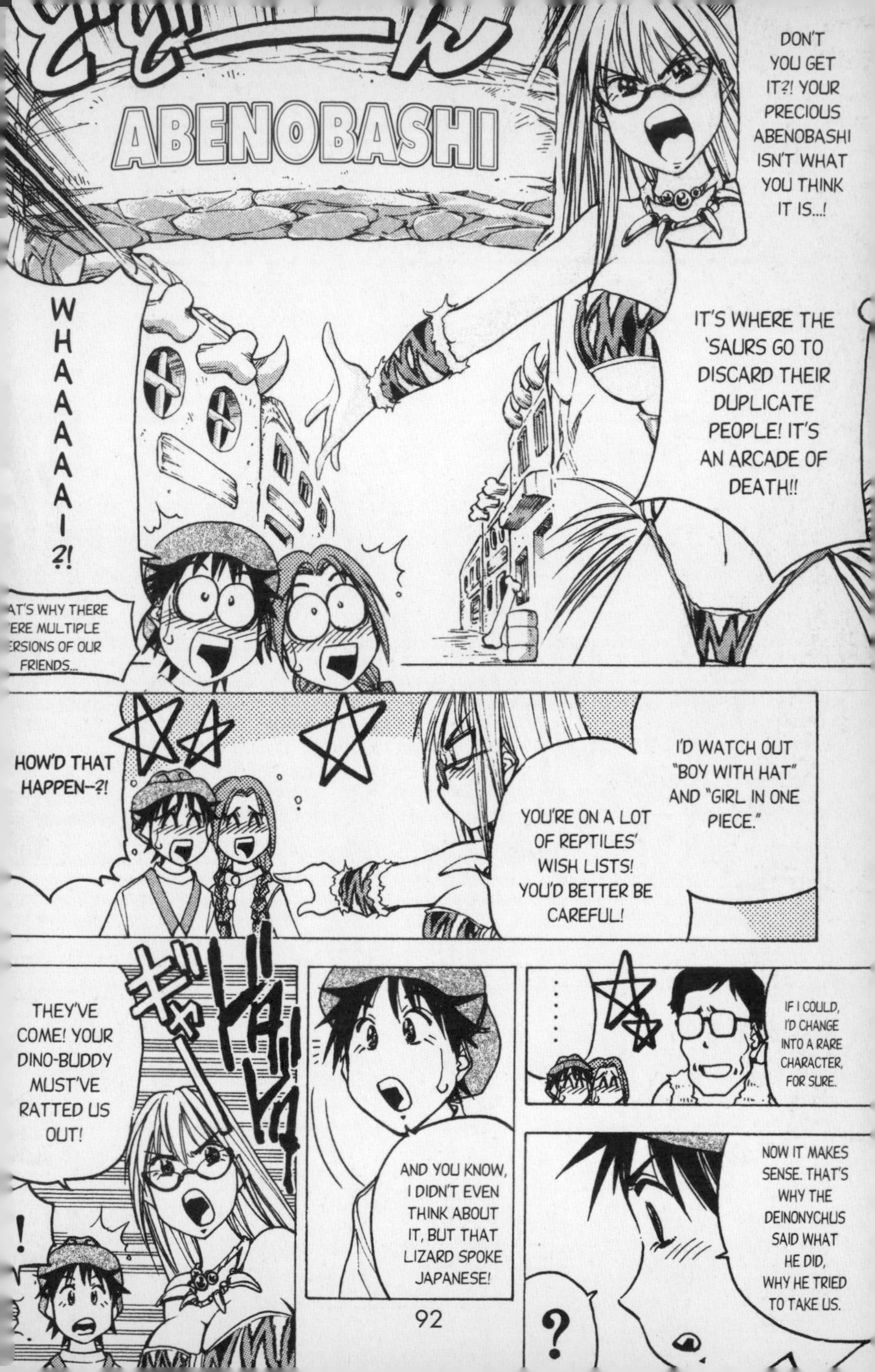
DON'T YOU GET IT?! YOUR PRECIOUS ABENOBASHI ISN'T WHAT YOU THINK IT IS...!
ABENOBASHI
IT'S WHERE THE 'SAURS GO TO DISCARD THEIR DUPLICATE PEOPLE! IT'S AN ARCADE OF DEATH!!
WHAAAAAAAI?!
AT'S WHY THERE ERE MULTIPLE ERSIONS OF OUR FRIENDS...
I'D WATCH OUT "BOY WITH HAT" AND "GIRL IN ONE PIECE."
YOU'RE ON A LOT OF REPTILES' WISH LISTS! YOU'D BETTER BE CAREFUL!
HOW'D THAT HAPPEN--?!
IF I COULD, I'D CHANGE INTO A RARE CHARACTER, FOR SURE.
......
NOW IT MAKES SENSE. THAT'S WHY THE DEINONYCHUS SAID WHAT HE DID, WHY HE TRIED TO TAKE US.
?
AND YOU KNOW, I DIDN'T EVEN THINK ABOUT IT, BUT THAT LIZARD SPOKE JAPANESE!
THEY'VE COME! YOUR DINO-BUDDY MUST'VE RATTED US OUT!
!

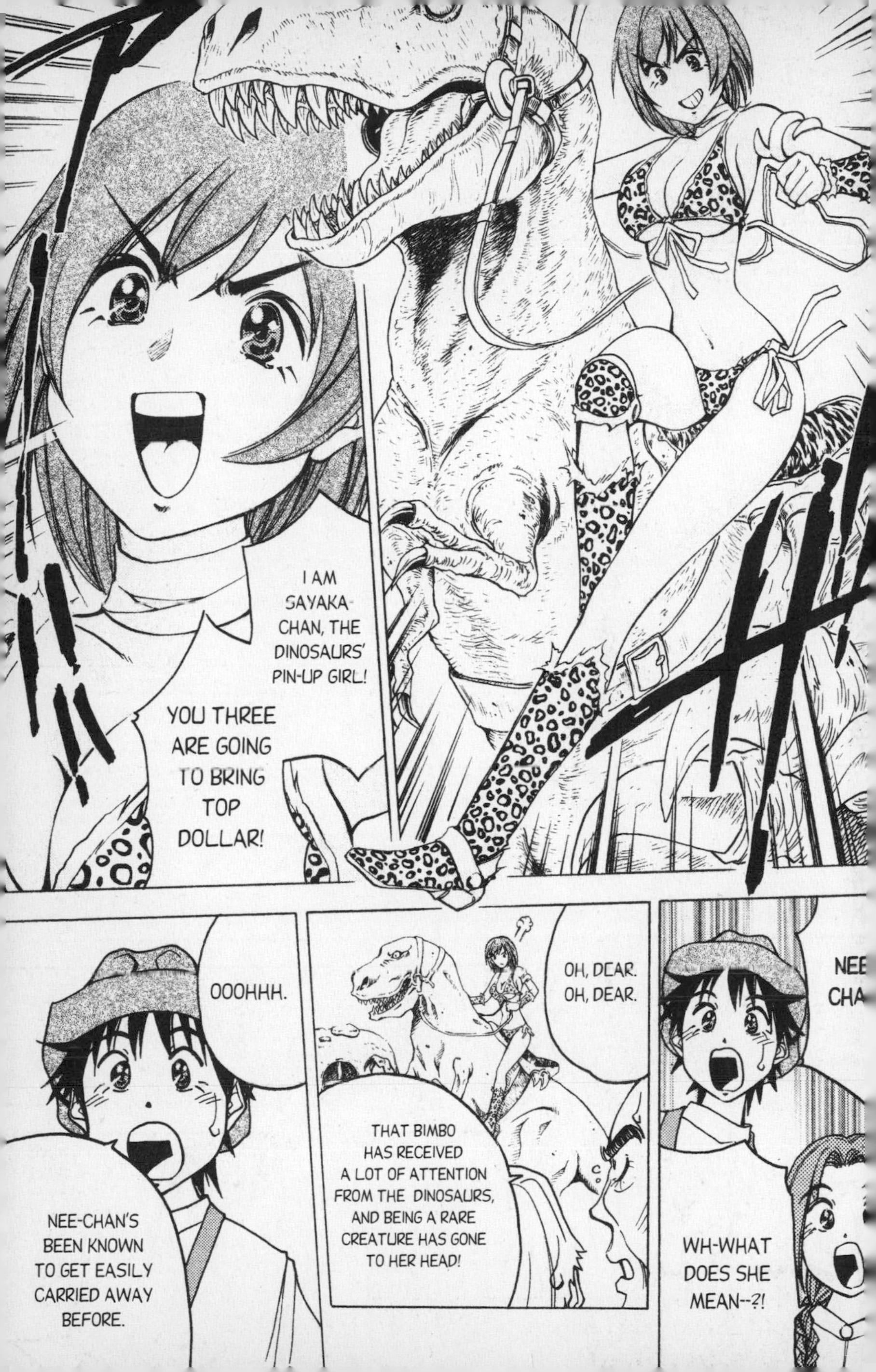
I AM SAYAKA-CHAN, THE DINOSAURS' PIN-UP GIRL!
YOU THREE ARE GOING TO BRING TOP DOLLAR!
NEE CHA
WH-WHAT DOES SHE MEAN--?!
OH, DEAR. OH, DEAR.
THAT BIMBO HAS RECEIVED A LOT OF ATTENTION FROM THE DINOSAURS, AND BEING A RARE CREATURE HAS GONE TO HER HEAD!
OOOHHH.
NEE-CHAN'S BEEN KNOWN TO GET EASILY CARRIED AWAY BEFORE.

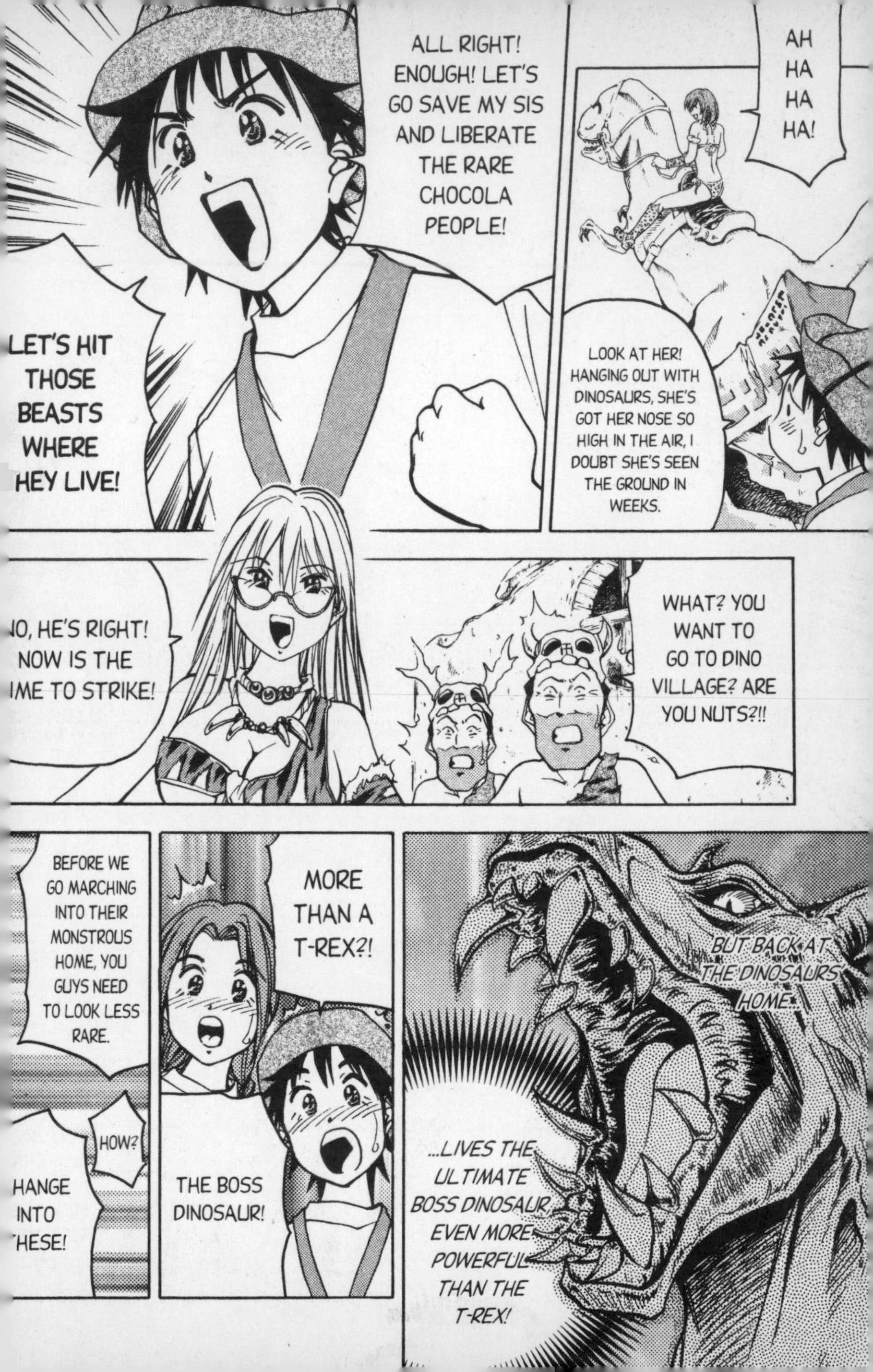
AH HA HA HA!
LOOK AT HER! HANGING OUT WITH DINOSAURS, SHE'S GOT HER NOSE SO HIGH IN THE AIR, I DOUBT SHE'S SEEN THE GROUND IN WEEKS.
ALL RIGHT! ENOUGH! LET'S GO SAVE MY SIS AND LIBERATE THE RARE CHOCOLA PEOPLE!
LET'S HIT THOSE BEASTS WHERE HEY LIVE!
WHAT? YOU WANT TO GO TO DINO VILLAGE? ARE YOU NUTS?!!
IO, HE'S RIGHT! NOW IS THE IME TO STRIKE!
BUT BACK AT THE DINOSAURS HOME...
...LIVES THE ULTIMATE BOSS DINOSAUR EVEN MORE POWERFUL THAN THE T-REX!
MORE THAN A T-REX?!
THE BOSS DINOSAUR!
BEFORE WE GO MARCHING INTO THEIR MONSTROUS HOME, YOU GUYS NEED TO LOOK LESS RARE.
HOW?
HANGE INTO HESE!

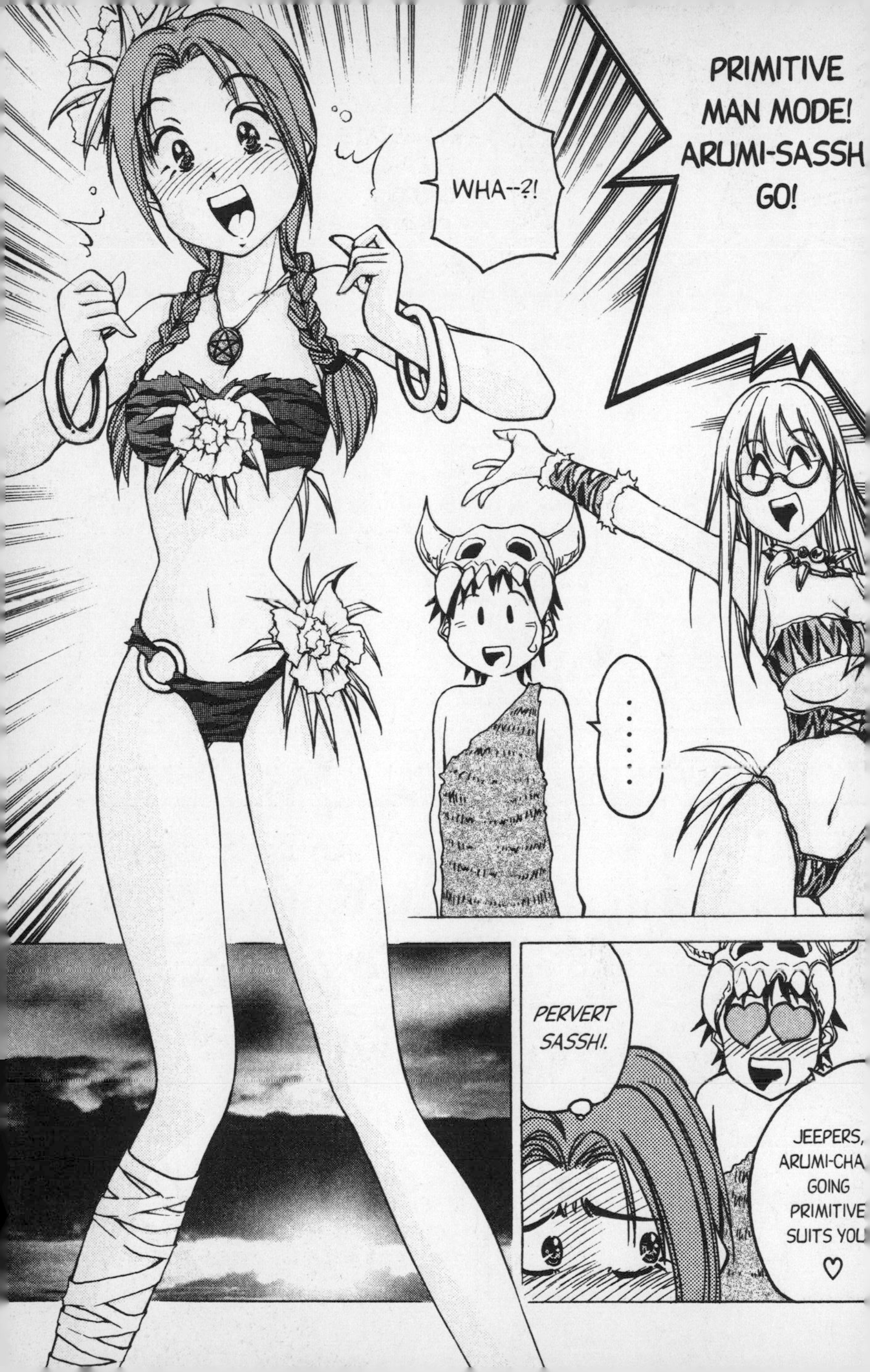
PRIMITIVE MAN MODE! ARUMI-SASSH GO!
WHA--?!
......
JEEPERS, ARUMI-CHA GOING PRIMITIVE SUITS YOU ♡
PERVERT SASSHI.

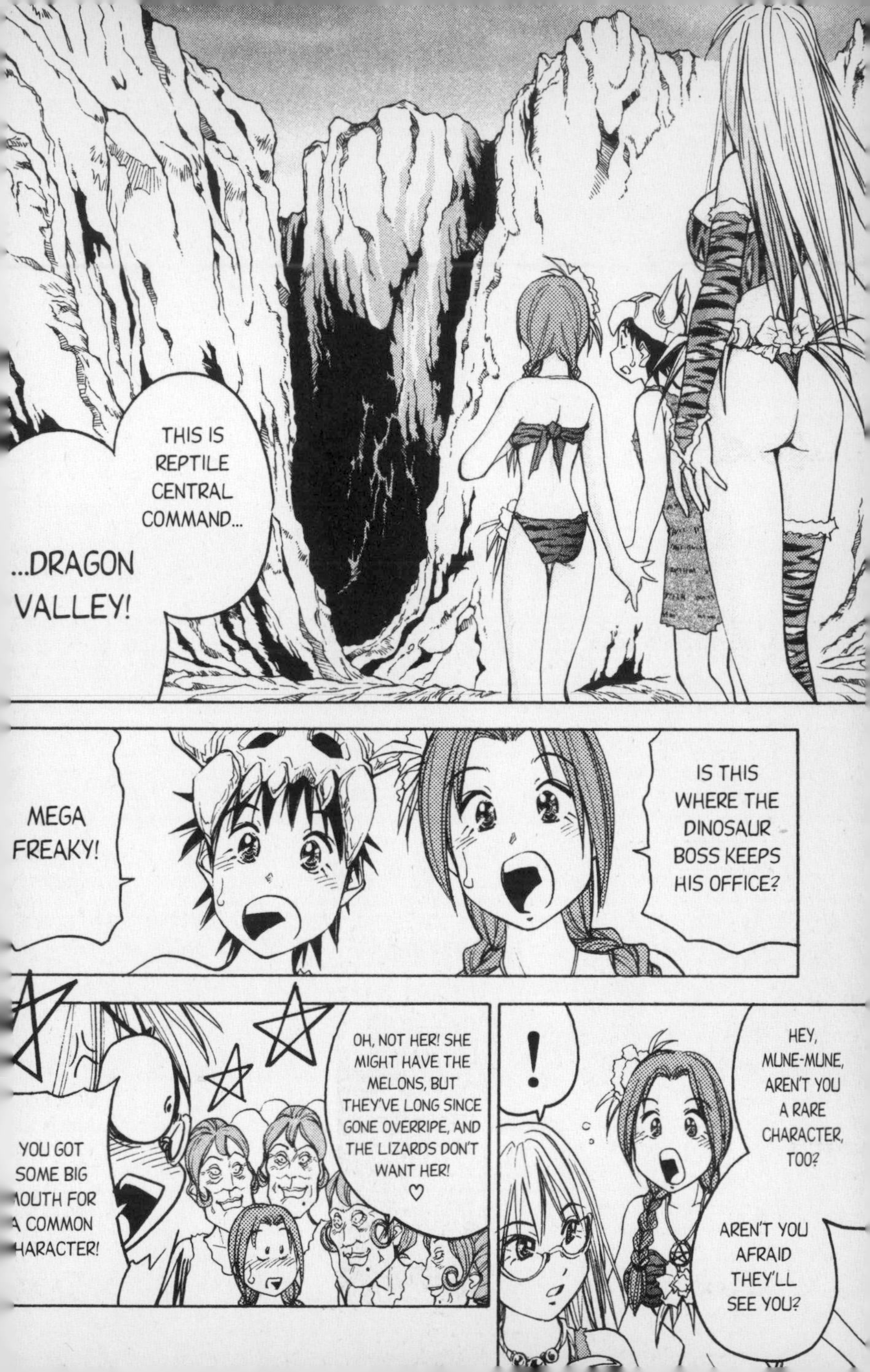
THIS IS REPTILE CENTRAL COMMAND...
...DRAGON VALLEY!
IS THIS WHERE THE DINOSAUR BOSS KEEPS HIS OFFICE?
MEGA FREAKY!
HEY, MUNE-MUNE, AREN'T YOU A RARE CHARACTER, TOO?
AREN'T YOU AFRAID THEY'LL SEE YOU?
!
OH, NOT HER! SHE MIGHT HAVE THE MELONS, BUT THEY'VE LONG SINCE GONE OVERRIPE, AND THE LIZARDS DON'T WANT HER! ♡
YOU GOT SOME BIG OUTH FOR A COMMON HARACTER!

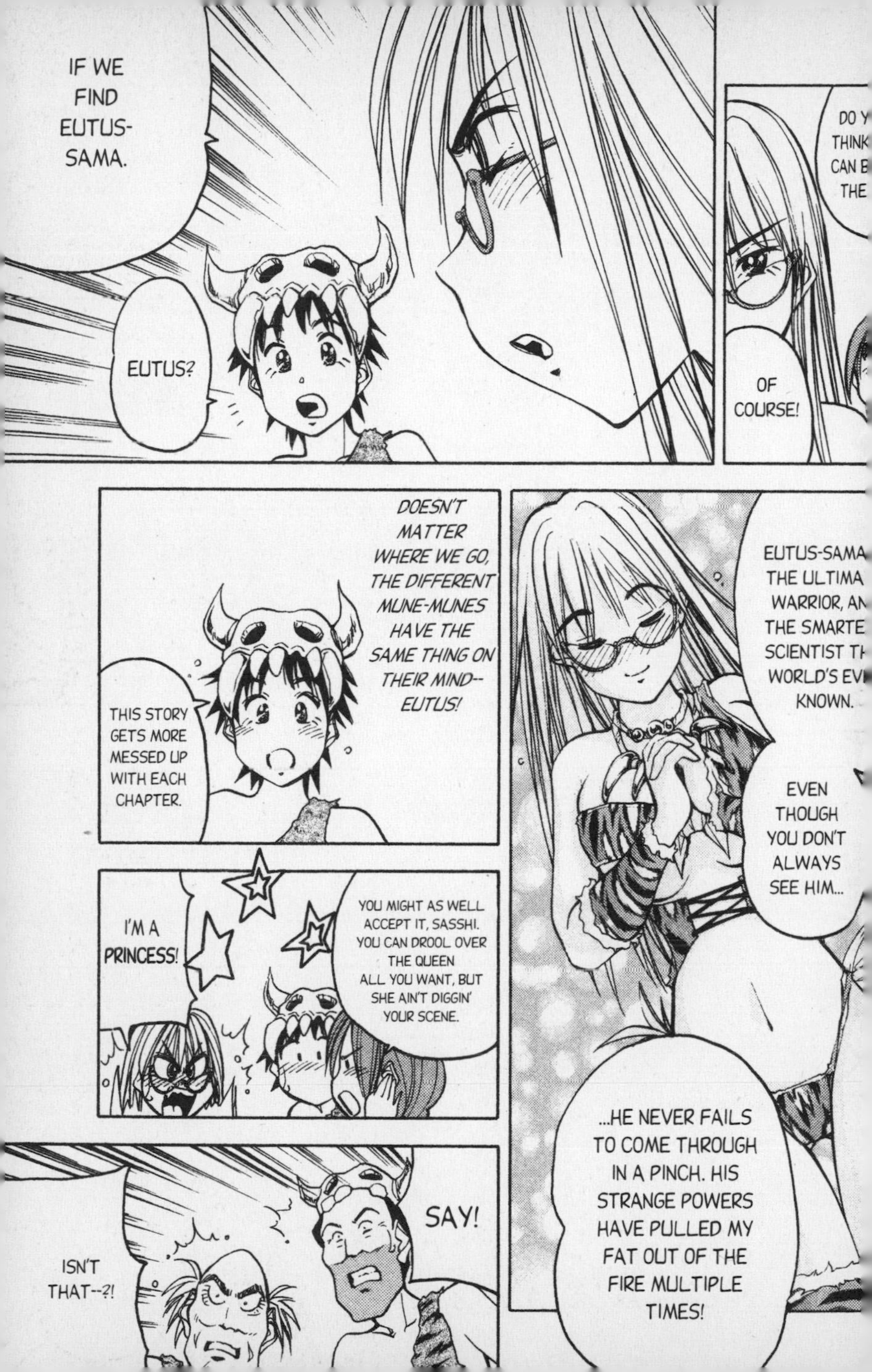
DO Y
THINK
CAN B
THE
OF COURSE!
IF WE FIND EUTUS-SAMA.
EUTUS?
EUTUS-SAMA THE ULTIMA WARRIOR, AN THE SMARTE SCIENTIST TH WORLD'S EV KNOWN.
EVEN THOUGH YOU DON'T ALWAYS SEE HIM...
...HE NEVER FAILS TO COME THROUGH IN A PINCH. HIS STRANGE POWERS HAVE PULLED MY FAT OUT OF THE FIRE MULTIPLE TIMES!
DOESN'T MATTER WHERE WE GO, THE DIFFERENT MUNE-MUNES HAVE THE SAME THING ON THEIR MIND-- EUTUS!
THIS STORY GETS MORE MESSED UP WITH EACH CHAPTER.
YOU MIGHT AS WELL ACCEPT IT, SASSHI. YOU CAN DROOL OVER THE QUEEN ALL YOU WANT, BUT SHE AIN'T DIGGIN' YOUR SCENE.
I'M A PRINCESS!
SAY!
ISN'T THAT--?!

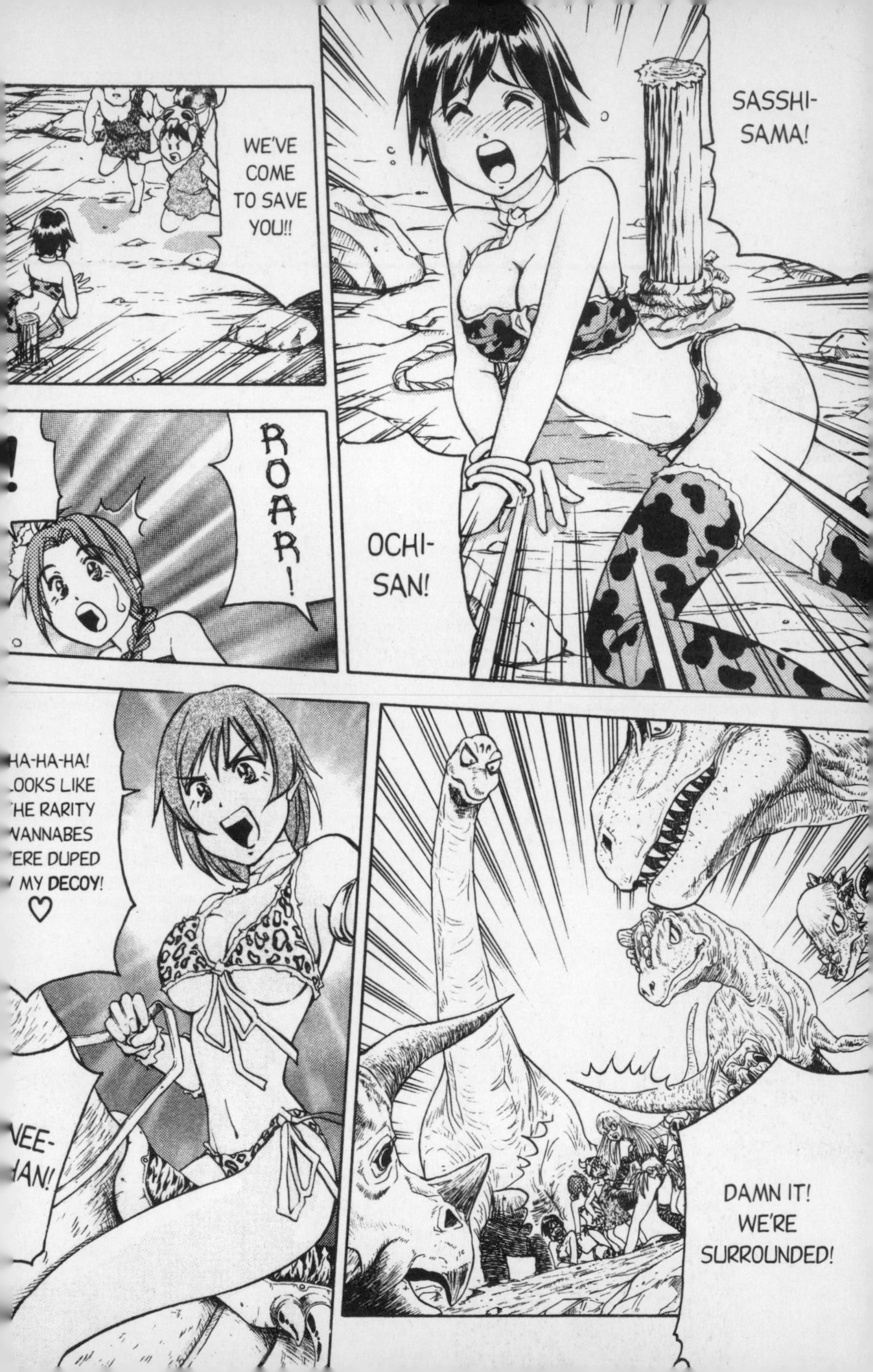
SASSHI-SAMA!
OCHI-SAN!
WE'VE COME TO SAVE YOU!!
ROAR!
DAMN IT! WE'RE SURROUNDED!
HA-HA-HA! OOKS LIKE HE RARITY ANNABES ERE DUPED MY DECOY! ♡
EE- AN!

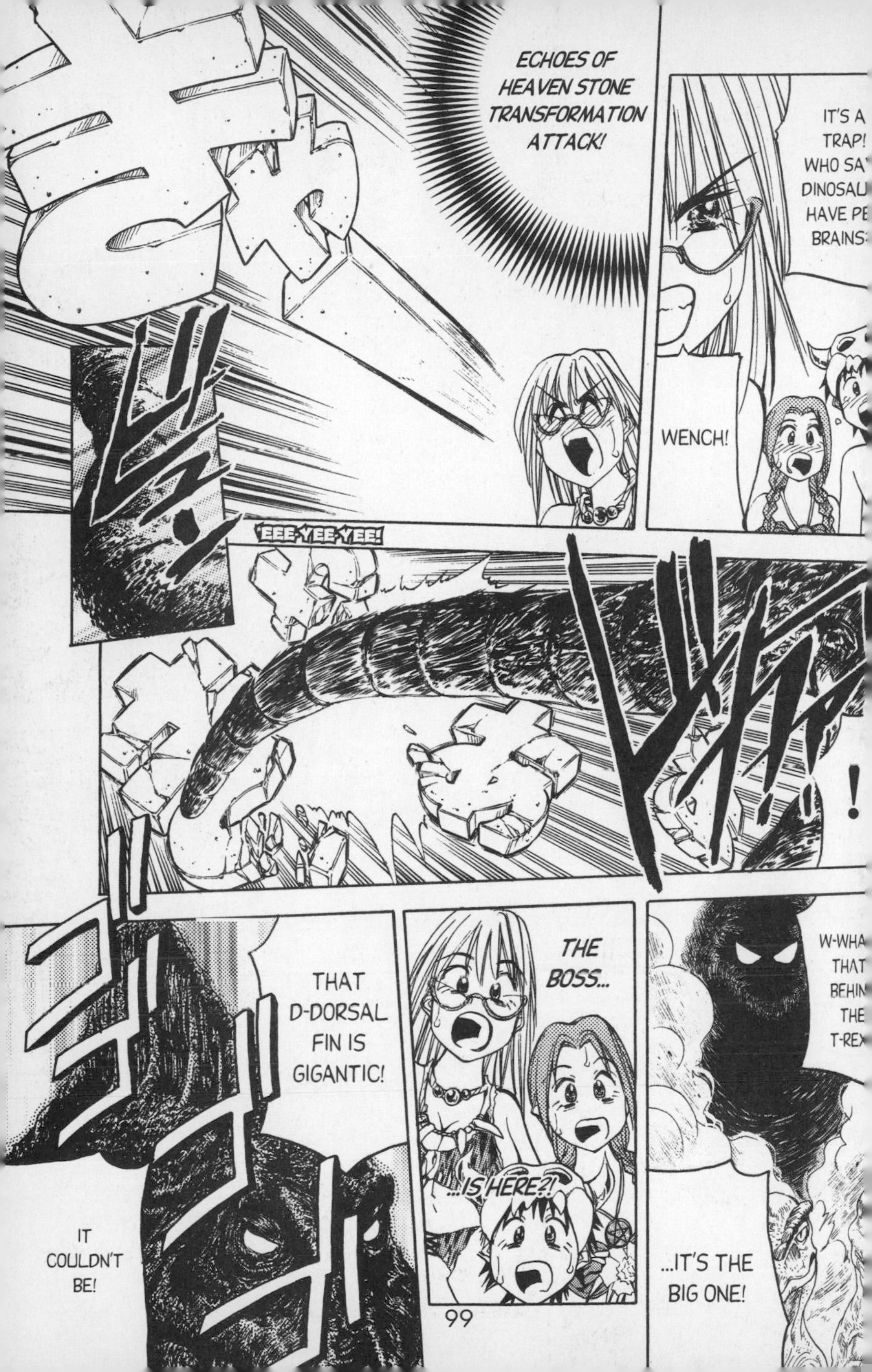
IT'S A TRAP! WHO SA DINOSAU HAVE PE BRAINS
WENCH!
ECHOES OF HEAVEN STONE TRANSFORMATION ATTACK!
EEE-YEE-YEE!
W-WHA THAT BEHIN THE T-REX
...IT'S THE BIG ONE!
THE BOSS...
...IS HERE?!
THAT D-DORSAL FIN IS GIGANTIC!
IT COULDN'T BE!

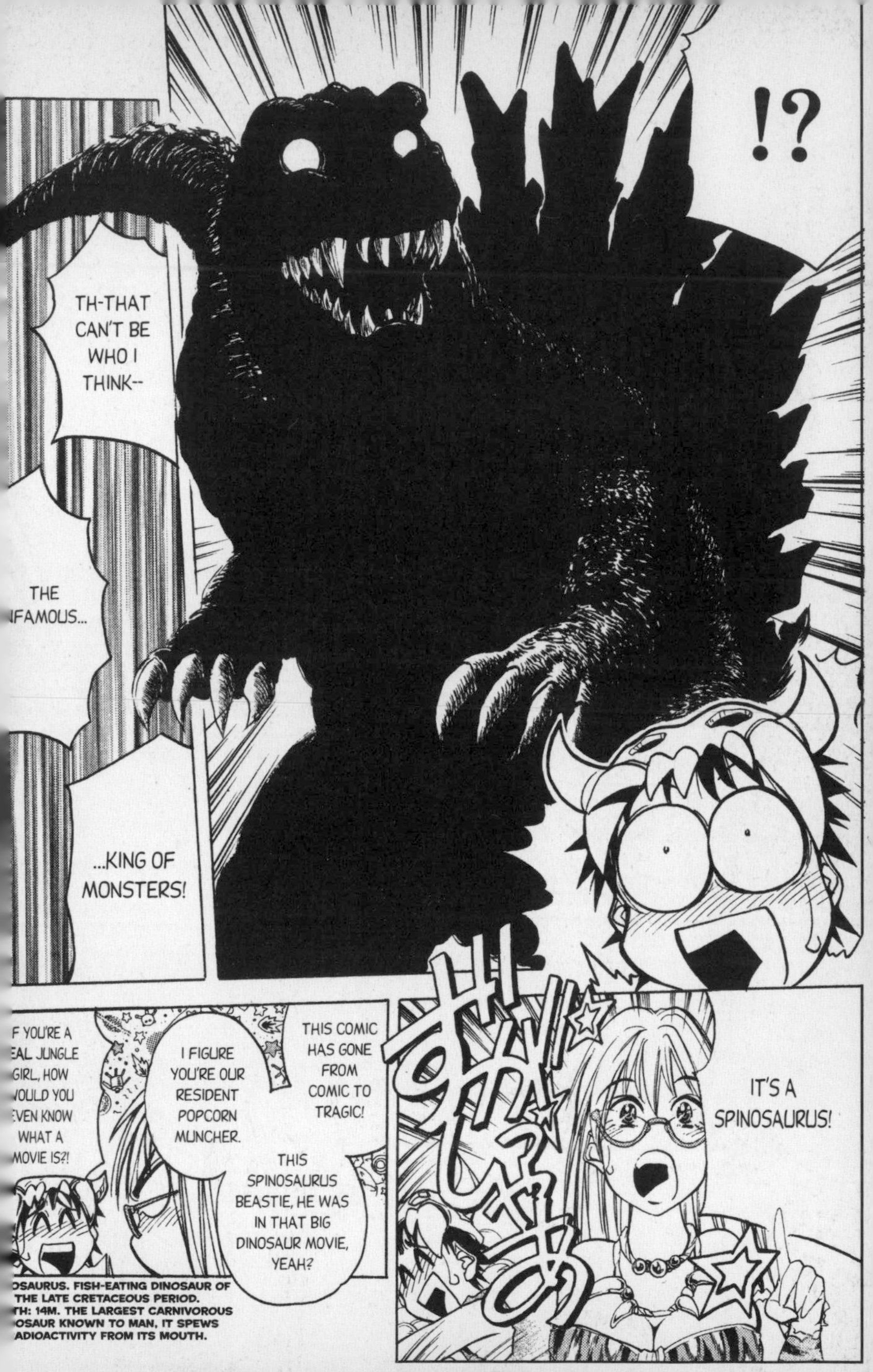
!?
TH-THAT CAN'T BE WHO I THINK--
THE NFAMOUS...
...KING OF MONSTERS!
IT'S A SPINOSAURUS!
THIS COMIC HAS GONE FROM COMIC TO TRAGIC!
I FIGURE YOU'RE OUR RESIDENT POPCORN MUNCHER.
THIS SPINOSAURUS BEASTIE, HE WAS IN THAT BIG DINOSAUR MOVIE, YEAH?
F YOU'RE A EAL JUNGLE GIRL, HOW VOULD YOU EVEN KNOW WHAT A MOVIE IS?!
OSAURUS. FISH-EATING DINOSAUR OF THE LATE CRETACEOUS PERIOD. TH: 14M. THE LARGEST CARNIVOROUS OSAUR KNOWN TO MAN, IT SPEWS ADIOACTIVITY FROM ITS MOUTH.

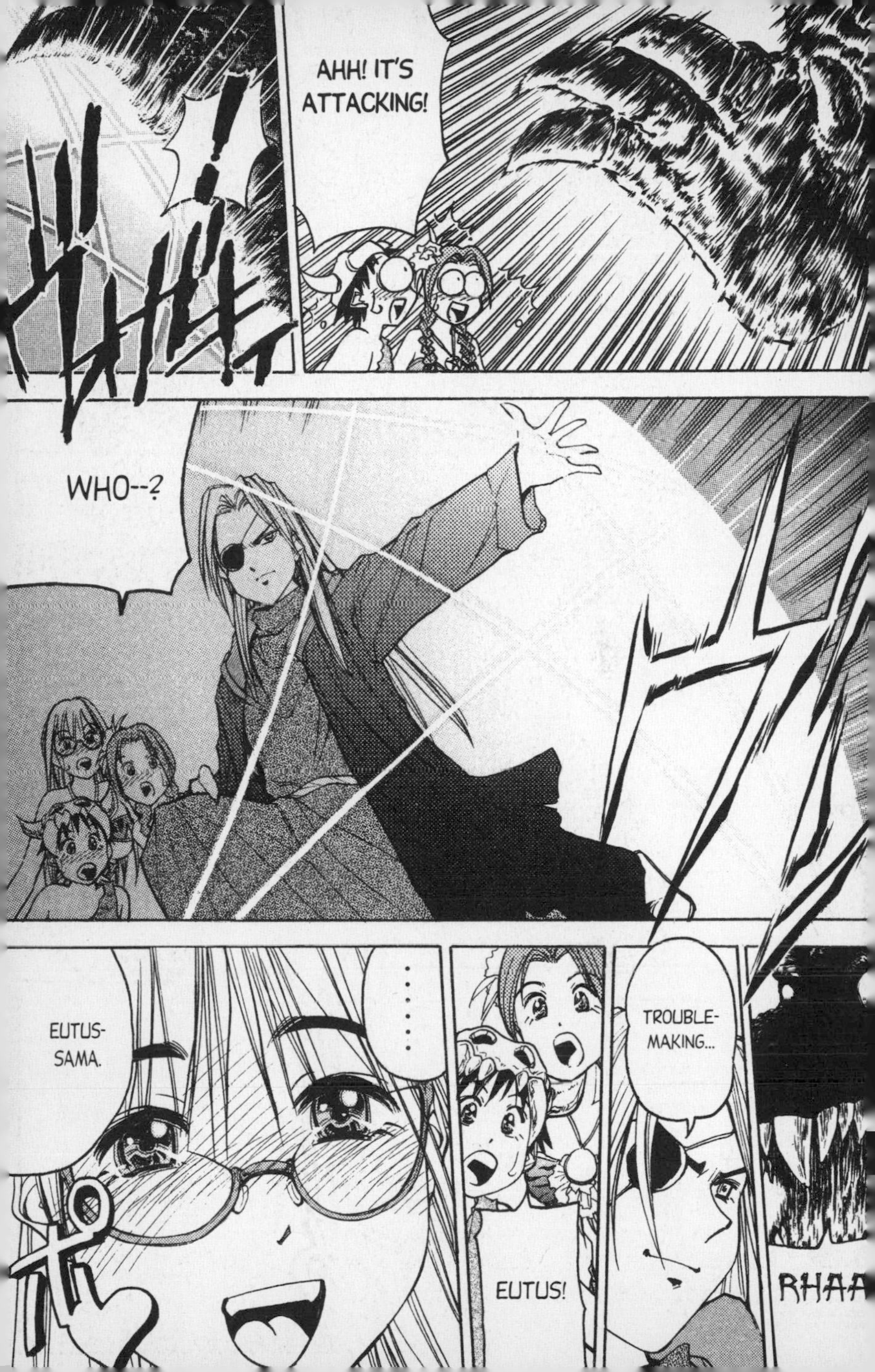
AHH! IT'S ATTACKING!
WHO--?
RHAA
TROUBLE-MAKING...
EUTUS!
......
EUTUS-SAMA.

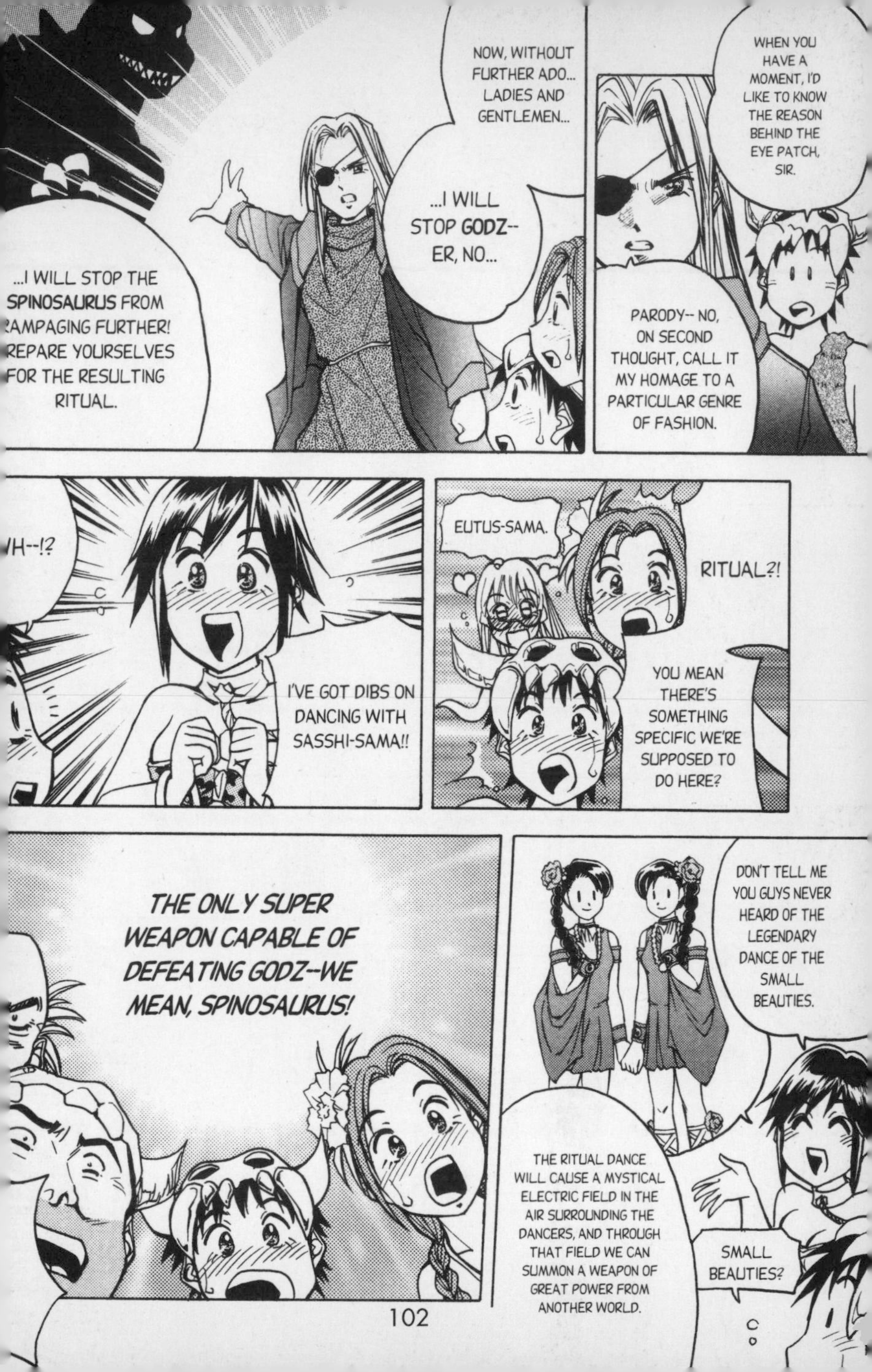
WHEN YOU HAVE A MOMENT, I'D LIKE TO KNOW THE REASON BEHIND THE EYE PATCH, SIR.
PARODY-- NO, ON SECOND THOUGHT, CALL IT MY HOMAGE TO A PARTICULAR GENRE OF FASHION.
NOW, WITHOUT FURTHER ADO... LADIES AND GENTLEMEN...
...I WILL STOP GODZ-- ER, NO...
...I WILL STOP THE SPINOSAURUS FROM AMPAGING FURTHER! REPARE YOURSELVES FOR THE RESULTING RITUAL.
EUTUS-SAMA.
RITUAL?!
YOU MEAN THERE'S SOMETHING SPECIFIC WE'RE SUPPOSED TO DO HERE?
H--!?
I'VE GOT DIBS ON DANCING WITH SASSHI-SAMA!!
DON'T TELL ME YOU GUYS NEVER HEARD OF THE LEGENDARY DANCE OF THE SMALL BEAUTIES.
SMALL BEAUTIES?
THE RITUAL DANCE WILL CAUSE A MYSTICAL ELECTRIC FIELD IN THE AIR SURROUNDING THE DANCERS, AND THROUGH THAT FIELD WE CAN SUMMON A WEAPON OF GREAT POWER FROM ANOTHER WORLD.
THE ONLY SUPER WEAPON CAPABLE OF DEFEATING GODZ--WE MEAN, SPINOSAURUS!

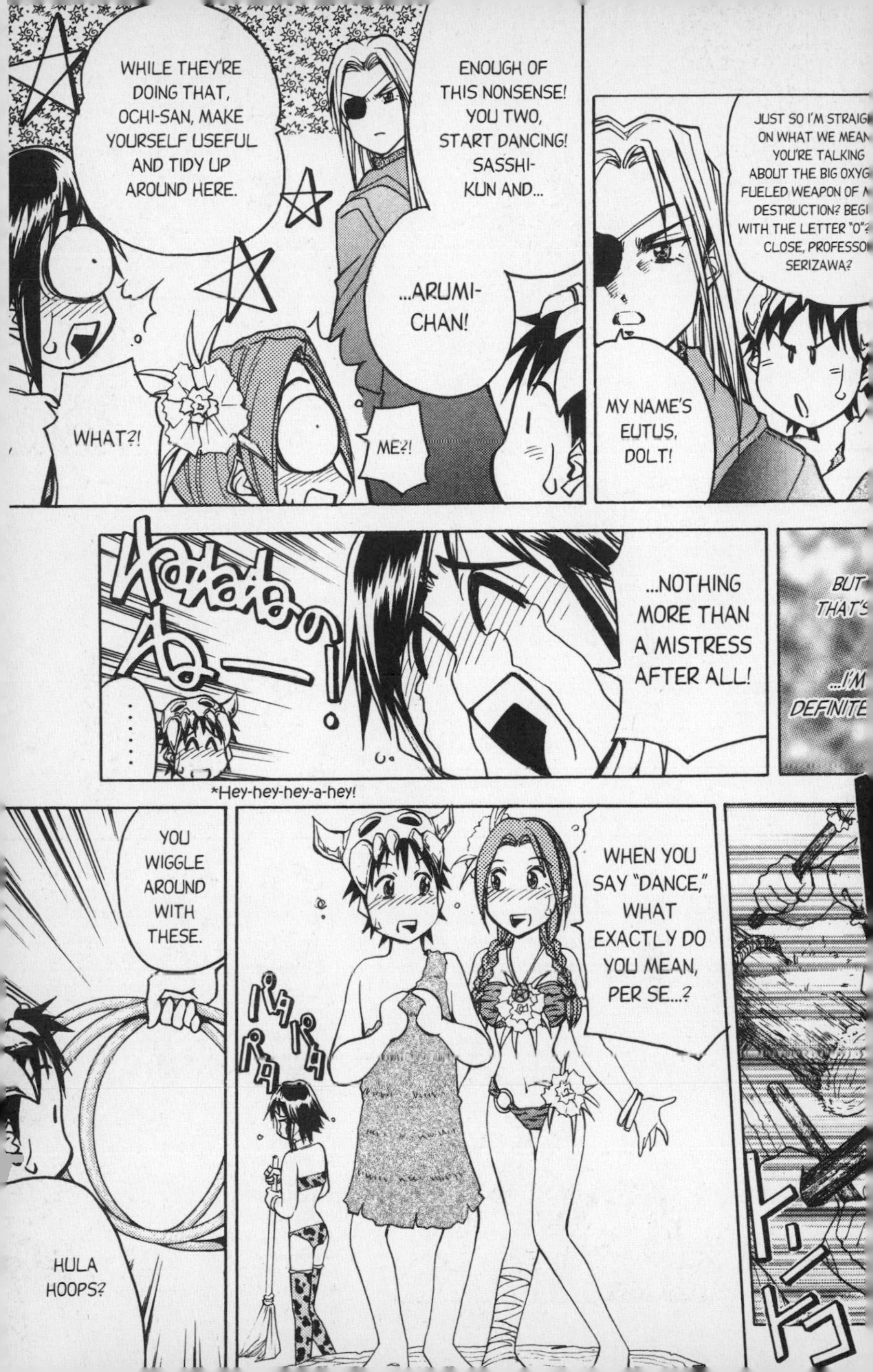
JUST SO I'M STRAIG
ON WHAT WE MEAN
YOU'RE TALKING
ABOUT THE BIG OXYG
FUELED WEAPON OF M
DESTRUCTION? BEGI
WITH THE LETTER "O"?
CLOSE, PROFESSO
SERIZAWA?
MY NAME'S EUTUS, DOLT!
ENOUGH OF THIS NONSENSE! YOU TWO, START DANCING! SASSHI-KUN AND...
...ARUMI-CHAN!
WHILE THEY'RE DOING THAT, OCHI-SAN, MAKE YOURSELF USEFUL AND TIDY UP AROUND HERE.
ME?!
WHAT?!
BUT THAT'S
...I'M DEFINITE
...NOTHING MORE THAN A MISTRESS AFTER ALL!
......
*Hey-hey-hey-a-hey!
WHEN YOU SAY "DANCE," WHAT EXACTLY DO YOU MEAN, PER SE...?
パタパタ
YOU WIGGLE AROUND WITH THESE.
HULA HOOPS?

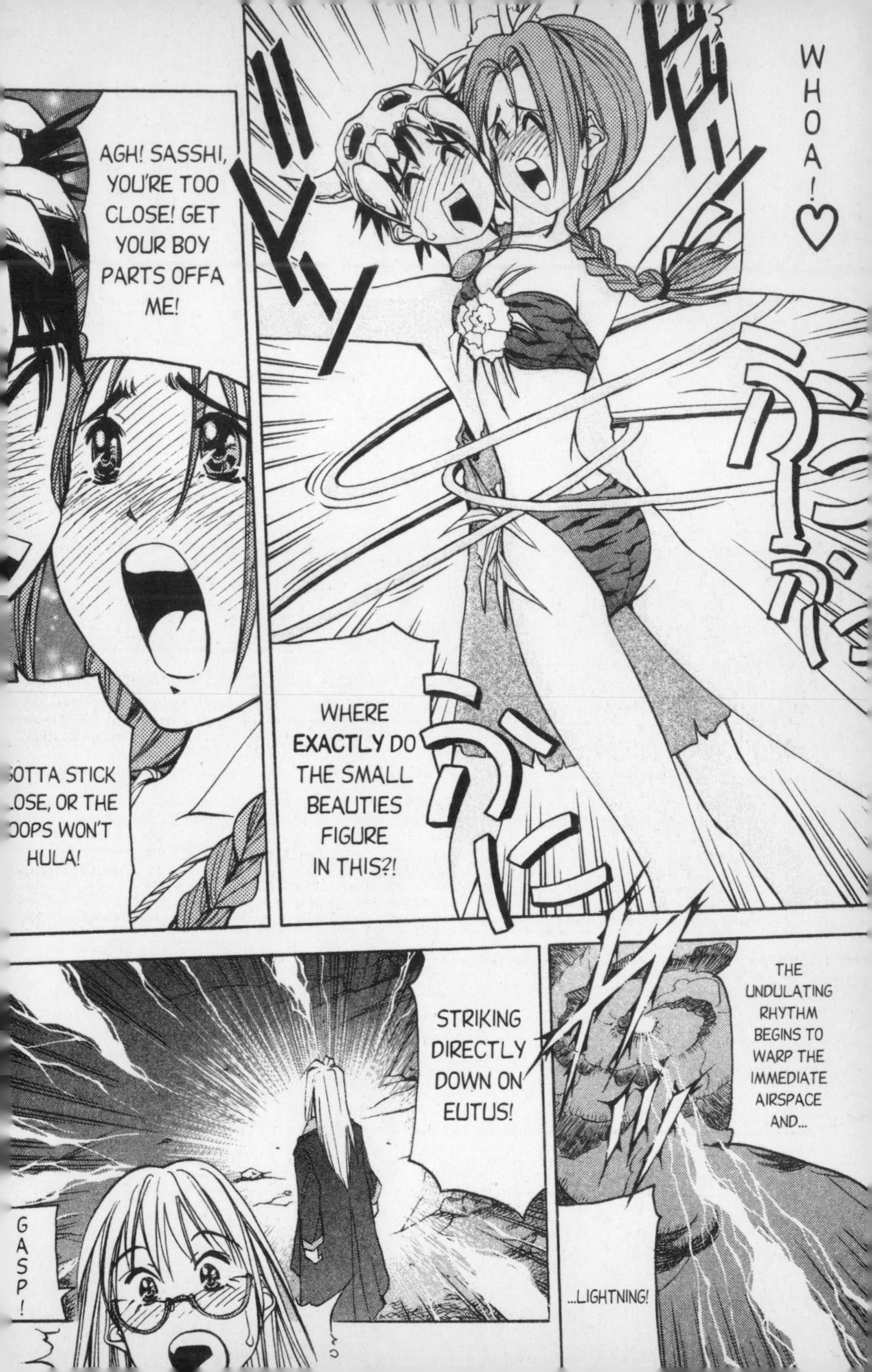
WHOA!♡
WHERE EXACTLY DO THE SMALL BEAUTIES FIGURE IN THIS?!
AGH! SASSHI, YOU'RE TOO CLOSE! GET YOUR BOY PARTS OFFA ME!
OTTA STICK LOSE, OR THE OOPS WON'T HULA!
THE UNDULATING RHYTHM BEGINS TO WARP THE IMMEDIATE AIRSPACE AND...
...LIGHTNING!
STRIKING DIRECTLY DOWN ON EUTUS!
GASP!

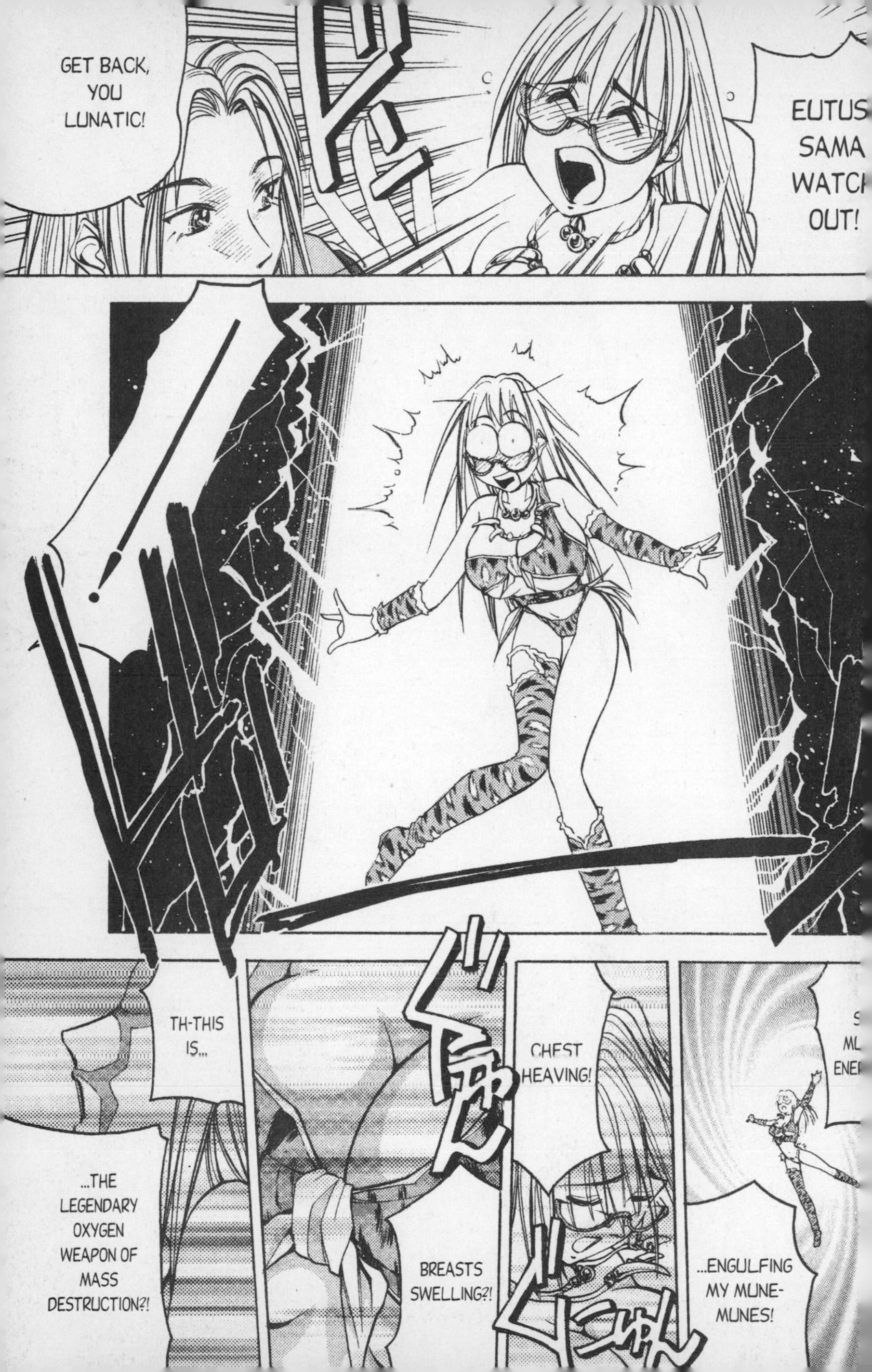
EUTUS SAMA WATCH OUT!
GET BACK, YOU LUNATIC!
...ENGULFING MY MUNE-MUNES!
CHEST HEAVING!
BREASTS SWELLING?!
TH-THIS IS...
...THE LEGENDARY OXYGEN WEAPON OF MASS DESTRUCTION?!

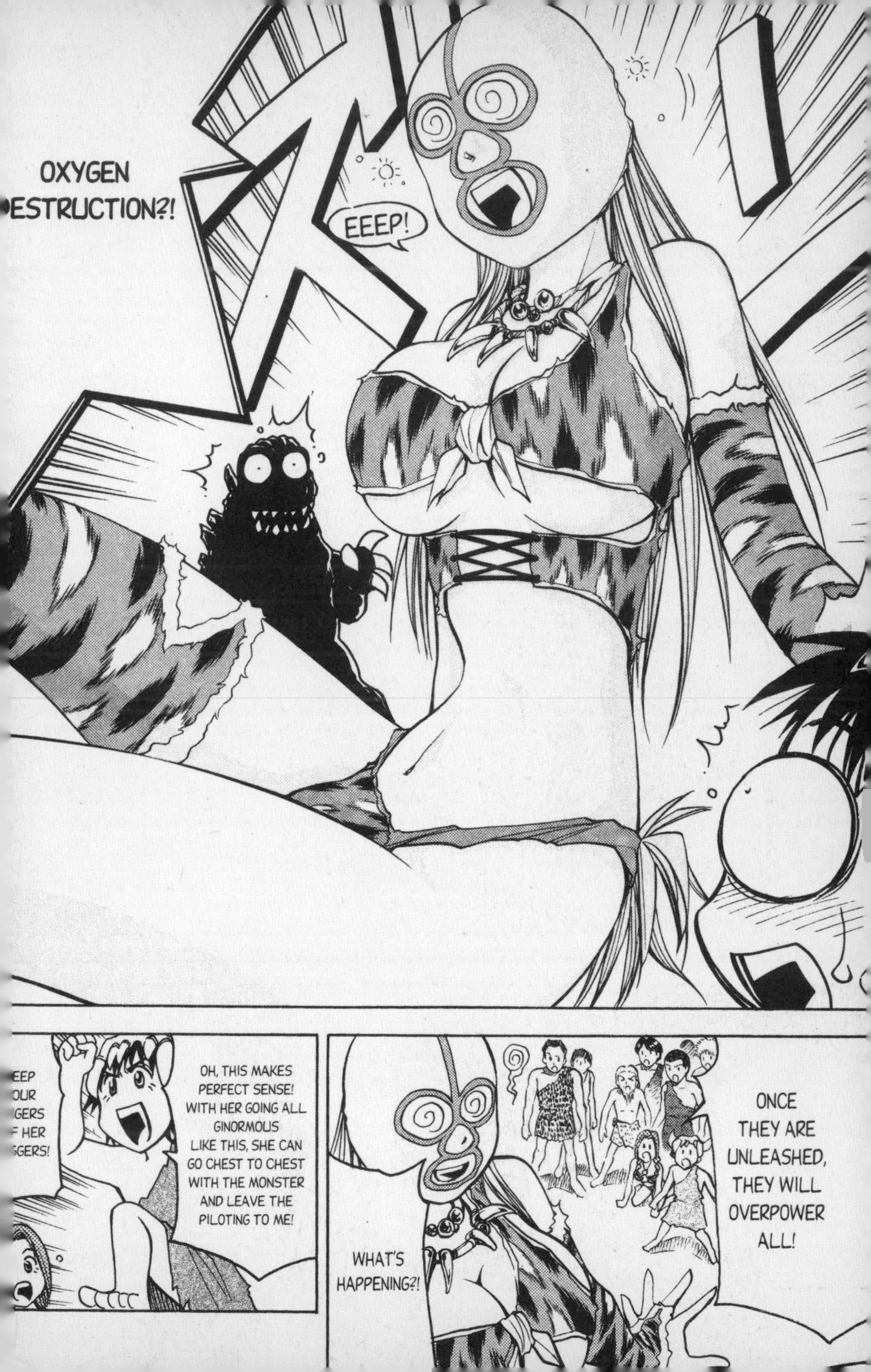
OXYGEN
ESTRUCTION?!
EEEP!
ONCE THEY ARE UNLEASHED, THEY WILL OVERPOWER ALL!
WHAT'S HAPPENING?!
OH, THIS MAKES PERFECT SENSE! WITH HER GOING ALL GINORMOUS LIKE THIS, SHE CAN GO CHEST TO CHEST WITH THE MONSTER AND LEAVE THE PILOTING TO ME!
EEP OUR IGERS F HER GGERS!

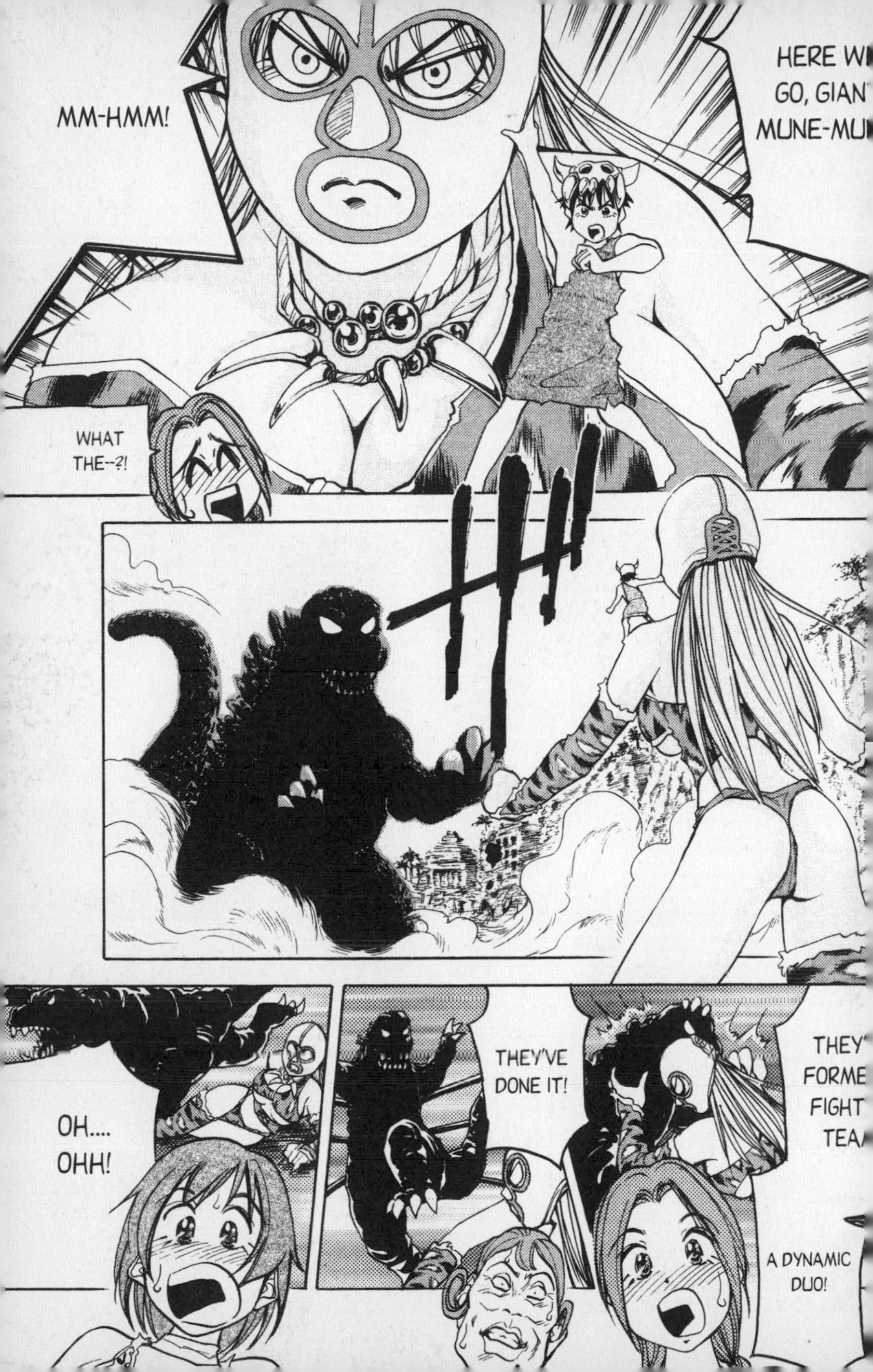
HERE WI
GO, GIAN
MUNE-MU
MM-HMM!
WHAT THE--?!
THEY'
FORME
FIGHT
TEA
A DYNAMIC DUO!
THEY'VE DONE IT!
OH.... OHH!

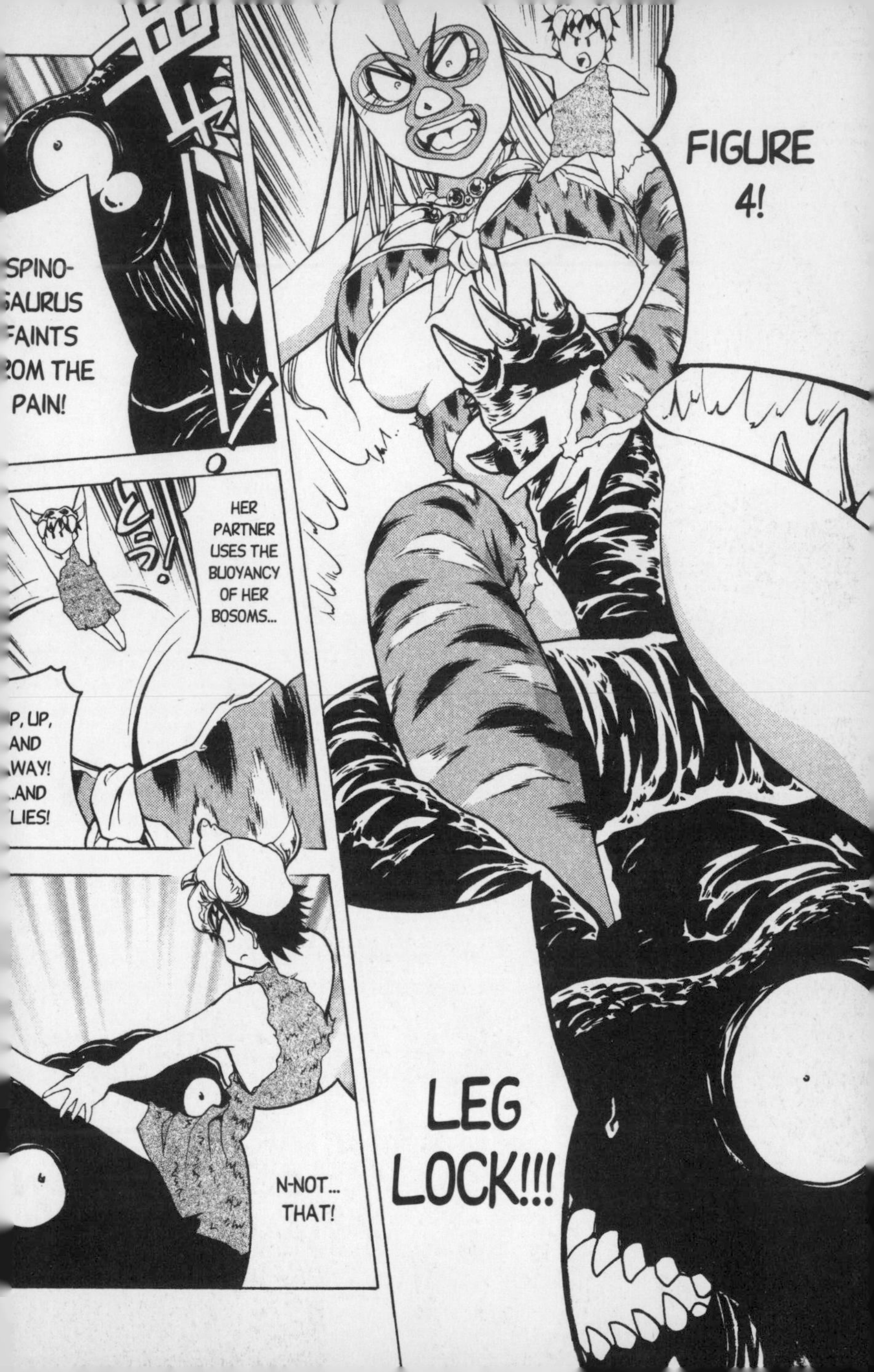
FIGURE 4!
LEG LOCK!!!
SPINO-SAURUS FAINTS ROM THE PAIN!
HER PARTNER USES THE BUOYANCY OF HER BOSOMS...
P, UP, AND WAY! ..AND LIES!
N-NOT... THAT!

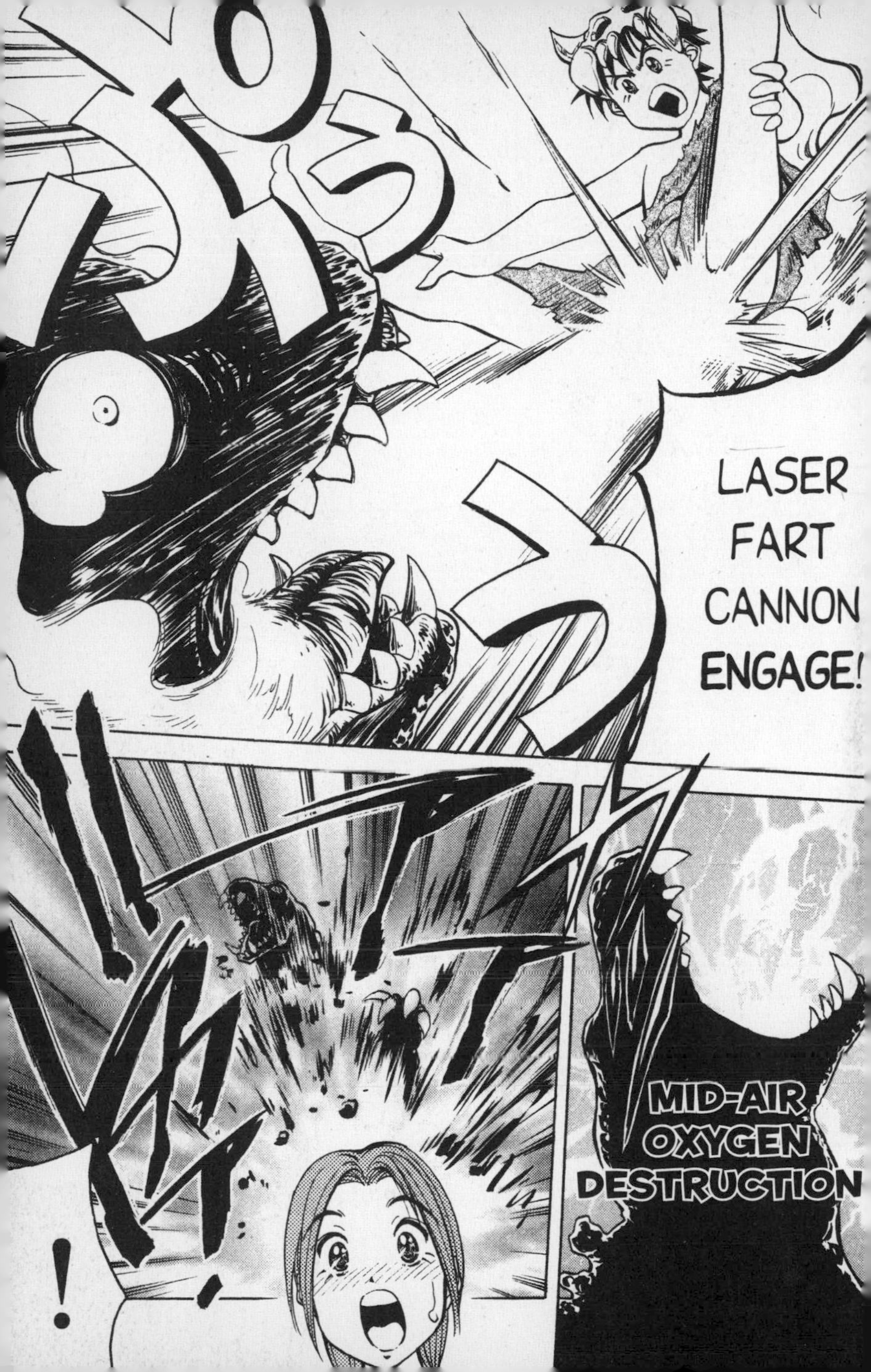
LASER FART CANNON ENGAGE!
MID-AIR OXYGEN DESTRUCTION

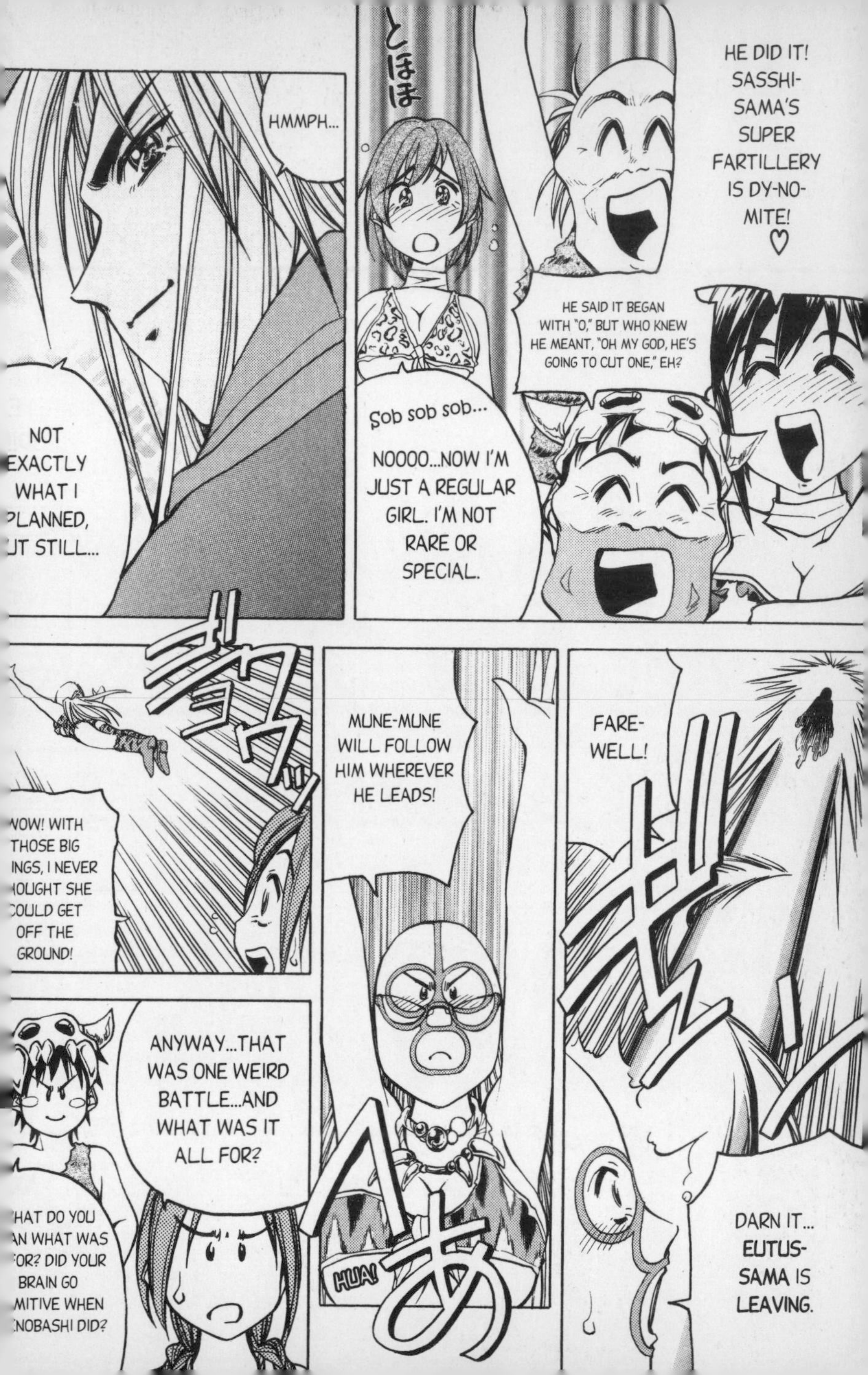
HE DID IT! SASSHI-SAMA'S SUPER FARTILLERY IS DY-NO-MITE! ♡
HE SAID IT BEGAN WITH "O," BUT WHO KNEW HE MEANT, "OH MY GOD, HE'S GOING TO CUT ONE," EH?
とほほ
Sob sob sob...
NOOOO...NOW I'M JUST A REGULAR GIRL. I'M NOT RARE OR SPECIAL.
HMMPH...
NOT EXACTLY WHAT I PLANNED, UT STILL...
FARE-WELL!
DARN IT... EUTUS-SAMA IS LEAVING.
MUNE-MUNE WILL FOLLOW HIM WHEREVER HE LEADS!
HUA!
あ
WOW! WITH THOSE BIG INGS, I NEVER HOUGHT SHE COULD GET OFF THE GROUND!
ANYWAY...THAT WAS ONE WEIRD BATTLE...AND WHAT WAS IT ALL FOR?
HAT DO YOU AN WHAT WAS FOR? DID YOUR BRAIN GO MITIVE WHEN NOBASHI DID?

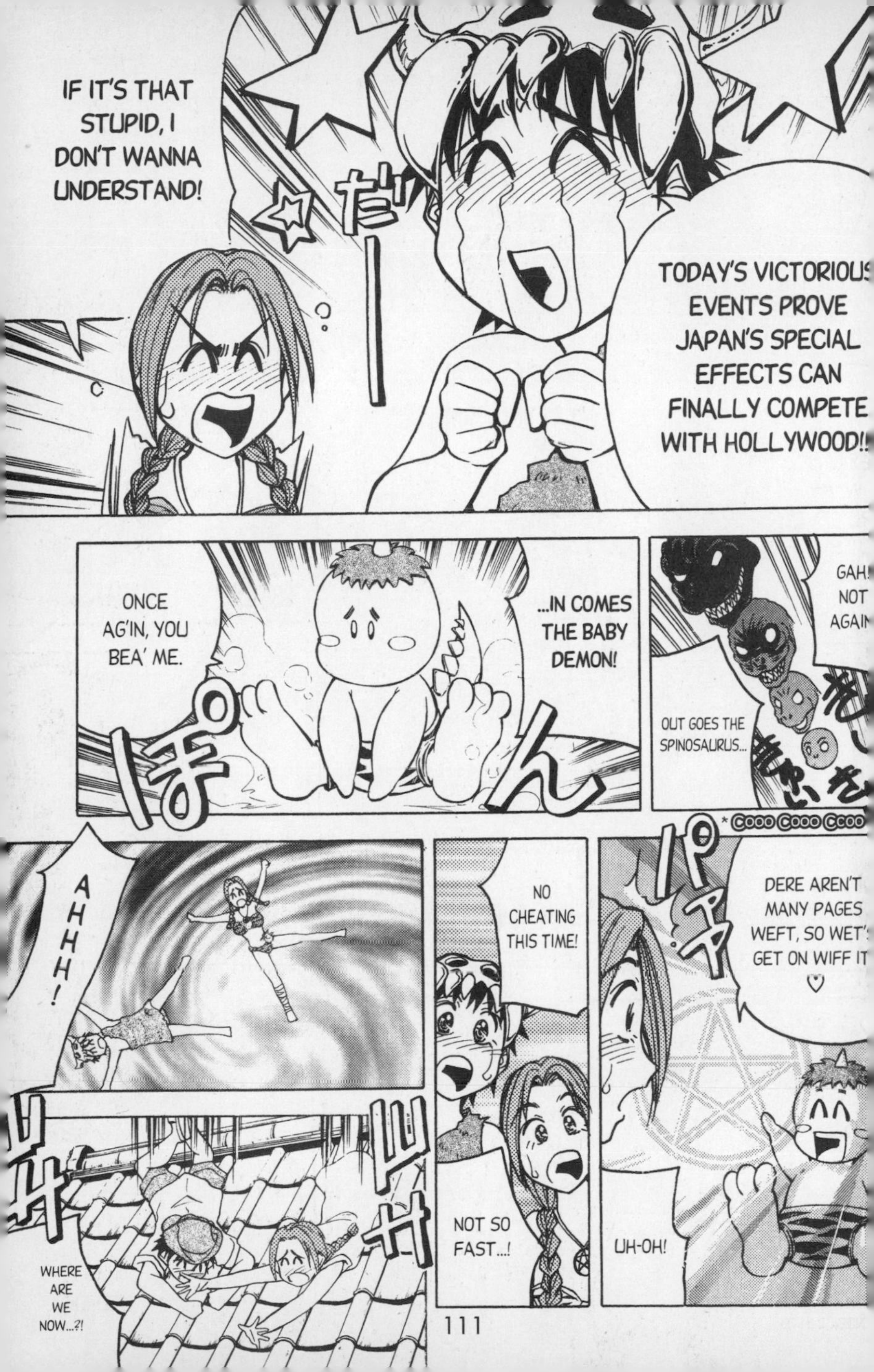
TODAY'S VICTORIOUS EVENTS PROVE JAPAN'S SPECIAL EFFECTS CAN FINALLY COMPETE WITH HOLLYWOOD!!
IF IT'S THAT STUPID, I DON'T WANNA UNDERSTAND!
GAH! NOT AGAIN
OUT GOES THE SPINOSAURUS...
* COOO COOO COOO
...IN COMES THE BABY DEMON!
ONCE AG'IN, YOU BEA' ME.
DERE AREN'T MANY PAGES WEFT, SO WET'S GET ON WIFF IT ♡
UH-OH!
NO CHEATING THIS TIME!
NOT SO FAST...!
AHHHH!
WHERE ARE WE NOW...?!

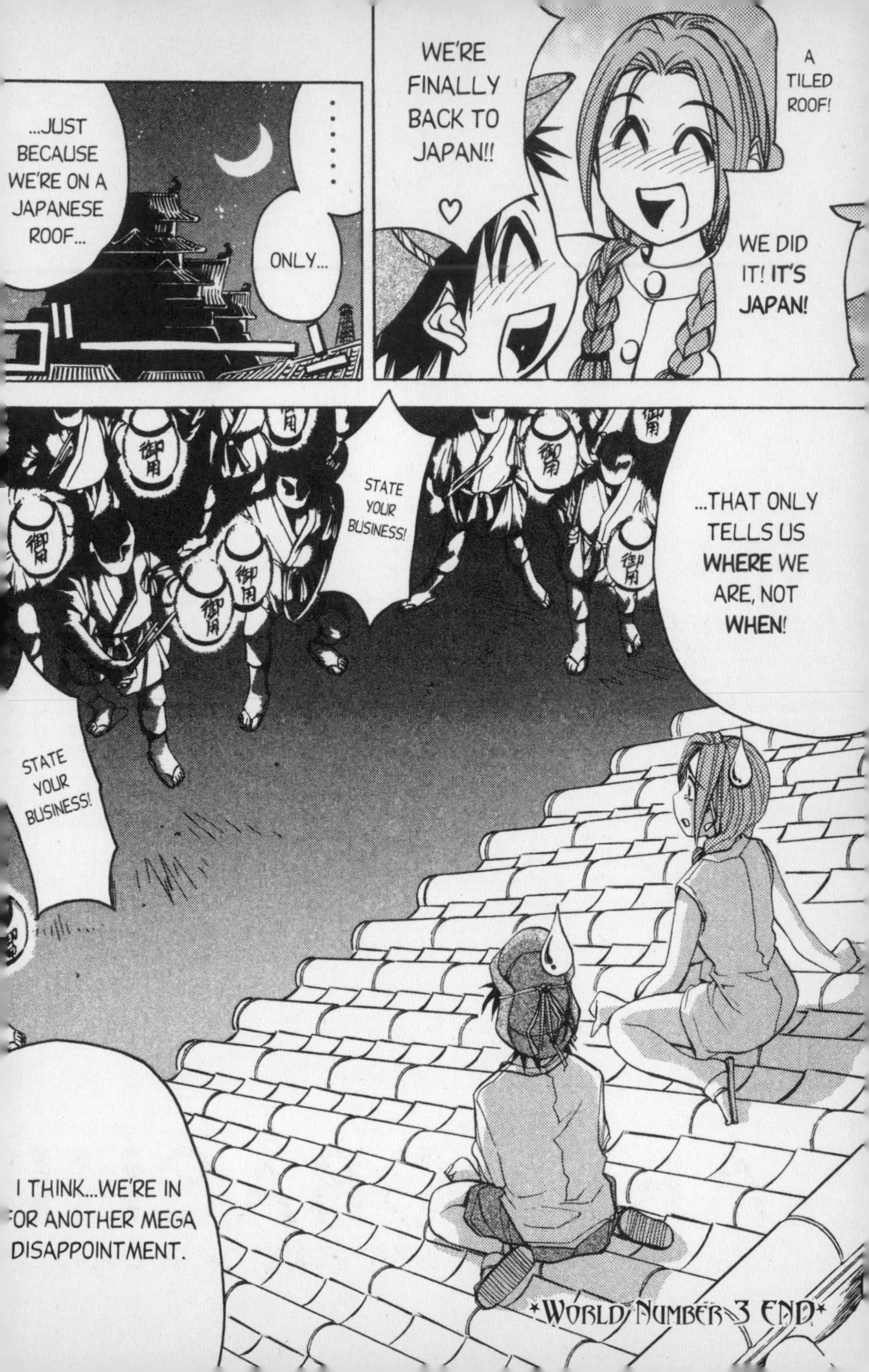
A TILED ROOF!
WE'RE FINALLY BACK TO JAPAN!! ♡
WE DID IT! IT'S JAPAN!
......
ONLY...
...JUST BECAUSE WE'RE ON A JAPANESE ROOF...
...THAT ONLY TELLS US WHERE WE ARE, NOT WHEN!
STATE YOUR BUSINESS!
STATE YOUR BUSINESS!
I THINK...WE'RE IN FOR ANOTHER MEGA DISAPPOINTMENT.
•WORLD NUMBER 3 END•

ABEN★BASHI
MAGICAL SHOPPING ARCADE

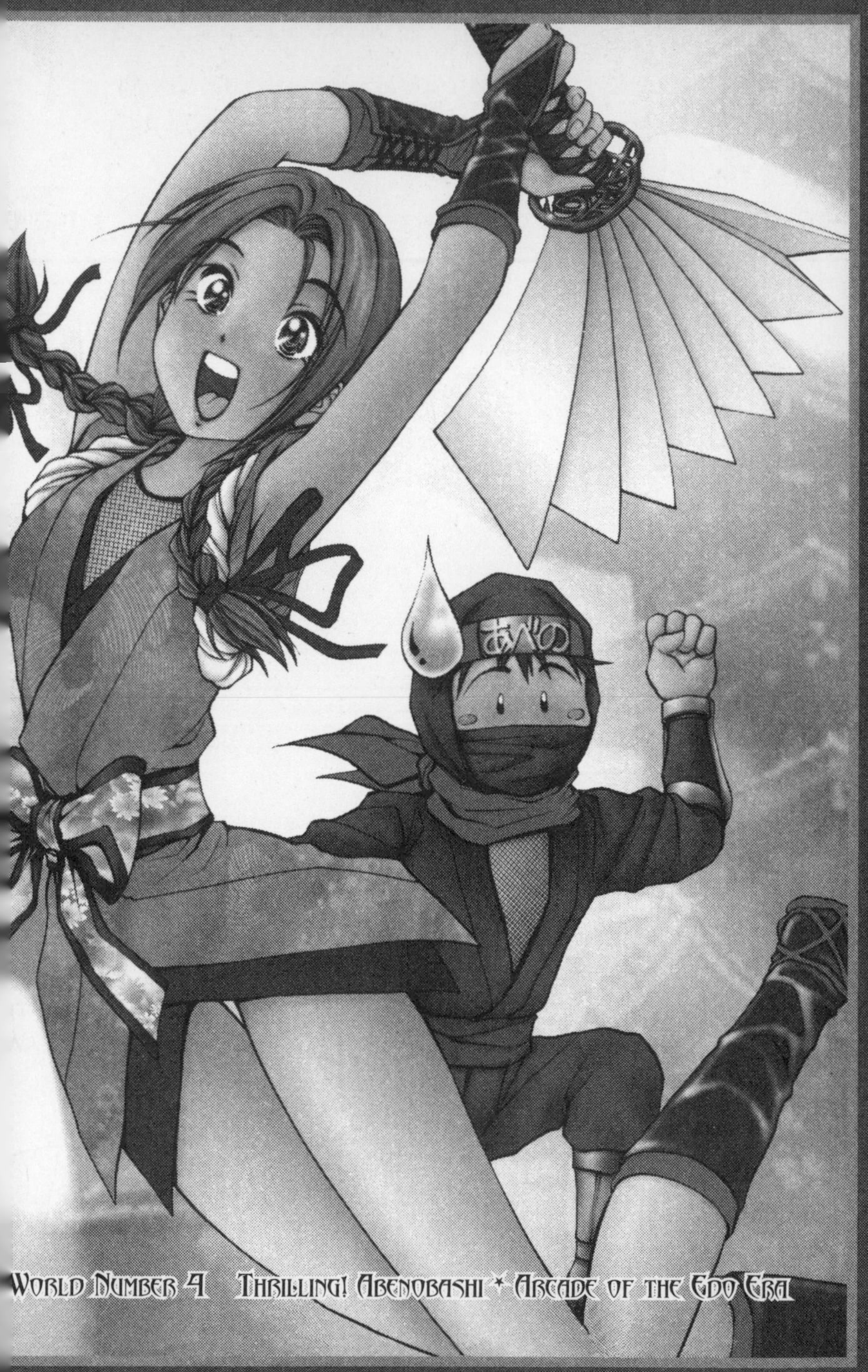
World Number 4 Thrilling! Abenobashi * Arcade of the Edo Era

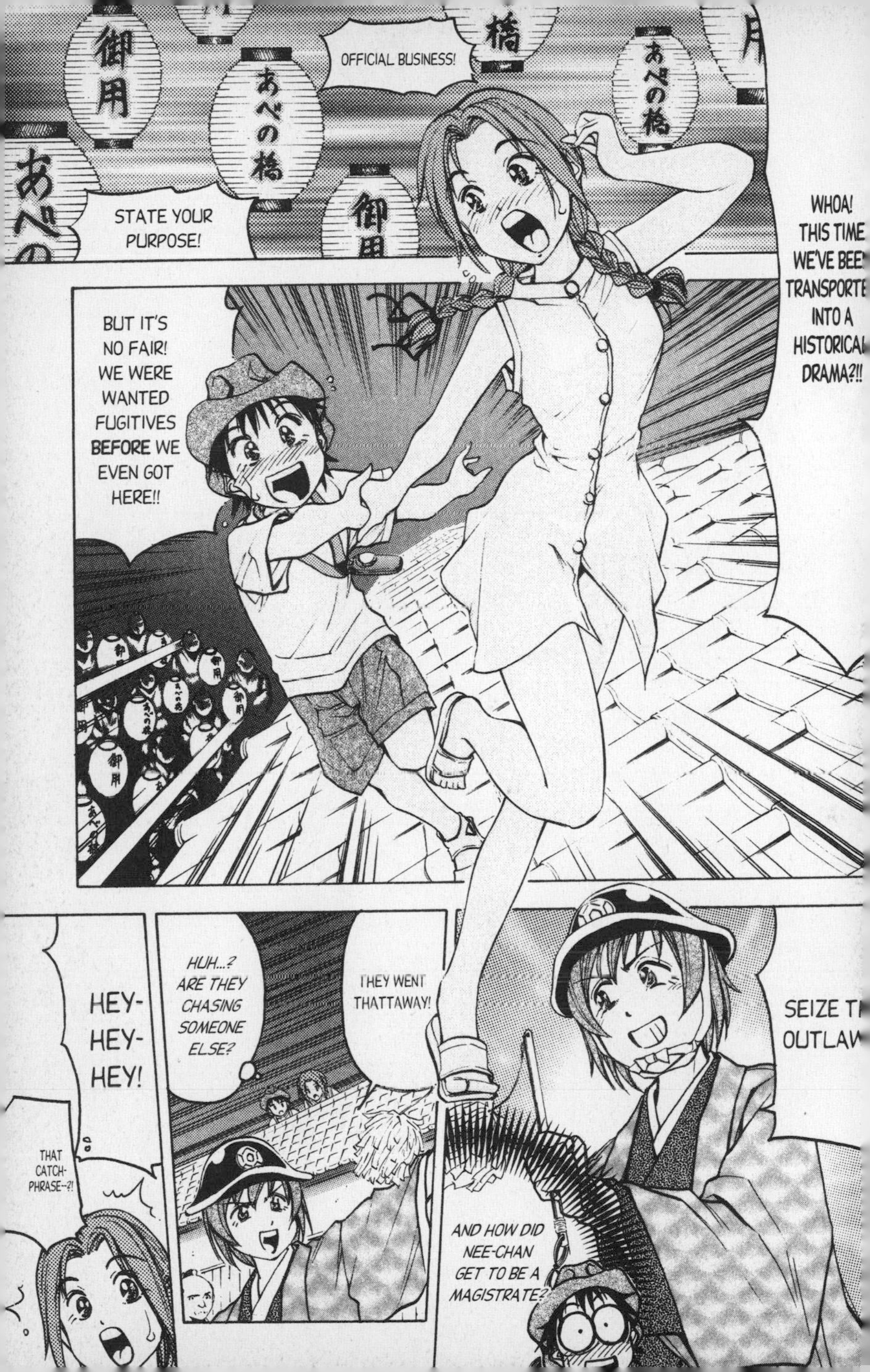
WHOA! THIS TIME WE'VE BEE TRANSPORTE INTO A HISTORICA DRAMA?!!
OFFICIAL BUSINESS!
STATE YOUR PURPOSE!
BUT IT'S NO FAIR! WE WERE WANTED FUGITIVES **BEFORE** WE EVEN GOT HERE!!
SEIZE TH OUTLAW
AND HOW DID NEE-CHAN GET TO BE A MAGISTRATE?
THEY WENT THATTAWAY!
HUH...? ARE THEY CHASING SOMEONE ELSE?
HEY-HEY-HEY!
THAT CATCH-PHRASE--?!

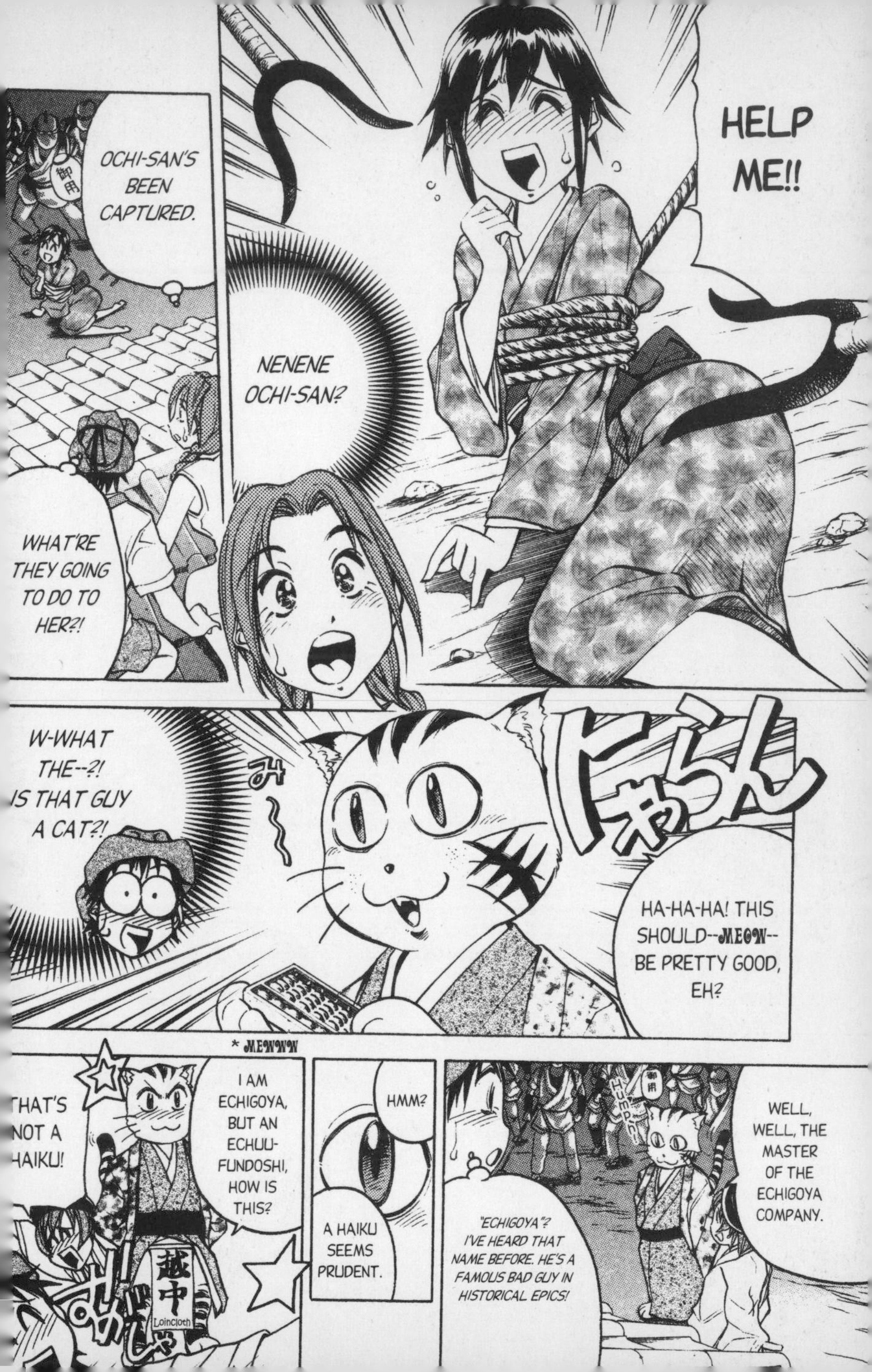
HELP ME!!
NENENE OCHI-SAN?
OCHI-SAN'S BEEN CAPTURED.
WHAT'RE THEY GOING TO DO TO HER?!
にゃらん
HA-HA-HA! THIS SHOULD--MEOW--BE PRETTY GOOD, EH?
みー
W-WHAT THE--?! IS THAT GUY A CAT?!
* MEWWW
WELL, WELL, THE MASTER OF THE ECHIGOYA COMPANY.
HUMPH!
"ECHIGOYA"? I'VE HEARD THAT NAME BEFORE. HE'S A FAMOUS BAD GUY IN HISTORICAL EPICS!
HMM?
A HAIKU SEEMS PRUDENT.
I AM ECHIGOYA, BUT AN ECHUU-FUNDOSHI, HOW IS THIS?
THAT'S NOT A HAIKU!
越中
Loincloth

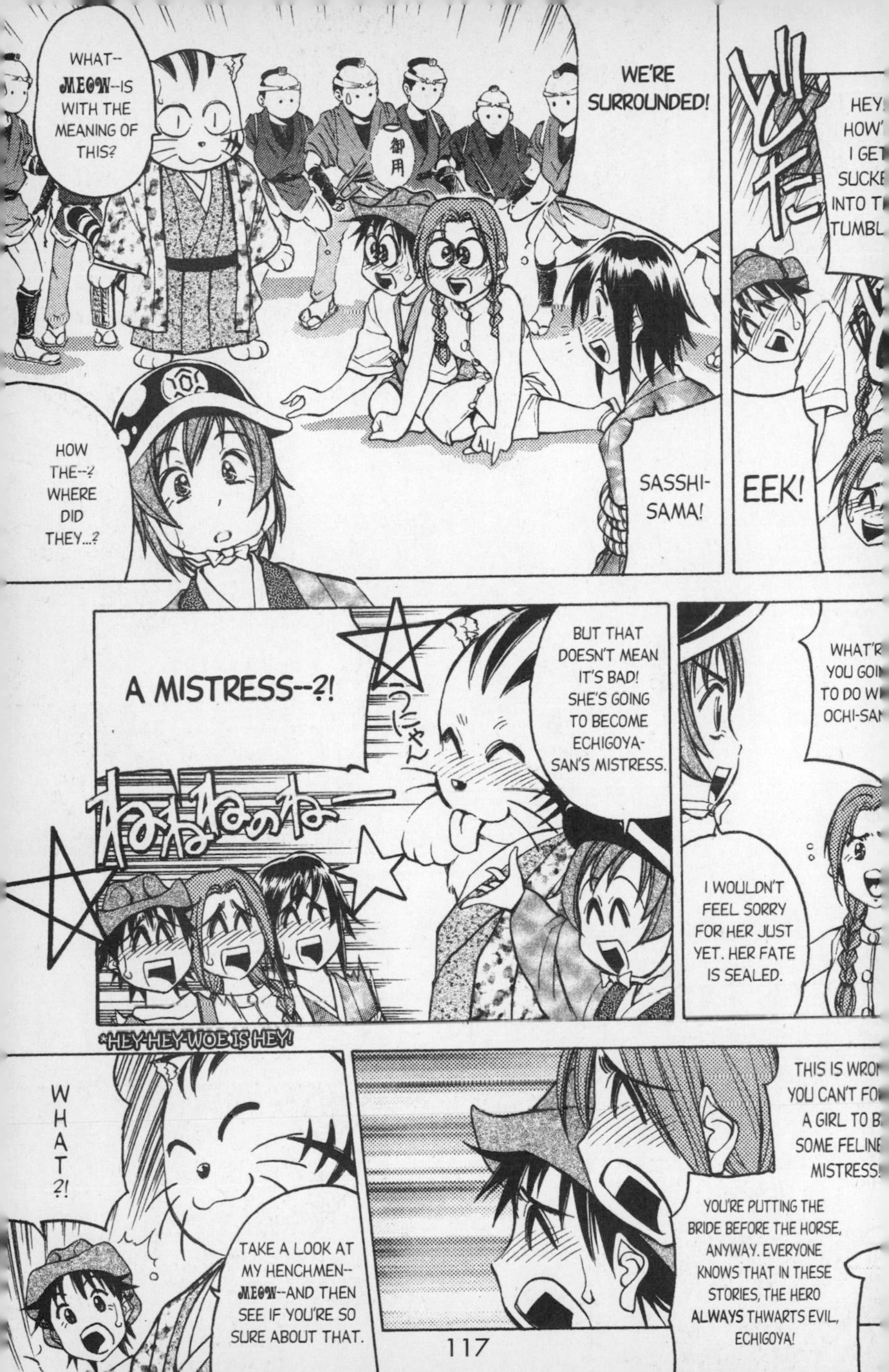
EEK!
HEY! HOW' I GET SUCKE INTO T TUMBL
WE'RE SURROUNDED!
WHAT-- MEOW--IS WITH THE MEANING OF THIS?
御用
SASSHI-SAMA!
HOW THE--? WHERE DID THEY...?
WHAT'R YOU GOI TO DO W OCHI-SA
I WOULDN'T FEEL SORRY FOR HER JUST YET. HER FATE IS SEALED.
BUT THAT DOESN'T MEAN IT'S BAD! SHE'S GOING TO BECOME ECHIGOYA-SAN'S MISTRESS.
うにゃん
A MISTRESS--?!
ねねねのね
*HEY-HEY-WOE IS HEY!
THIS IS WRO YOU CAN'T FO A GIRL TO B SOME FELINE MISTRESS!
YOU'RE PUTTING THE BRIDE BEFORE THE HORSE, ANYWAY. EVERYONE KNOWS THAT IN THESE STORIES, THE HERO ALWAYS THWARTS EVIL, ECHIGOYA!
TAKE A LOOK AT MY HENCHMEN-- MEOW--AND THEN SEE IF YOU'RE SO SURE ABOUT THAT.
WHAT?!

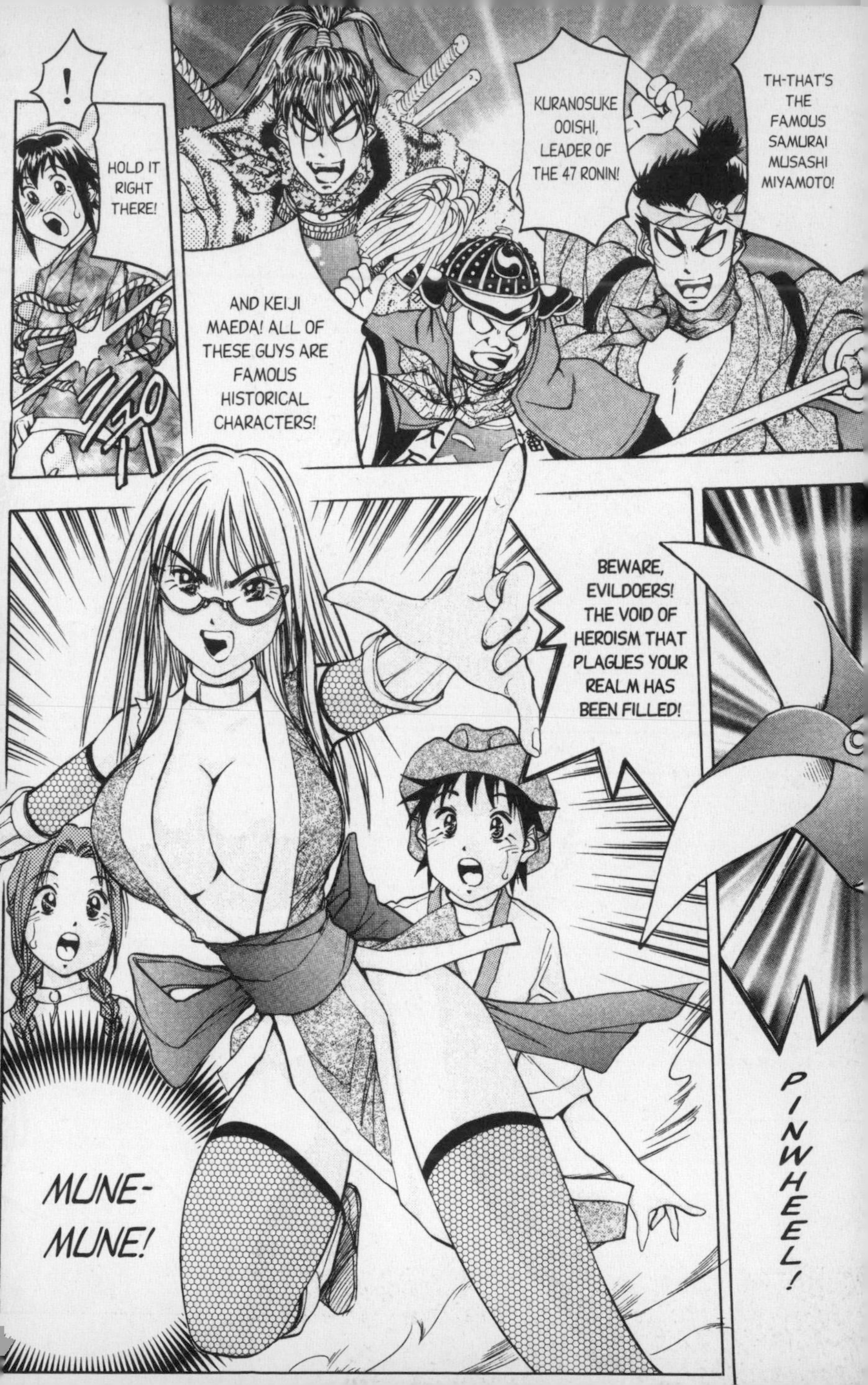
TH-THAT'S THE FAMOUS SAMURAI MUSASHI MIYAMOTO!
KURANOSUKE OOISHI, LEADER OF THE 47 RONIN!
AND KEIJI MAEDA! ALL OF THESE GUYS ARE FAMOUS HISTORICAL CHARACTERS!
!
HOLD IT RIGHT THERE!
PINWHEEL!
BEWARE, EVILDOERS! THE VOID OF HEROISM THAT PLAGUES YOUR REALM HAS BEEN FILLED!
MUNE-MUNE!

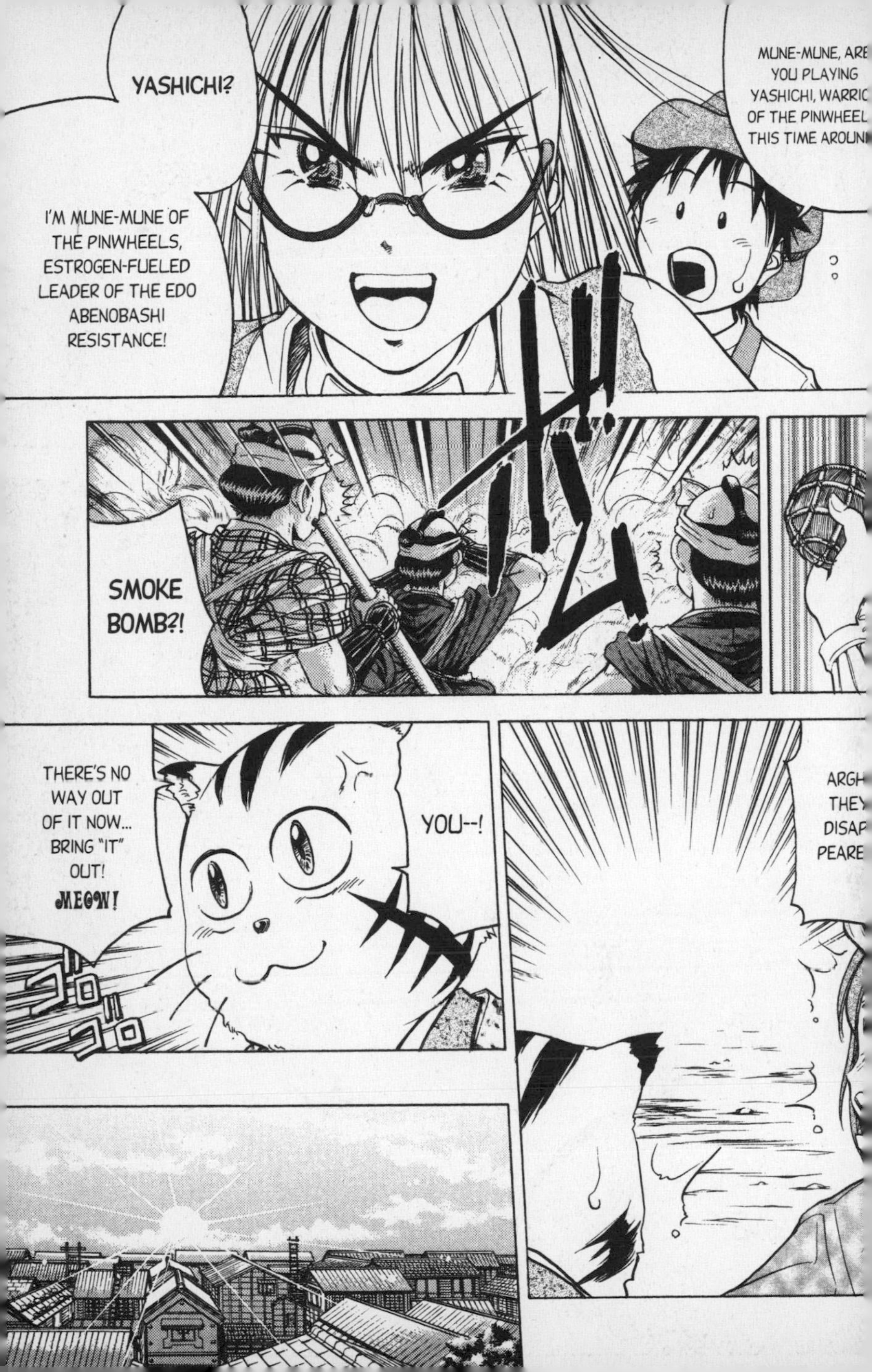

MUNE-MUNE, ARE YOU PLAYING YASHICHI, WARRIC OF THE PINWHEEL THIS TIME AROUN
YASHICHI?
I'M MUNE-MUNE OF THE PINWHEELS, ESTROGEN-FUELED LEADER OF THE EDO ABENOBASHI RESISTANCE!
SMOKE BOMB?!
ARGH THEY DISAP PEARE
YOU--!
THERE'S NO WAY OUT OF IT NOW... BRING "IT" OUT!
MEOW!

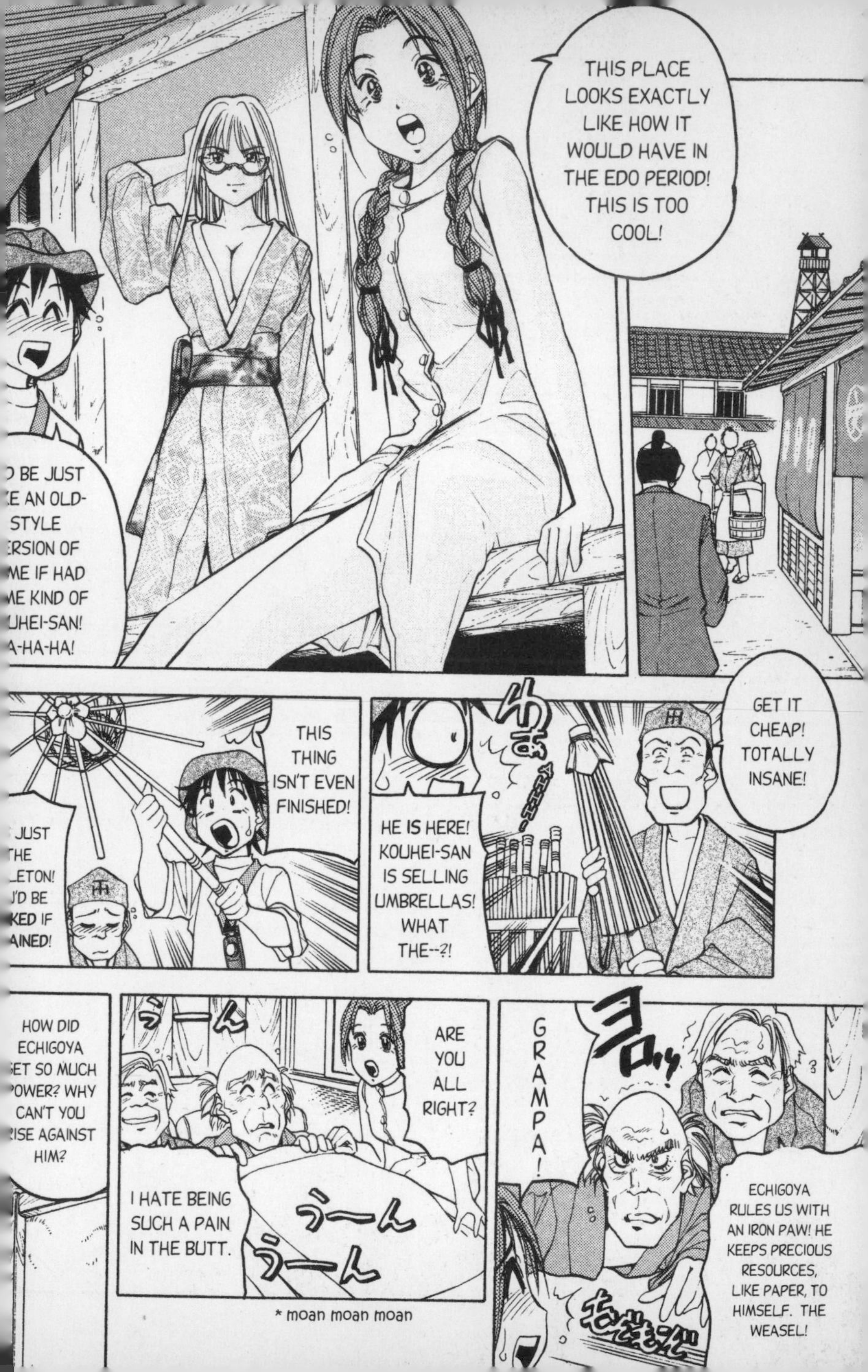
THIS PLACE LOOKS EXACTLY LIKE HOW IT WOULD HAVE IN THE EDO PERIOD! THIS IS TOO COOL!
D BE JUST E AN OLD-STYLE ERSION OF ME IF HAD ME KIND OF UHEI-SAN! A-HA-HA!
GET IT CHEAP! TOTALLY INSANE!
HE IS HERE! KOUHEI-SAN IS SELLING UMBRELLAS! WHAT THE--?!
THIS THING ISN'T EVEN FINISHED!
JUST THE LETON! U'D BE KED IF AINED!
ヨロッ
GRAMPA!
ECHIGOYA RULES US WITH AN IRON PAW! HE KEEPS PRECIOUS RESOURCES, LIKE PAPER, TO HIMSELF. THE WEASEL!
うーん
ARE YOU ALL RIGHT?
I HATE BEING SUCH A PAIN IN THE BUTT.
うーん
うーん
* moan moan moan
HOW DID ECHIGOYA GET SO MUCH POWER? WHY CAN'T YOU RISE AGAINST HIM?

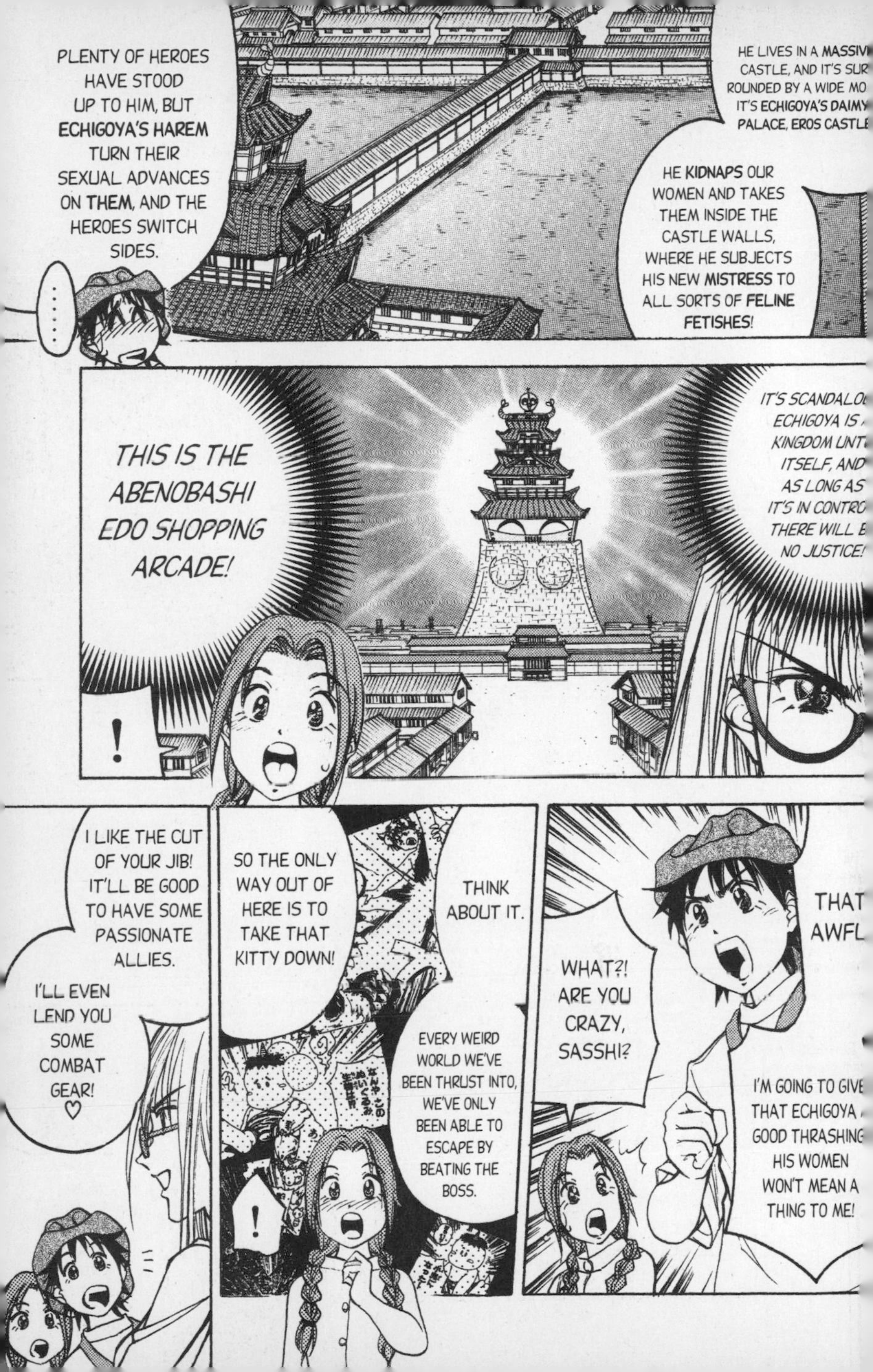
HE LIVES IN A MASSIV
CASTLE, AND IT'S SUR
ROUNDED BY A WIDE MO
IT'S ECHIGOYA'S DAIMY
PALACE, EROS CASTL
HE KIDNAPS OUR WOMEN AND TAKES THEM INSIDE THE CASTLE WALLS, WHERE HE SUBJECTS HIS NEW MISTRESS TO ALL SORTS OF FELINE FETISHES!
PLENTY OF HEROES HAVE STOOD UP TO HIM, BUT ECHIGOYA'S HAREM TURN THEIR SEXUAL ADVANCES ON THEM, AND THE HEROES SWITCH SIDES.
......
IT'S SCANDALO
ECHIGOYA IS
KINGDOM UNT
ITSELF, AND
AS LONG AS
IT'S IN CONTRO
THERE WILL B
NO JUSTICE!
THIS IS THE ABENOBASHI EDO SHOPPING ARCADE!
!
THAT
AWFL
I'M GOING TO GIVE
THAT ECHIGOYA
GOOD THRASHING
HIS WOMEN
WON'T MEAN A
THING TO ME!
WHAT?! ARE YOU CRAZY, SASSHI?
THINK ABOUT IT.
SO THE ONLY WAY OUT OF HERE IS TO TAKE THAT KITTY DOWN!
EVERY WEIRD WORLD WE'VE BEEN THRUST INTO, WE'VE ONLY BEEN ABLE TO ESCAPE BY BEATING THE BOSS.
!
I LIKE THE CUT OF YOUR JIB! IT'LL BE GOOD TO HAVE SOME PASSIONATE ALLIES.
I'LL EVEN LEND YOU SOME COMBAT GEAR! ♡

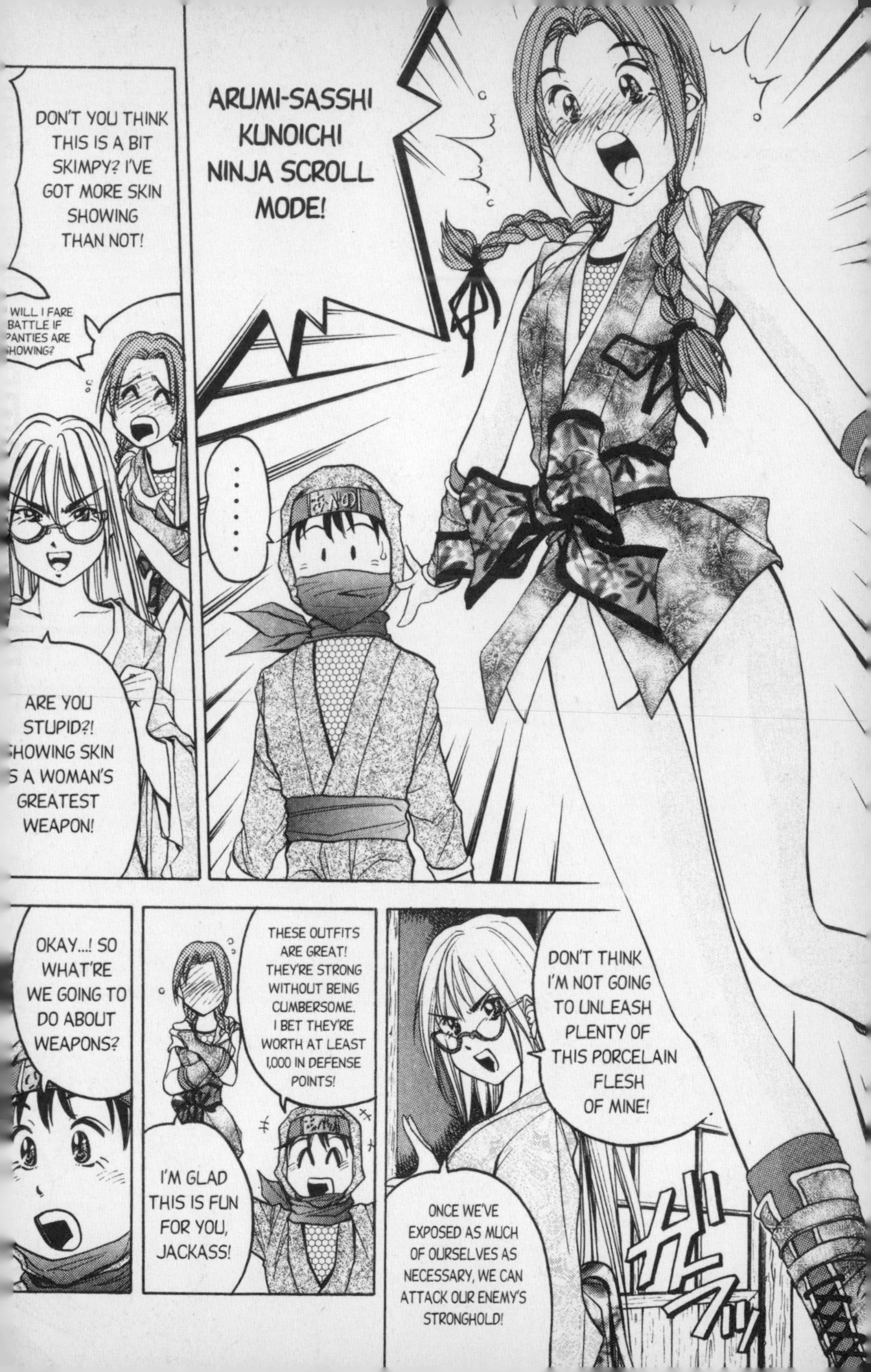
ARUMI-SASSHI KUNOICHI NINJA SCROLL MODE!
......
DON'T YOU THINK THIS IS A BIT SKIMPY? I'VE GOT MORE SKIN SHOWING THAN NOT!
WILL I FARE BATTLE IF PANTIES ARE SHOWING?
ARE YOU STUPID?! SHOWING SKIN S A WOMAN'S GREATEST WEAPON!
DON'T THINK I'M NOT GOING TO UNLEASH PLENTY OF THIS PORCELAIN FLESH OF MINE!
ONCE WE'VE EXPOSED AS MUCH OF OURSELVES AS NECESSARY, WE CAN ATTACK OUR ENEMY'S STRONGHOLD!
THESE OUTFITS ARE GREAT! THEY'RE STRONG WITHOUT BEING CUMBERSOME. I BET THEY'RE WORTH AT LEAST 1,000 IN DEFENSE POINTS!
I'M GLAD THIS IS FUN FOR YOU, JACKASS!
OKAY...! SO WHAT'RE WE GOING TO DO ABOUT WEAPONS?

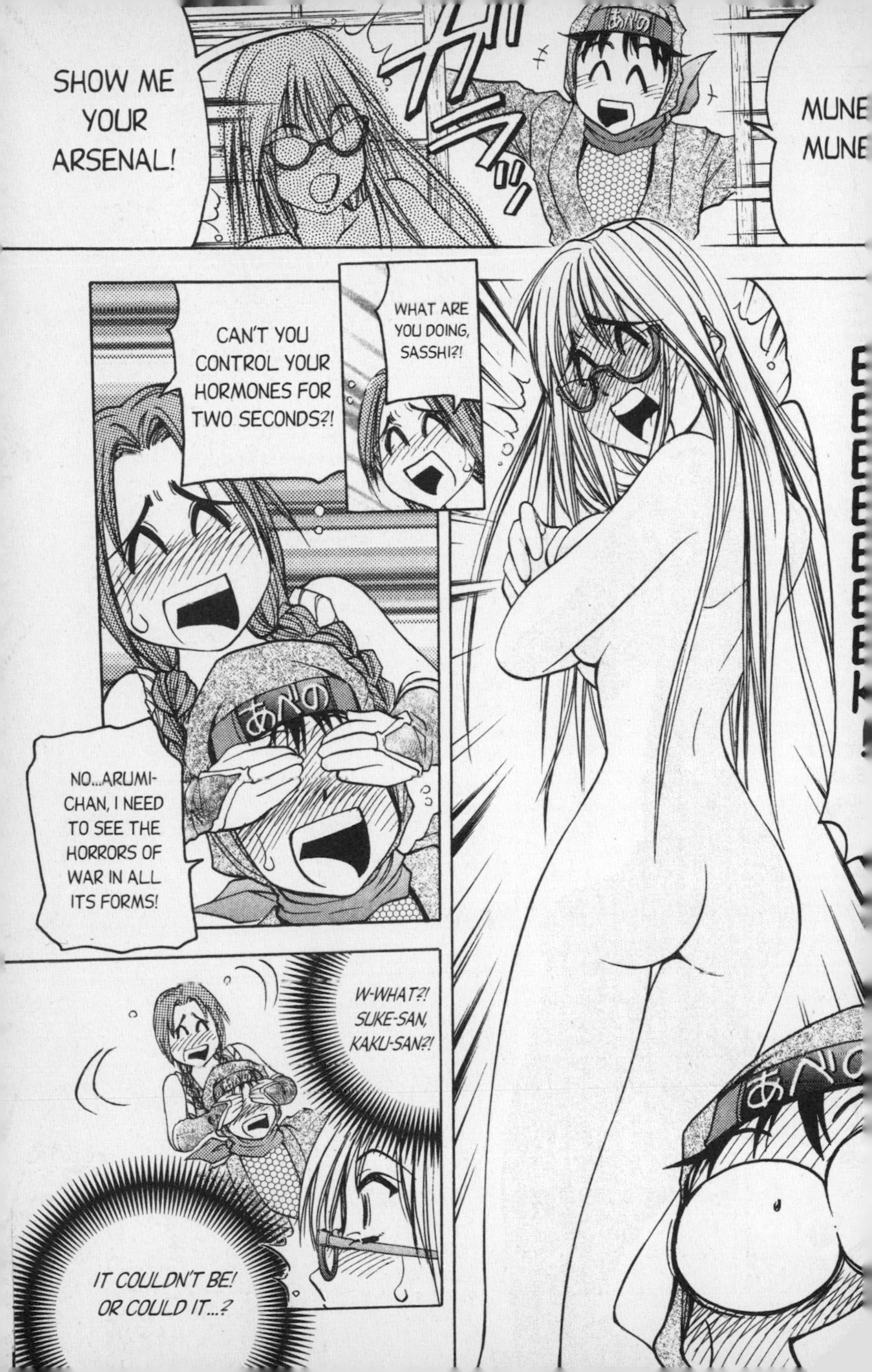
MUNE MUNE
SHOW ME YOUR ARSENAL!
EEEEEEEK!
WHAT ARE YOU DOING, SASSHI?!
CAN'T YOU CONTROL YOUR HORMONES FOR TWO SECONDS?!
NO...ARUMI-CHAN, I NEED TO SEE THE HORRORS OF WAR IN ALL ITS FORMS!
W-WHAT?! SUKE-SAN, KAKU-SAN?!
IT COULDN'T BE! OR COULD IT...?

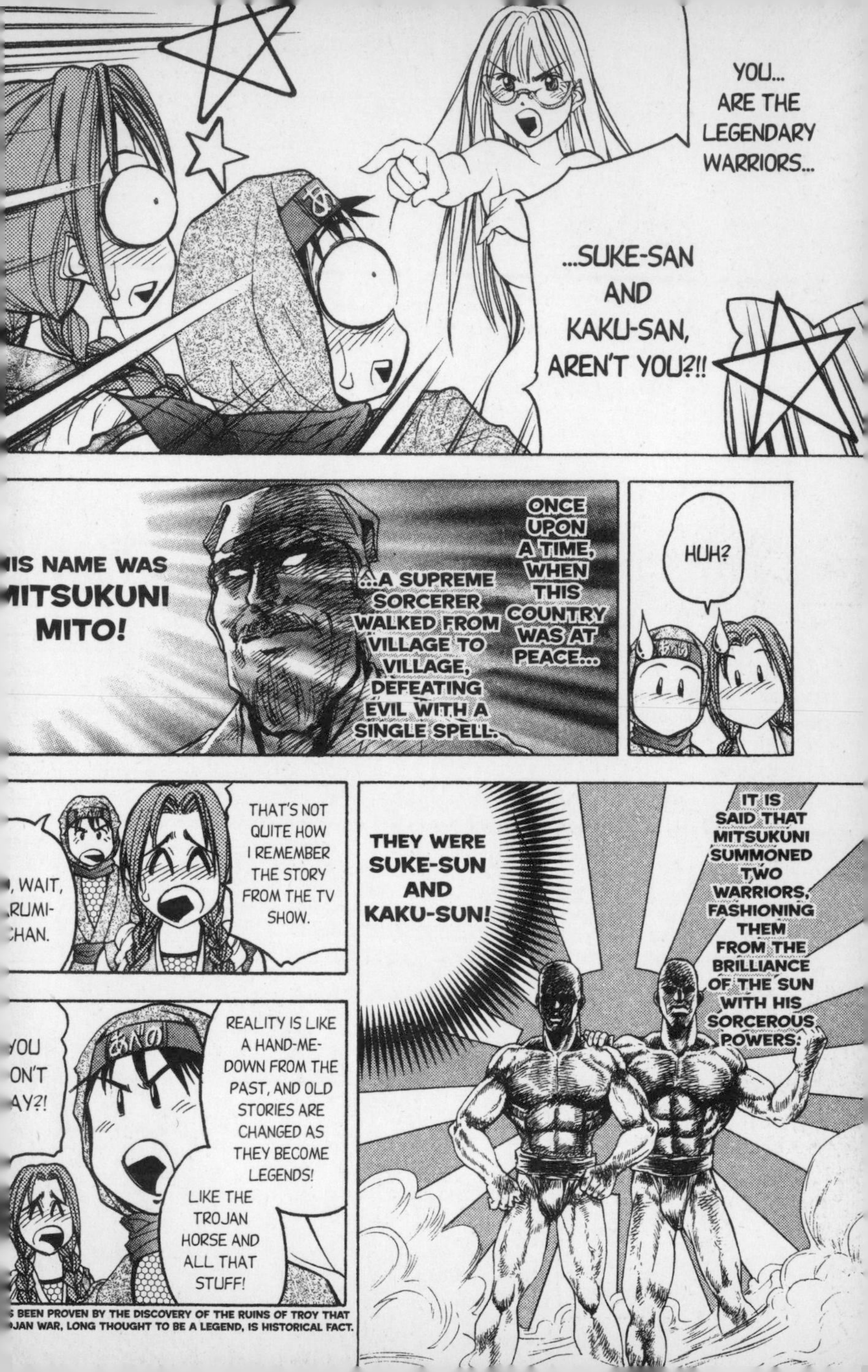
YOU... ARE THE LEGENDARY WARRIORS...
...SUKE-SAN AND KAKU-SAN, AREN'T YOU?!!
HUH?
ONCE UPON A TIME, WHEN THIS COUNTRY WAS AT PEACE...
...A SUPREME SORCERER WALKED FROM VILLAGE TO VILLAGE, DEFEATING EVIL WITH A SINGLE SPELL.
IS NAME WAS ITSUKUNI MITO!
IT IS SAID THAT MITSUKUNI SUMMONED TWO WARRIORS, FASHIONING THEM FROM THE BRILLIANCE OF THE SUN WITH HIS SORCEROUS POWERS.
THEY WERE SUKE-SUN AND KAKU-SUN!
THAT'S NOT QUITE HOW I REMEMBER THE STORY FROM THE TV SHOW.
, WAIT, RUMI- CHAN.
REALITY IS LIKE A HAND-ME-DOWN FROM THE PAST, AND OLD STORIES ARE CHANGED AS THEY BECOME LEGENDS!
YOU ON'T AY?!
LIKE THE TROJAN HORSE AND ALL THAT STUFF!
S BEEN PROVEN BY THE DISCOVERY OF THE RUINS OF TROY THAT
OJAN WAR, LONG THOUGHT TO BE A LEGEND, IS HISTORICAL FACT.

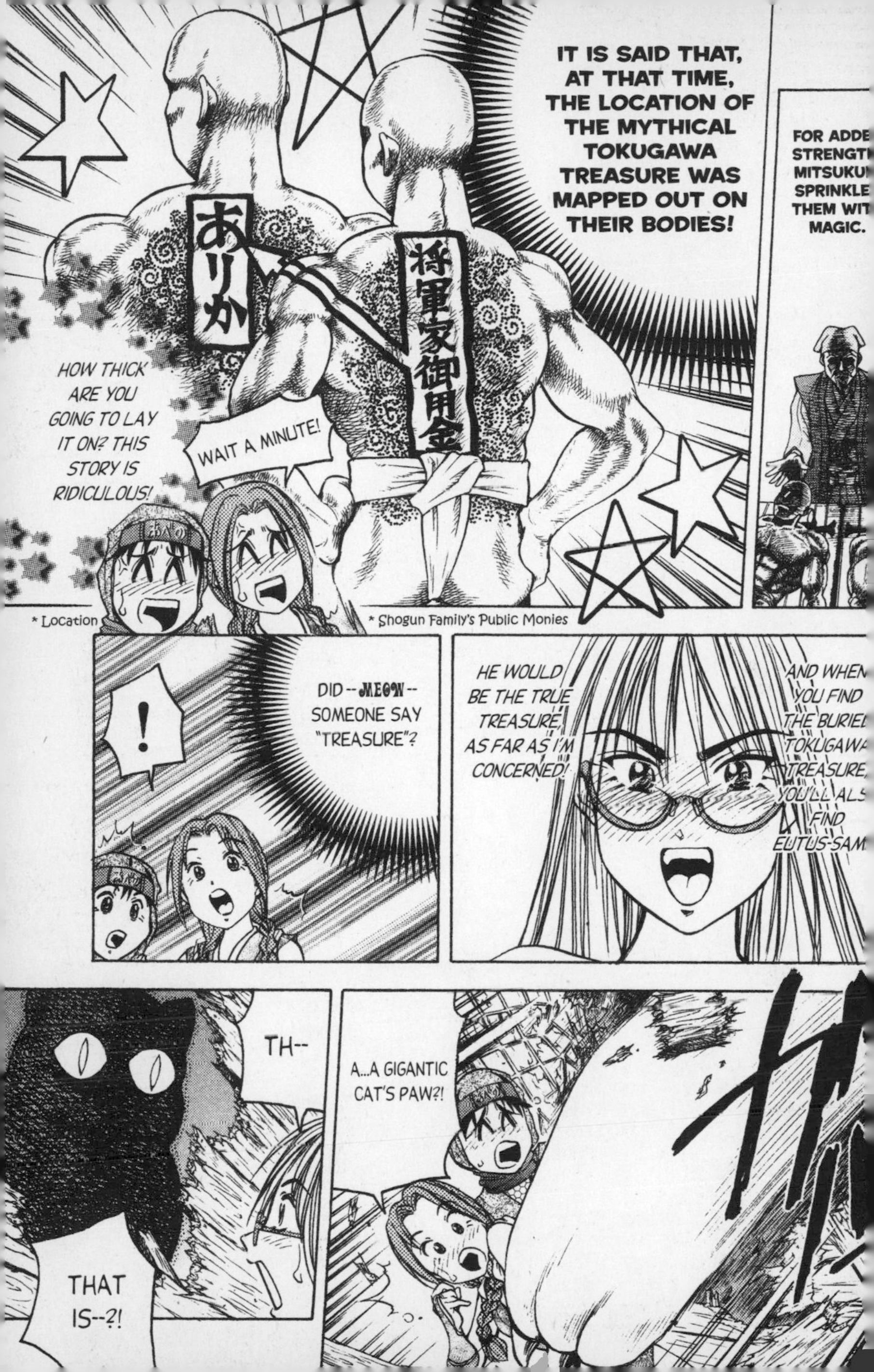
FOR ADDE STRENGT MITSUKU SPRINKLE THEM WIT MAGIC.
IT IS SAID THAT, AT THAT TIME, THE LOCATION OF THE MYTHICAL TOKUGAWA TREASURE WAS MAPPED OUT ON THEIR BODIES!
将軍家御用金
ありか
WAIT A MINUTE!
HOW THICK ARE YOU GOING TO LAY IT ON? THIS STORY IS RIDICULOUS!
* Shogun Family's Public Monies
* Location
AND WHEN YOU FIND THE BURIE TOKUGAWA TREASURE, YOU'LL ALS FIND EUTUS-SAM
HE WOULD BE THE TRUE TREASURE, AS FAR AS I'M CONCERNED!
DID --MEOW-- SOMEONE SAY "TREASURE"?
!
A...A GIGANTIC CAT'S PAW?!
TH--
THAT IS--?!

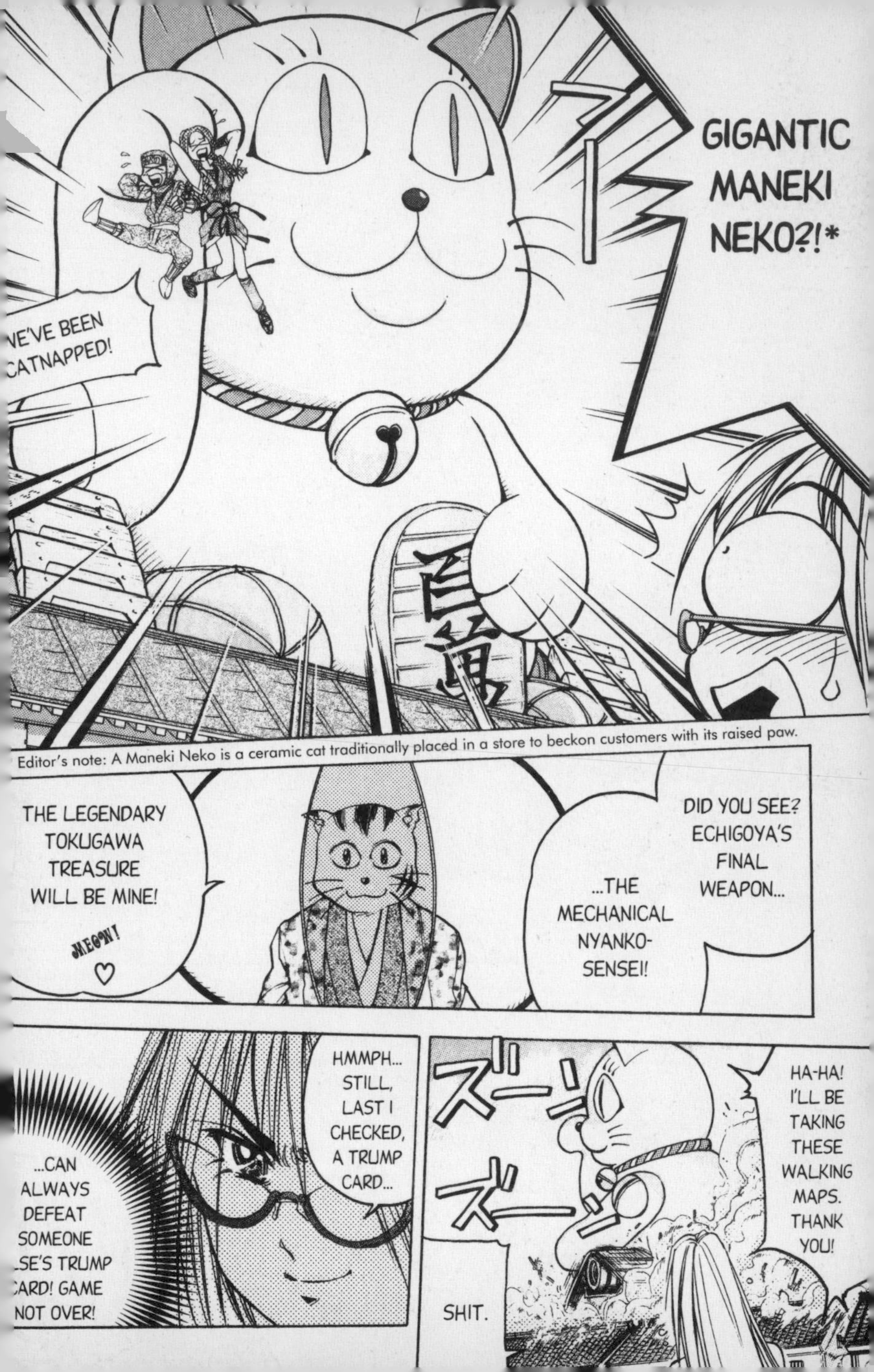
GIGANTIC MANEKI NEKO?!*
WE'VE BEEN CATNAPPED!
DID YOU SEE? ECHIGOYA'S FINAL WEAPON...
...THE MECHANICAL NYANKO-SENSEI!
THE LEGENDARY TOKUGAWA TREASURE WILL BE MINE!
MEOW! ♡
HA-HA! I'LL BE TAKING THESE WALKING MAPS. THANK YOU!
ズーン
ズーン
SHIT.
HMMPH... STILL, LAST I CHECKED, A TRUMP CARD...
...CAN ALWAYS DEFEAT SOMEONE ELSE'S TRUMP CARD! GAME NOT OVER!

Editor's note: A Maneki Neko is a ceramic cat traditionally placed in a store to beckon customers with its raised paw.

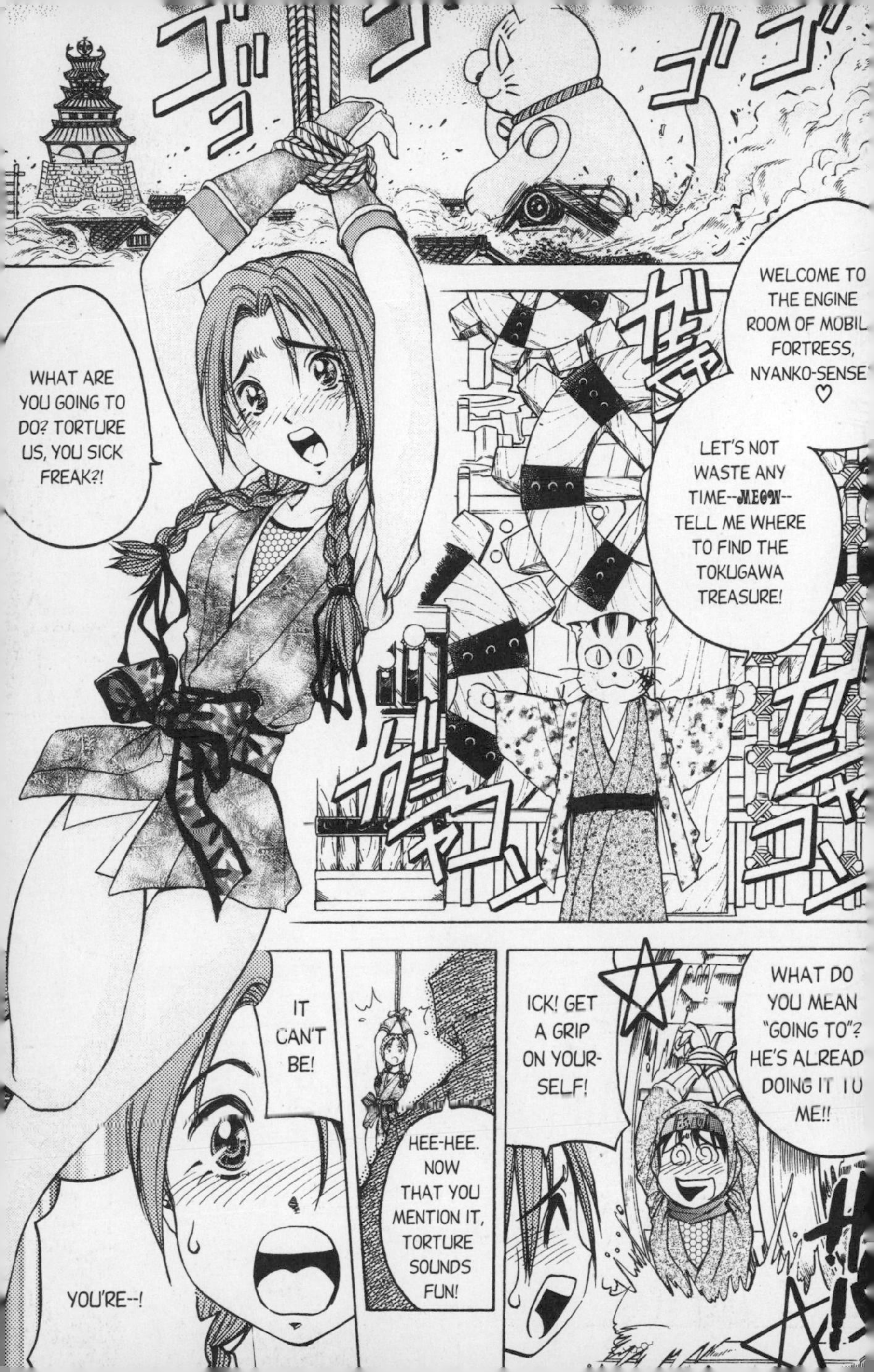
WELCOME TO THE ENGINE ROOM OF MOBIL FORTRESS, NYANKO-SENSE ♡
LET'S NOT WASTE ANY TIME--MEOW--TELL ME WHERE TO FIND THE TOKUGAWA TREASURE!
WHAT ARE YOU GOING TO DO? TORTURE US, YOU SICK FREAK?!
WHAT DO YOU MEAN "GOING TO"? HE'S ALREAD DOING IT TO ME!!
ICK! GET A GRIP ON YOUR-SELF!
IT CAN'T BE!
HEE-HEE. NOW THAT YOU MENTION IT, TORTURE SOUNDS FUN!
YOU'RE--!

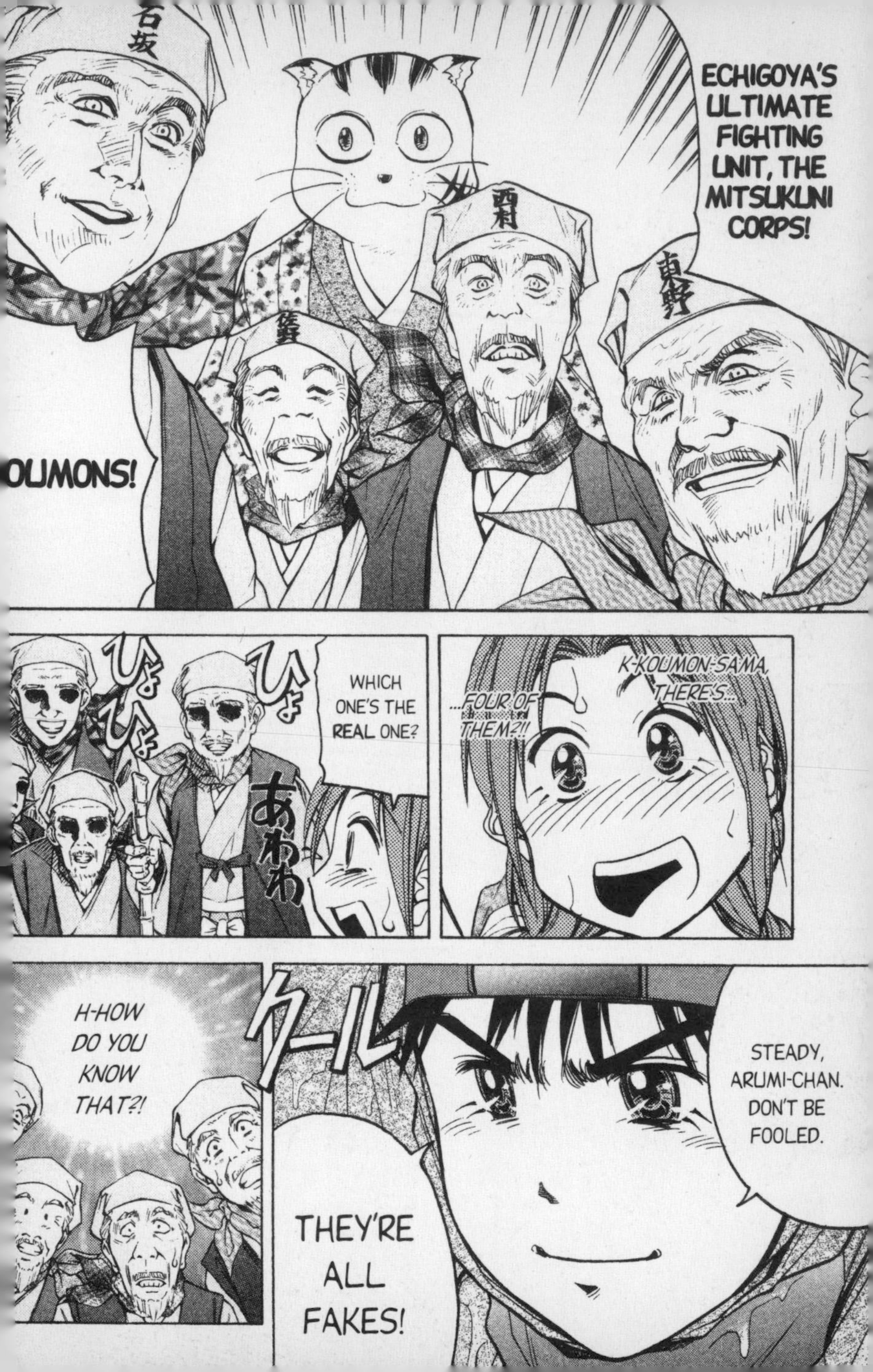

石坂
西村
東野
ECHIGOYA'S ULTIMATE FIGHTING UNIT, THE MITSUKUNI CORPS!
OUMONS!
K-KOUMON-SAMA, THERE'S...
...FOUR OF THEM?!!
ひょ
ひょひょ
WHICH ONE'S THE REAL ONE?
あわわ
クール
STEADY, ARUMI-CHAN. DON'T BE FOOLED.
THEY'RE ALL FAKES!
H-HOW DO YOU KNOW THAT?!

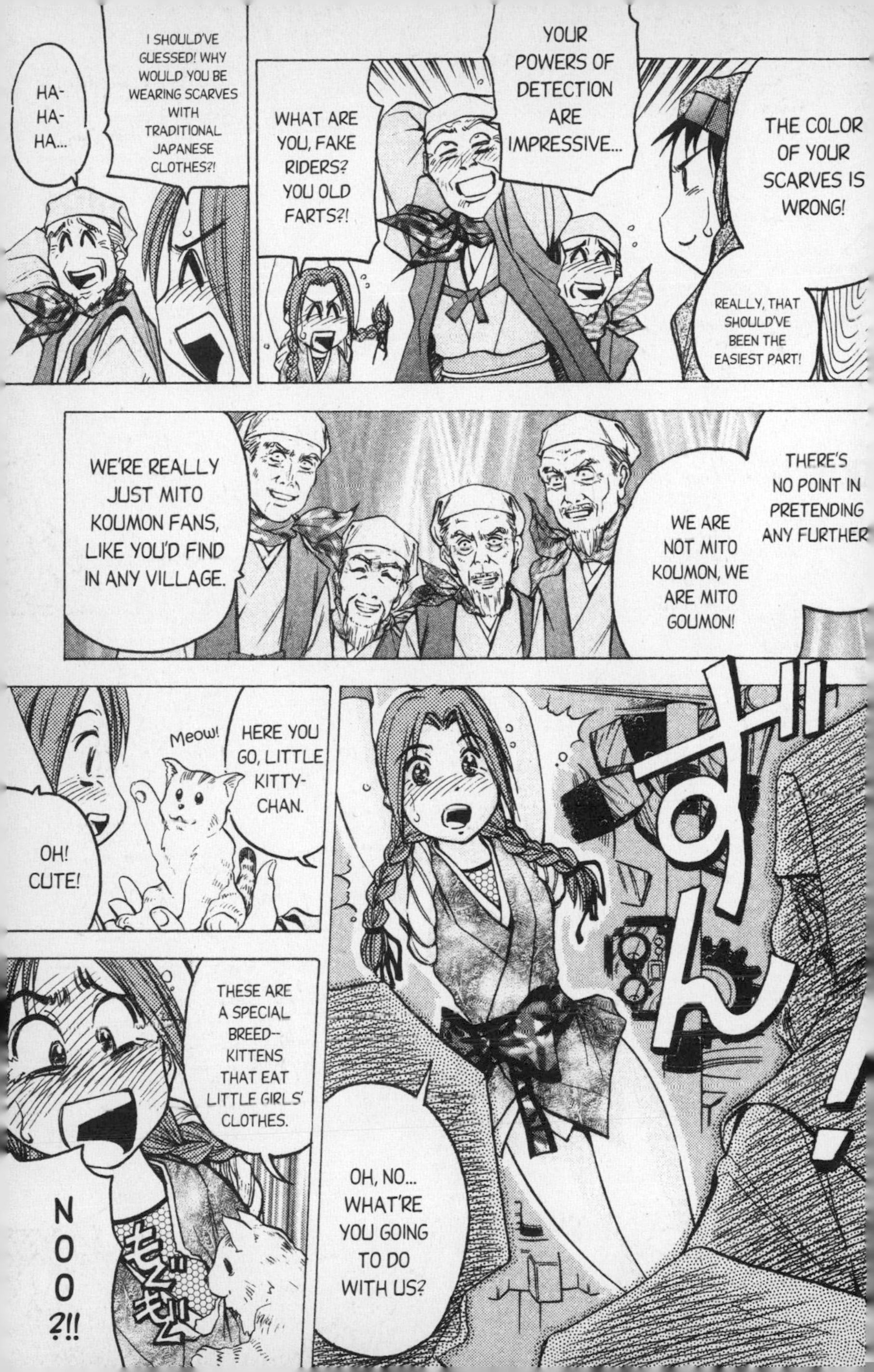
THE COLOR OF YOUR SCARVES IS WRONG!
REALLY, THAT SHOULD'VE BEEN THE EASIEST PART!
YOUR POWERS OF DETECTION ARE IMPRESSIVE...
WHAT ARE YOU, FAKE RIDERS? YOU OLD FARTS?!
I SHOULD'VE GUESSED! WHY WOULD YOU BE WEARING SCARVES WITH TRADITIONAL JAPANESE CLOTHES?!
HA-HA-HA...
THERE'S NO POINT IN PRETENDING ANY FURTHER
WE ARE NOT MITO KOUMON, WE ARE MITO GOUMON!
WE'RE REALLY JUST MITO KOUMON FANS, LIKE YOU'D FIND IN ANY VILLAGE.
OH, NO... WHAT'RE YOU GOING TO DO WITH US?
HERE YOU GO, LITTLE KITTY-CHAN.
Meow!
OH! CUTE!
THESE ARE A SPECIAL BREED--KITTENS THAT EAT LITTLE GIRLS' CLOTHES.
NOOO?!!

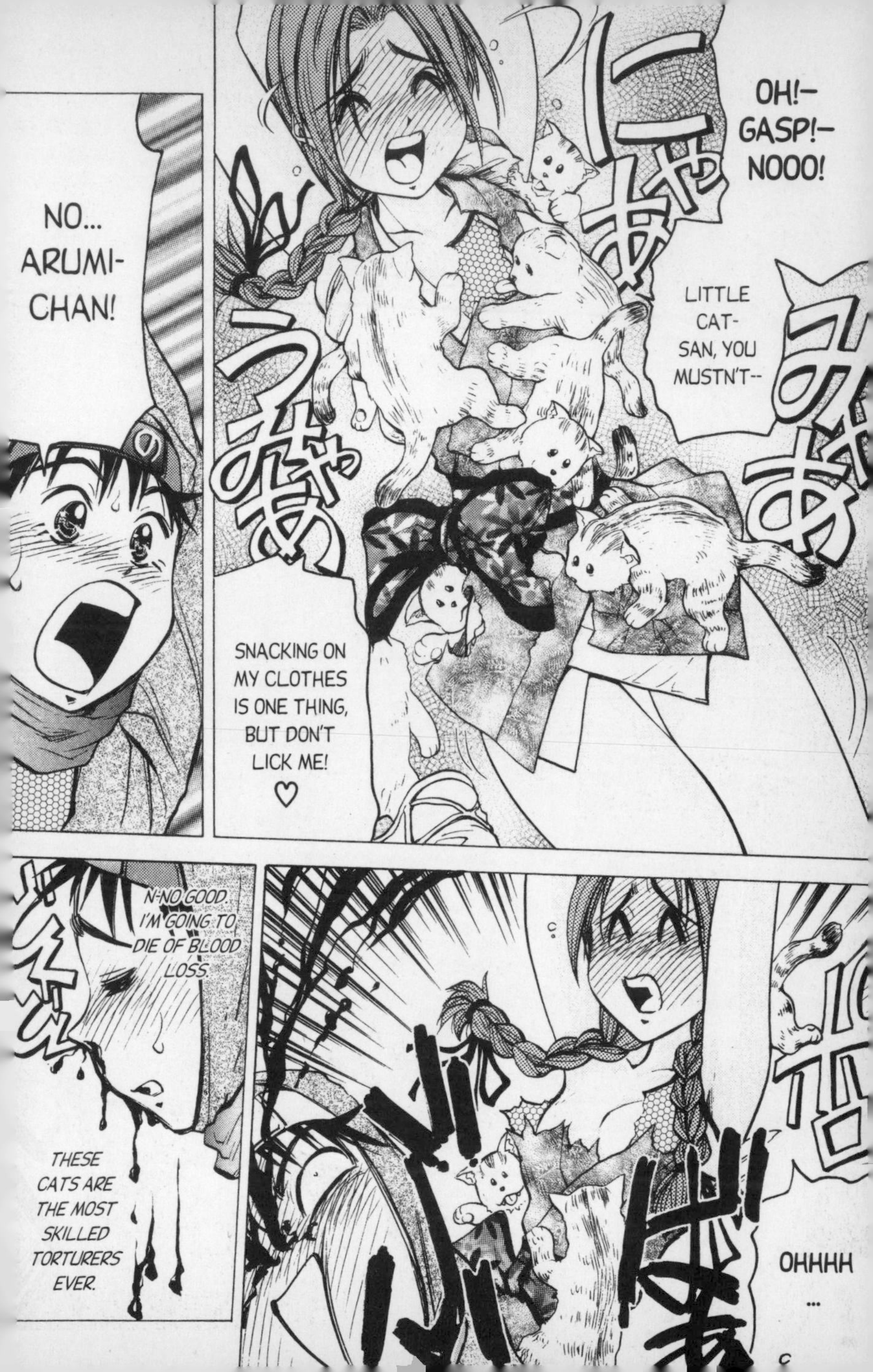

にゃあ
OH!—GASP!—NOOO!
みゃあ
LITTLE CAT-SAN, YOU MUSTN'T--
うみゃあ
SNACKING ON MY CLOTHES IS ONE THING, BUT DON'T LICK ME! ♡
NO... ARUMI-CHAN!
OHHHH ...
N-NO GOOD. I'M GOING TO DIE OF BLOOD LOSS.
THESE CATS ARE THE MOST SKILLED TORTURERS EVER.

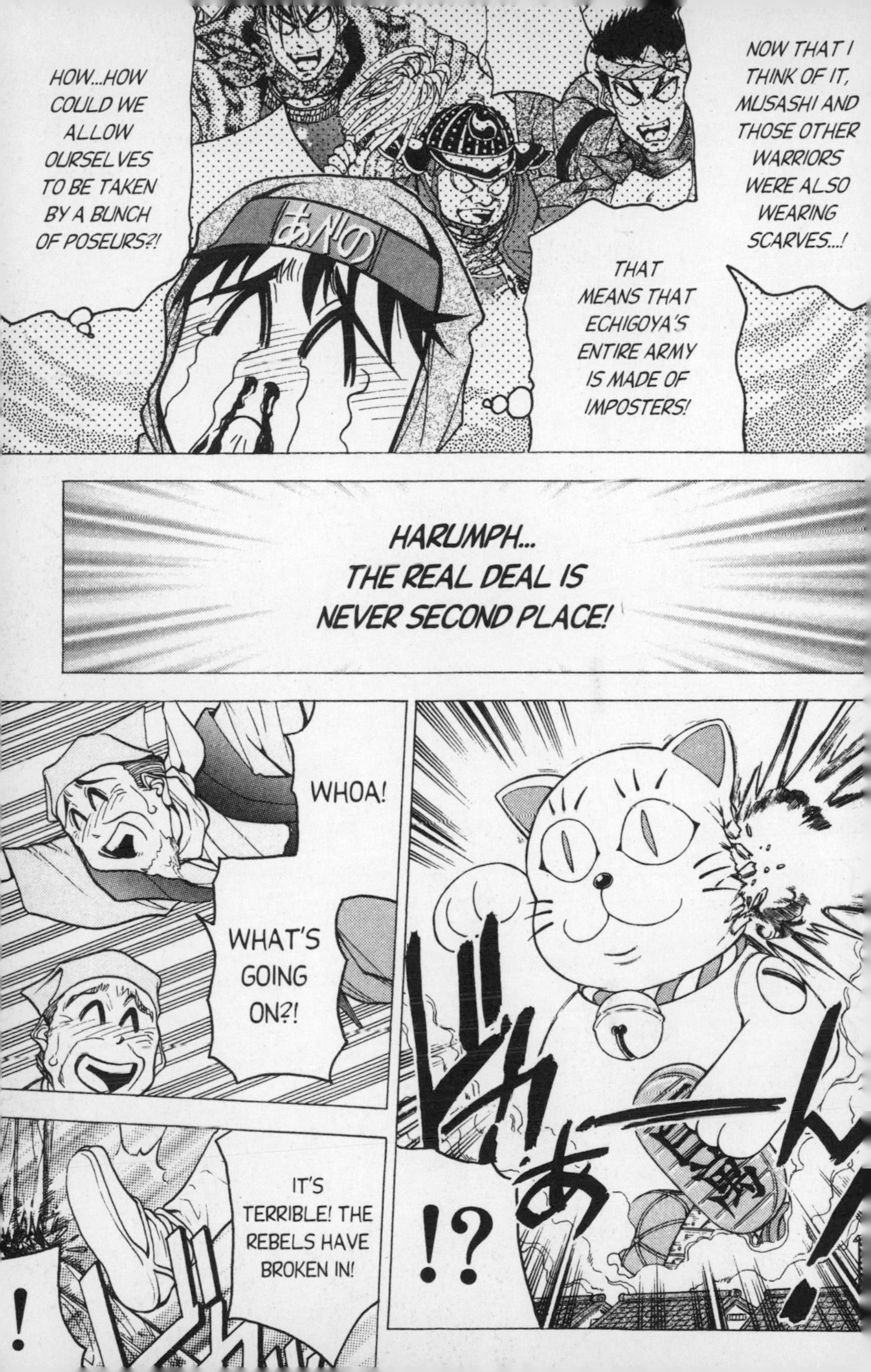
NOW THAT I THINK OF IT, MUSASHI AND THOSE OTHER WARRIORS WERE ALSO WEARING SCARVES...!
THAT MEANS THAT ECHIGOYA'S ENTIRE ARMY IS MADE OF IMPOSTERS!
HOW...HOW COULD WE ALLOW OURSELVES TO BE TAKEN BY A BUNCH OF POSEURS?!
HARUMPH... THE REAL DEAL IS NEVER SECOND PLACE!
!?
WHOA!
WHAT'S GOING ON?!
IT'S TERRIBLE! THE REBELS HAVE BROKEN IN!
!

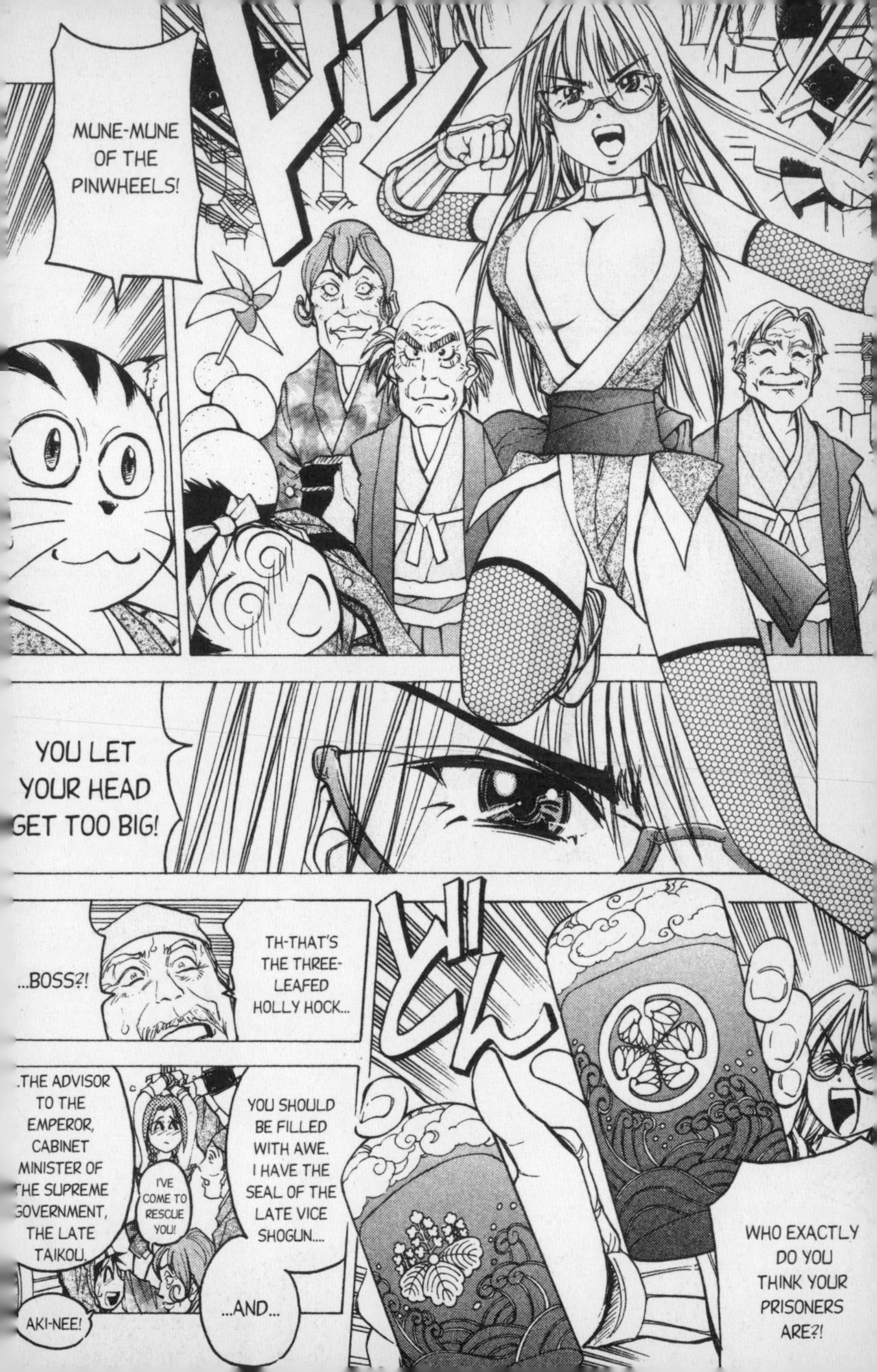
MUNE-MUNE OF THE PINWHEELS!
YOU LET YOUR HEAD GET TOO BIG!
どん
YOU SHOULD BE FILLED WITH AWE. I HAVE THE SEAL OF THE LATE VICE SHOGUN....
...AND...
TH-THAT'S THE THREE-LEAFED HOLLY HOCK...
...BOSS?!
..THE ADVISOR TO THE EMPEROR, CABINET MINISTER OF THE SUPREME GOVERNMENT, THE LATE TAIKOU.
I'VE COME TO RESCUE YOU!
AKI-NEE!
WHO EXACTLY DO YOU THINK YOUR PRISONERS ARE?!

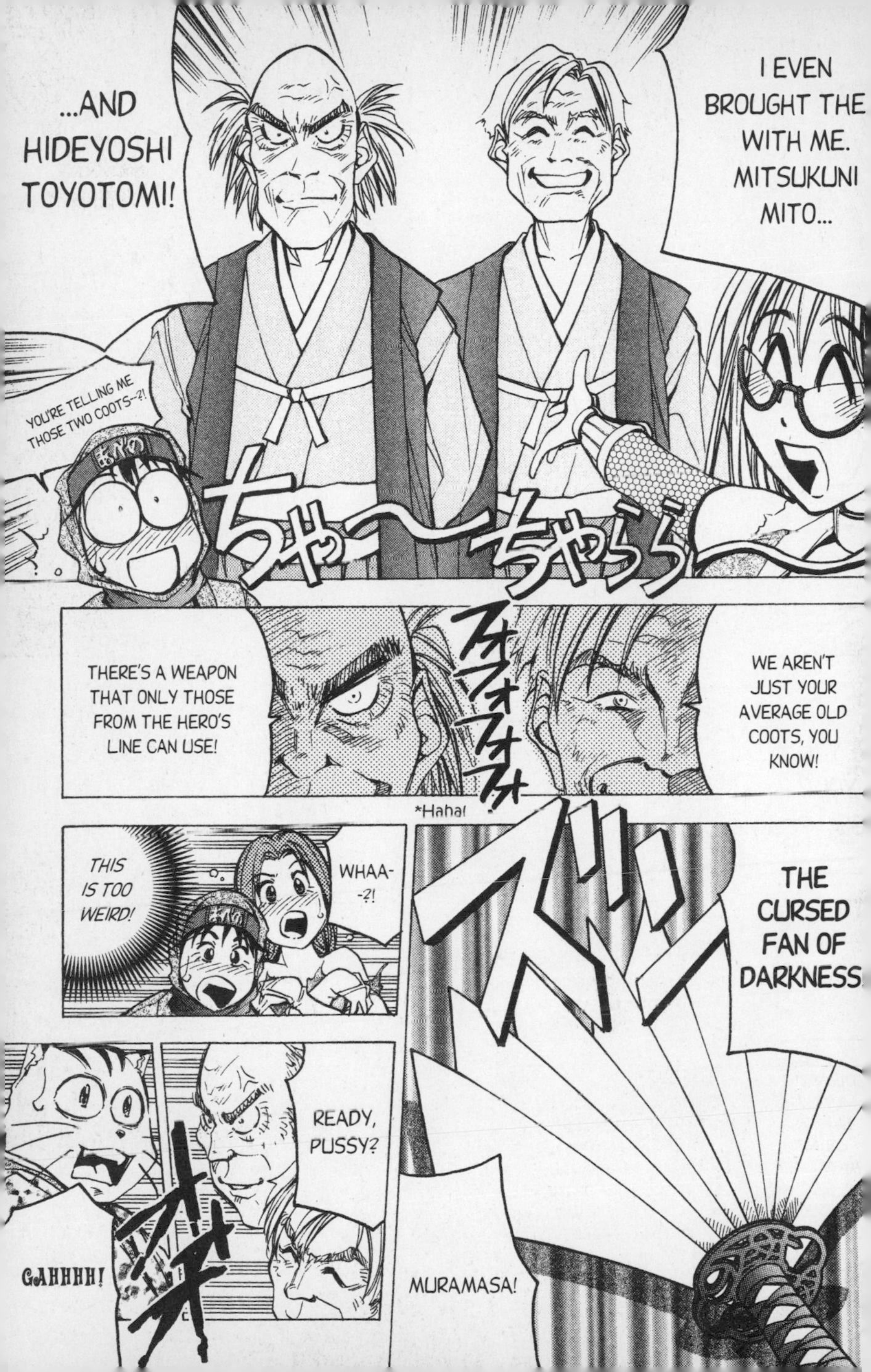
I EVEN BROUGHT THE WITH ME. MITSUKUNI MITO...
...AND HIDEYOSHI TOYOTOMI!
YOU'RE TELLING ME THOSE TWO COOTS--?!
ちゃ〜〜ちゃらら
WE AREN'T JUST YOUR AVERAGE OLD COOTS, YOU KNOW!
THERE'S A WEAPON THAT ONLY THOSE FROM THE HERO'S LINE CAN USE!
*Haha!
THE CURSED FAN OF DARKNESS.
WHAA--?!
THIS IS TOO WEIRD!
MURAMASA!
READY, PUSSY?
GAHHHH!

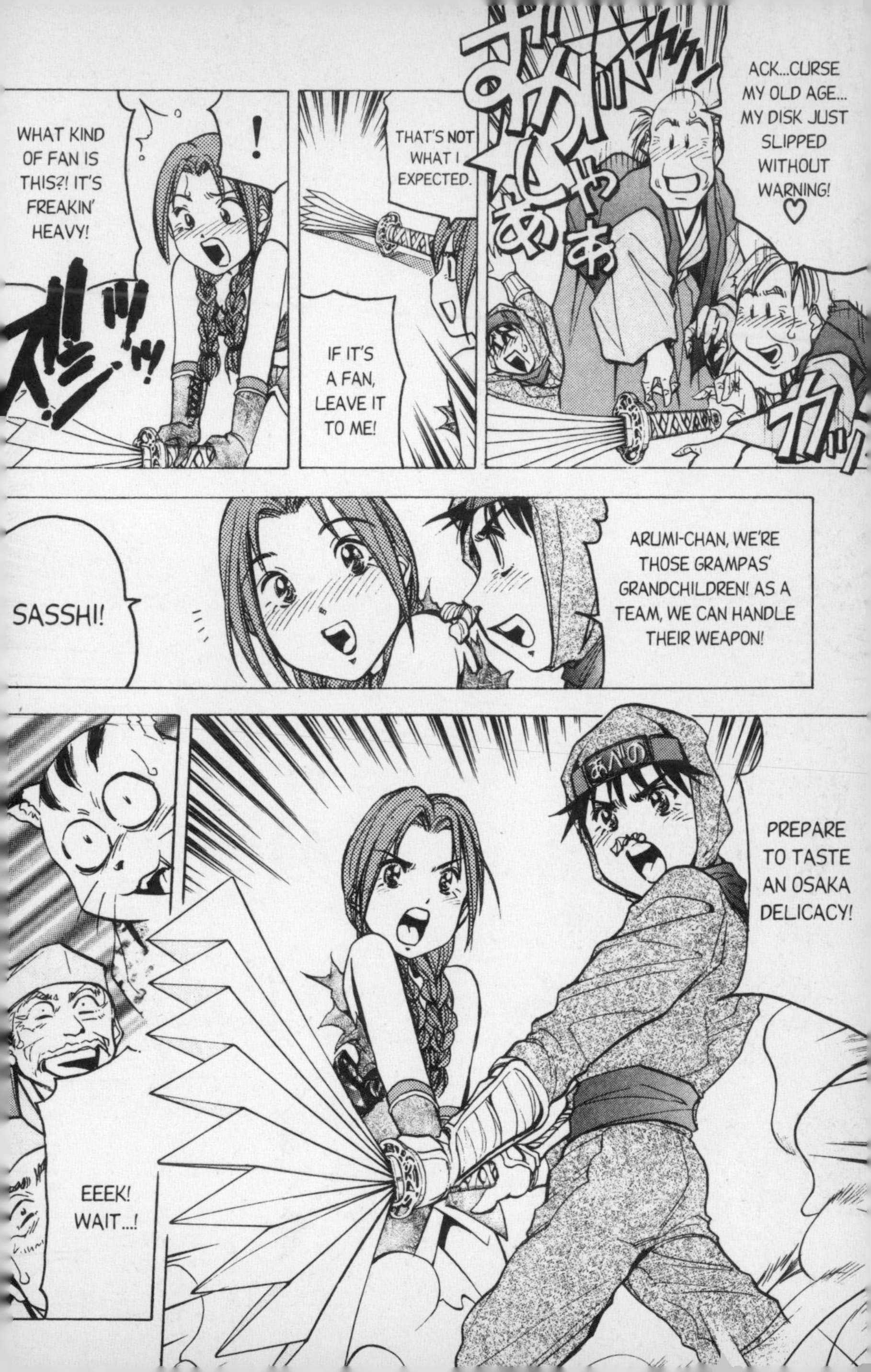
ACK...CURSE MY OLD AGE... MY DISK JUST SLIPPED WITHOUT WARNING! ♡
THAT'S NOT WHAT I EXPECTED.
IF IT'S A FAN, LEAVE IT TO ME!
!
WHAT KIND OF FAN IS THIS?! IT'S FREAKIN' HEAVY!
ARUMI-CHAN, WE'RE THOSE GRAMPAS' GRANDCHILDREN! AS A TEAM, WE CAN HANDLE THEIR WEAPON!
SASSHI!
PREPARE TO TASTE AN OSAKA DELICACY!
EEEK! WAIT...!

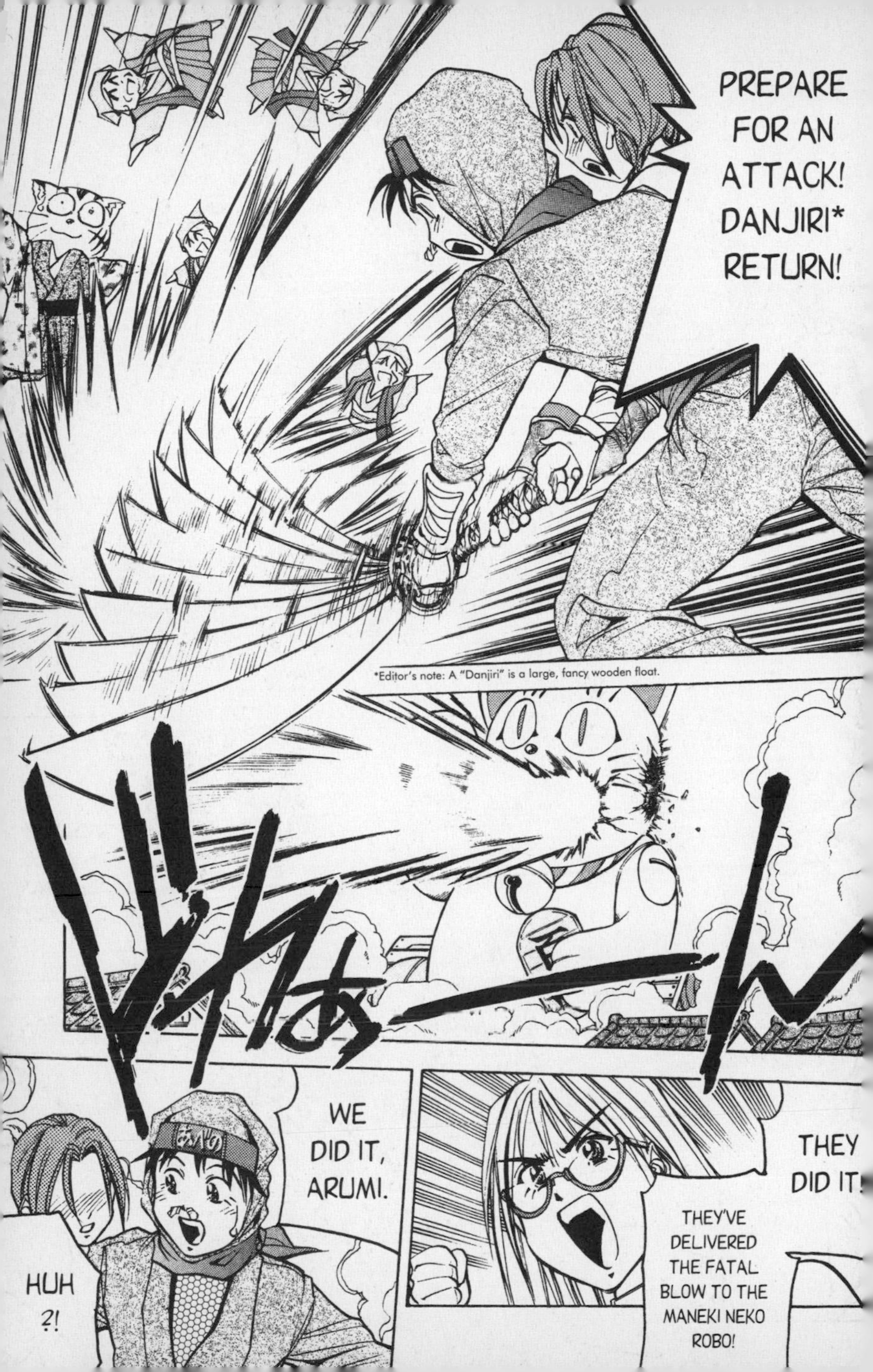
PREPARE FOR AN ATTACK! DANJIRI* RETURN!
*Editor's note: A "Danjiri" is a large, fancy wooden float.
THEY DID IT!
THEY'VE DELIVERED THE FATAL BLOW TO THE MANEKI NEKO ROBO!
WE DID IT, ARUMI.
HUH ?!

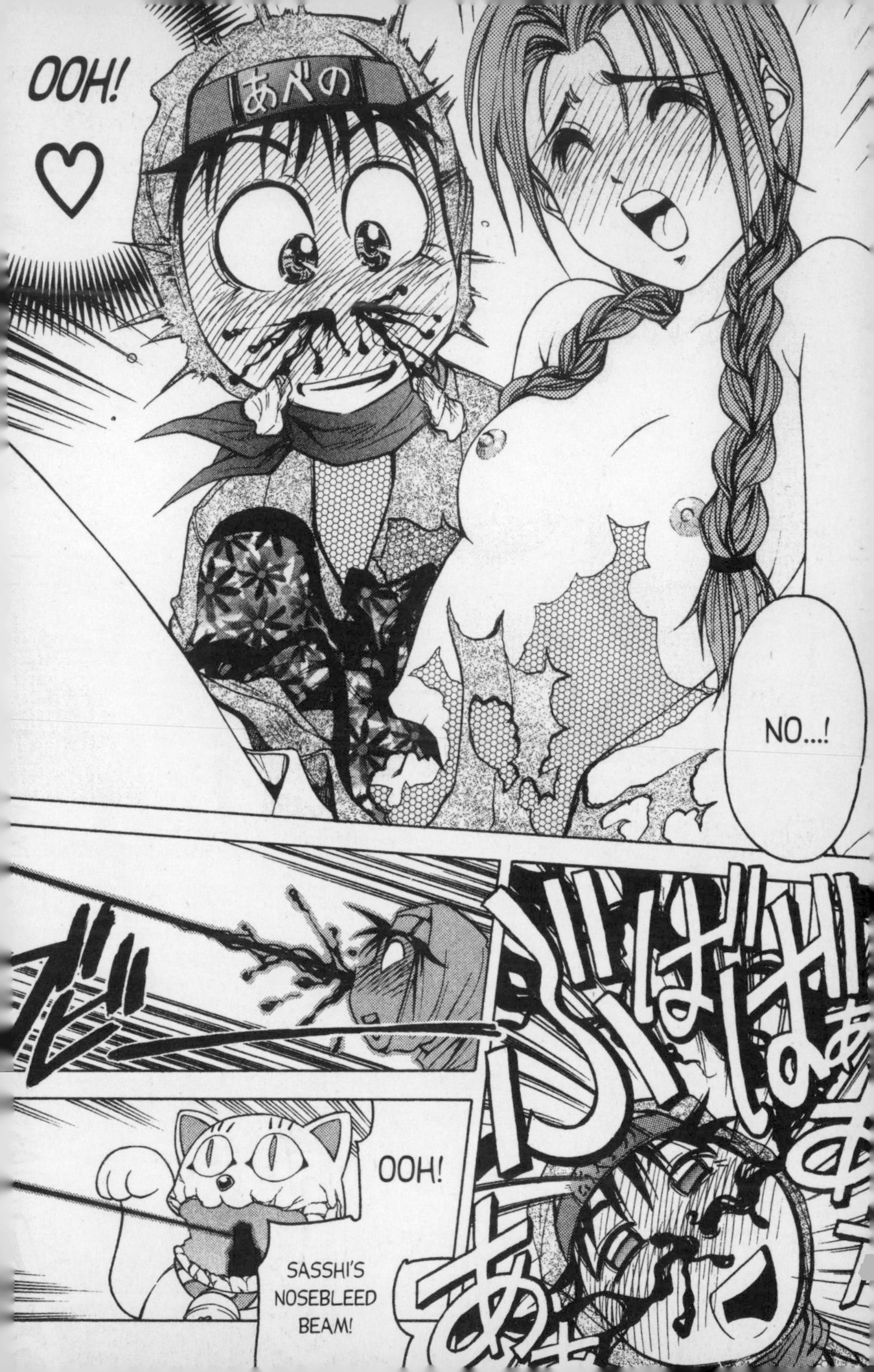
NO...!
あべの
OOH! ♡
OOH!
SASSHI'S NOSEBLEED BEAM!

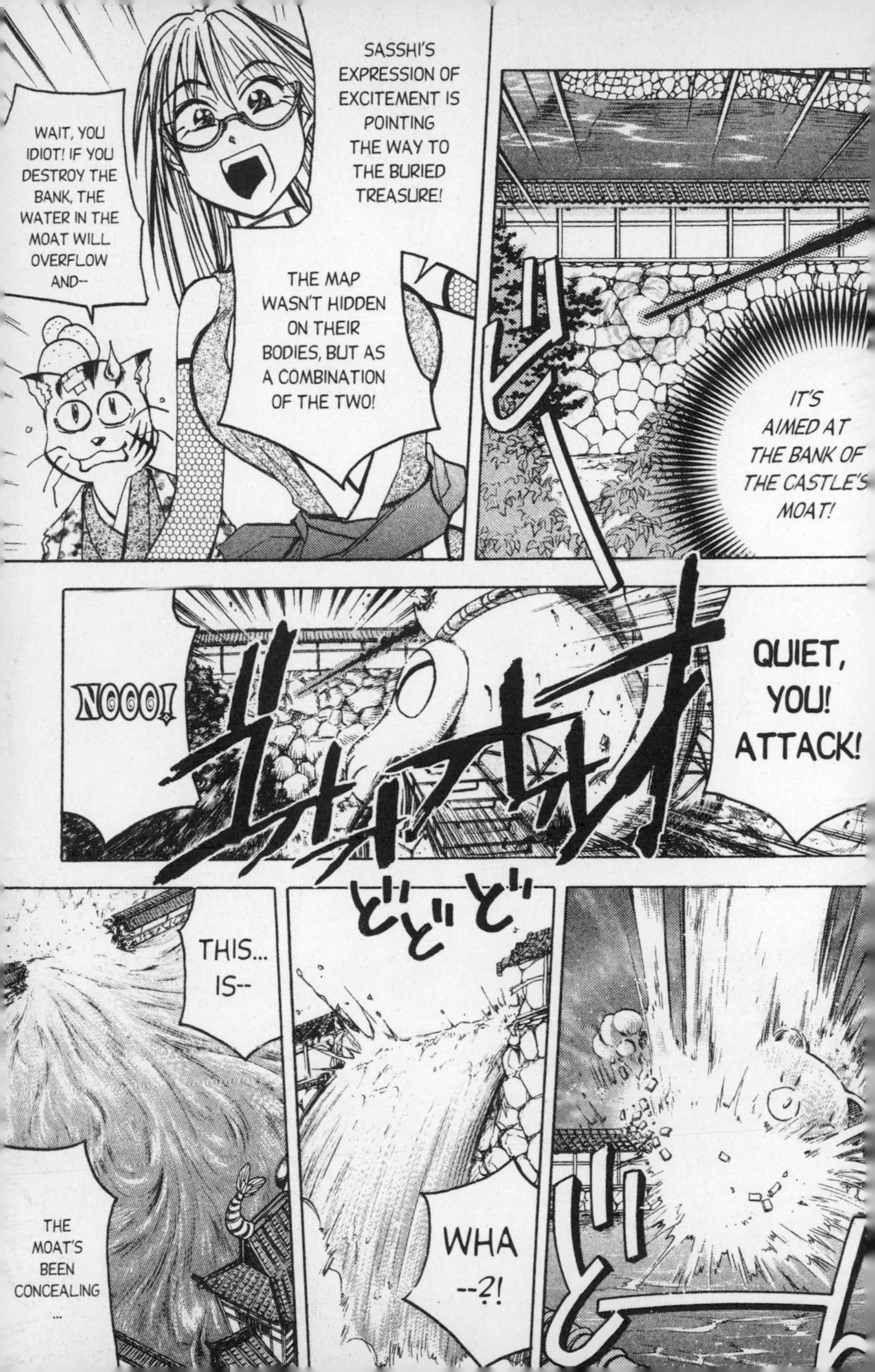

IT'S AIMED AT THE BANK OF THE CASTLE'S MOAT!
SASSHI'S EXPRESSION OF EXCITEMENT IS POINTING THE WAY TO THE BURIED TREASURE!
THE MAP WASN'T HIDDEN ON THEIR BODIES, BUT AS A COMBINATION OF THE TWO!
WAIT, YOU IDIOT! IF YOU DESTROY THE BANK, THE WATER IN THE MOAT WILL OVERFLOW AND--
QUIET, YOU! ATTACK!
NOOO!
どどど
WHA --?!
THIS... IS--
THE MOAT'S BEEN CONCEALING ...

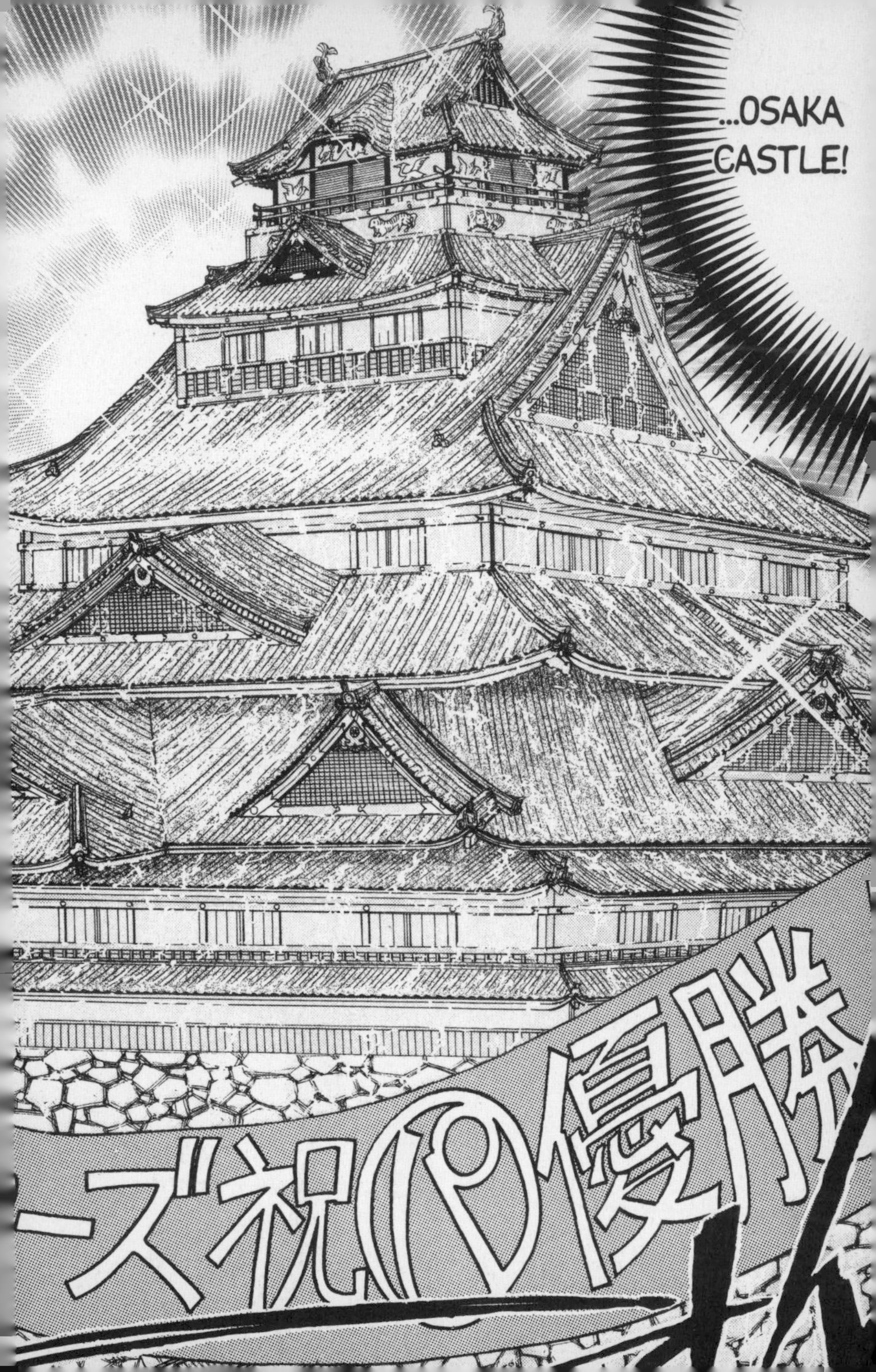
...OSAKA CASTLE!
ーズ祝の優勝

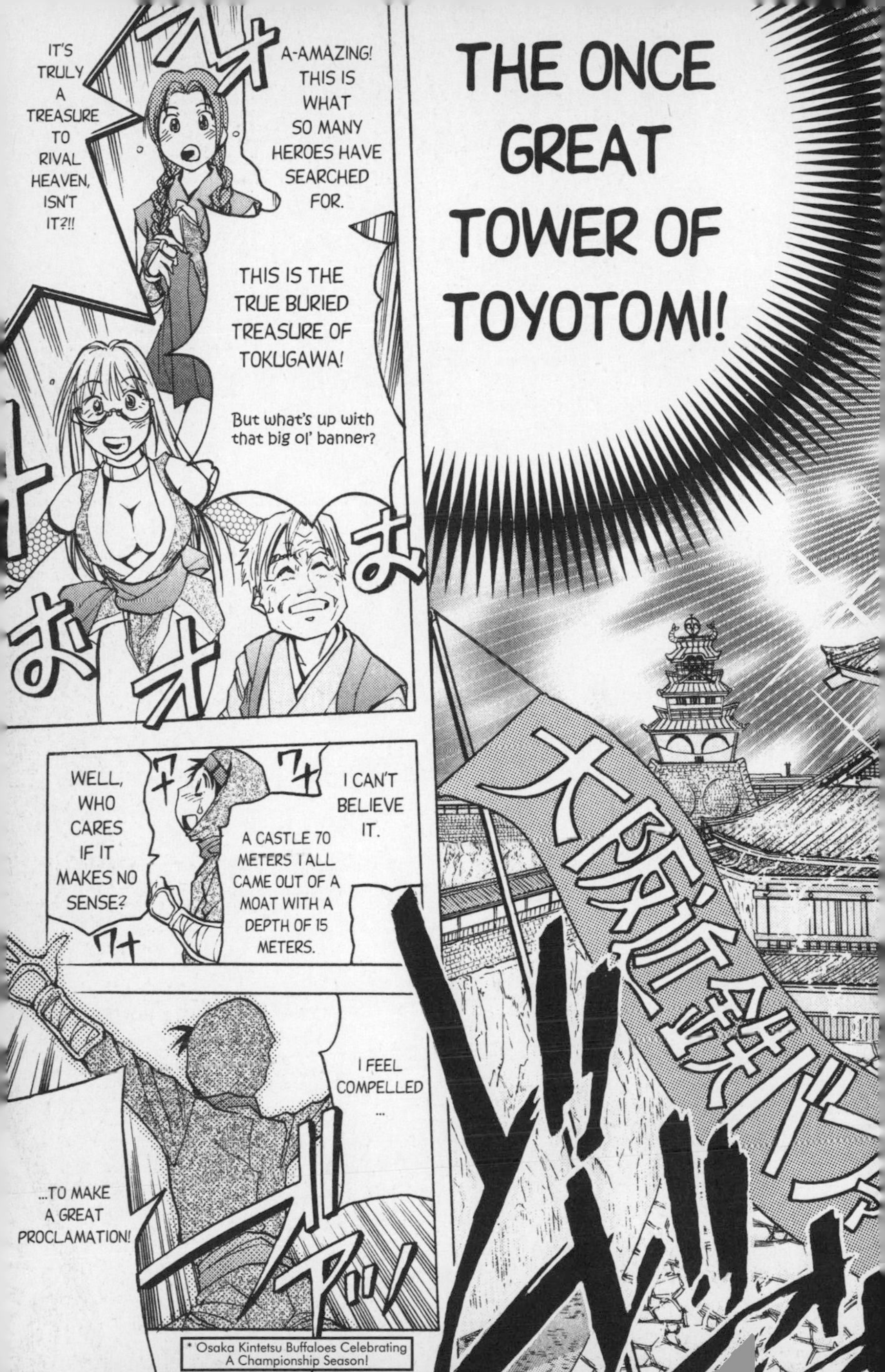
THE ONCE GREAT TOWER OF TOYOTOMI!
A-AMAZING! THIS IS WHAT SO MANY HEROES HAVE SEARCHED FOR.
IT'S TRULY A TREASURE TO RIVAL HEAVEN, ISN'T IT?!!
THIS IS THE TRUE BURIED TREASURE OF TOKUGAWA!
But what's up with that big ol' banner?
I CAN'T BELIEVE IT.
A CASTLE 70 METERS TALL CAME OUT OF A MOAT WITH A DEPTH OF 15 METERS.
WELL, WHO CARES IF IT MAKES NO SENSE?
I FEEL COMPELLED ...
...TO MAKE A GREAT PROCLAMATION!

* Osaka Kintetsu Buffaloes Celebrating A Championship Season!

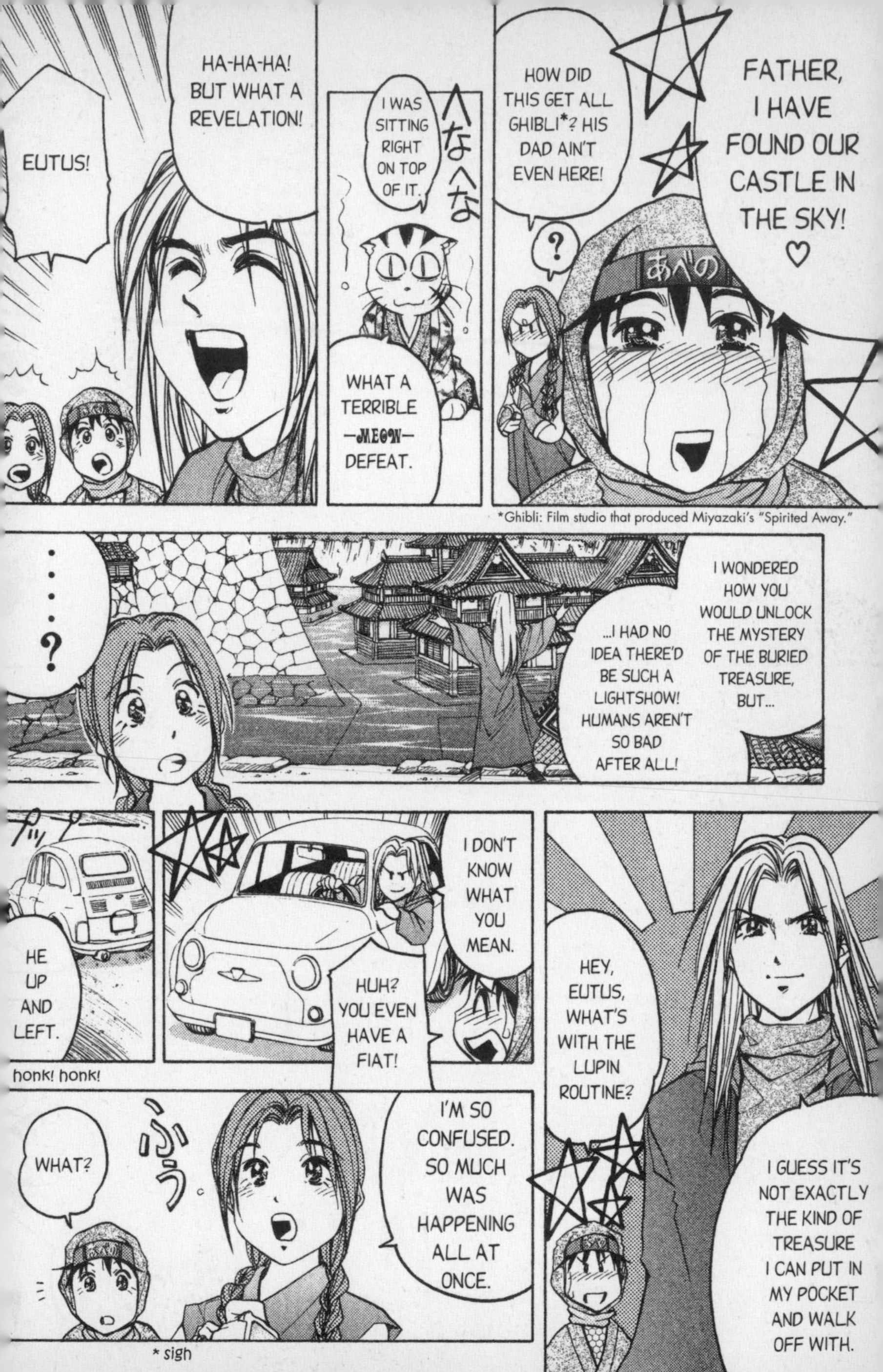
FATHER, I HAVE FOUND OUR CASTLE IN THE SKY! ♡
あべの
HOW DID THIS GET ALL GHIBLI*? HIS DAD AIN'T EVEN HERE!
?
へなへな
I WAS SITTING RIGHT ON TOP OF IT.
WHAT A TERRIBLE —MEOW— DEFEAT.
HA-HA-HA! BUT WHAT A REVELATION!
EUTUS!
I WONDERED HOW YOU WOULD UNLOCK THE MYSTERY OF THE BURIED TREASURE, BUT...
...I HAD NO IDEA THERE'D BE SUCH A LIGHTSHOW! HUMANS AREN'T SO BAD AFTER ALL!
......?
I GUESS IT'S NOT EXACTLY THE KIND OF TREASURE I CAN PUT IN MY POCKET AND WALK OFF WITH.
HEY, EUTUS, WHAT'S WITH THE LUPIN ROUTINE?
I DON'T KNOW WHAT YOU MEAN.
HUH? YOU EVEN HAVE A FIAT!
HE UP AND LEFT.
honk! honk!
I'M SO CONFUSED. SO MUCH WAS HAPPENING ALL AT ONCE.
ふぅ
WHAT?
* sigh
*Ghibli: Film studio that produced Miyazaki's "Spirited Away."

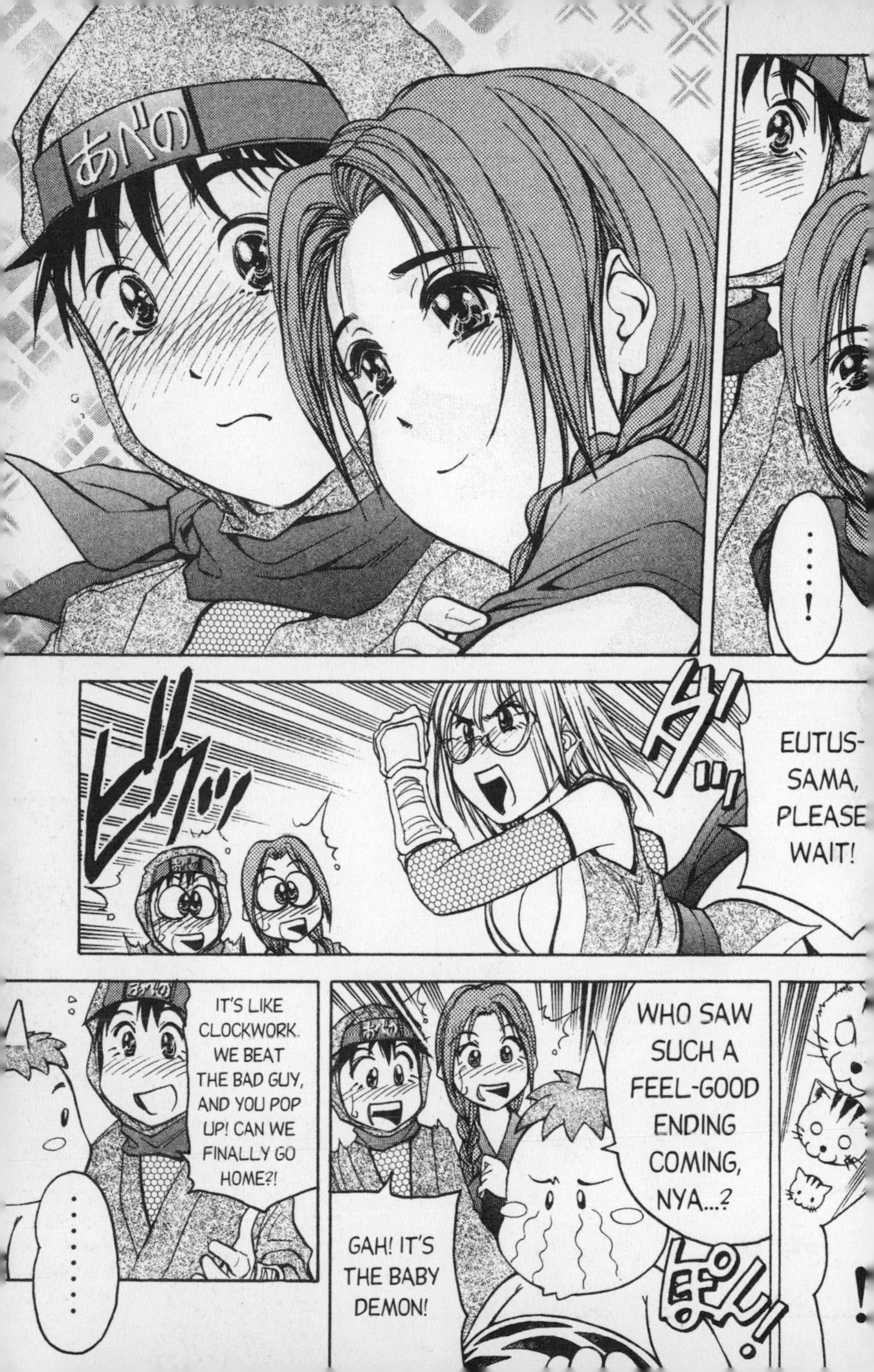
....!
あべの
EUTUS-SAMA, PLEASE WAIT!
!
WHO SAW SUCH A FEEL-GOOD ENDING COMING, NYA...?
GAH! IT'S THE BABY DEMON!
IT'S LIKE CLOCKWORK. WE BEAT THE BAD GUY, AND YOU POP UP! CAN WE FINALLY GO HOME?!
......

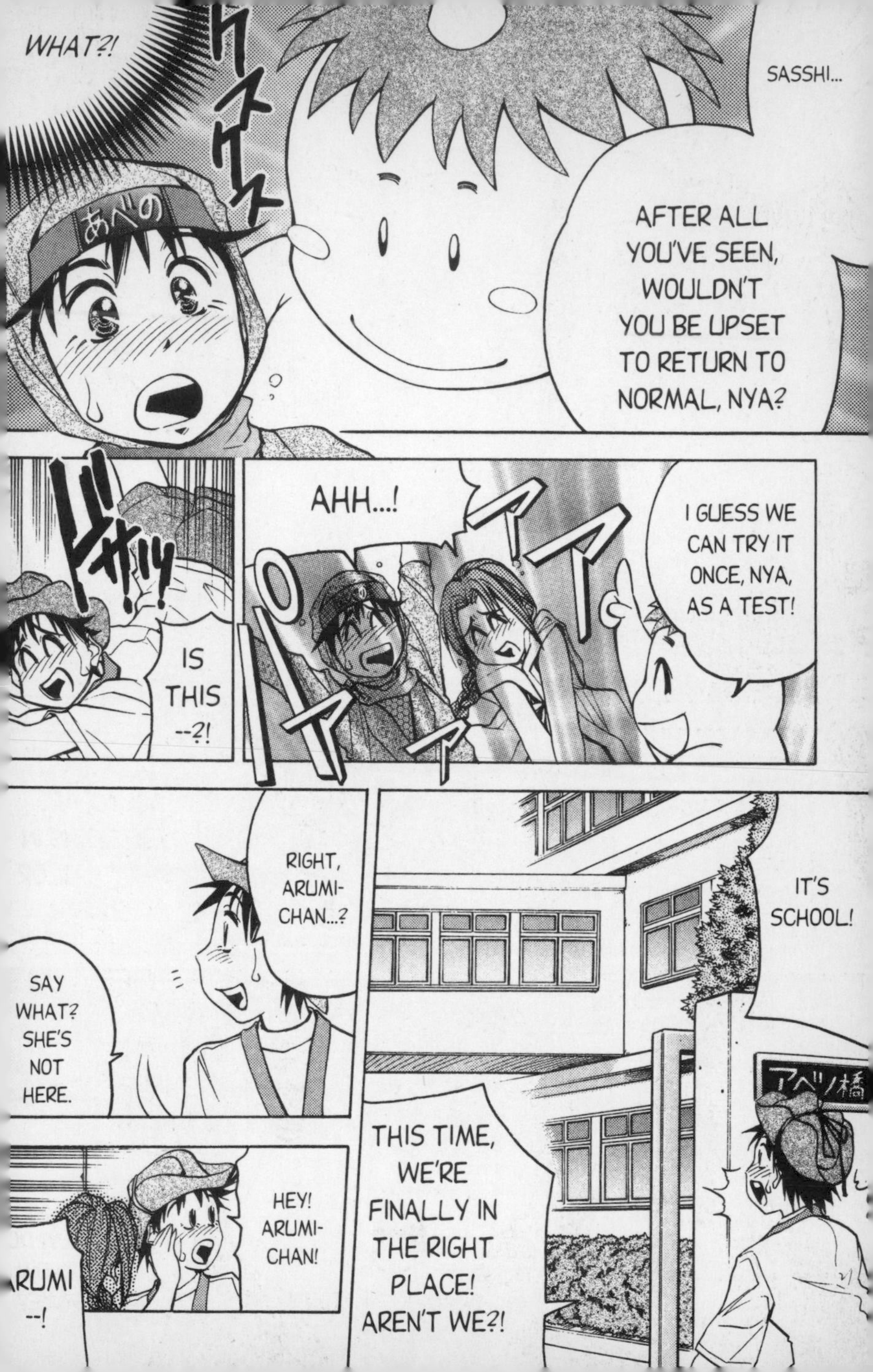
SASSHI...
AFTER ALL YOU'VE SEEN, WOULDN'T YOU BE UPSET TO RETURN TO NORMAL, NYA?
WHAT?!
あべの
I GUESS WE CAN TRY IT ONCE, NYA, AS A TEST!
AHH...!
IS THIS --?!
IT'S SCHOOL!
アベノ橋
THIS TIME, WE'RE FINALLY IN THE RIGHT PLACE! AREN'T WE?!
RIGHT, ARUMI-CHAN...?
SAY WHAT? SHE'S NOT HERE.
HEY! ARUMI-CHAN!
ARUMI --!

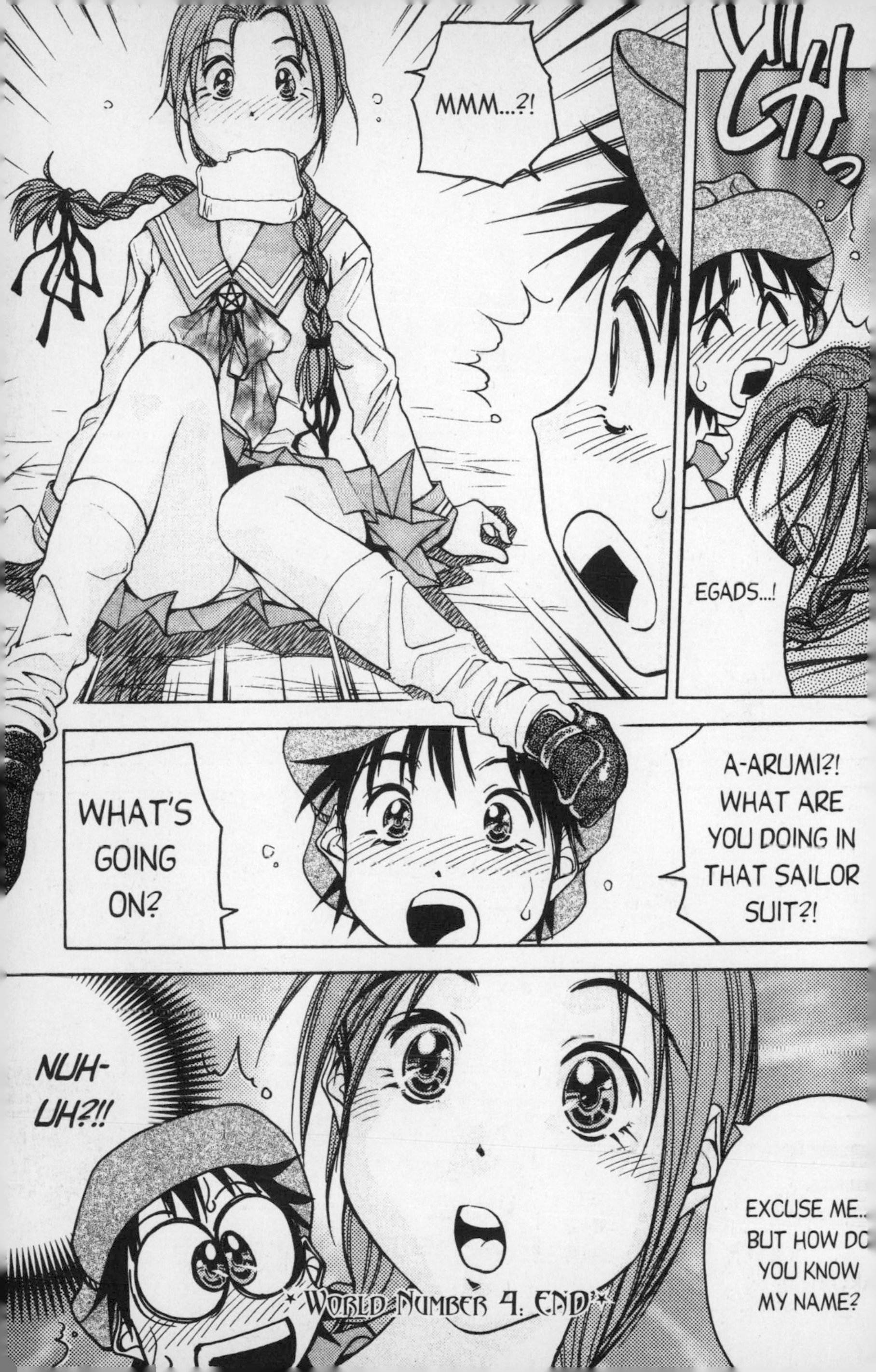
EGADS...!
MMM...?!
A-ARUMI?! WHAT ARE YOU DOING IN THAT SAILOR SUIT?!
WHAT'S GOING ON?
EXCUSE ME... BUT HOW DO YOU KNOW MY NAME?
NUH-UH?!!
World Number 4. End

ABENOBASHI

MAGICAL SHOPPING ARCADE

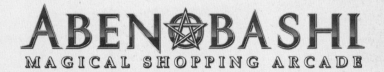

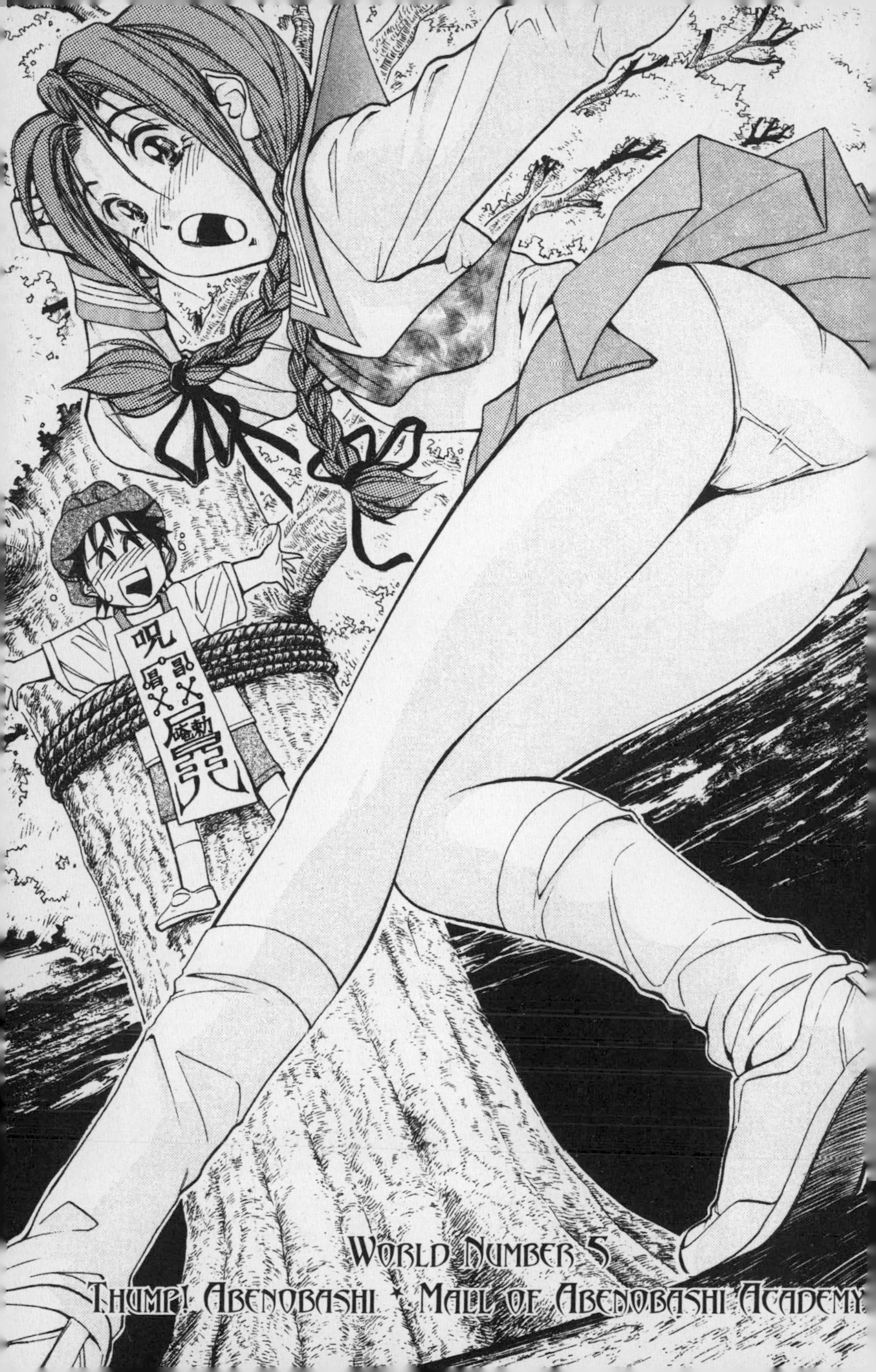

World Number 5
Thump! Abenobashi • Mall of Abenobashi Academy

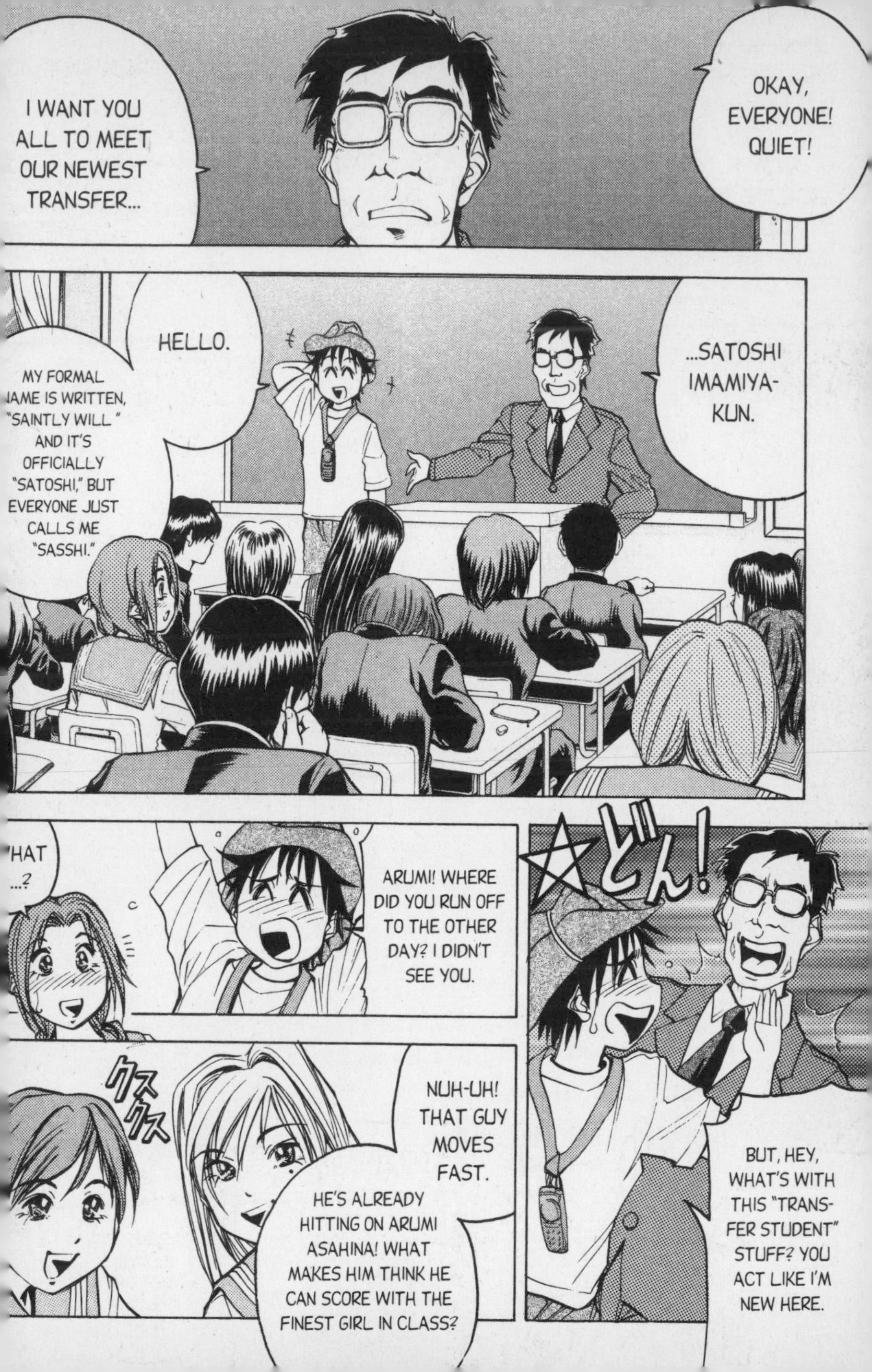
OKAY, EVERYONE! QUIET!
I WANT YOU ALL TO MEET OUR NEWEST TRANSFER...
...SATOSHI IMAMIYA-KUN.
HELLO.
MY FORMAL IAME IS WRITTEN, "SAINTLY WILL" AND IT'S OFFICIALLY "SATOSHI," BUT EVERYONE JUST CALLS ME "SASSHI."
どん!
BUT, HEY, WHAT'S WITH THIS "TRANS-FER STUDENT" STUFF? YOU ACT LIKE I'M NEW HERE.
ARUMI! WHERE DID YOU RUN OFF TO THE OTHER DAY? I DIDN'T SEE YOU.
'HAT ...?
NUH-UH! THAT GUY MOVES FAST.
HE'S ALREADY HITTING ON ARUMI ASAHINA! WHAT MAKES HIM THINK HE CAN SCORE WITH THE FINEST GIRL IN CLASS?
クスクス

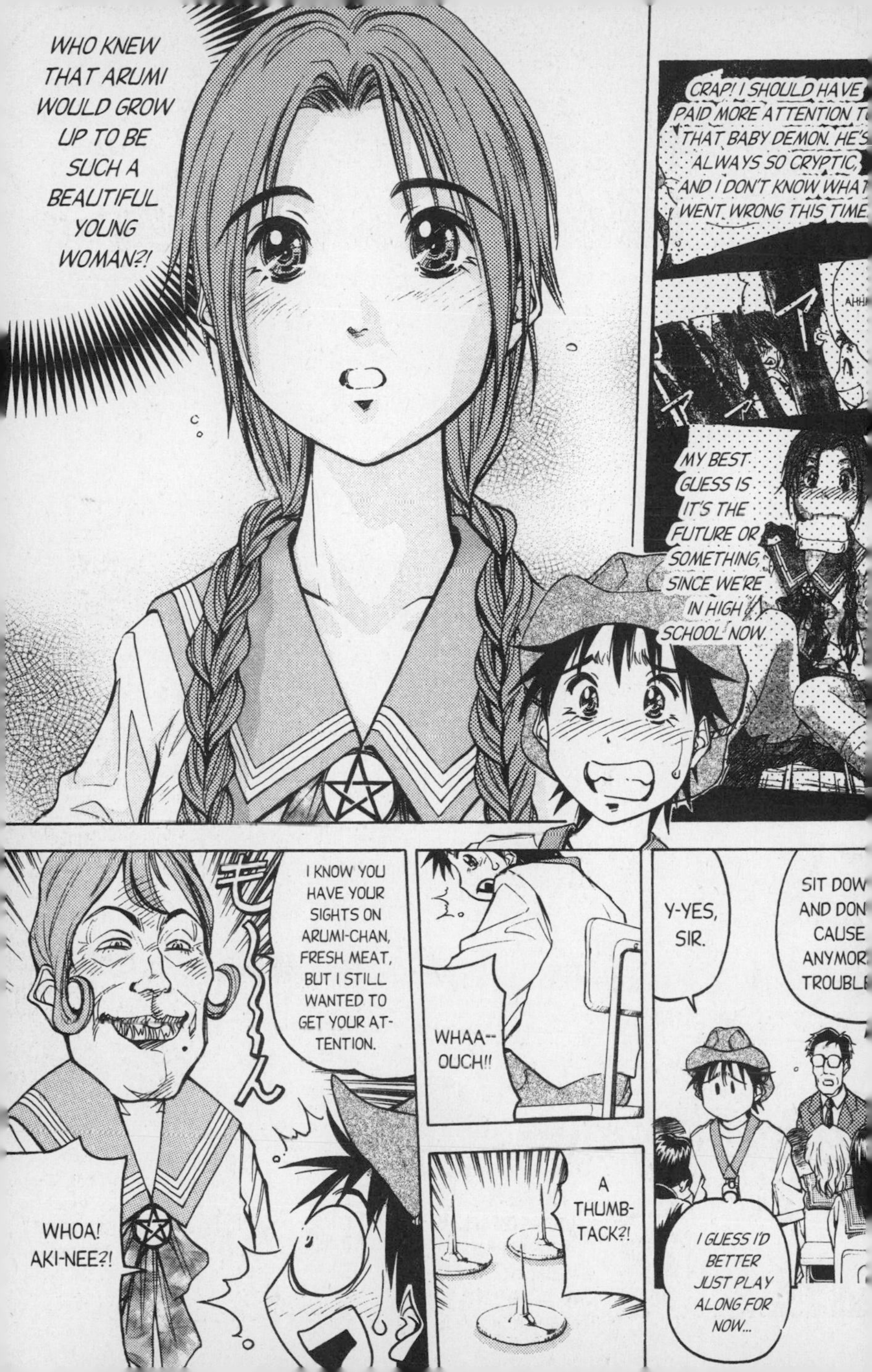
CRAP! I SHOULD HAVE PAID MORE ATTENTION TO THAT BABY DEMON. HE'S ALWAYS SO CRYPTIC, AND I DON'T KNOW WHAT WENT WRONG THIS TIME.
MY BEST GUESS IS IT'S THE FUTURE OR SOMETHING, SINCE WE'RE IN HIGH SCHOOL NOW.
WHO KNEW THAT ARUMI WOULD GROW UP TO BE SUCH A BEAUTIFUL YOUNG WOMAN?!
SIT DOW AND DON CAUSE ANYMOR TROUBL
Y-YES, SIR.
I GUESS I'D BETTER JUST PLAY ALONG FOR NOW...
WHAA-- OUCH!!
A THUMB-TACK?!
I KNOW YOU HAVE YOUR SIGHTS ON ARUMI-CHAN, FRESH MEAT, BUT I STILL WANTED TO GET YOUR AT-TENTION.
WHOA! AKI-NEE?!

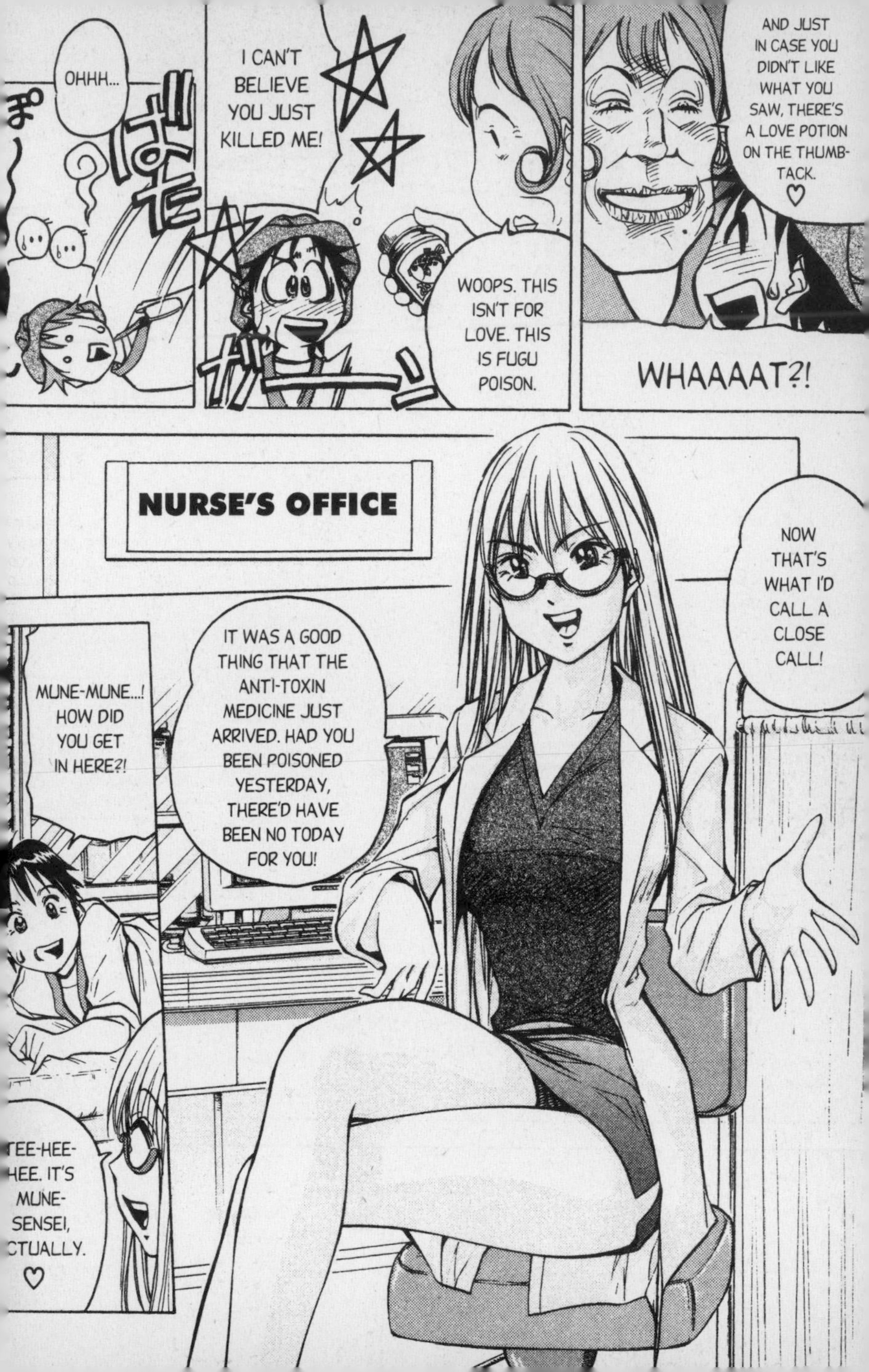
AND JUST IN CASE YOU DIDN'T LIKE WHAT YOU SAW, THERE'S A LOVE POTION ON THE THUMB-TACK. ♡
WHAAAAT?!
WOOPS. THIS ISN'T FOR LOVE. THIS IS FUGU POISON.
I CAN'T BELIEVE YOU JUST KILLED ME!
OHHH...
ぱたっ
ぽ~
NOW THAT'S WHAT I'D CALL A CLOSE CALL!
NURSE'S OFFICE
IT WAS A GOOD THING THAT THE ANTI-TOXIN MEDICINE JUST ARRIVED. HAD YOU BEEN POISONED YESTERDAY, THERE'D HAVE BEEN NO TODAY FOR YOU!
MUNE-MUNE...! HOW DID YOU GET IN HERE?!
TEE-HEE-HEE. IT'S MUNE-SENSEI, CTUALLY. ♡

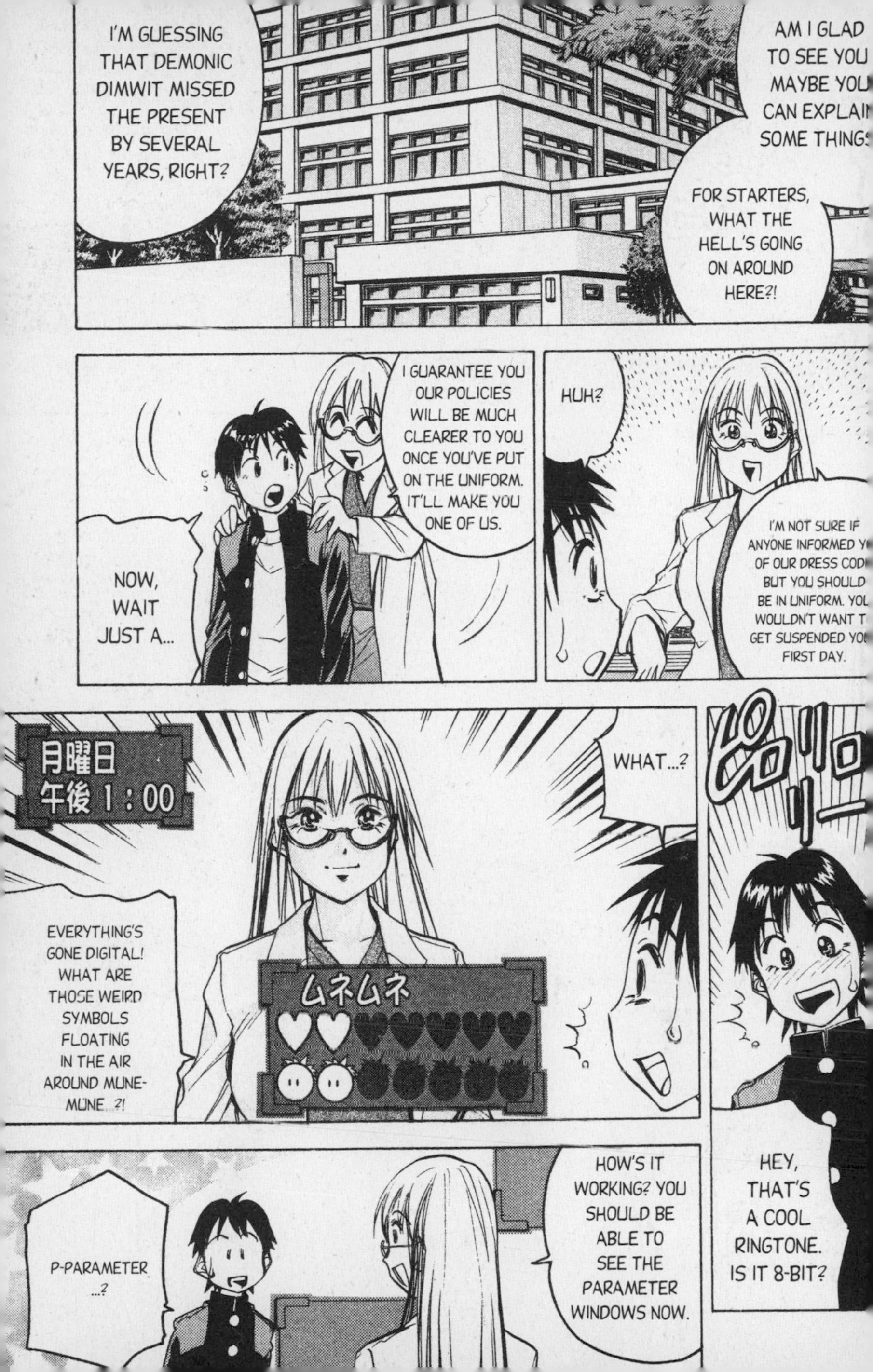
AM I GLAD TO SEE YOU MAYBE YOU CAN EXPLAI SOME THINGS
FOR STARTERS, WHAT THE HELL'S GOING ON AROUND HERE?!
I'M GUESSING THAT DEMONIC DIMWIT MISSED THE PRESENT BY SEVERAL YEARS, RIGHT?
HUH?
I'M NOT SURE IF ANYONE INFORMED Y OF OUR DRESS COD BUT YOU SHOULD BE IN UNIFORM. YO WOULDN'T WANT T GET SUSPENDED YO FIRST DAY.
I GUARANTEE YOU OUR POLICIES WILL BE MUCH CLEARER TO YOU ONCE YOU'VE PUT ON THE UNIFORM. IT'LL MAKE YOU ONE OF US.
NOW, WAIT JUST A...
ピロリロリー
HEY, THAT'S A COOL RINGTONE. IS IT 8-BIT?
WHAT...?
月曜日 午後 1：00
EVERYTHING'S GONE DIGITAL! WHAT ARE THOSE WEIRD SYMBOLS FLOATING IN THE AIR AROUND MUNE-MUNE...?!
ムネムネ
HOW'S IT WORKING? YOU SHOULD BE ABLE TO SEE THE PARAMETER WINDOWS NOW.
P-PARAMETER ...?

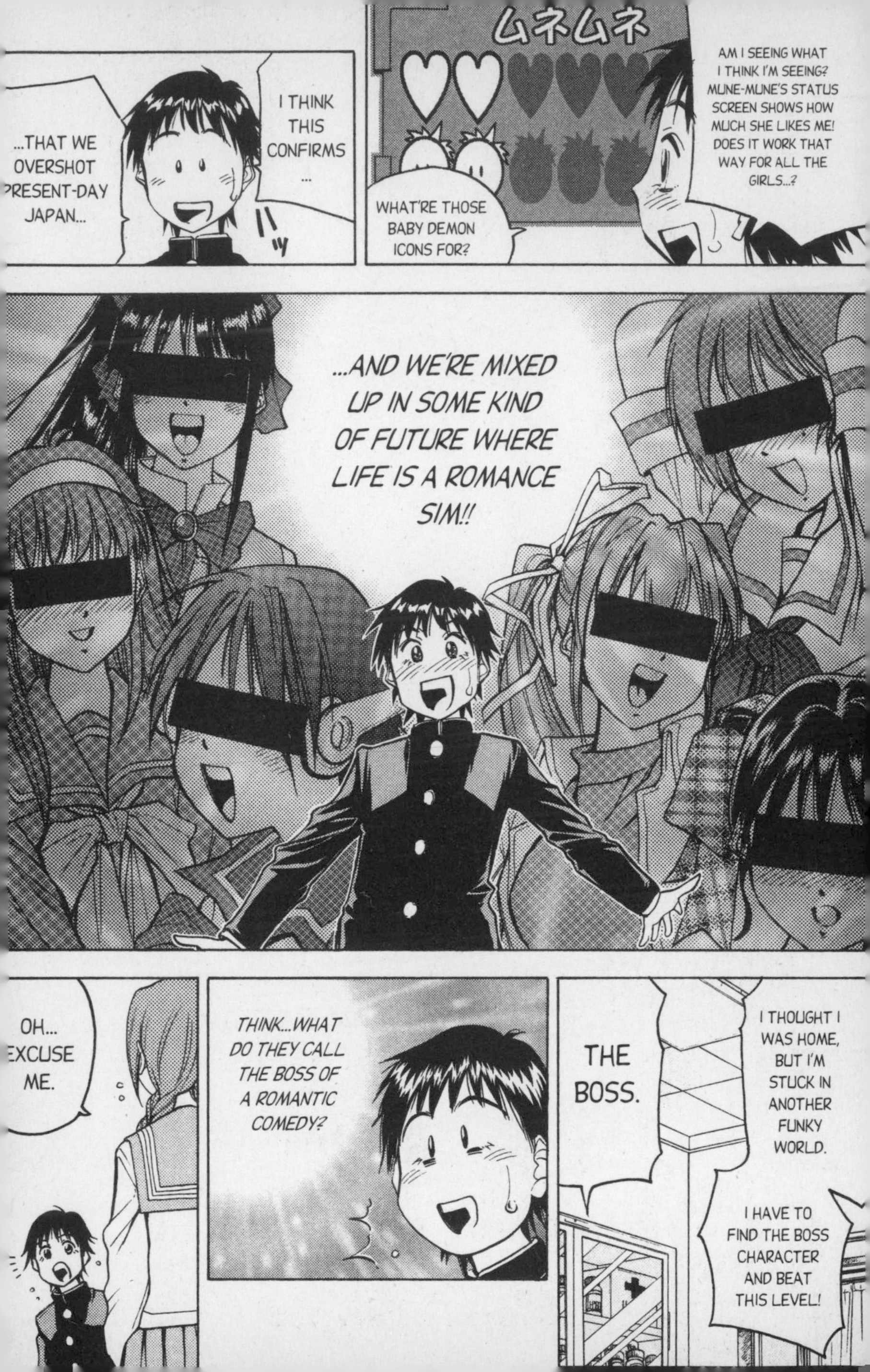
ムネムネ
AM I SEEING WHAT I THINK I'M SEEING? MUNE-MUNE'S STATUS SCREEN SHOWS HOW MUCH SHE LIKES ME! DOES IT WORK THAT WAY FOR ALL THE GIRLS...?
WHAT'RE THOSE BABY DEMON ICONS FOR?
I THINK THIS CONFIRMS ...
...THAT WE OVERSHOT PRESENT-DAY JAPAN...
ハッ
...AND WE'RE MIXED UP IN SOME KIND OF FUTURE WHERE LIFE IS A ROMANCE SIM!!
I THOUGHT I WAS HOME, BUT I'M STUCK IN ANOTHER FUNKY WORLD.
I HAVE TO FIND THE BOSS CHARACTER AND BEAT THIS LEVEL!
THE BOSS.
THINK...WHAT DO THEY CALL THE BOSS OF A ROMANTIC COMEDY?
OH... EXCUSE ME.

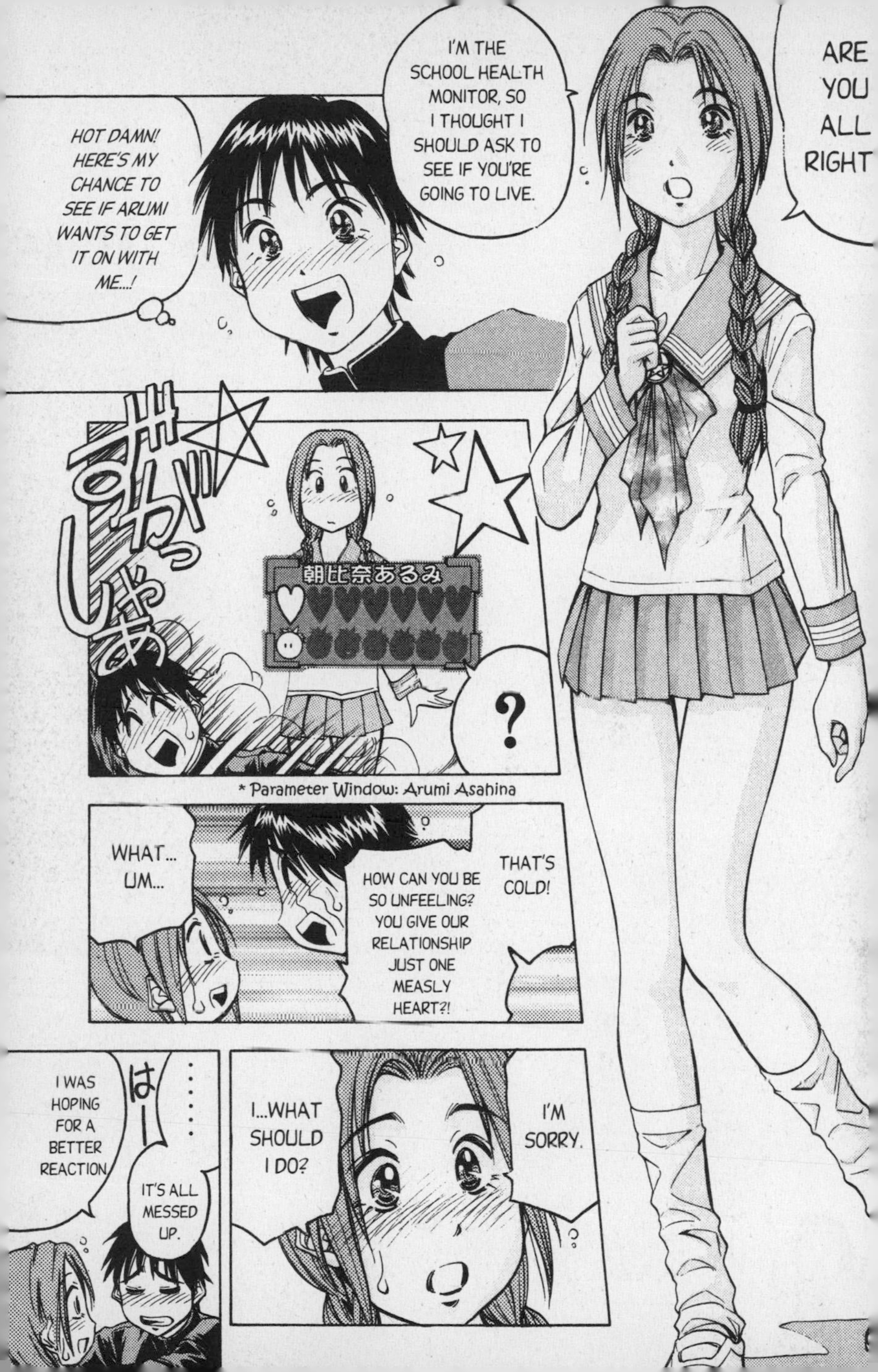
ARE YOU ALL RIGHT
I'M THE SCHOOL HEALTH MONITOR, SO I THOUGHT I SHOULD ASK TO SEE IF YOU'RE GOING TO LIVE.
HOT DAMN! HERE'S MY CHANCE TO SEE IF ARUMI WANTS TO GET IT ON WITH ME...!
朝比奈あるみ
?
* Parameter Window: Arumi Asahina
THAT'S COLD!
HOW CAN YOU BE SO UNFEELING? YOU GIVE OUR RELATIONSHIP JUST ONE MEASLY HEART?!
WHAT... UM...
I'M SORRY.
I...WHAT SHOULD I DO?
......
はー
I WAS HOPING FOR A BETTER REACTION.
IT'S ALL MESSED UP.

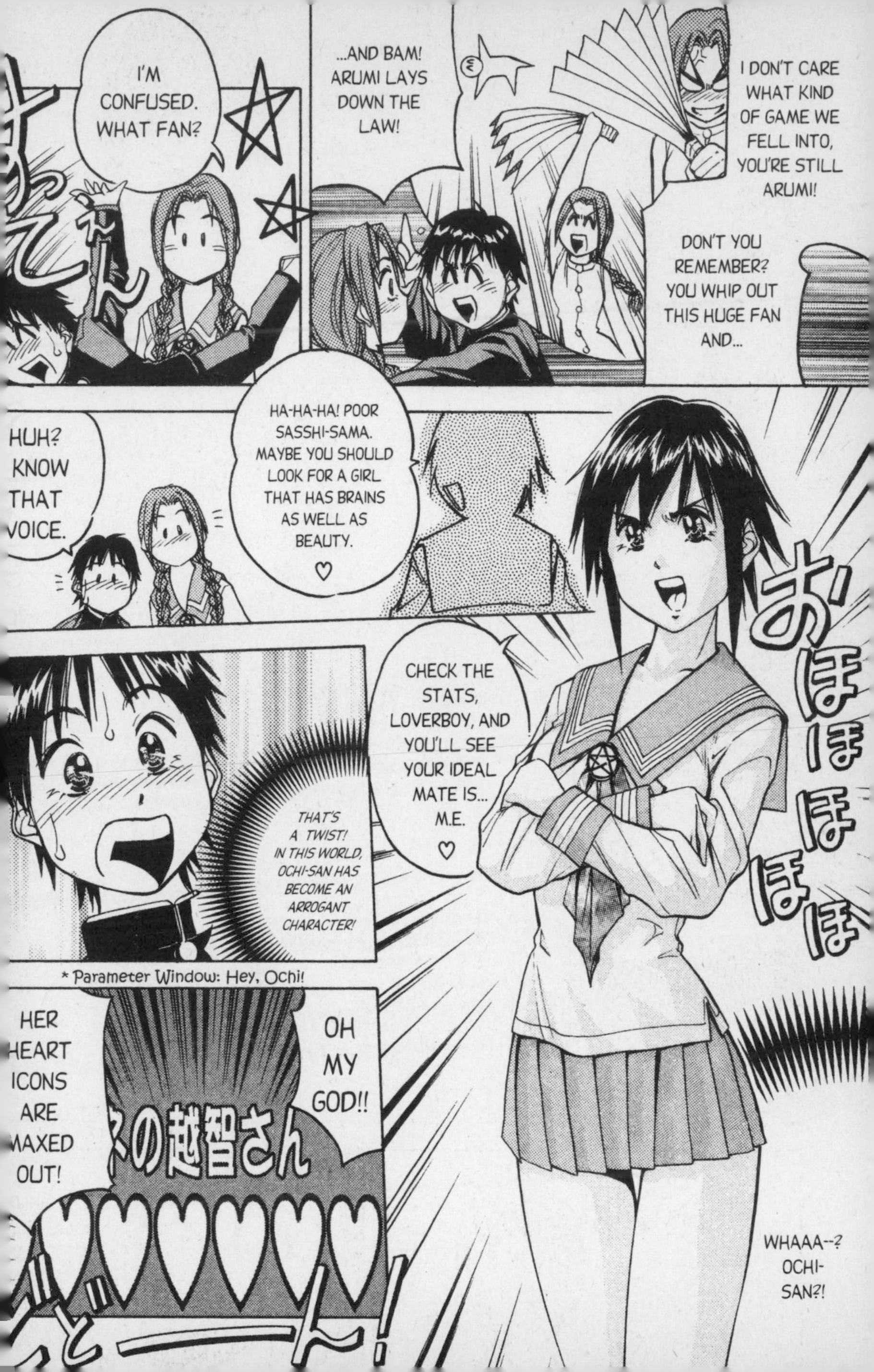

I DON'T CARE WHAT KIND OF GAME WE FELL INTO, YOU'RE STILL ARUMI!
DON'T YOU REMEMBER? YOU WHIP OUT THIS HUGE FAN AND...
...AND BAM! ARUMI LAYS DOWN THE LAW!
I'M CONFUSED. WHAT FAN?
HA-HA-HA! POOR SASSHI-SAMA. MAYBE YOU SHOULD LOOK FOR A GIRL THAT HAS BRAINS AS WELL AS BEAUTY. ♡
HUH? KNOW THAT VOICE.
おほほほほほ
CHECK THE STATS, LOVERBOY, AND YOU'LL SEE YOUR IDEAL MATE IS... M.E. ♡
WHAAA--? OCHI-SAN?!
THAT'S A TWIST! IN THIS WORLD, OCHI-SAN HAS BECOME AN ARROGANT CHARACTER!
* Parameter Window: Hey, Ochi!
OH MY GOD!!
HER HEART ICONS ARE MAXED OUT!

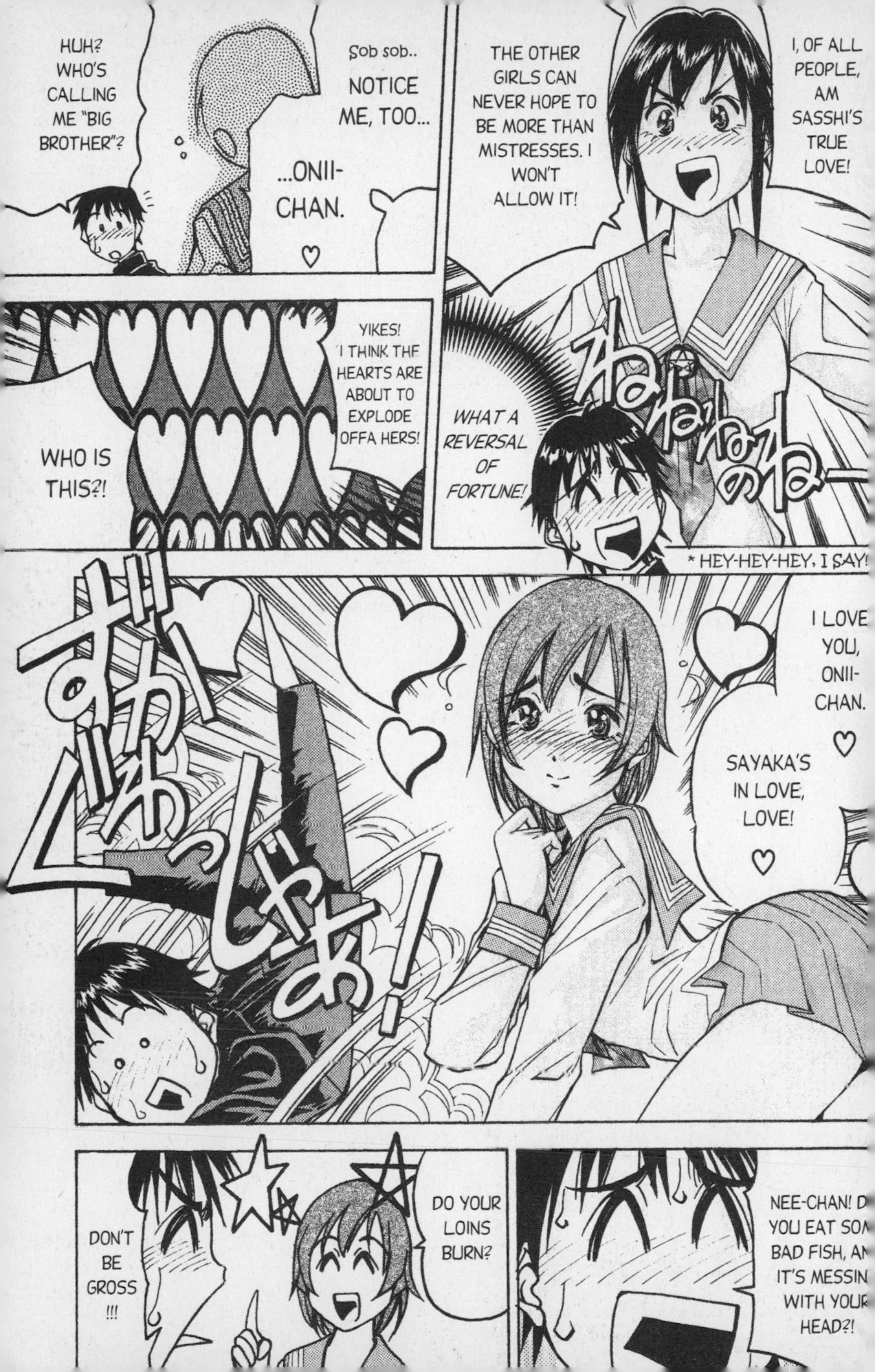
I, OF ALL PEOPLE, AM SASSHI'S TRUE LOVE!
THE OTHER GIRLS CAN NEVER HOPE TO BE MORE THAN MISTRESSES. I WON'T ALLOW IT!
WHAT A REVERSAL OF FORTUNE!
* HEY-HEY-HEY, I SAY!
Sob sob.. NOTICE ME, TOO...
...ONII-CHAN. ♡
HUH? WHO'S CALLING ME "BIG BROTHER"?
YIKES! I THINK THE HEARTS ARE ABOUT TO EXPLODE OFFA HERS!
WHO IS THIS?!
I LOVE YOU, ONII-CHAN. ♡
SAYAKA'S IN LOVE, LOVE! ♡
NEE-CHAN! D YOU EAT SOM BAD FISH, AN IT'S MESSIN WITH YOUR HEAD?!
DO YOUR LOINS BURN?
DON'T BE GROSS !!!

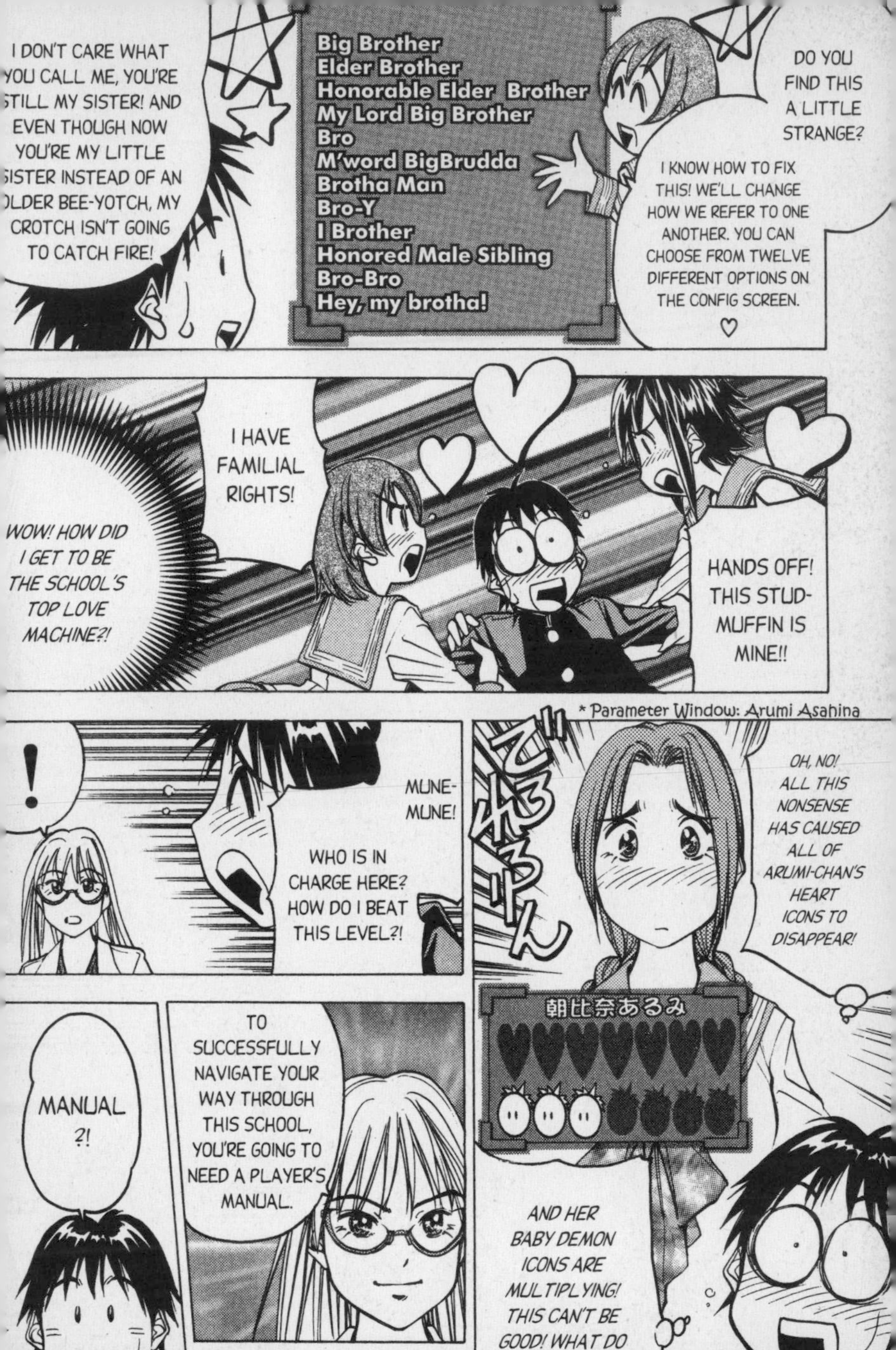
DO YOU FIND THIS A LITTLE STRANGE?
I KNOW HOW TO FIX THIS! WE'LL CHANGE HOW WE REFER TO ONE ANOTHER. YOU CAN CHOOSE FROM TWELVE DIFFERENT OPTIONS ON THE CONFIG SCREEN. ♡
Big Brother
Elder Brother
Honorable Elder Brother
My Lord Big Brother
Bro
M'word BigBrudda
Brotha Man
Bro-Y
I Brother
Honored Male Sibling
Bro-Bro
Hey, my brotha!
I DON'T CARE WHAT YOU CALL ME, YOU'RE STILL MY SISTER! AND EVEN THOUGH NOW YOU'RE MY LITTLE SISTER INSTEAD OF AN OLDER BEE-YOTCH, MY CROTCH ISN'T GOING TO CATCH FIRE!
HANDS OFF! THIS STUD-MUFFIN IS MINE!!
I HAVE FAMILIAL RIGHTS!
WOW! HOW DID I GET TO BE THE SCHOOL'S TOP LOVE MACHINE?!
* Parameter Window: Arumi Asahina
OH, NO! ALL THIS NONSENSE HAS CAUSED ALL OF ARUMI-CHAN'S HEART ICONS TO DISAPPEAR!
朝比奈あるみ
AND HER BABY DEMON ICONS ARE MULTIPLYING! THIS CAN'T BE GOOD! WHAT DO THOSE MEAN?!
MUNE-MUNE!
WHO IS IN CHARGE HERE? HOW DO I BEAT THIS LEVEL?!
!
TO SUCCESSFULLY NAVIGATE YOUR WAY THROUGH THIS SCHOOL, YOU'RE GOING TO NEED A PLAYER'S MANUAL.
MANUAL ?!

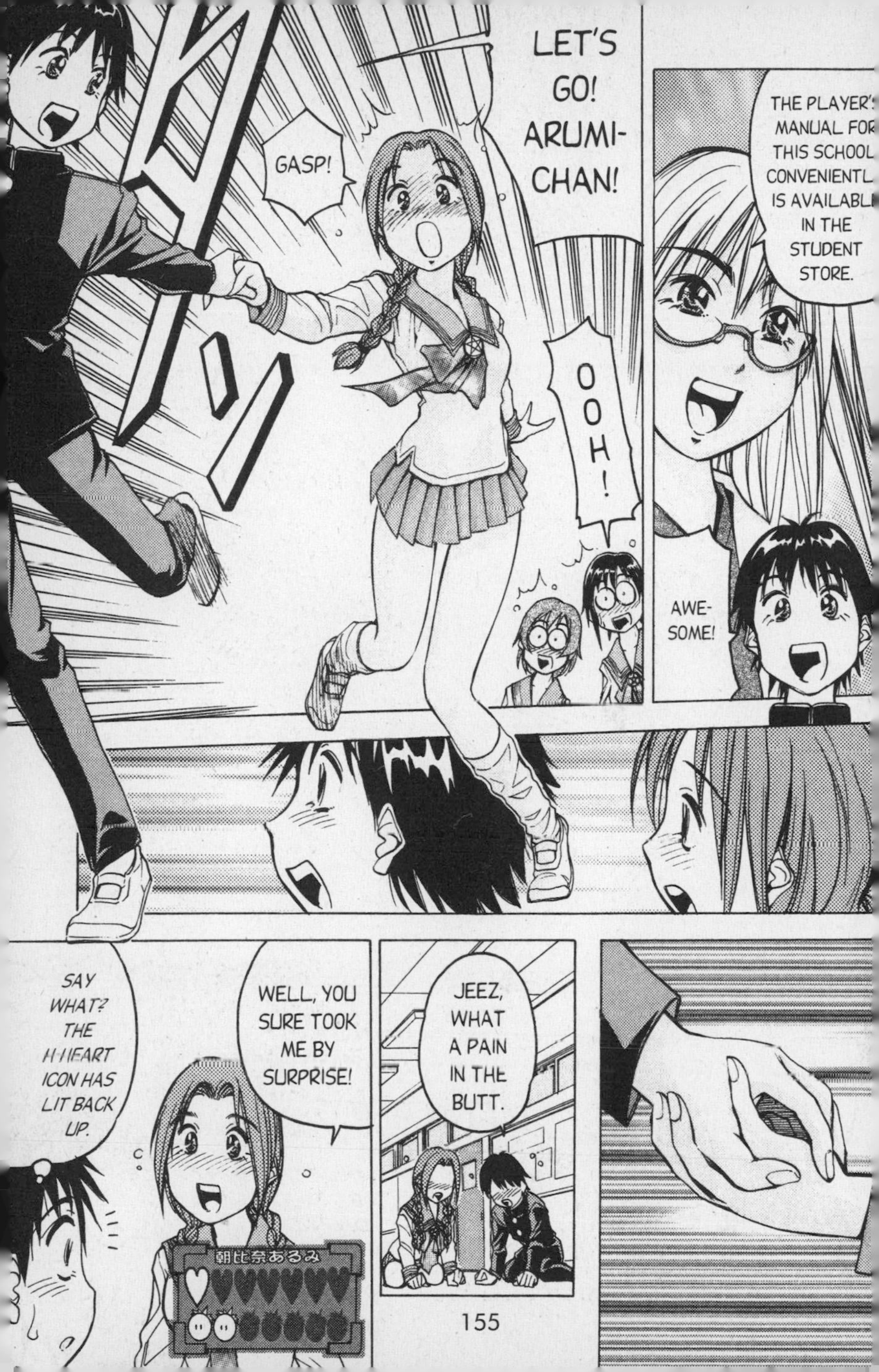
THE PLAYER'S MANUAL FOR THIS SCHOOL CONVENIENTL IS AVAILABL IN THE STUDENT STORE.
AWE-SOME!
LET'S GO! ARUMI-CHAN!
GASP!
OOH!
JEEZ, WHAT A PAIN IN THE BUTT.
WELL, YOU SURE TOOK ME BY SURPRISE!
SAY WHAT? THE H-HEART ICON HAS LIT BACK UP.
朝比奈あるみ

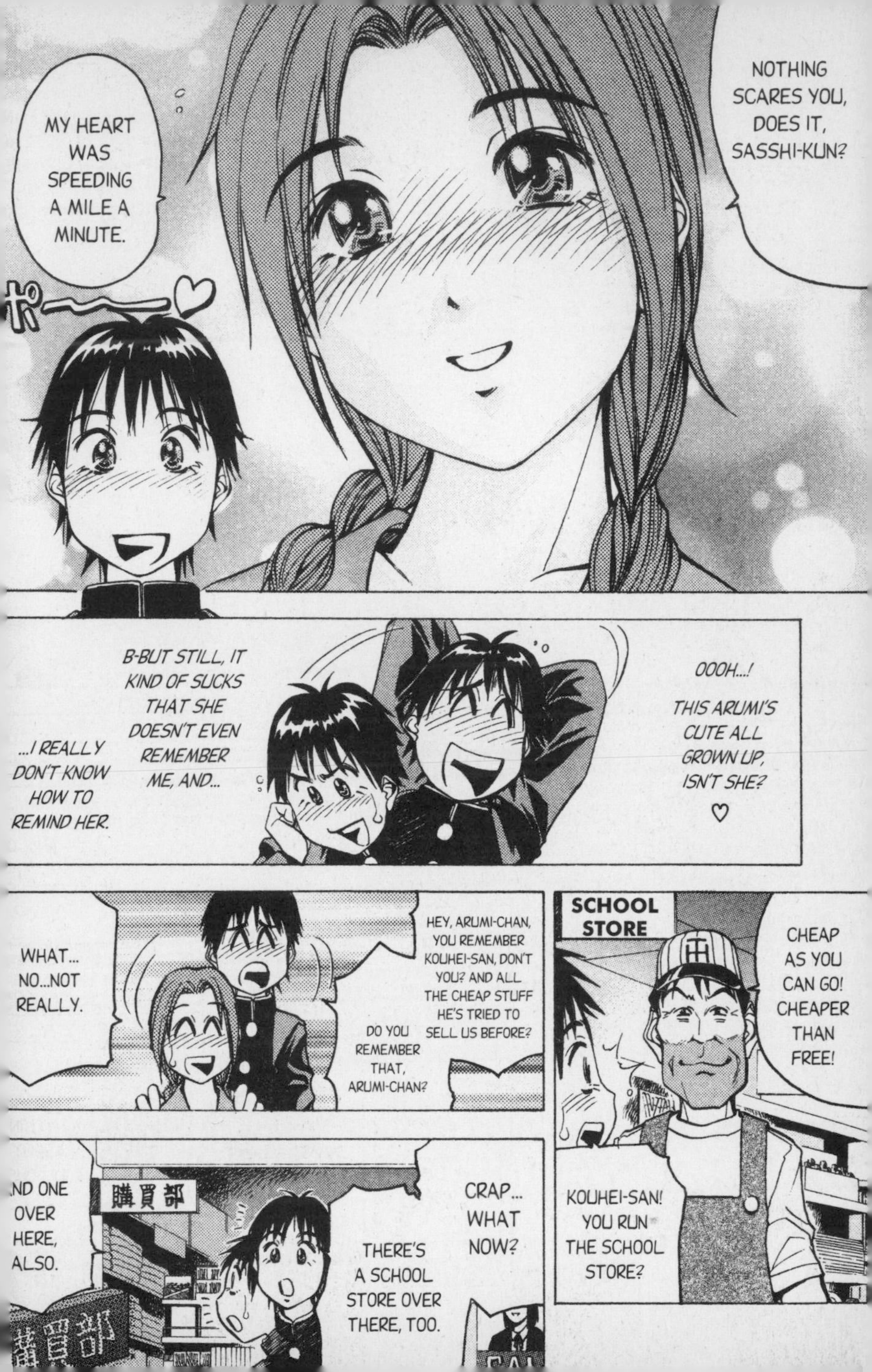

NOTHING SCARES YOU, DOES IT, SASSHI-KUN?
MY HEART WAS SPEEDING A MILE A MINUTE.
ポーーー♡
OOOH...!
THIS ARUMI'S CUTE ALL GROWN UP, ISN'T SHE? ♡
B-BUT STILL, IT KIND OF SUCKS THAT SHE DOESN'T EVEN REMEMBER ME, AND...
...I REALLY DON'T KNOW HOW TO REMIND HER.
SCHOOL STORE
CHEAP AS YOU CAN GO! CHEAPER THAN FREE!
KOUHEI-SAN! YOU RUN THE SCHOOL STORE?
HEY, ARUMI-CHAN, YOU REMEMBER KOUHEI-SAN, DON'T YOU? AND ALL THE CHEAP STUFF HE'S TRIED TO SELL US BEFORE?
DO YOU REMEMBER THAT, ARUMI-CHAN?
WHAT... NO...NOT REALLY.
CRAP... WHAT NOW?
購買部
THERE'S A SCHOOL STORE OVER THERE, TOO.
ND ONE OVER HERE, ALSO.

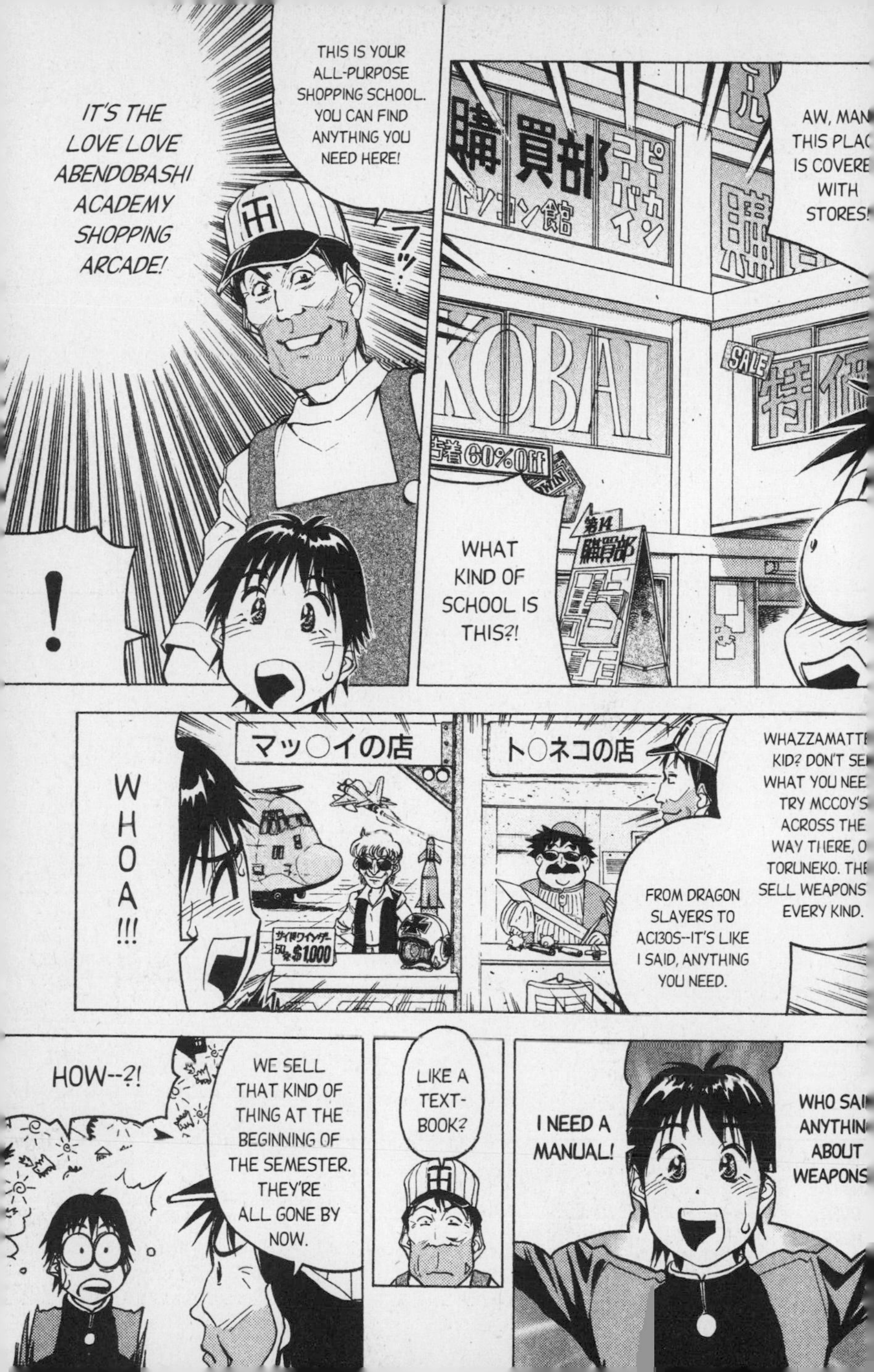

購買部
パソコン館
KOBAI
SALE
60%Off
第14
購買部
AW, MAN THIS PLAC IS COVERE WITH STORES!
WHAT KIND OF SCHOOL IS THIS?!
THIS IS YOUR ALL-PURPOSE SHOPPING SCHOOL. YOU CAN FIND ANYTHING YOU NEED HERE!
IT'S THE LOVE LOVE ABENDOBASHI ACADEMY SHOPPING ARCADE!
!
ト○ネコの店
マッ○イの店
WHAZZAMATTE KID? DON'T SE WHAT YOU NEE TRY MCCOY'S ACROSS THE WAY THERE, O TORUNEKO. THE SELL WEAPONS EVERY KIND.
FROM DRAGON SLAYERS TO AC130S--IT'S LIKE I SAID, ANYTHING YOU NEED.
$1,000
WHOA!!!
WHO SAI ANYTHIN ABOUT WEAPONS
I NEED A MANUAL!
LIKE A TEXT-BOOK?
WE SELL THAT KIND OF THING AT THE BEGINNING OF THE SEMESTER. THEY'RE ALL GONE BY NOW.
HOW--?!

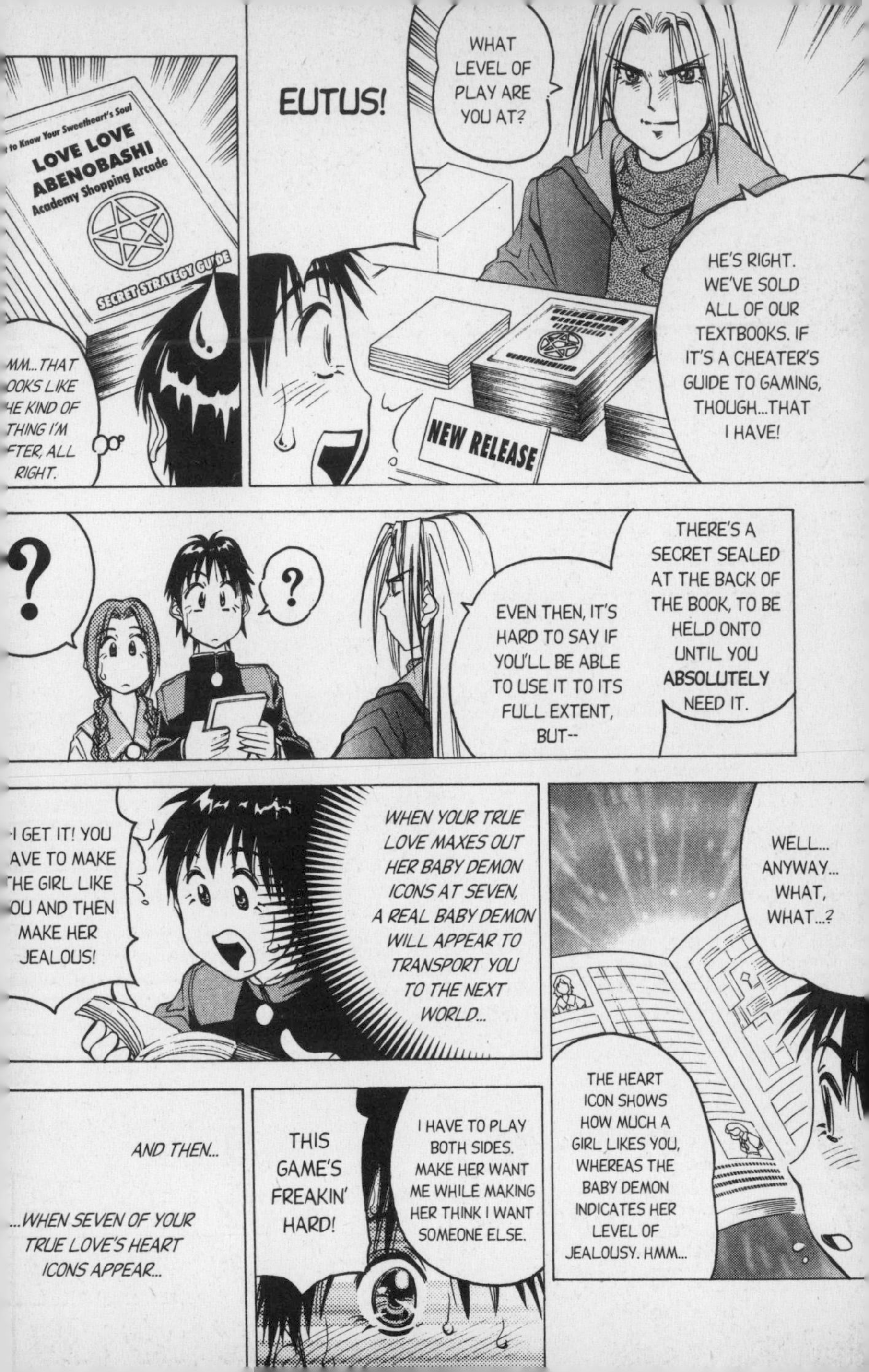
HE'S RIGHT. WE'VE SOLD ALL OF OUR TEXTBOOKS. IF IT'S A CHEATER'S GUIDE TO GAMING, THOUGH...THAT I HAVE!
WHAT LEVEL OF PLAY ARE YOU AT?
EUTUS!
NEW RELEASE
to Know Your Sweetheart's Soul
LOVE LOVE ABENOBASHI
Academy Shopping Arcade
SECRET STRATEGY GUIDE
MM...THAT OOKS LIKE HE KIND OF THING I'M FTER, ALL RIGHT.
THERE'S A SECRET SEALED AT THE BACK OF THE BOOK, TO BE HELD ONTO UNTIL YOU ABSOLUTELY NEED IT.
EVEN THEN, IT'S HARD TO SAY IF YOU'LL BE ABLE TO USE IT TO ITS FULL EXTENT, BUT--
?
?
WELL... ANYWAY... WHAT, WHAT...?
THE HEART ICON SHOWS HOW MUCH A GIRL LIKES YOU, WHEREAS THE BABY DEMON INDICATES HER LEVEL OF JEALOUSY. HMM...
WHEN YOUR TRUE LOVE MAXES OUT HER BABY DEMON ICONS AT SEVEN, A REAL BABY DEMON WILL APPEAR TO TRANSPORT YOU TO THE NEXT WORLD...
-I GET IT! YOU AVE TO MAKE THE GIRL LIKE OU AND THEN MAKE HER JEALOUS!
I HAVE TO PLAY BOTH SIDES. MAKE HER WANT ME WHILE MAKING HER THINK I WANT SOMEONE ELSE.
THIS GAME'S FREAKIN' HARD!
AND THEN...
...WHEN SEVEN OF YOUR TRUE LOVE'S HEART ICONS APPEAR...

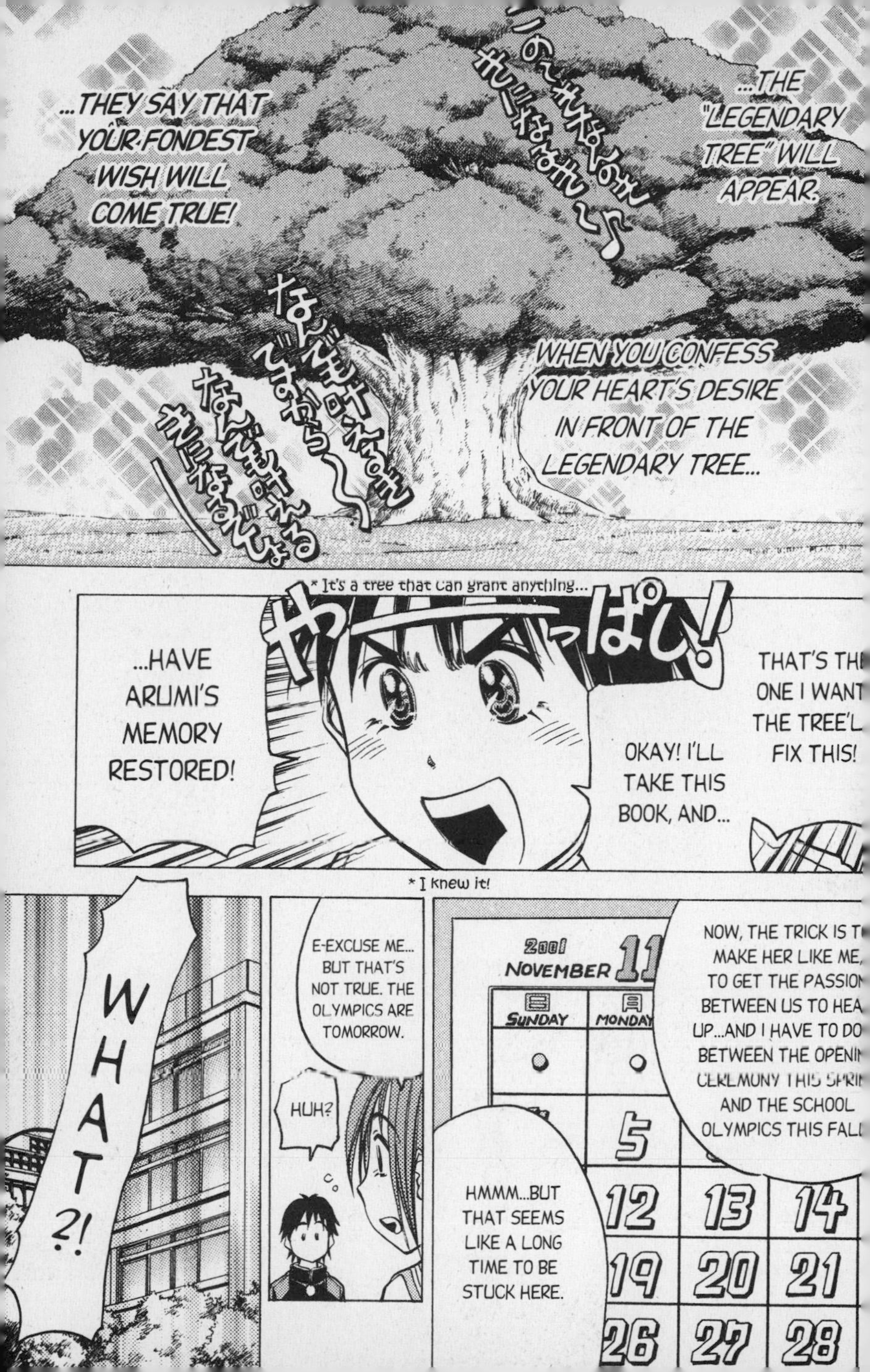
..."THE "LEGENDARY TREE" WILL APPEAR.
この木なんの木 木になる木～♪
...THEY SAY THAT YOUR FONDEST WISH WILL COME TRUE!
WHEN YOU CONFESS YOUR HEART'S DESIRE IN FRONT OF THE LEGENDARY TREE...
なんでも叶える木ですから～
なんでも叶える木になるでしょ
* It's a tree that can grant anything...
THAT'S TH ONE I WANT THE TREE'L FIX THIS!
OKAY! I'LL TAKE THIS BOOK, AND...
やっぱし!
...HAVE ARUMI'S MEMORY RESTORED!
* I knew it!
2001 NOVEMBER 11
SUNDAY MONDAY
5 12 13 14 19 20 21 26 27 28
NOW, THE TRICK IS T MAKE HER LIKE ME, TO GET THE PASSION BETWEEN US TO HEA UP...AND I HAVE TO DO BETWEEN THE OPENIN CEREMONY THIS SPRIN AND THE SCHOOL OLYMPICS THIS FALL
HMMM...BUT THAT SEEMS LIKE A LONG TIME TO BE STUCK HERE.
E-EXCUSE ME... BUT THAT'S NOT TRUE. THE OLYMPICS ARE TOMORROW.
HUH?
WHAT?!

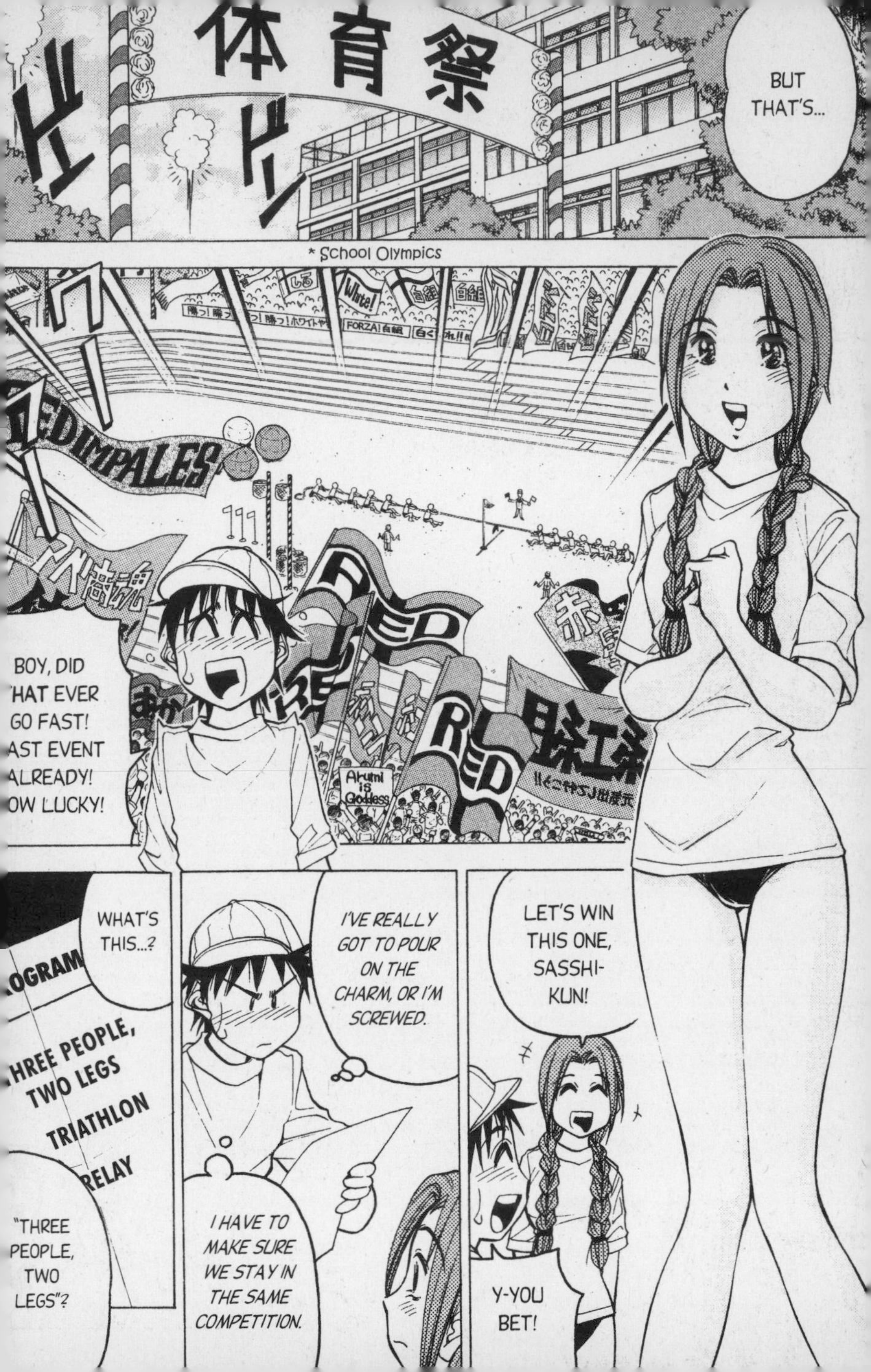
BUT THAT'S...
体育祭
ドドン
* School Olympics
BOY, DID 'HAT EVER GO FAST! AST EVENT ALREADY! OW LUCKY!
Arumi is Goddess
RED
LET'S WIN THIS ONE, SASSHI-KUN!
Y-YOU BET!
I'VE REALLY GOT TO POUR ON THE CHARM, OR I'M SCREWED.
I HAVE TO MAKE SURE WE STAY IN THE SAME COMPETITION.
WHAT'S THIS...?
ROGRAM
THREE PEOPLE, TWO LEGS
TRIATHLON
RELAY
"THREE PEOPLE, TWO LEGS"?

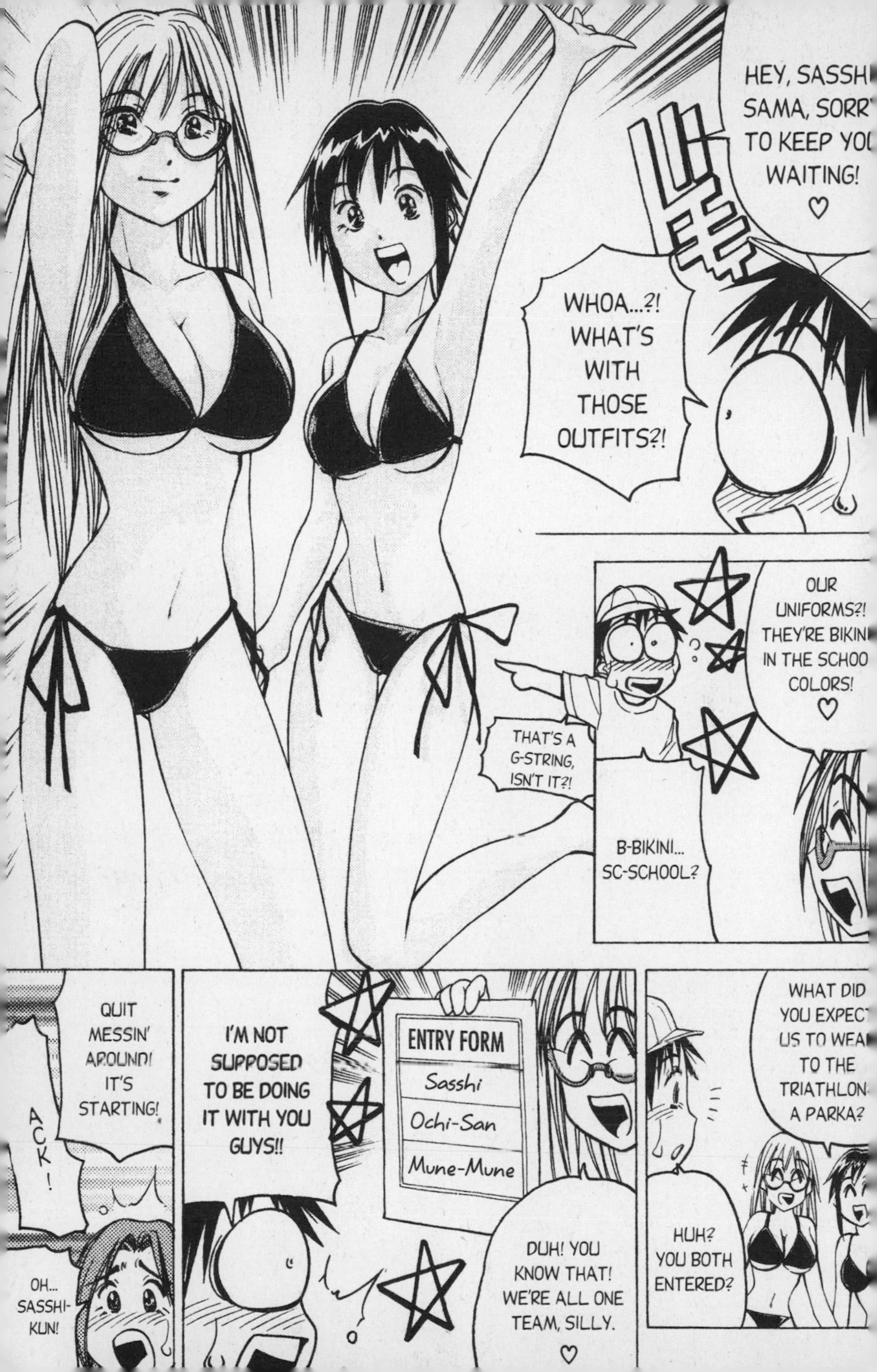
HEY, SASSHI SAMA, SORR TO KEEP YOU WAITING! ♡
WHOA...?! WHAT'S WITH THOSE OUTFITS?!
OUR UNIFORMS?! THEY'RE BIKINI IN THE SCHOO COLORS! ♡
THAT'S A G-STRING, ISN'T IT?!
B-BIKINI... SC-SCHOOL?
WHAT DID YOU EXPECT US TO WEA TO THE TRIATHLON A PARKA?
HUH? YOU BOTH ENTERED?
ENTRY FORM
Sasshi
Ochi-San
Mune-Mune
DUH! YOU KNOW THAT! WE'RE ALL ONE TEAM, SILLY. ♡
I'M NOT SUPPOSED TO BE DOING IT WITH YOU GUYS!!
QUIT MESSIN' AROUND! IT'S STARTING!
ACK!
OH... SASSHI-KUN!

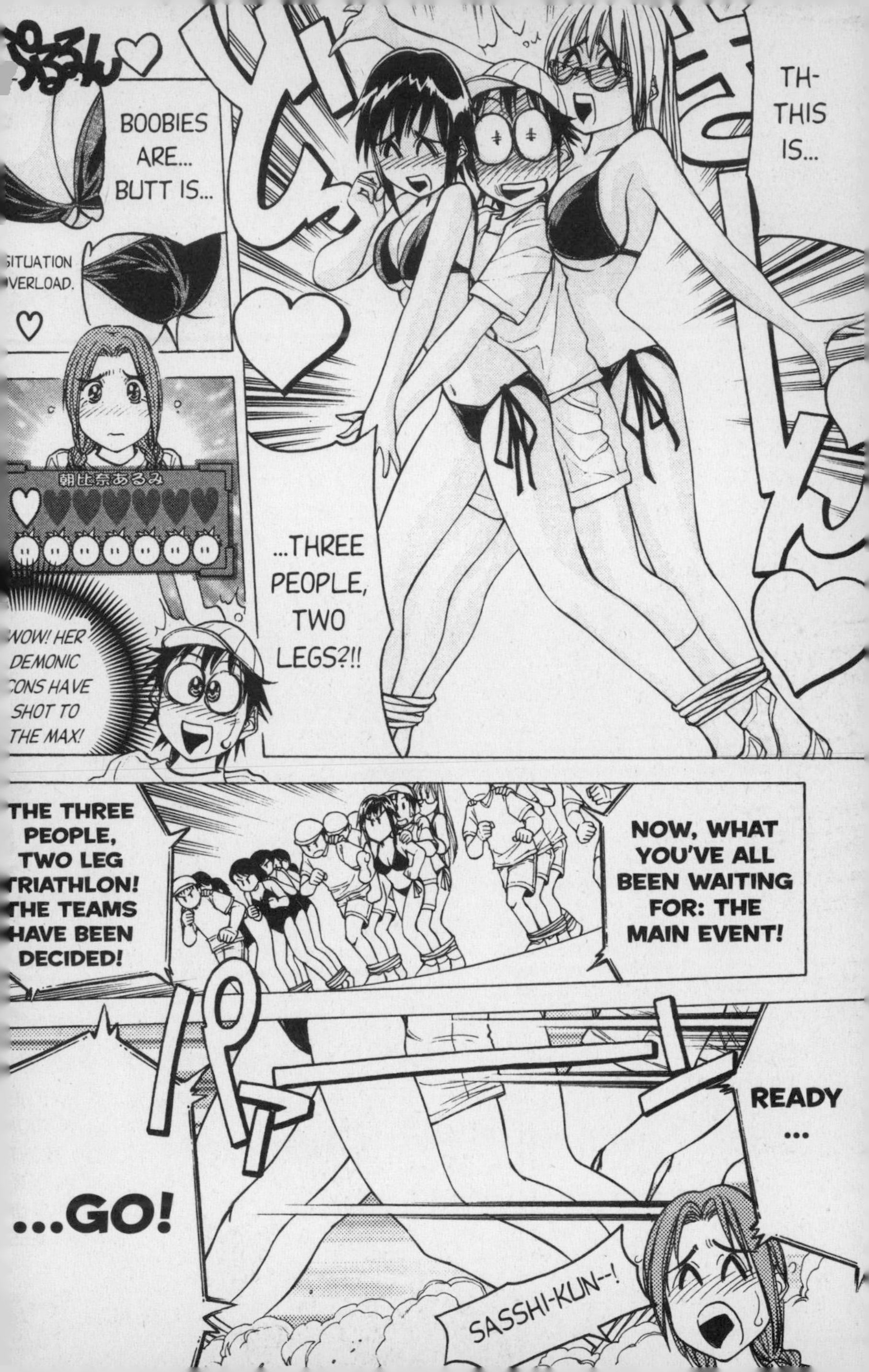
TH- THIS IS...
...THREE PEOPLE, TWO LEGS?!!
ぷるるん♡
BOOBIES ARE... BUTT IS...
SITUATION OVERLOAD.
朝比奈あるみ
NOW! HER DEMONIC CONS HAVE SHOT TO THE MAX!
NOW, WHAT YOU'VE ALL BEEN WAITING FOR: THE MAIN EVENT!
THE THREE PEOPLE, TWO LEG TRIATHLON! THE TEAMS HAVE BEEN DECIDED!
READY...
...GO!
SASSHI-KUN--!

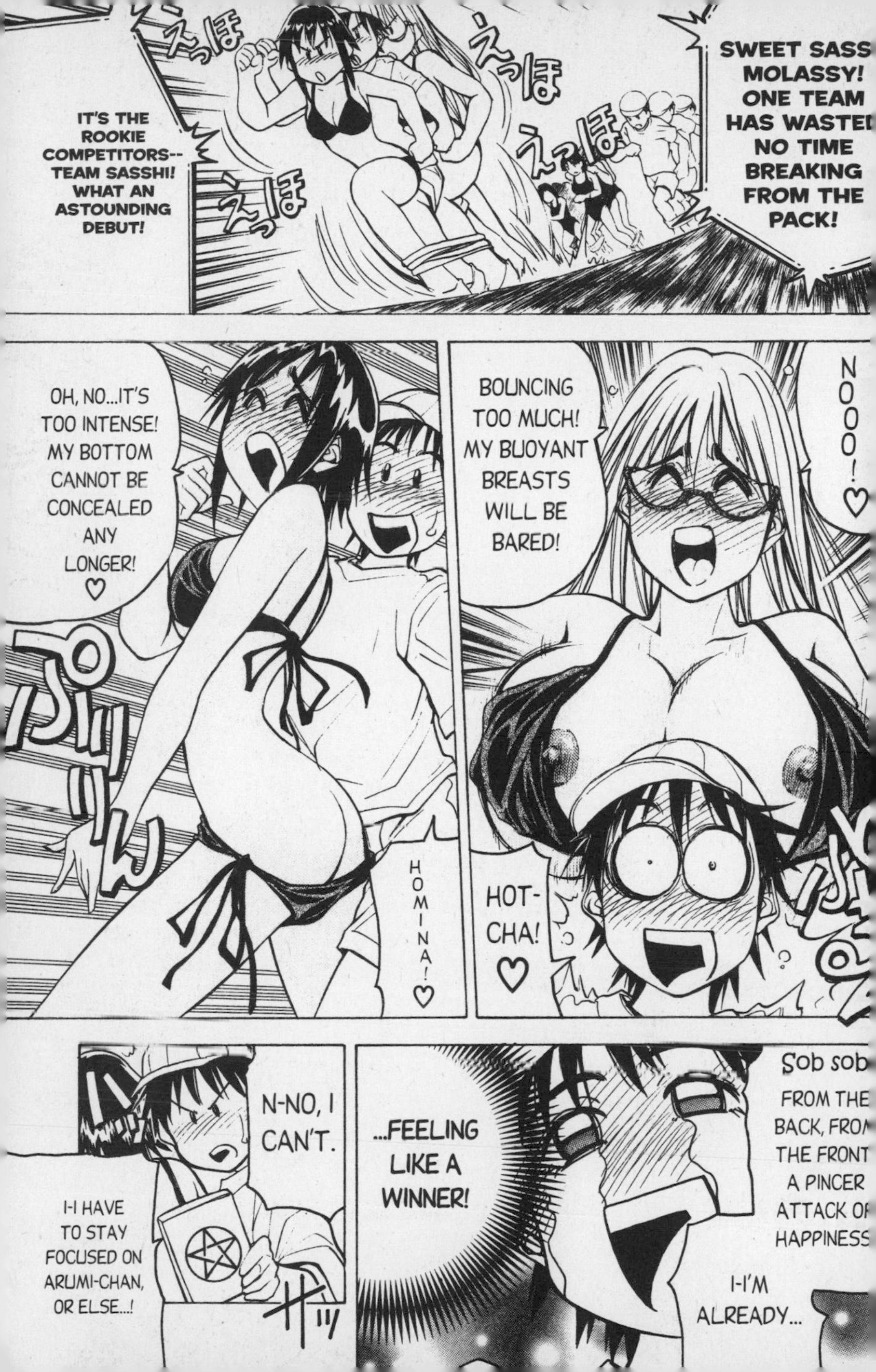
SWEET SASS MOLASSY! ONE TEAM HAS WASTED NO TIME BREAKING FROM THE PACK!
えっほ
えっほ
えっほ
えっほ
IT'S THE ROOKIE COMPETITORS--TEAM SASSHI! WHAT AN ASTOUNDING DEBUT!
NOOO! ♡
BOUNCING TOO MUCH! MY BUOYANT BREASTS WILL BE BARED!
HOT-CHA! ♡
OH, NO...IT'S TOO INTENSE! MY BOTTOM CANNOT BE CONCEALED ANY LONGER! ♡
HOMINA! ♡
Sob sob
FROM THE BACK, FROM THE FRONT A PINCER ATTACK OF HAPPINESS
I-I'M ALREADY...
...FEELING LIKE A WINNER!
N-NO, I CAN'T.
I-I HAVE TO STAY FOCUSED ON ARUMI-CHAN, OR ELSE...!

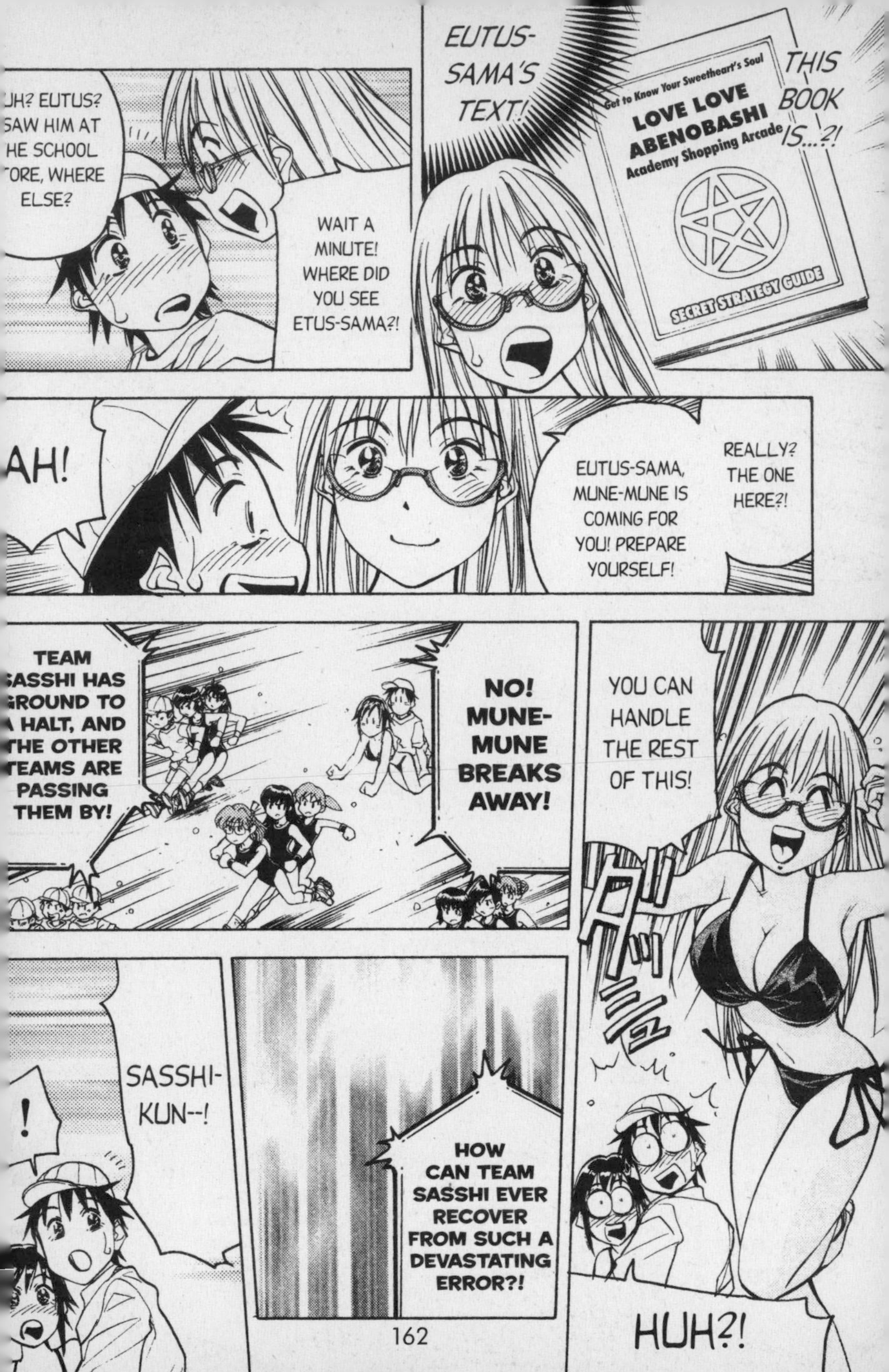
THIS BOOK IS...?!
EUTUS-SAMA'S TEXT!
Get to Know Your Sweetheart's Soul
LOVE LOVE ABENOBASHI
Academy Shopping Arcade
SECRET STRATEGY GUIDE
WAIT A MINUTE! WHERE DID YOU SEE ETUS-SAMA?!
UH? EUTUS? SAW HIM AT HE SCHOOL TORE, WHERE ELSE?
REALLY? THE ONE HERE?!
EUTUS-SAMA, MUNE-MUNE IS COMING FOR YOU! PREPARE YOURSELF!
AH!
YOU CAN HANDLE THE REST OF THIS!
HUH?!
NO! MUNE-MUNE BREAKS AWAY!
TEAM SASSHI HAS GROUND TO A HALT, AND THE OTHER TEAMS ARE PASSING THEM BY!
HOW CAN TEAM SASSHI EVER RECOVER FROM SUCH A DEVASTATING ERROR?!
SASSHI-KUN--!
!

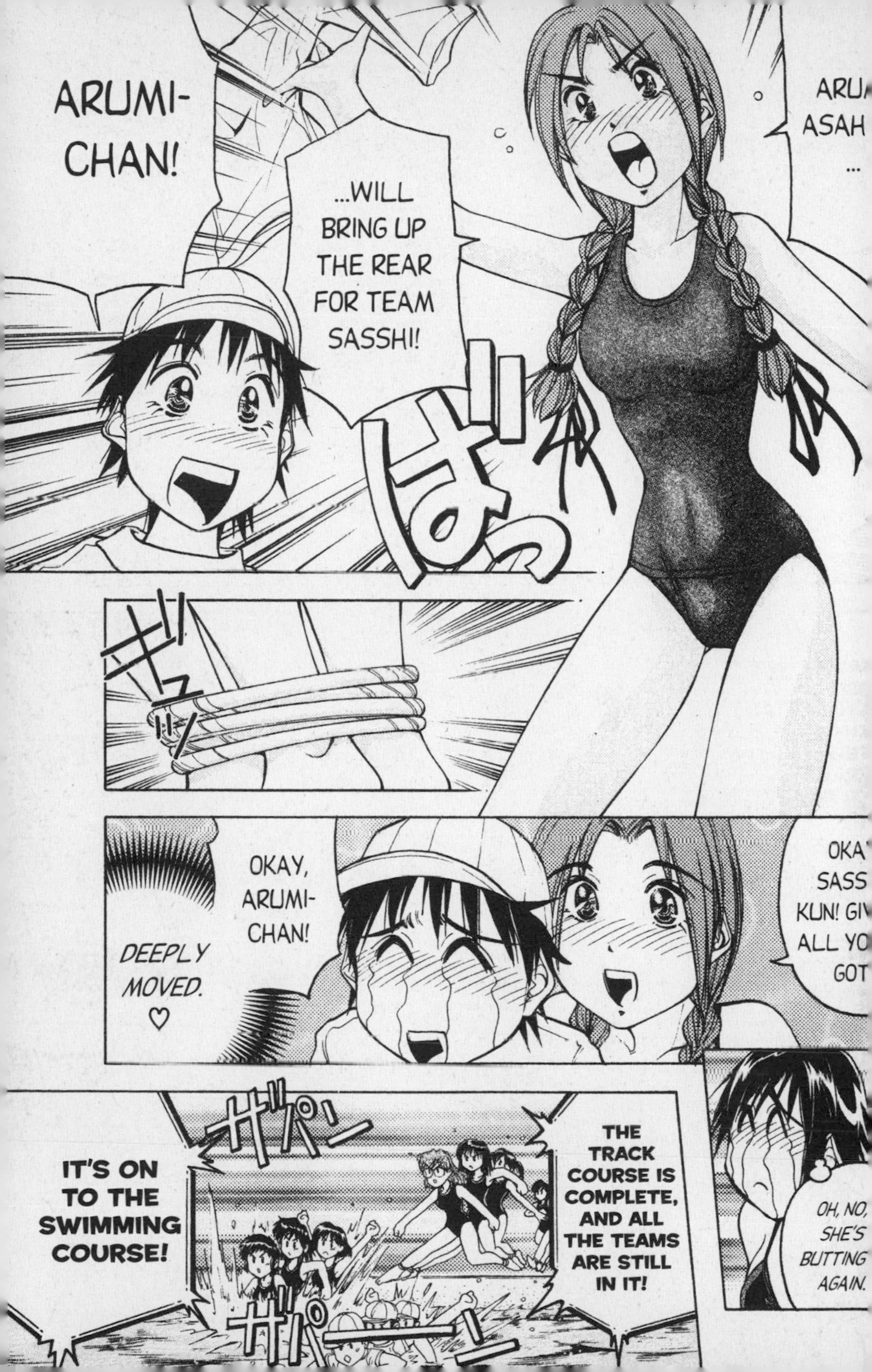
ARU
ASAH
...
...WILL BRING UP THE REAR FOR TEAM SASSHI!
ARUMI-CHAN!
ぱっ
ギュッ
OKA
SASS
KUN! GIV
ALL YO
GOT
OKAY, ARUMI-CHAN!
DEEPLY MOVED. ♡
OH, NO, SHE'S BUTTING AGAIN.
THE TRACK COURSE IS COMPLETE, AND ALL THE TEAMS ARE STILL IN IT!
ザパーン
IT'S ON TO THE SWIMMING COURSE!
ザパーー

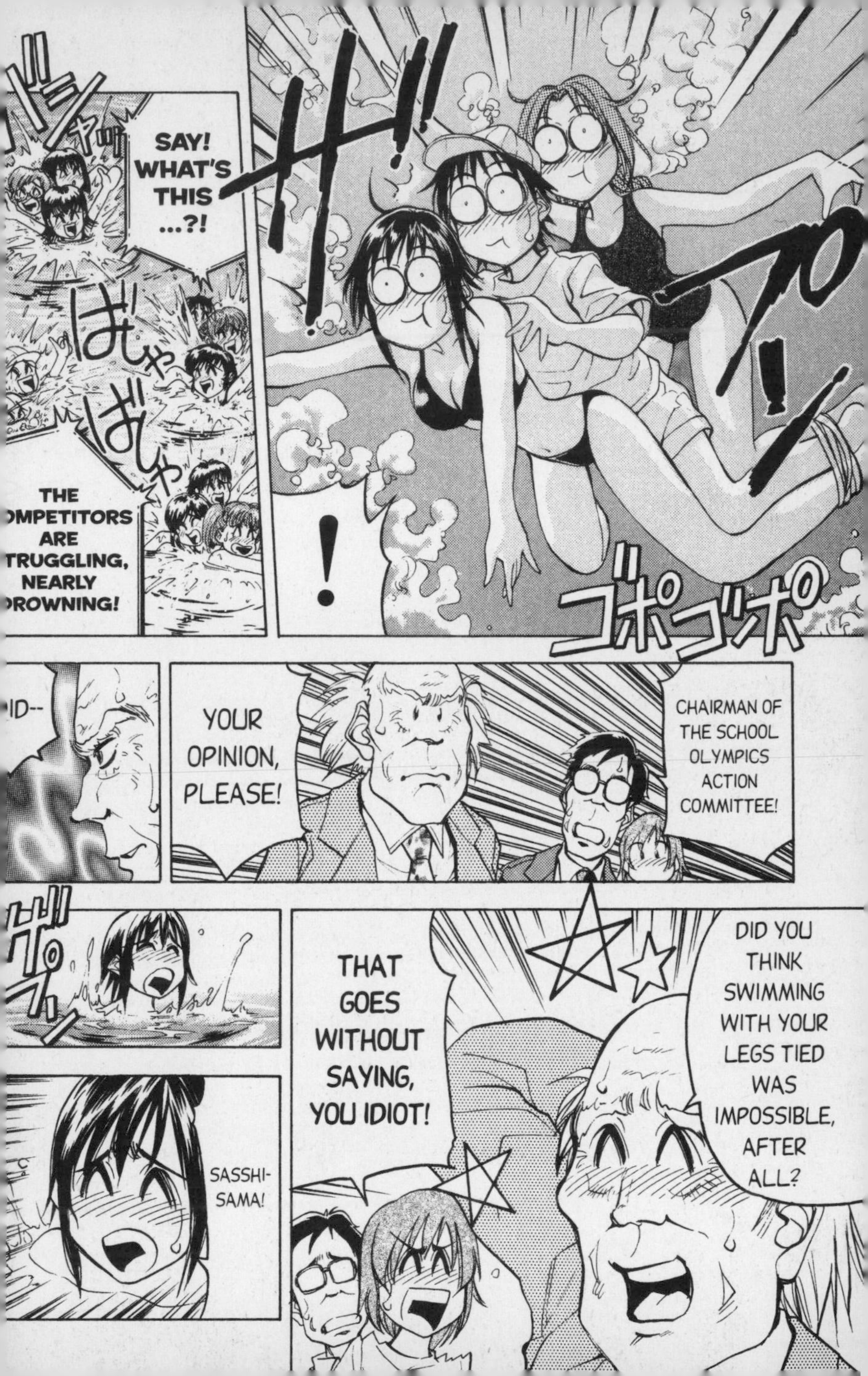
ゴポゴポ
SAY! WHAT'S THIS ...?!
ばしゃばしゃ
THE OMPETITORS ARE TRUGGLING, NEARLY ROWNING!
CHAIRMAN OF THE SCHOOL OLYMPICS ACTION COMMITTEE!
YOUR OPINION, PLEASE!
ID--
DID YOU THINK SWIMMING WITH YOUR LEGS TIED WAS IMPOSSIBLE, AFTER ALL?
THAT GOES WITHOUT SAYING, YOU IDIOT!
SASSHI-SAMA!

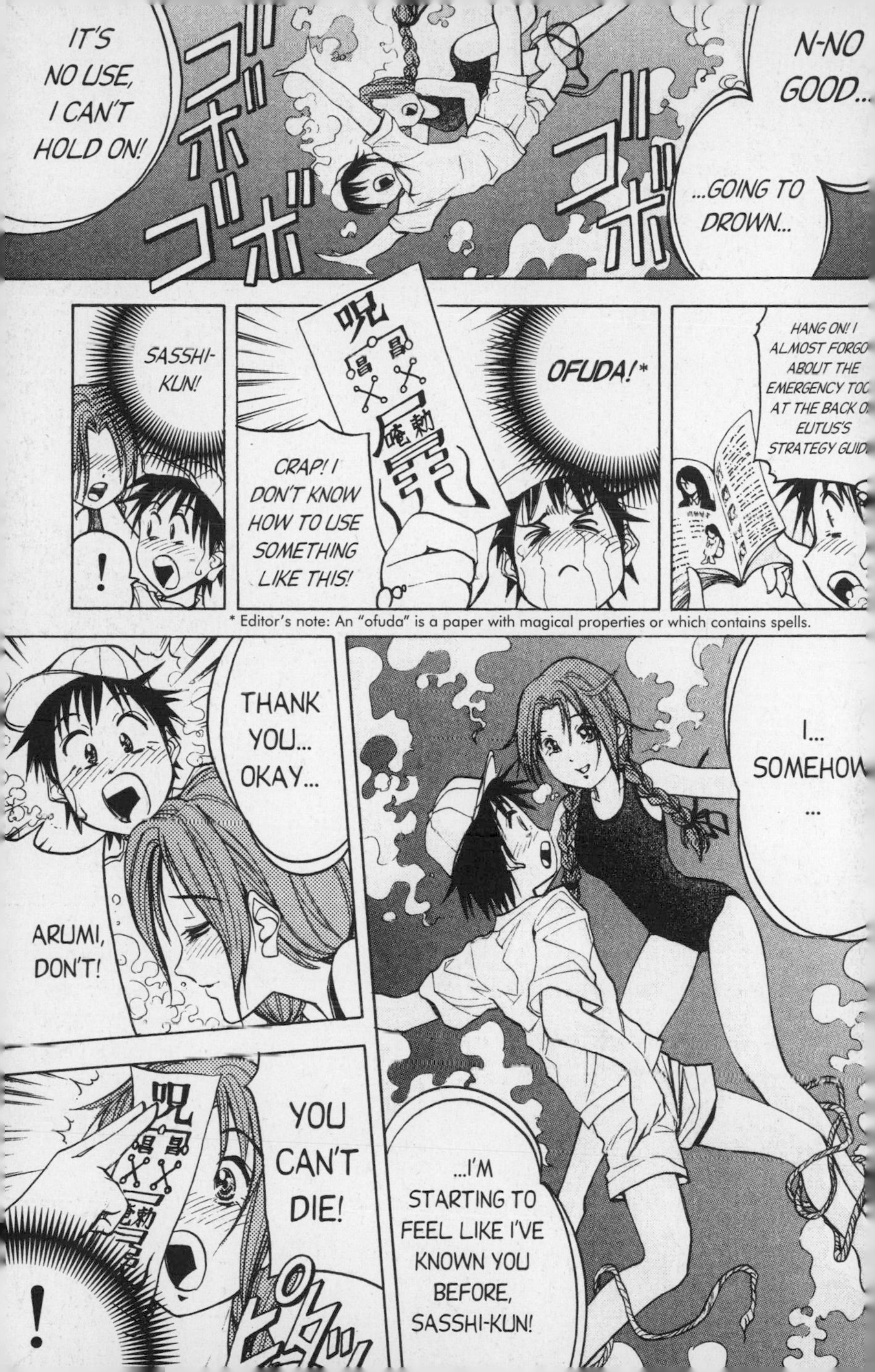
ゴボ
N-NO GOOD...
...GOING TO DROWN...
ゴボゴボ
IT'S NO USE, I CAN'T HOLD ON!
HANG ON! I ALMOST FORGO ABOUT THE EMERGENCY TOO AT THE BACK O EUTUS'S STRATEGY GUID
OFUDA!*
CRAP! I DON'T KNOW HOW TO USE SOMETHING LIKE THIS!
SASSHI-KUN!
!
I... SOMEHOW ...
...I'M STARTING TO FEEL LIKE I'VE KNOWN YOU BEFORE, SASSHI-KUN!
THANK YOU... OKAY...
ARUMI, DON'T!
YOU CAN'T DIE!
!

* Editor's note: An "ofuda" is a paper with magical properties or which contains spells.

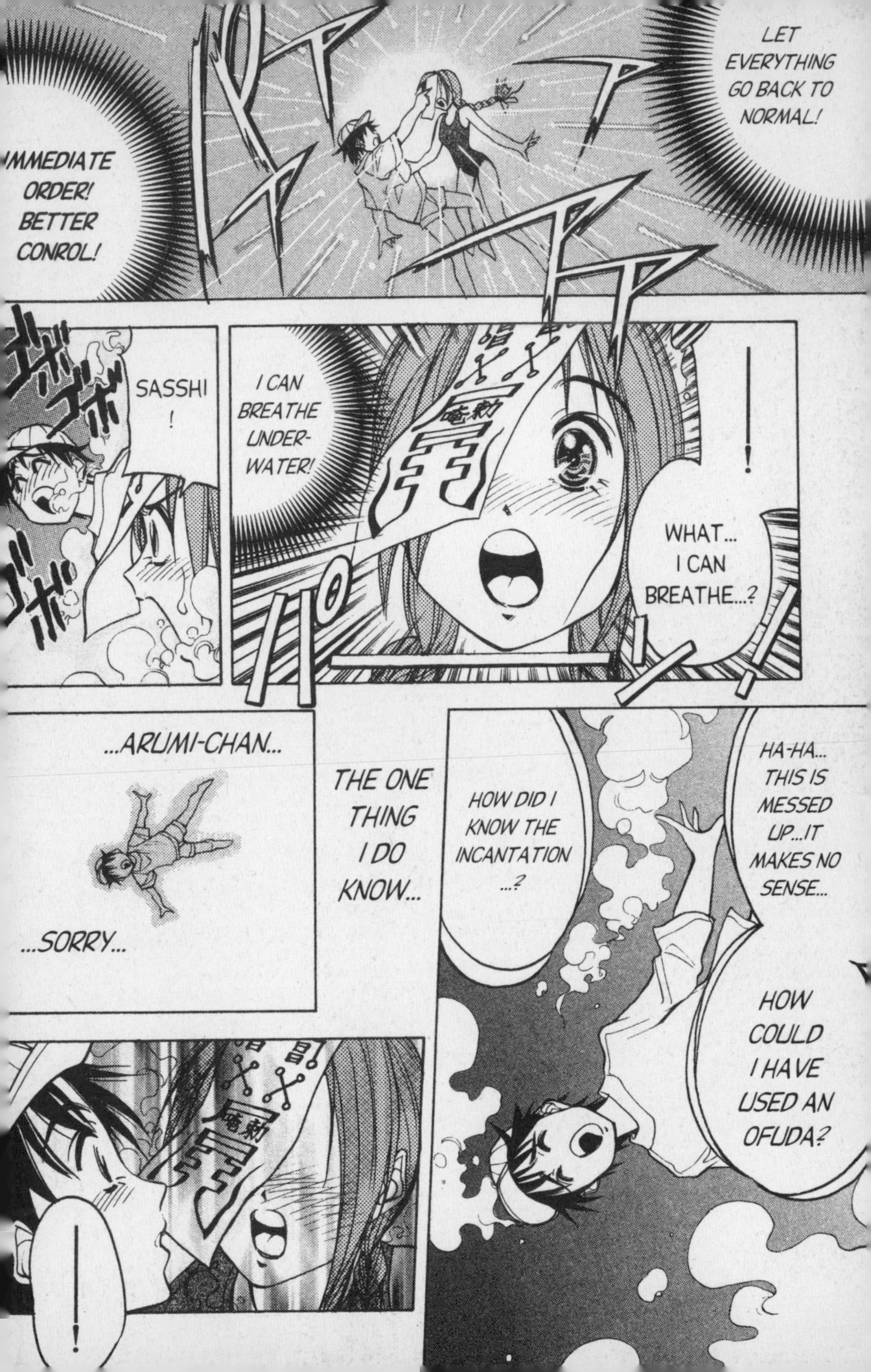
LET EVERYTHING GO BACK TO NORMAL!
IMMEDIATE ORDER! BETTER CONROL!
!
WHAT... I CAN BREATHE...?
I CAN BREATHE UNDER-WATER!
SASSHI!
HA-HA... THIS IS MESSED UP...IT MAKES NO SENSE...
HOW COULD I HAVE USED AN OFUDA?
HOW DID I KNOW THE INCANTATION ...?
THE ONE THING I DO KNOW...
...ARUMI-CHAN...
...SORRY...
!

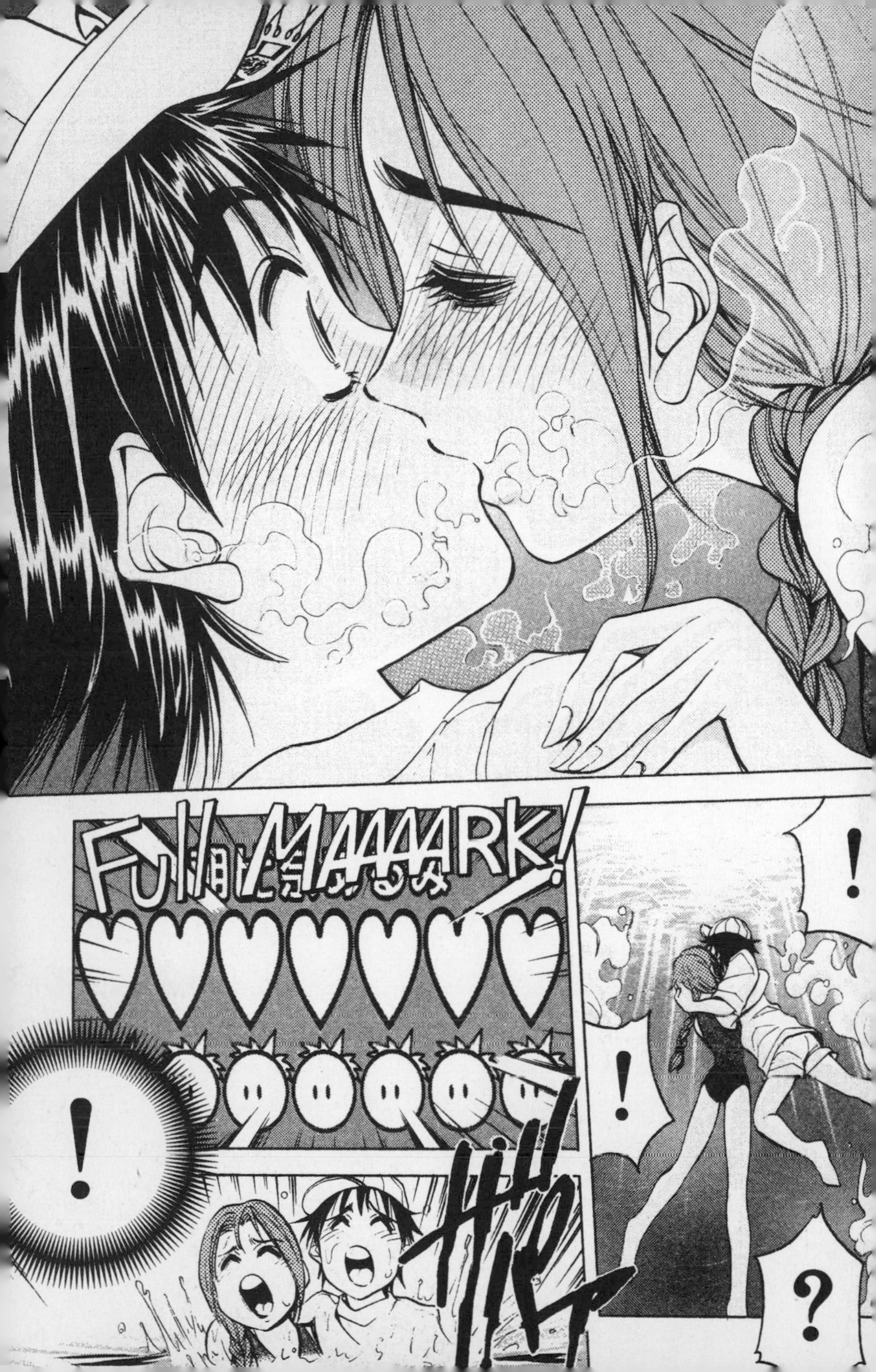
!
!
?
FULL MAAAARK!
!

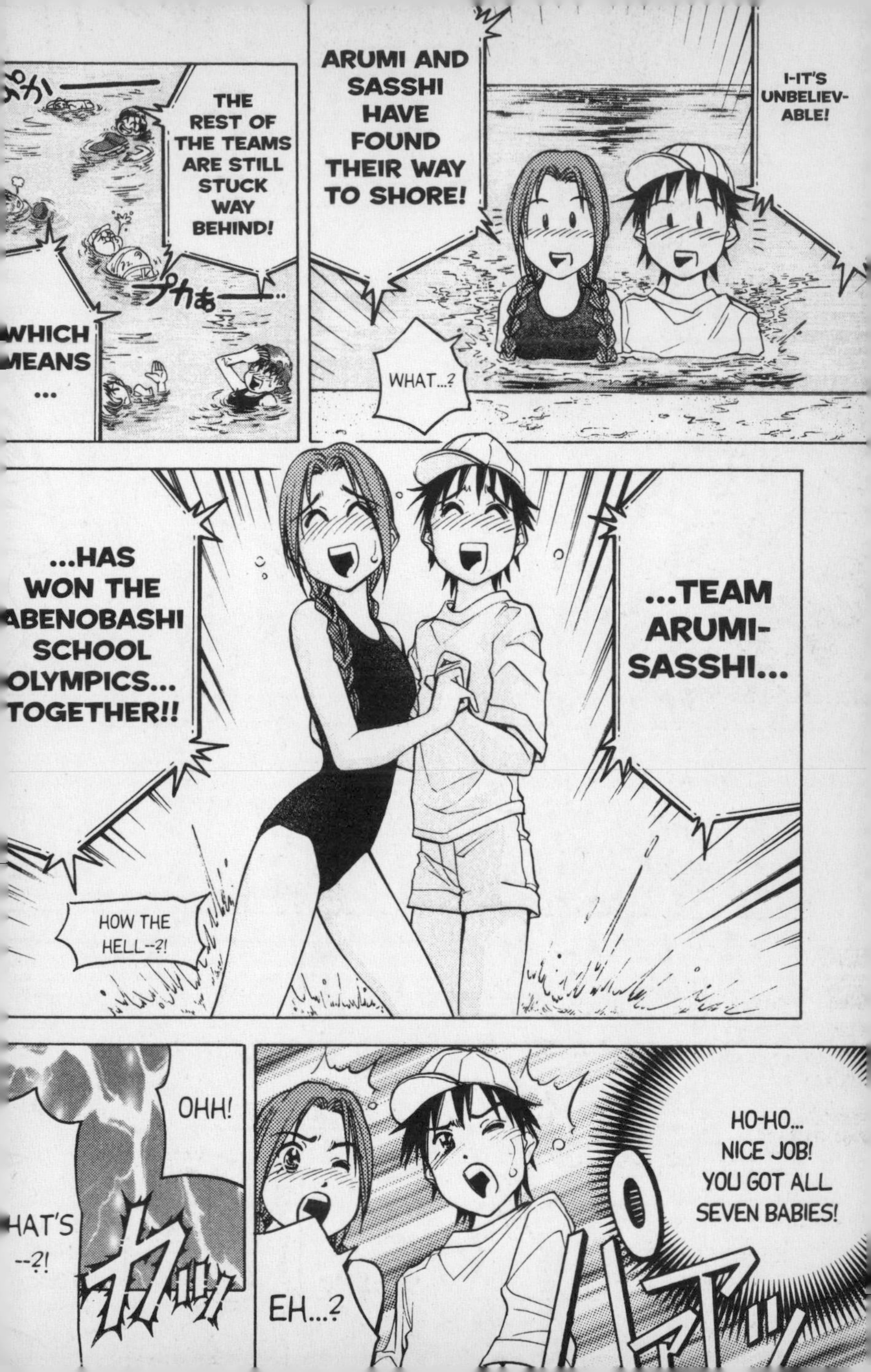
I-IT'S UNBELIEVABLE!
ARUMI AND SASSHI HAVE FOUND THEIR WAY TO SHORE!
WHAT...?
THE REST OF THE TEAMS ARE STILL STUCK WAY BEHIND!
WHICH MEANS ...
...TEAM ARUMI-SASSHI...
...HAS WON THE ABENOBASHI SCHOOL OLYMPICS... TOGETHER!!
HOW THE HELL--?!
HO-HO... NICE JOB! YOU GOT ALL SEVEN BABIES!
EH...?
OHH!
HAT'S --?!

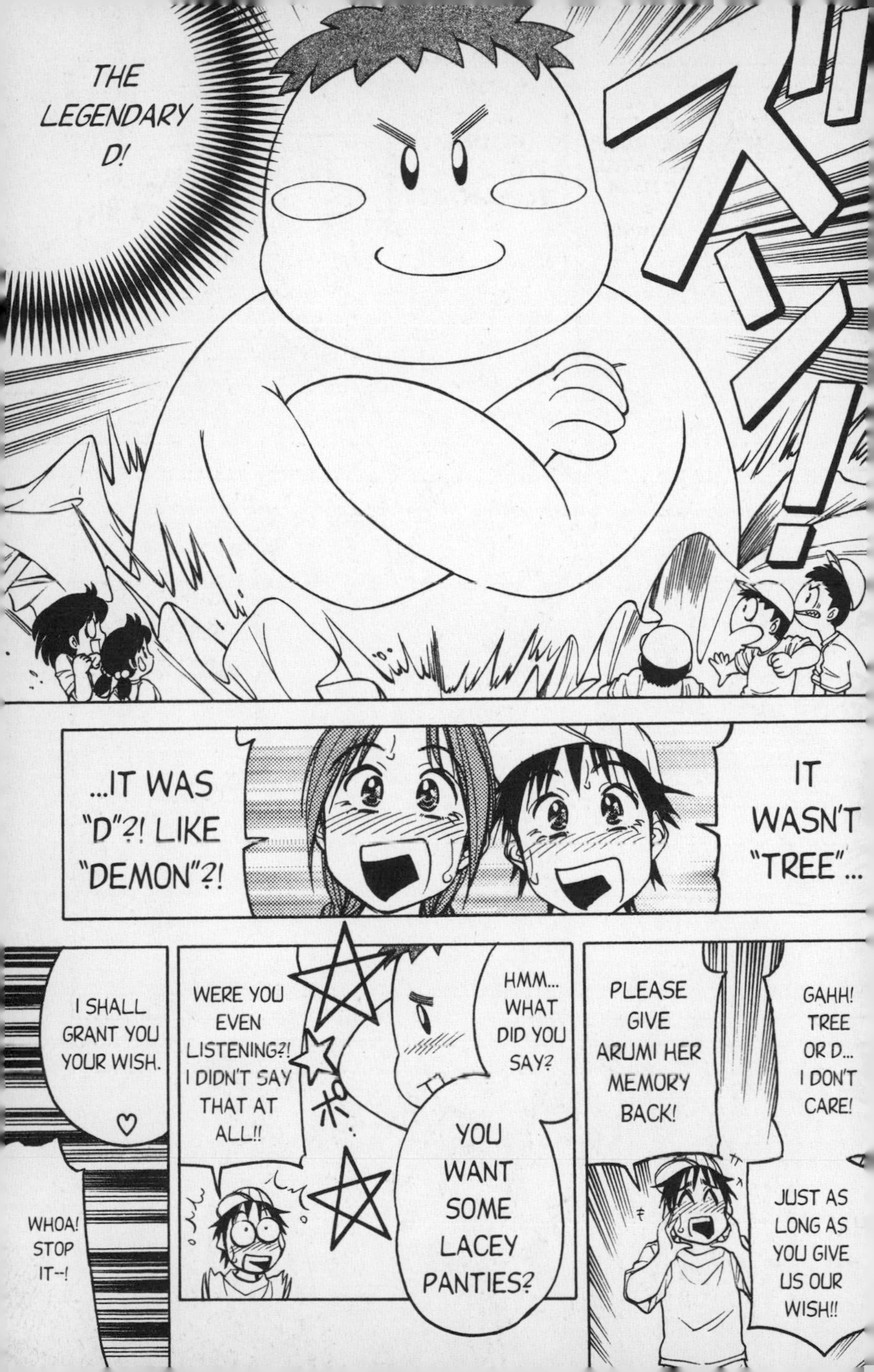
THE LEGENDARY D!
IT WASN'T "TREE"...
...IT WAS "D"?! LIKE "DEMON"?!
GAHH! TREE OR D... I DON'T CARE!
PLEASE GIVE ARUMI HER MEMORY BACK!
JUST AS LONG AS YOU GIVE US OUR WISH!!
HMM... WHAT DID YOU SAY?
YOU WANT SOME LACEY PANTIES?
WERE YOU EVEN LISTENING?! I DIDN'T SAY THAT AT ALL!!
I SHALL GRANT YOU YOUR WISH. ♡
WHOA! STOP IT--!

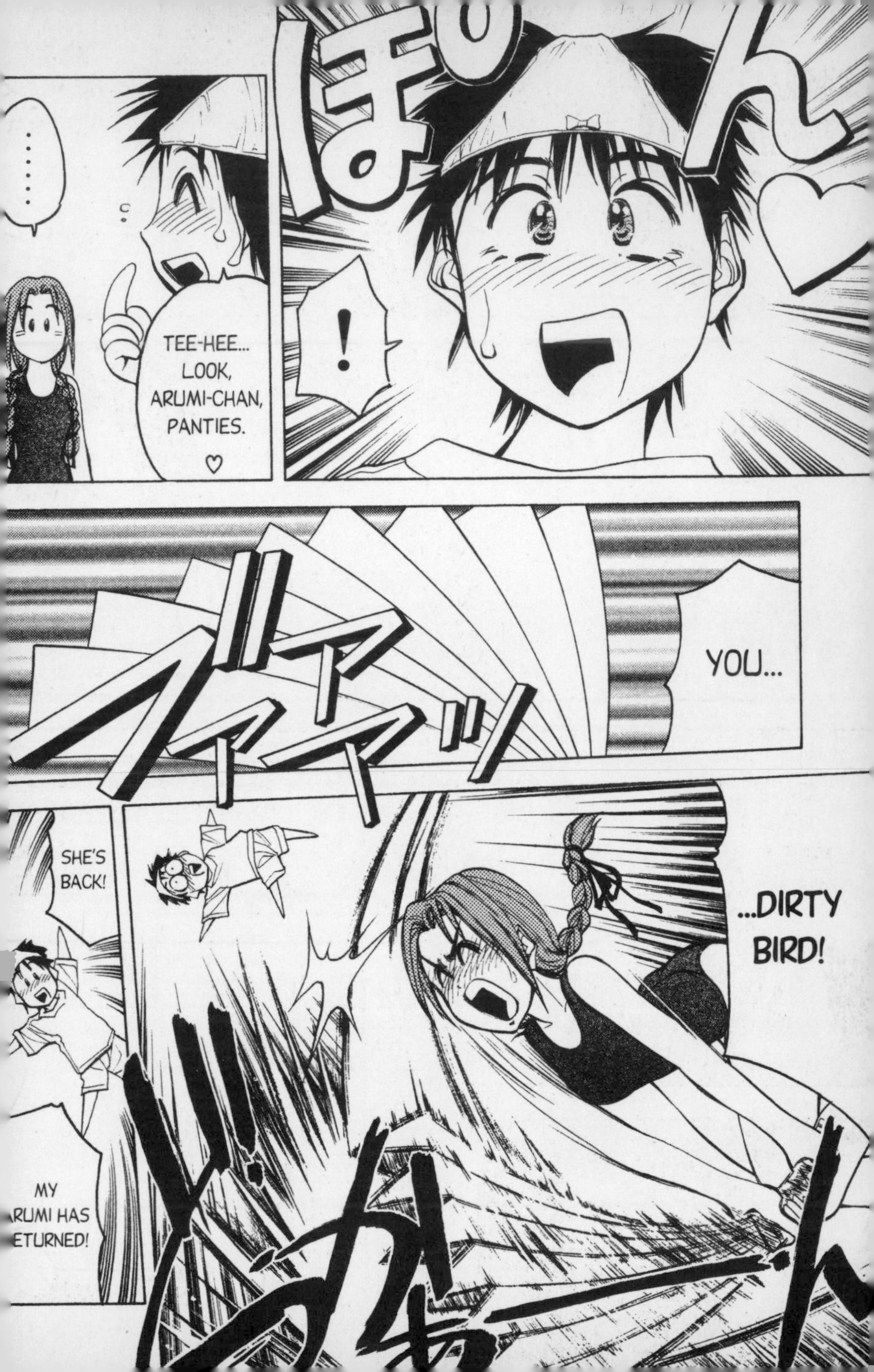
!
TEE-HEE... LOOK, ARUMI-CHAN, PANTIES. ♡
......
YOU...
...DIRTY BIRD!
SHE'S BACK!
MY ARUMI HAS ETURNED!

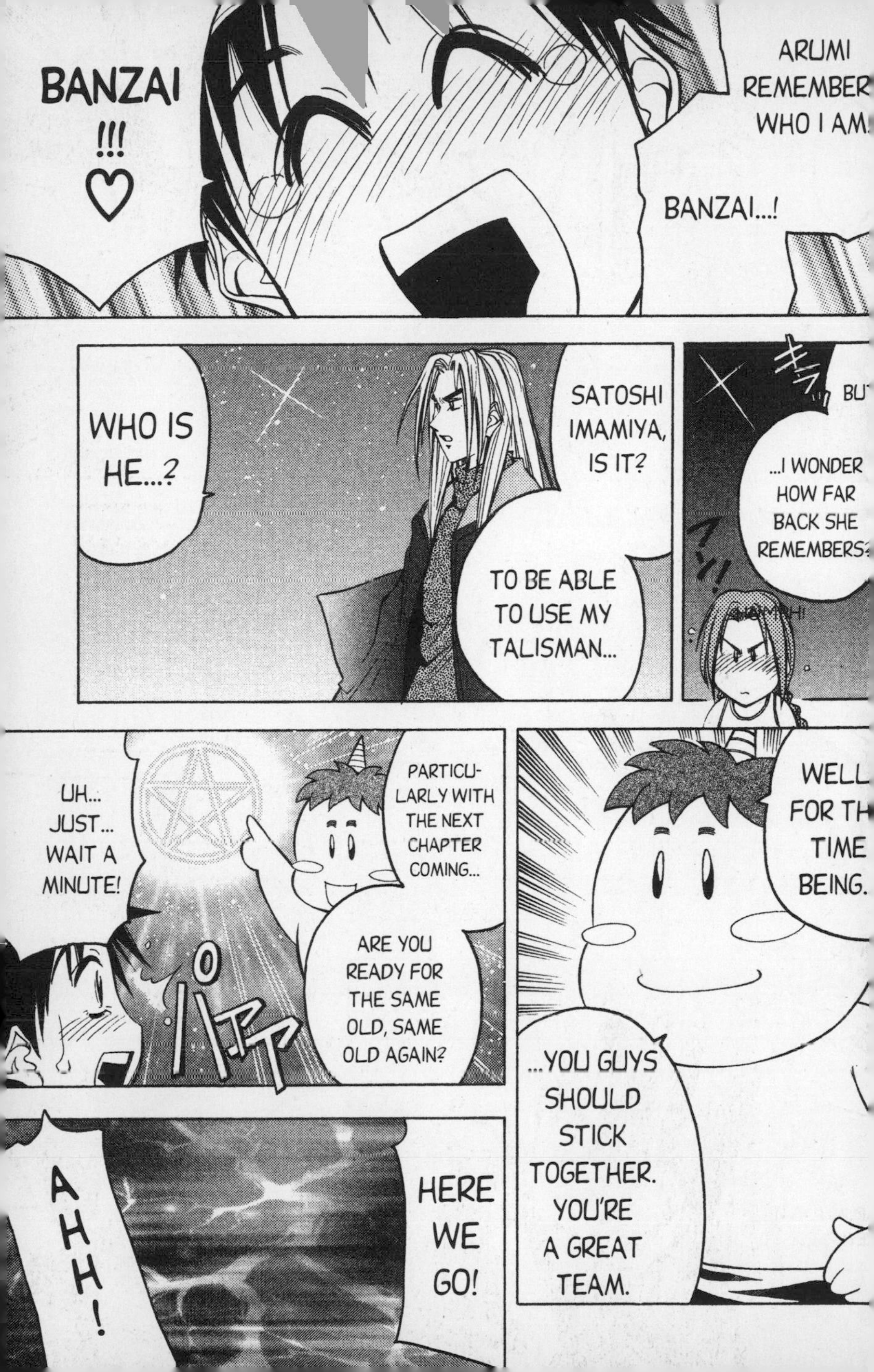
ARUMI REMEMBER WHO I AM!
BANZAI...!
BANZAI !!! ♡
BU
...I WONDER HOW FAR BACK SHE REMEMBERS?
SATOSHI IMAMIYA, IS IT?
TO BE ABLE TO USE MY TALISMAN...
WHO IS HE...?
WELL FOR TH TIME BEING.
...YOU GUYS SHOULD STICK TOGETHER. YOU'RE A GREAT TEAM.
PARTICU-LARLY WITH THE NEXT CHAPTER COMING...
ARE YOU READY FOR THE SAME OLD, SAME OLD AGAIN?
UH... JUST... WAIT A MINUTE!
HERE WE GO!
AHH!

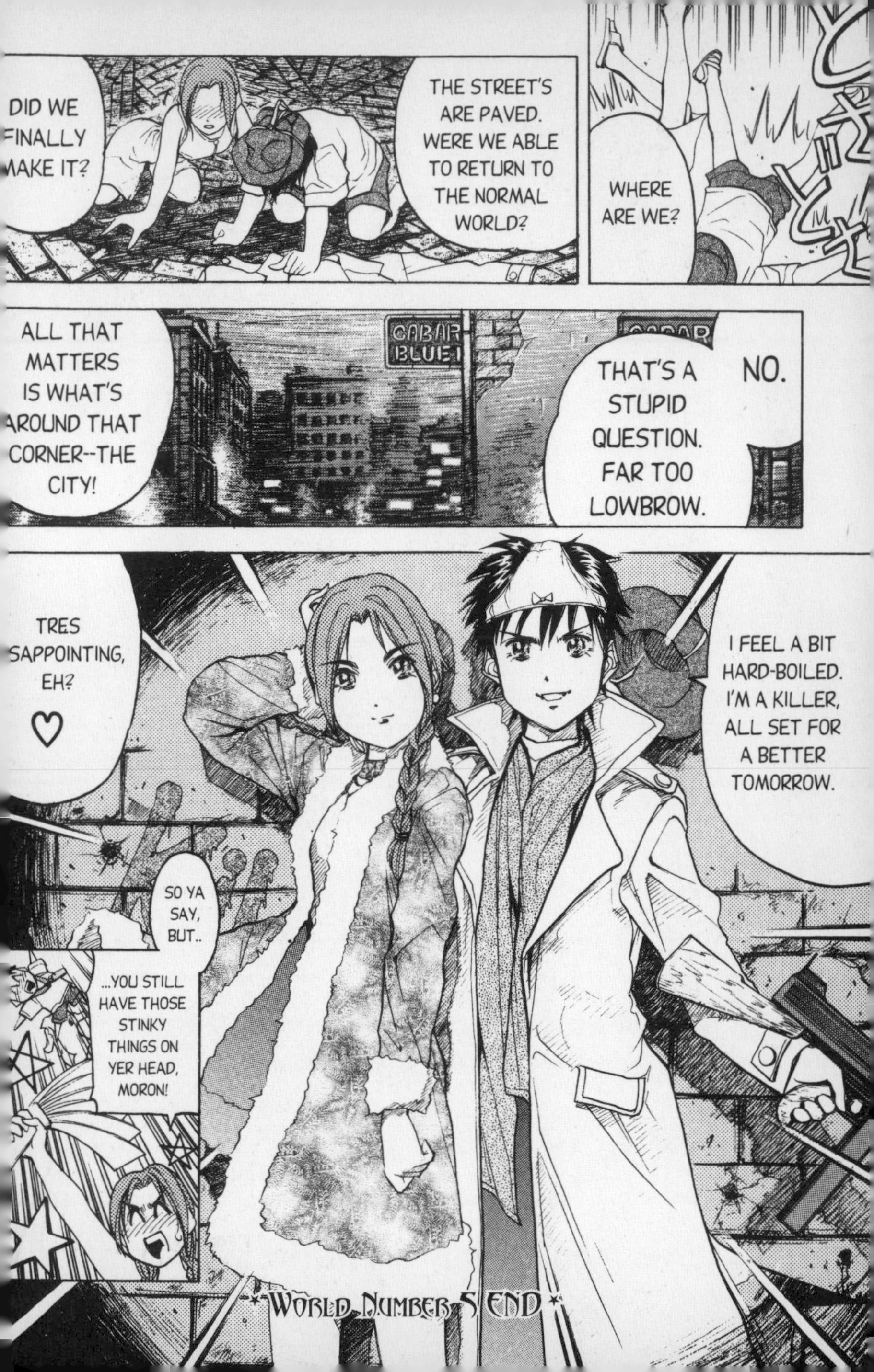
WHERE ARE WE?
THE STREET'S ARE PAVED. WERE WE ABLE TO RETURN TO THE NORMAL WORLD?
DID WE FINALLY MAKE IT?
NO.
THAT'S A STUPID QUESTION. FAR TOO LOWBROW.
CABAR BLUE
ALL THAT MATTERS IS WHAT'S AROUND THAT CORNER--THE CITY!
I FEEL A BIT HARD-BOILED. I'M A KILLER, ALL SET FOR A BETTER TOMORROW.
TRES SAPPOINTING, EH? ♡
SO YA SAY, BUT..
...YOU STILL HAVE THOSE STINKY THINGS ON YER HEAD, MORON!
WORLD NUMBER 5 END

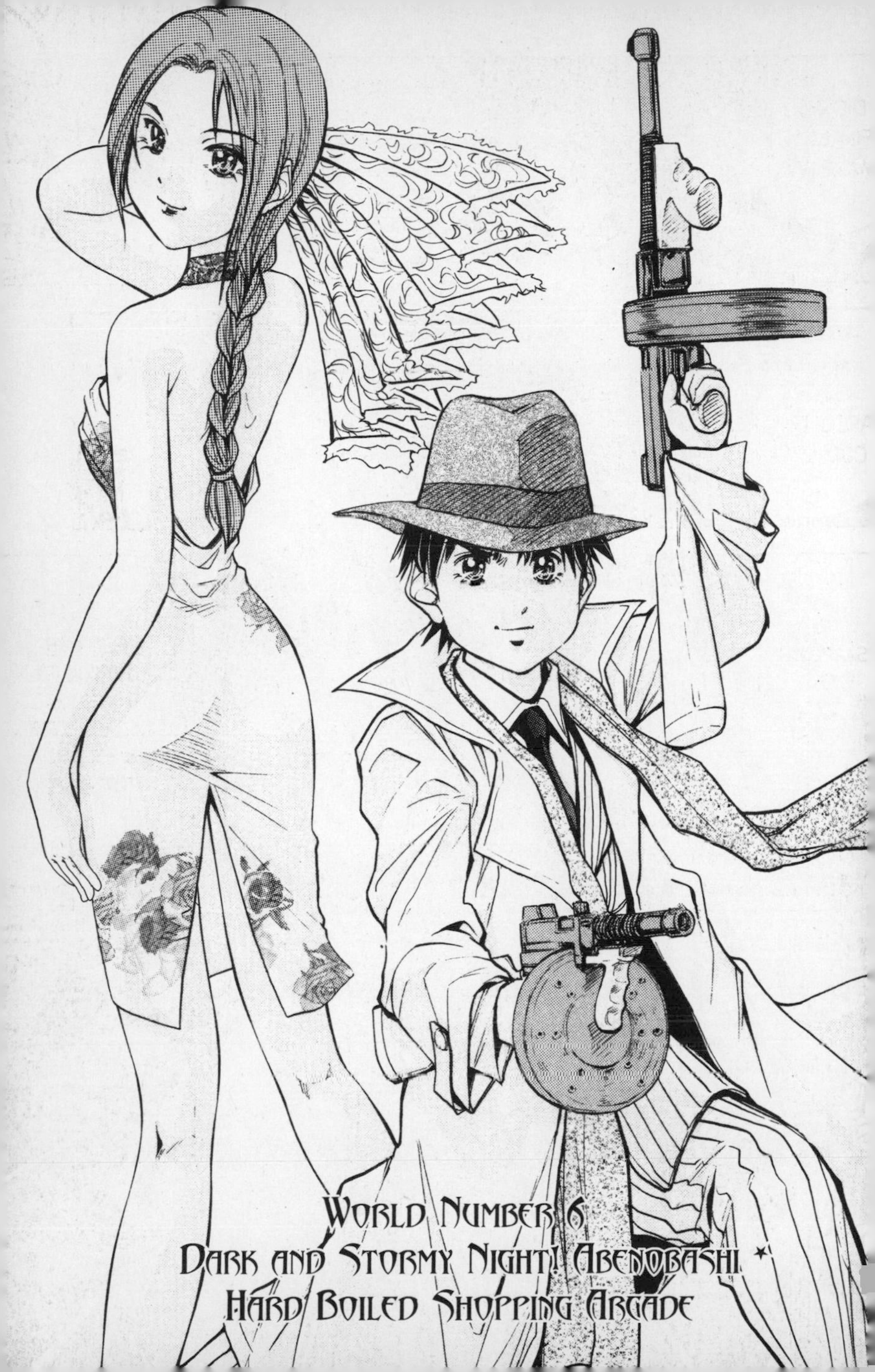

World Number 6
Dark and Stormy Night! Abenobashi ★ Hard Boiled Shopping Arcade

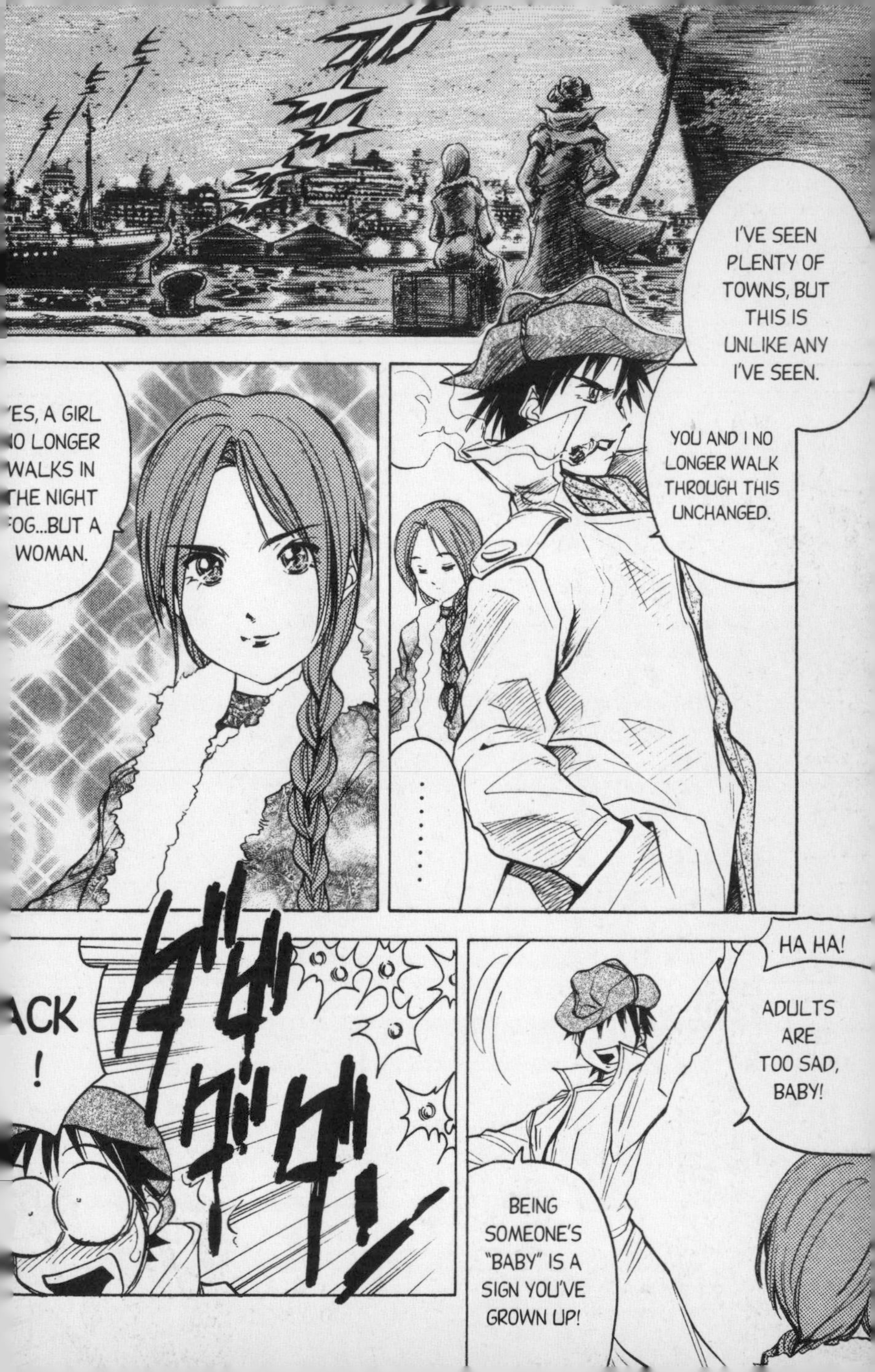
I'VE SEEN PLENTY OF TOWNS, BUT THIS IS UNLIKE ANY I'VE SEEN.
YOU AND I NO LONGER WALK THROUGH THIS UNCHANGED.
......
ES, A GIRL O LONGER WALKS IN THE NIGHT OG...BUT A WOMAN.
HA HA!
ADULTS ARE TOO SAD, BABY!
BEING SOMEONE'S "BABY" IS A SIGN YOU'VE GROWN UP!
ACK !

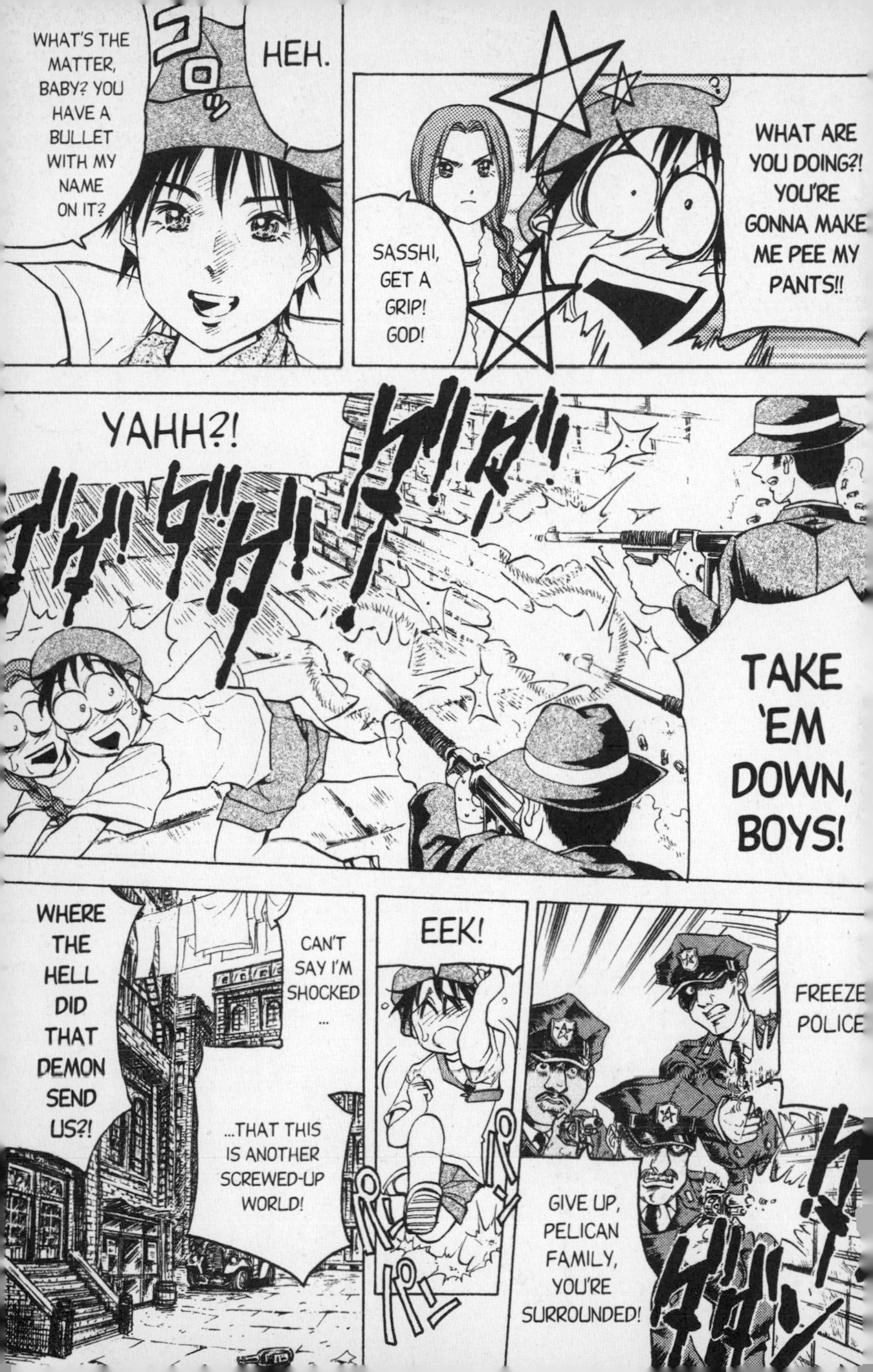
WHAT ARE YOU DOING?! YOU'RE GONNA MAKE ME PEE MY PANTS!!
SASSHI, GET A GRIP! GOD!
HEH.
WHAT'S THE MATTER, BABY? YOU HAVE A BULLET WITH MY NAME ON IT?
TAKE 'EM DOWN, BOYS!
YAHH?!
FREEZE POLICE
GIVE UP, PELICAN FAMILY, YOU'RE SURROUNDED!
EEK!
CAN'T SAY I'M SHOCKED ...
WHERE THE HELL DID THAT DEMON SEND US?!
...THAT THIS IS ANOTHER SCREWED-UP WORLD!

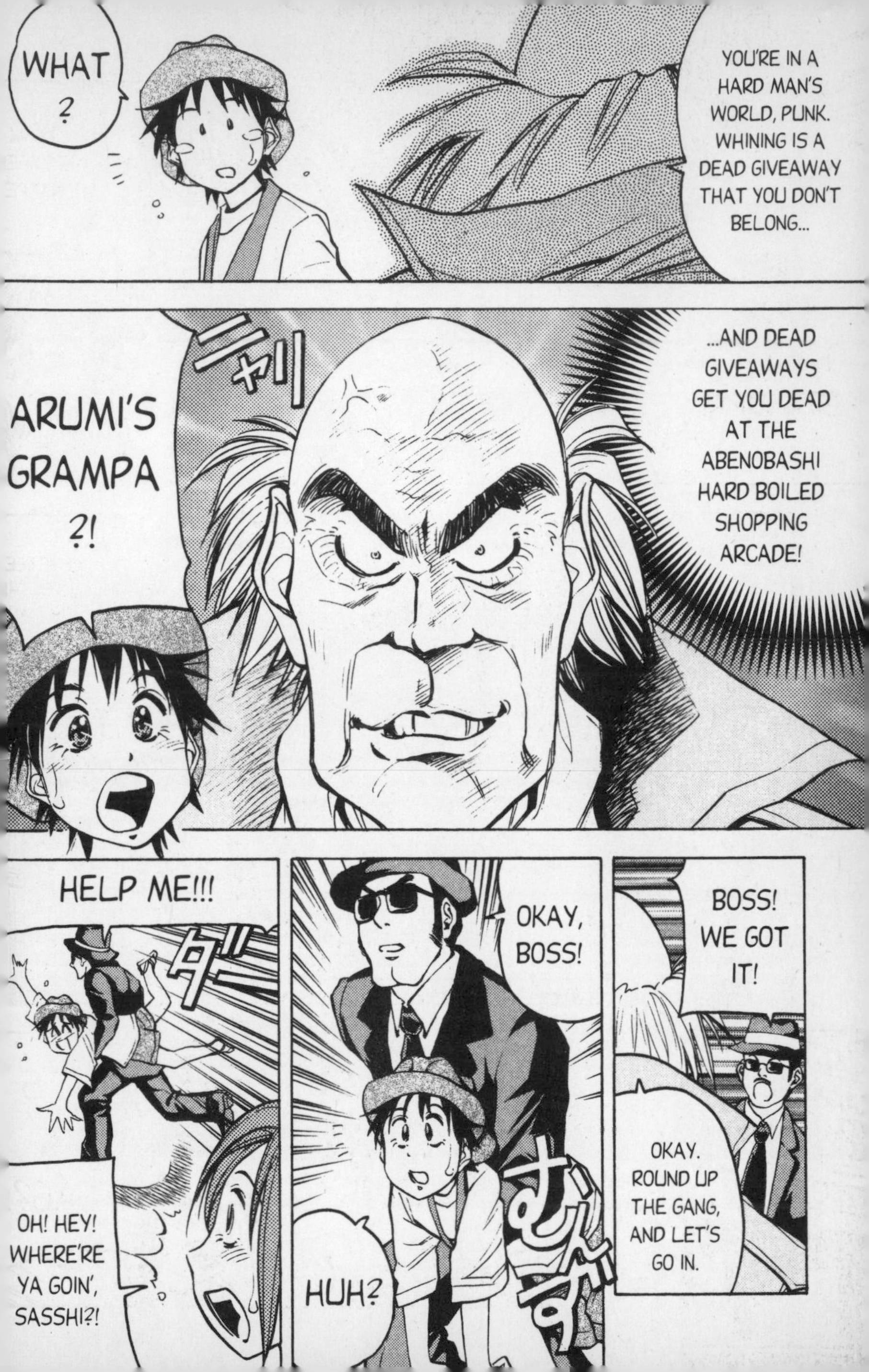
YOU'RE IN A HARD MAN'S WORLD, PUNK. WHINING IS A DEAD GIVEAWAY THAT YOU DON'T BELONG...
WHAT ?
...AND DEAD GIVEAWAYS GET YOU DEAD AT THE ABENOBASHI HARD BOILED SHOPPING ARCADE!
ニャリ
ARUMI'S GRAMPA ?!
BOSS! WE GOT IT!
OKAY. ROUND UP THE GANG, AND LET'S GO IN.
OKAY, BOSS!
むんず
HUH?
HELP ME!!!
ダッ
OH! HEY! WHERE'RE YA GOIN', SASSHI?!

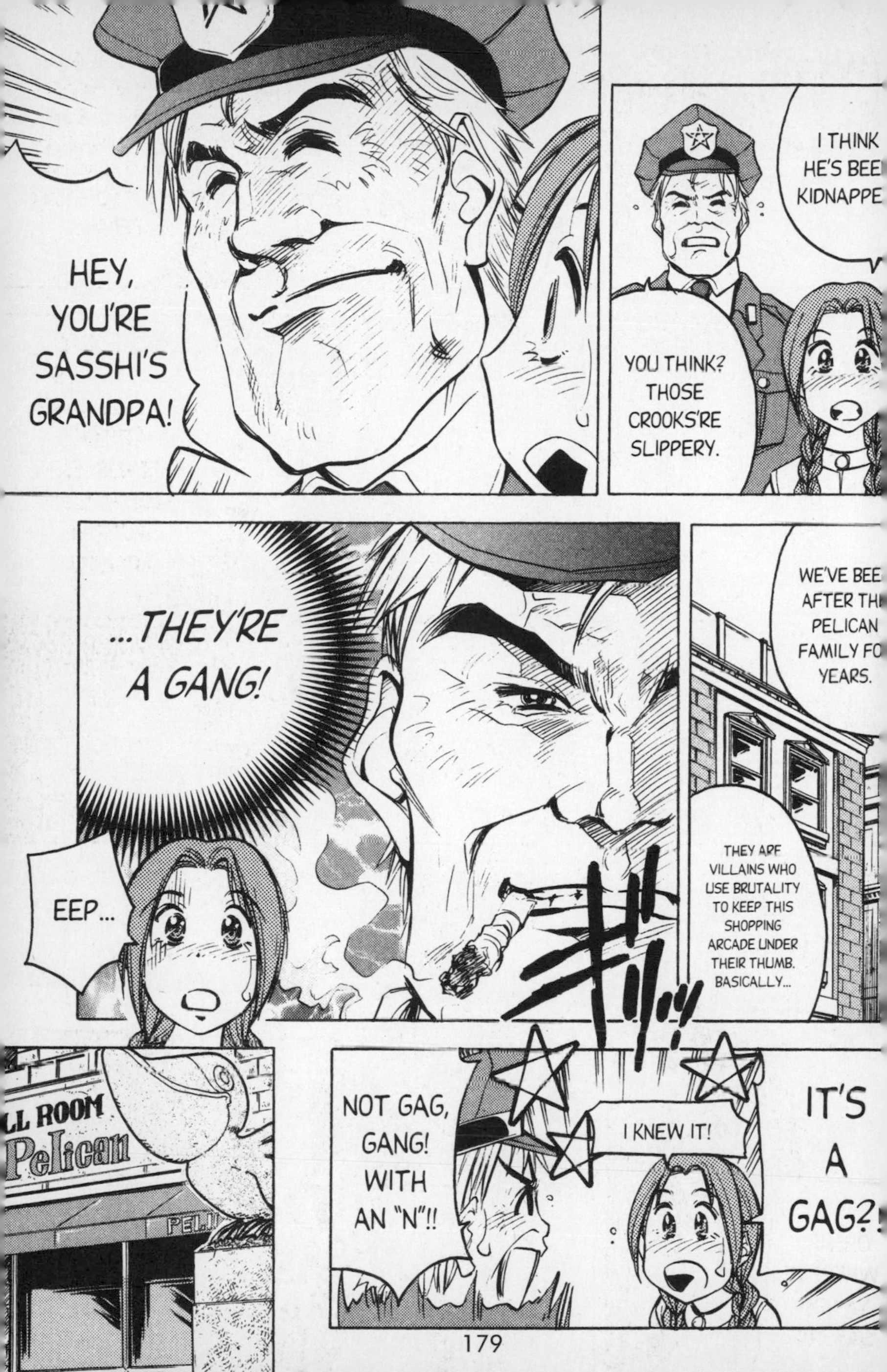
I THINK HE'S BEE KIDNAPPE
YOU THINK? THOSE CROOKS'RE SLIPPERY.
HEY, YOU'RE SASSHI'S GRANDPA!
WE'VE BEE AFTER TH PELICAN FAMILY FO YEARS.
THEY ARE VILLAINS WHO USE BRUTALITY TO KEEP THIS SHOPPING ARCADE UNDER THEIR THUMB. BASICALLY...
...THEY'RE A GANG!
EEP...
IT'S A GAG?!
I KNEW IT!
NOT GAG, GANG! WITH AN "N"!!
LL ROOM
Pelican
PELI

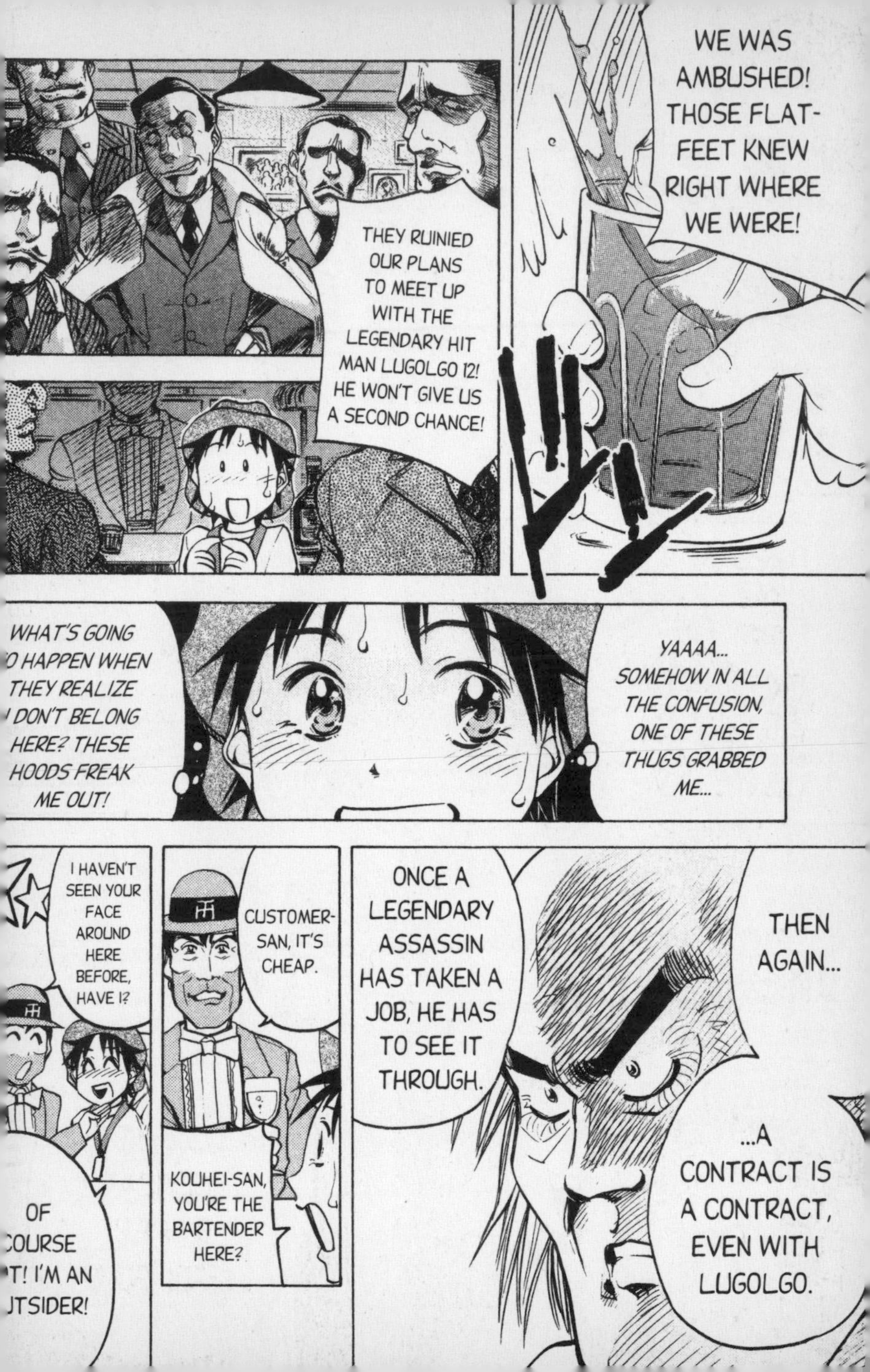
WE WAS AMBUSHED! THOSE FLAT-FEET KNEW RIGHT WHERE WE WERE!
THEY RUINIED OUR PLANS TO MEET UP WITH THE LEGENDARY HIT MAN LUGOLGO 12! HE WON'T GIVE US A SECOND CHANCE!
YAAAA... SOMEHOW IN ALL THE CONFUSION, ONE OF THESE THUGS GRABBED ME...
WHAT'S GOING O HAPPEN WHEN THEY REALIZE DON'T BELONG HERE? THESE HOODS FREAK ME OUT!
THEN AGAIN...
ONCE A LEGENDARY ASSASSIN HAS TAKEN A JOB, HE HAS TO SEE IT THROUGH.
...A CONTRACT IS A CONTRACT, EVEN WITH LUGOLGO.
CUSTOMER-SAN, IT'S CHEAP.
KOUHEI-SAN, YOU'RE THE BARTENDER HERE?
I HAVEN'T SEEN YOUR FACE AROUND HERE BEFORE, HAVE I?
OF OURSE T! I'M AN UTSIDER!

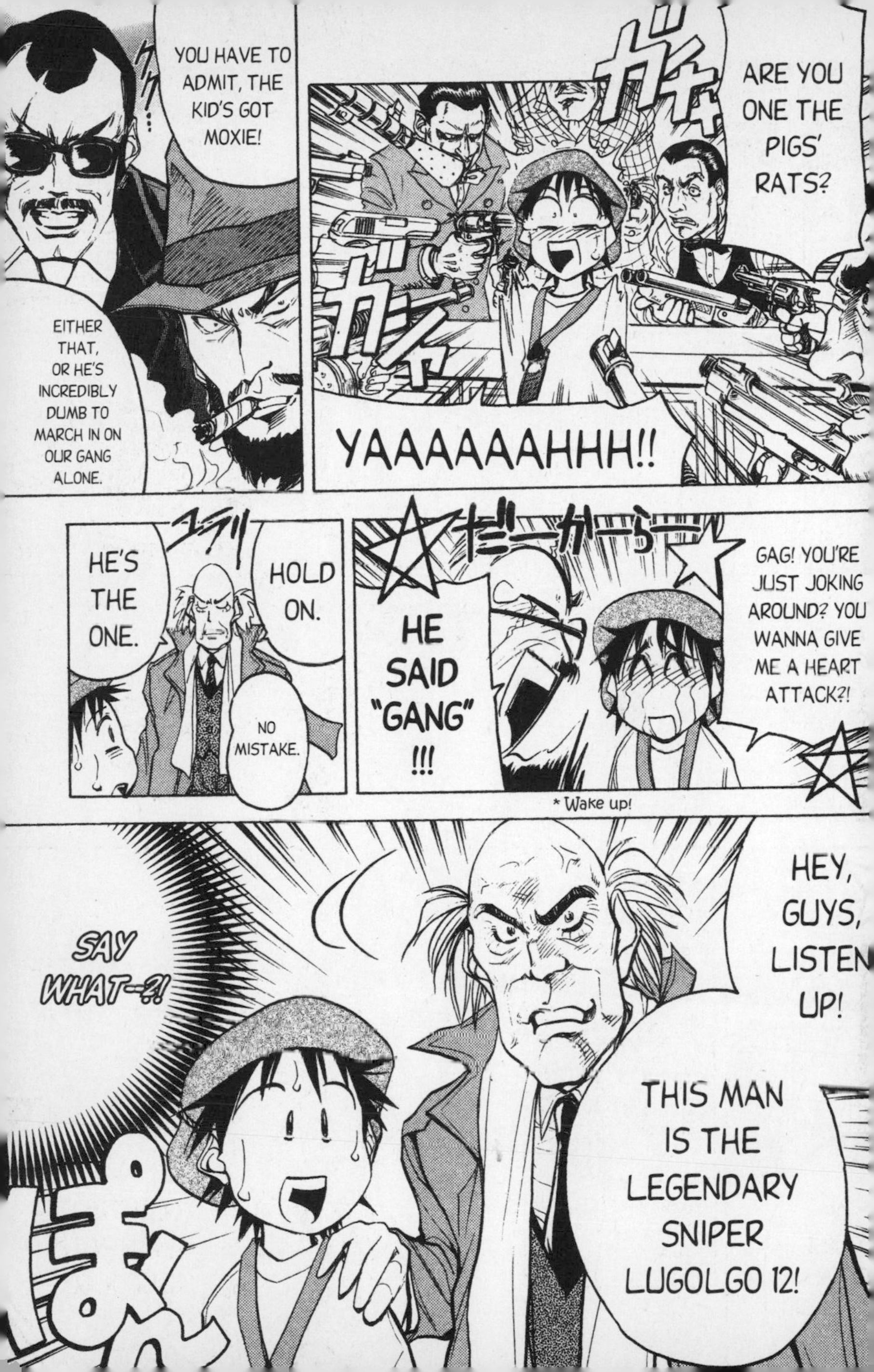
ARE YOU ONE THE PIGS' RATS?
YAAAAAAHHH!!
YOU HAVE TO ADMIT, THE KID'S GOT MOXIE!
EITHER THAT, OR HE'S INCREDIBLY DUMB TO MARCH IN ON OUR GANG ALONE.
GAG! YOU'RE JUST JOKING AROUND? YOU WANNA GIVE ME A HEART ATTACK?!
だーかーらー
HE SAID "GANG" !!!
* Wake up!
HOLD ON.
HE'S THE ONE.
NO MISTAKE.
HEY, GUYS, LISTEN UP!
THIS MAN IS THE LEGENDARY SNIPER LUGOLGO 12!
SAY WHAT--?!

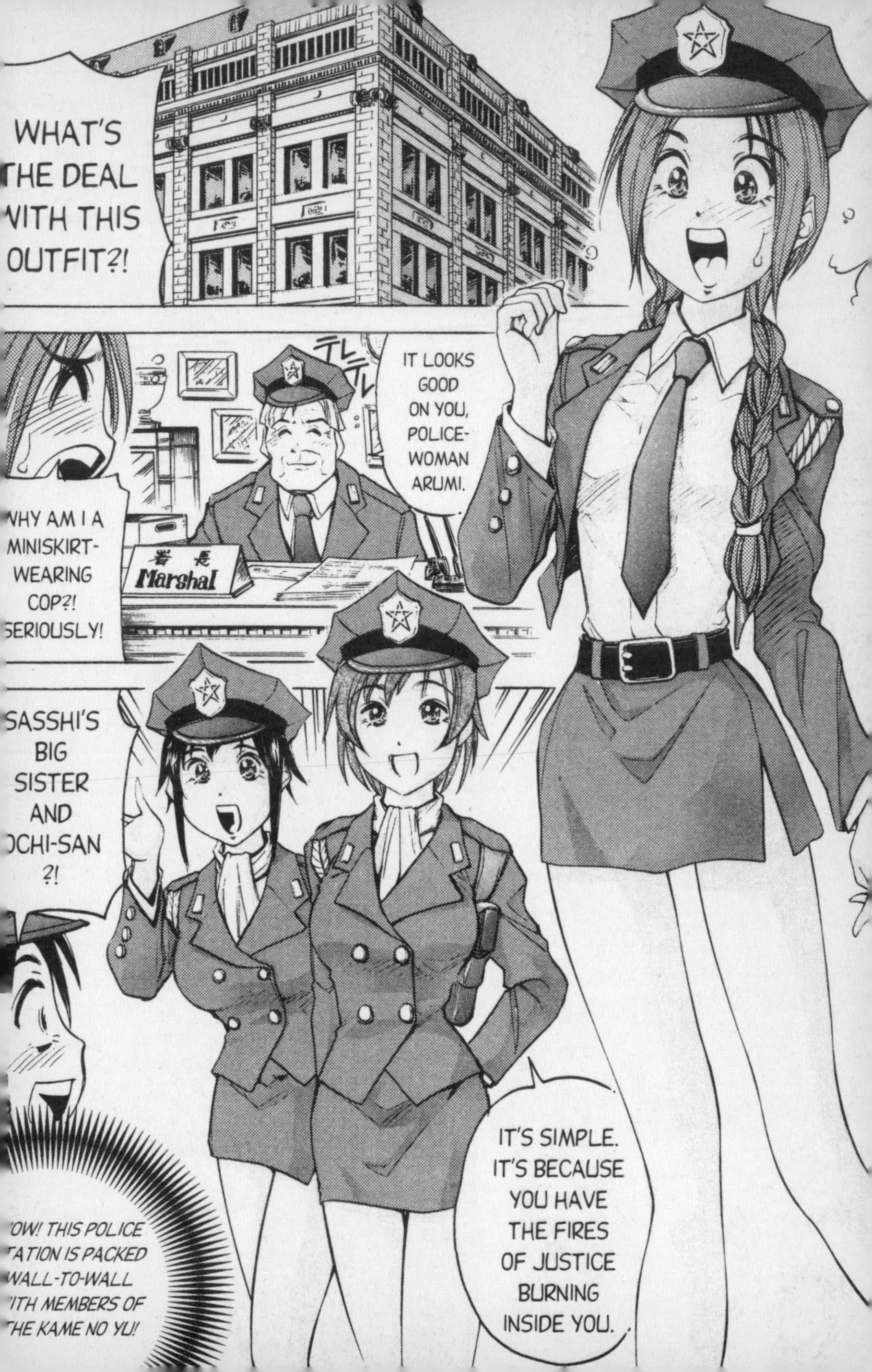
WHAT'S THE DEAL WITH THIS OUTFIT?!
テレテレ
IT LOOKS GOOD ON YOU, POLICE-WOMAN ARUMI.
署長
Marshal
WHY AM I A MINISKIRT-WEARING COP?! SERIOUSLY!
SASSHI'S BIG SISTER AND OCHI-SAN ?!
IT'S SIMPLE. IT'S BECAUSE YOU HAVE THE FIRES OF JUSTICE BURNING INSIDE YOU.
WOW! THIS POLICE STATION IS PACKED WALL-TO-WALL WITH MEMBERS OF THE KAME NO YU!

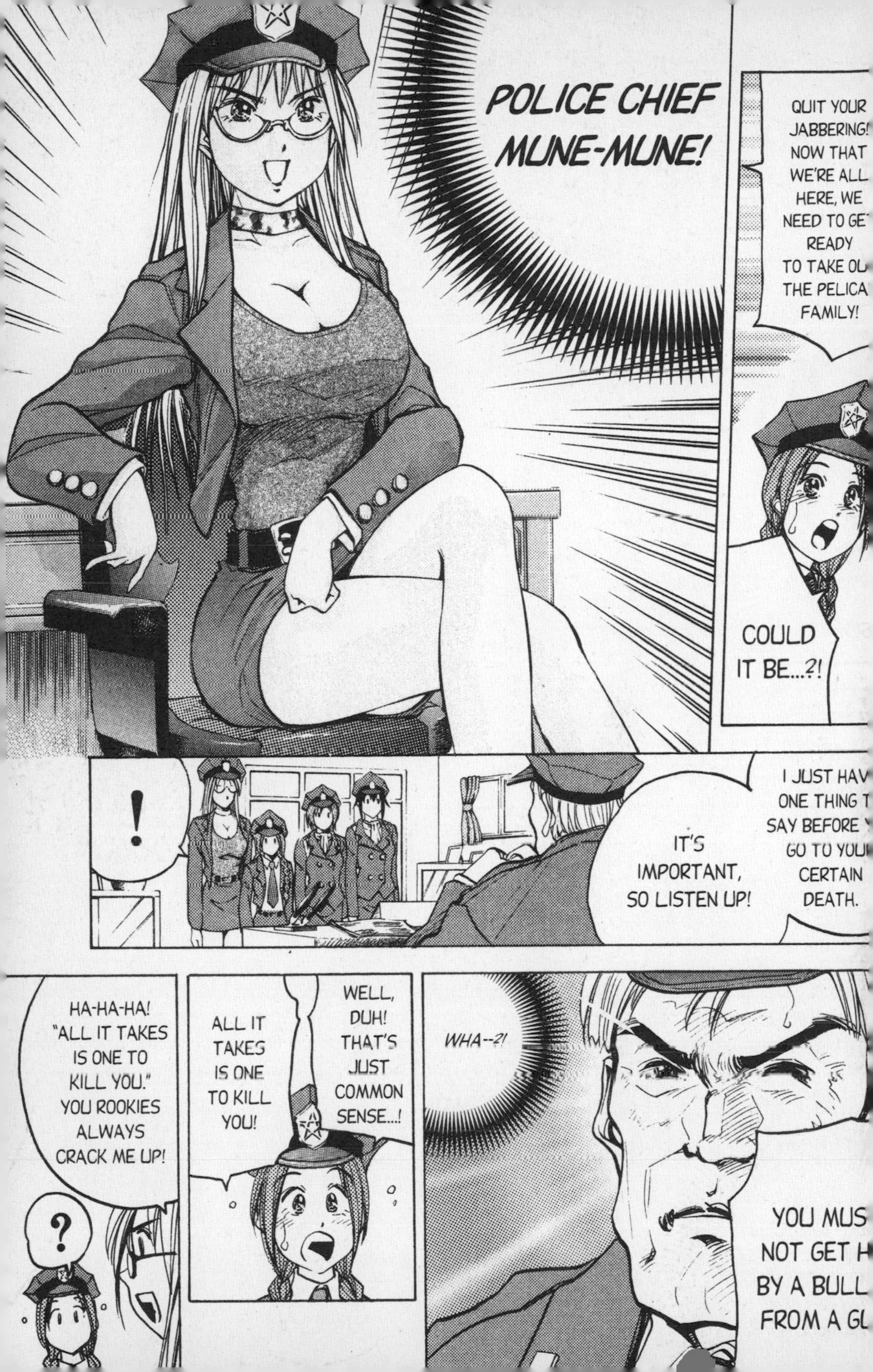
QUIT YOUR JABBERING! NOW THAT WE'RE ALL HERE, WE NEED TO GE READY TO TAKE OU THE PELICA FAMILY!
COULD IT BE...?!
POLICE CHIEF MUNE-MUNE!
I JUST HAV ONE THING T SAY BEFORE GO TO YOU CERTAIN DEATH.
IT'S IMPORTANT, SO LISTEN UP!
!
WHA--?!
YOU MUS NOT GET H BY A BULL FROM A GU
WELL, DUH! THAT'S JUST COMMON SENSE...!
ALL IT TAKES IS ONE TO KILL YOU!
HA-HA-HA! "ALL IT TAKES IS ONE TO KILL YOU." YOU ROOKIES ALWAYS CRACK ME UP!
?

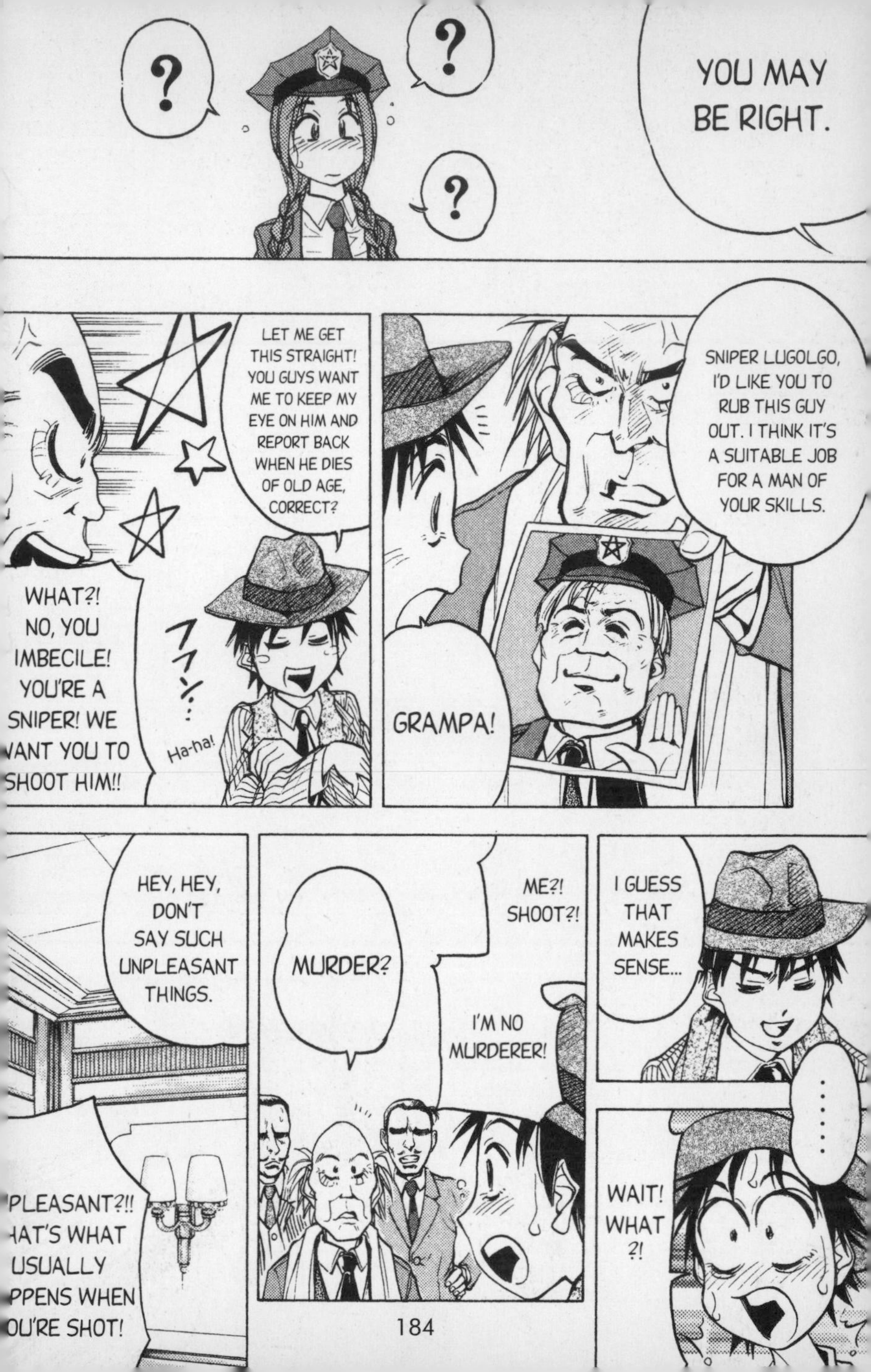
YOU MAY BE RIGHT.
?
?
?
SNIPER LUGOLGO, I'D LIKE YOU TO RUB THIS GUY OUT. I THINK IT'S A SUITABLE JOB FOR A MAN OF YOUR SKILLS.
GRAMPA!
LET ME GET THIS STRAIGHT! YOU GUYS WANT ME TO KEEP MY EYE ON HIM AND REPORT BACK WHEN HE DIES OF OLD AGE, CORRECT?
WHAT?! NO, YOU IMBECILE! YOU'RE A SNIPER! WE VANT YOU TO SHOOT HIM!!
Ha-ha!
I GUESS THAT MAKES SENSE...
......
WAIT! WHAT?!
ME?! SHOOT?!
I'M NO MURDERER!
MURDER?
HEY, HEY, DON'T SAY SUCH UNPLEASANT THINGS.
PLEASANT?!! HAT'S WHAT USUALLY PPENS WHEN OU'RE SHOT!

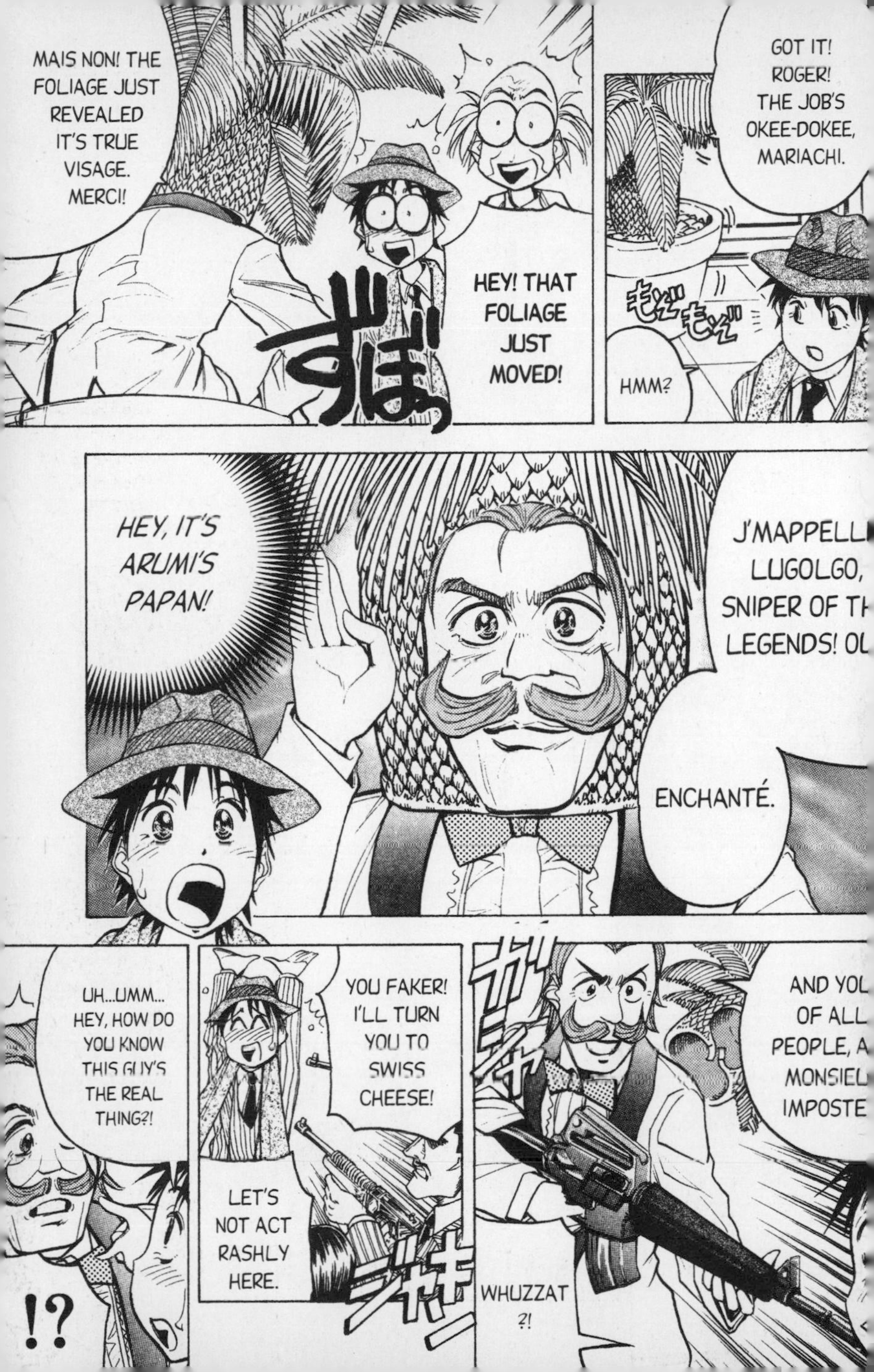
GOT IT! ROGER! THE JOB'S OKEE-DOKEE, MARIACHI.
もぞもぞ
HMM?
HEY! THAT FOLIAGE JUST MOVED!
すぽっ
MAIS NON! THE FOLIAGE JUST REVEALED IT'S TRUE VISAGE. MERCI!
J'MAPPELL LUGOLGO, SNIPER OF TH LEGENDS! OU
ENCHANTÉ.
HEY, IT'S ARUMI'S PAPAN!
AND YO OF ALL PEOPLE, A MONSIEU IMPOSTE
ガシャ
WHUZZAT ?!
YOU FAKER! I'LL TURN YOU TO SWISS CHEESE!
LET'S NOT ACT RASHLY HERE.
ジャキ
UH...UMM... HEY, HOW DO YOU KNOW THIS GUY'S THE REAL THING?!
!?

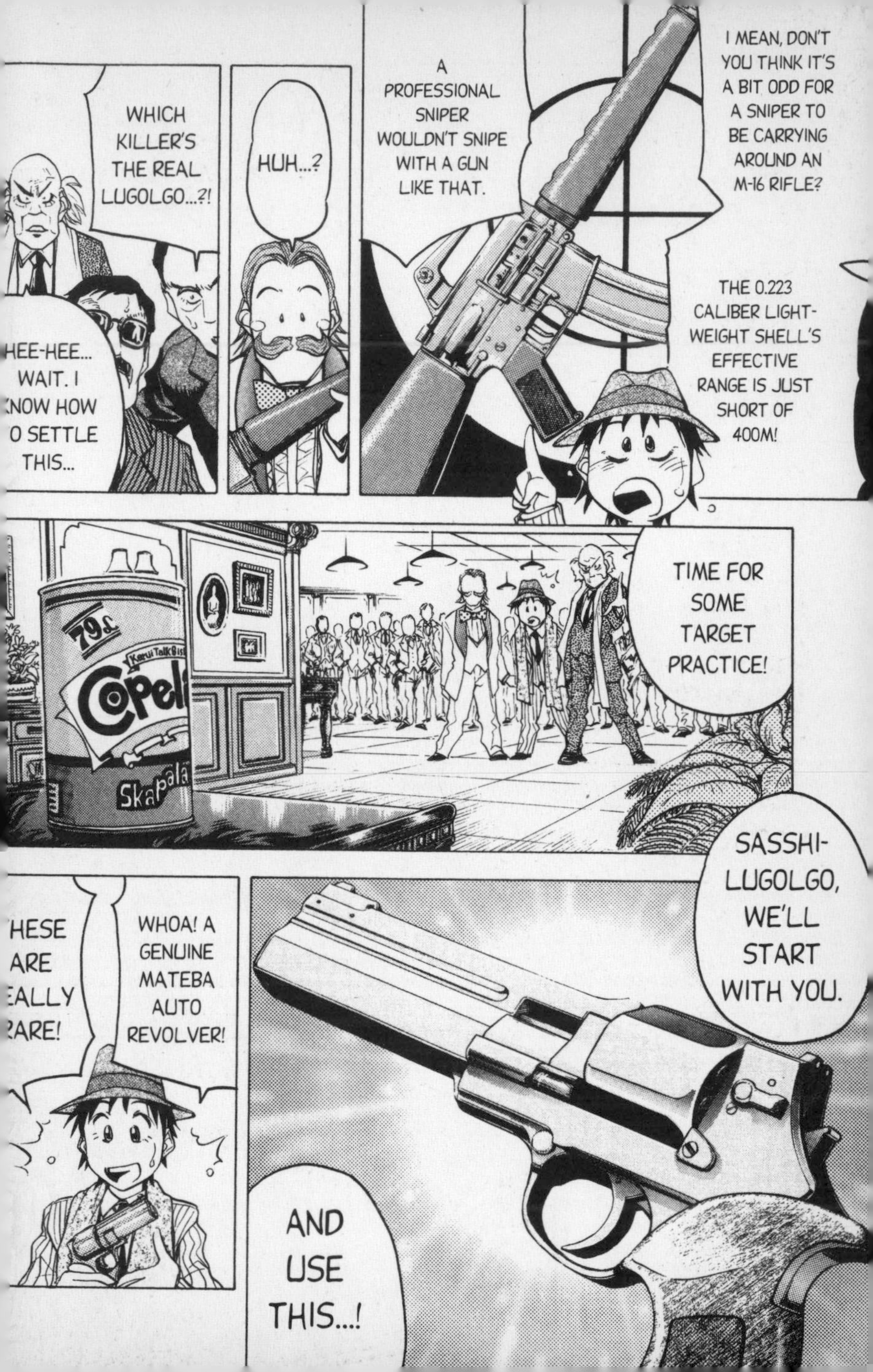
I MEAN, DON'T YOU THINK IT'S A BIT ODD FOR A SNIPER TO BE CARRYING AROUND AN M-16 RIFLE?
THE 0.223 CALIBER LIGHT-WEIGHT SHELL'S EFFECTIVE RANGE IS JUST SHORT OF 400M!
A PROFESSIONAL SNIPER WOULDN'T SNIPE WITH A GUN LIKE THAT.
HUH...?
WHICH KILLER'S THE REAL LUGOLGO...?!
HEE-HEE... WAIT. I NOW HOW O SETTLE THIS...
TIME FOR SOME TARGET PRACTICE!
SASSHI-LUGOLGO, WE'LL START WITH YOU.
AND USE THIS...!
WHOA! A GENUINE MATEBA AUTO REVOLVER!
HESE ARE EALLY RARE!

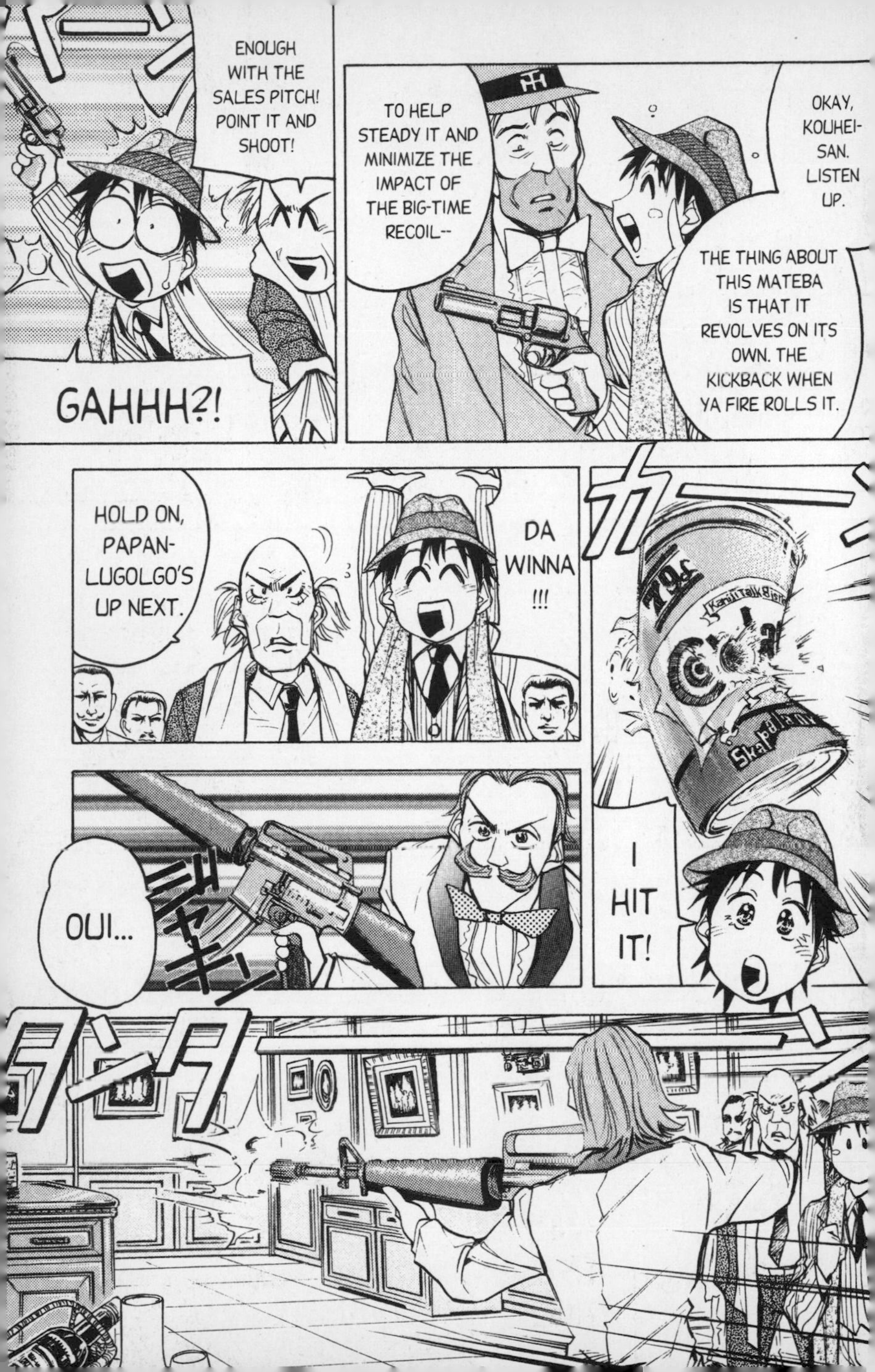
OKAY, KOUHEI-SAN. LISTEN UP.
THE THING ABOUT THIS MATEBA IS THAT IT REVOLVES ON ITS OWN. THE KICKBACK WHEN YA FIRE ROLLS IT.
TO HELP STEADY IT AND MINIMIZE THE IMPACT OF THE BIG-TIME RECOIL--
ENOUGH WITH THE SALES PITCH! POINT IT AND SHOOT!
GAHHH?!
I HIT IT!
DA WINNA!!!
HOLD ON, PAPAN-LUGOLGO'S UP NEXT.
OUI...

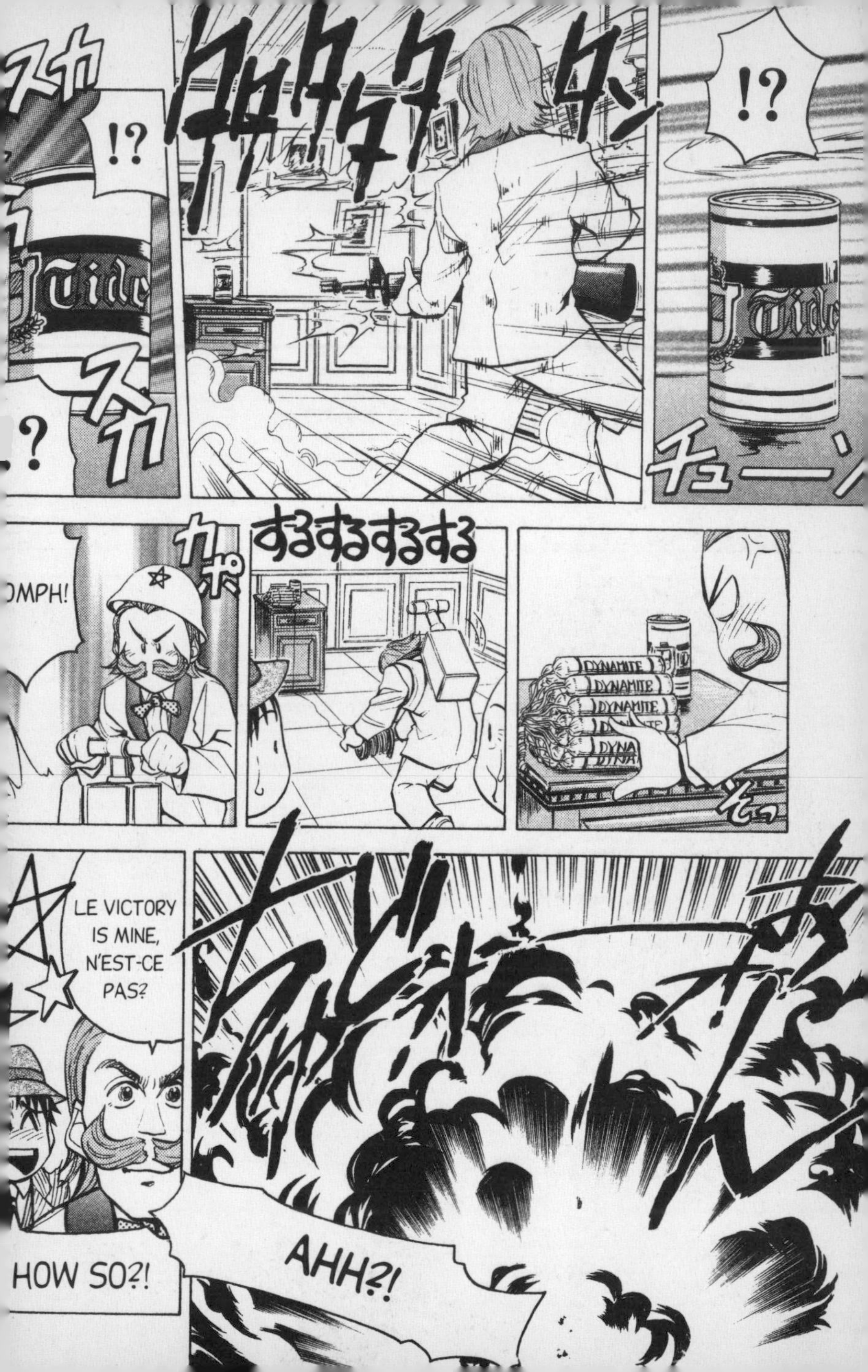

!?
チューン
!?
スカ
スカ
?
そっ
するするするする
カポ
OMPH!
AHH?!
LE VICTORY IS MINE, N'EST-CE PAS?
HOW SO?!

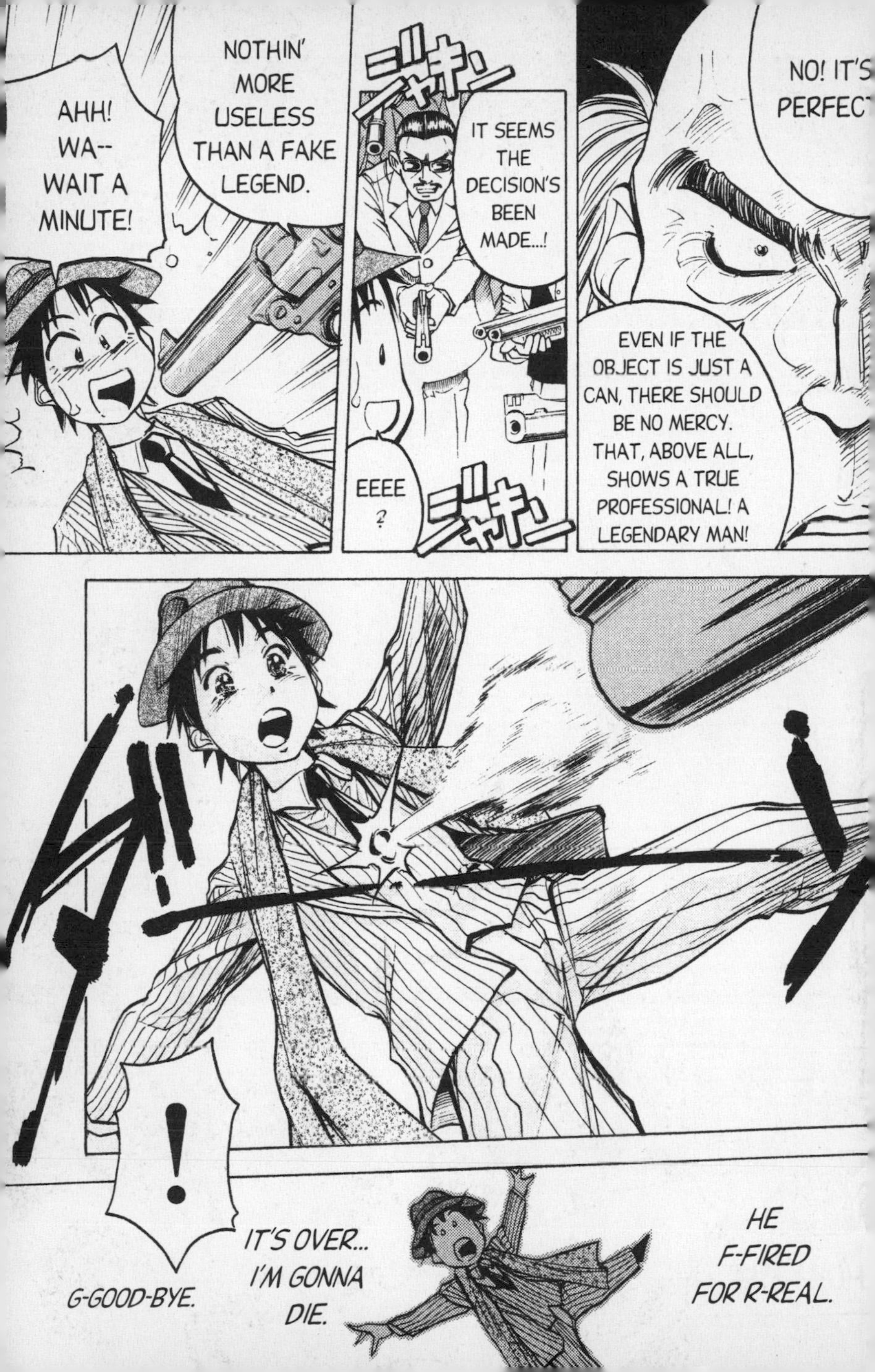
NO! IT'S PERFECT
EVEN IF THE OBJECT IS JUST A CAN, THERE SHOULD BE NO MERCY. THAT, ABOVE ALL, SHOWS A TRUE PROFESSIONAL! A LEGENDARY MAN!
IT SEEMS THE DECISION'S BEEN MADE...!
EEEE ?
NOTHIN' MORE USELESS THAN A FAKE LEGEND.
AHH! WA-- WAIT A MINUTE!
!
HE F-FIRED FOR R-REAL.
IT'S OVER... I'M GONNA DIE.
G-GOOD-BYE.

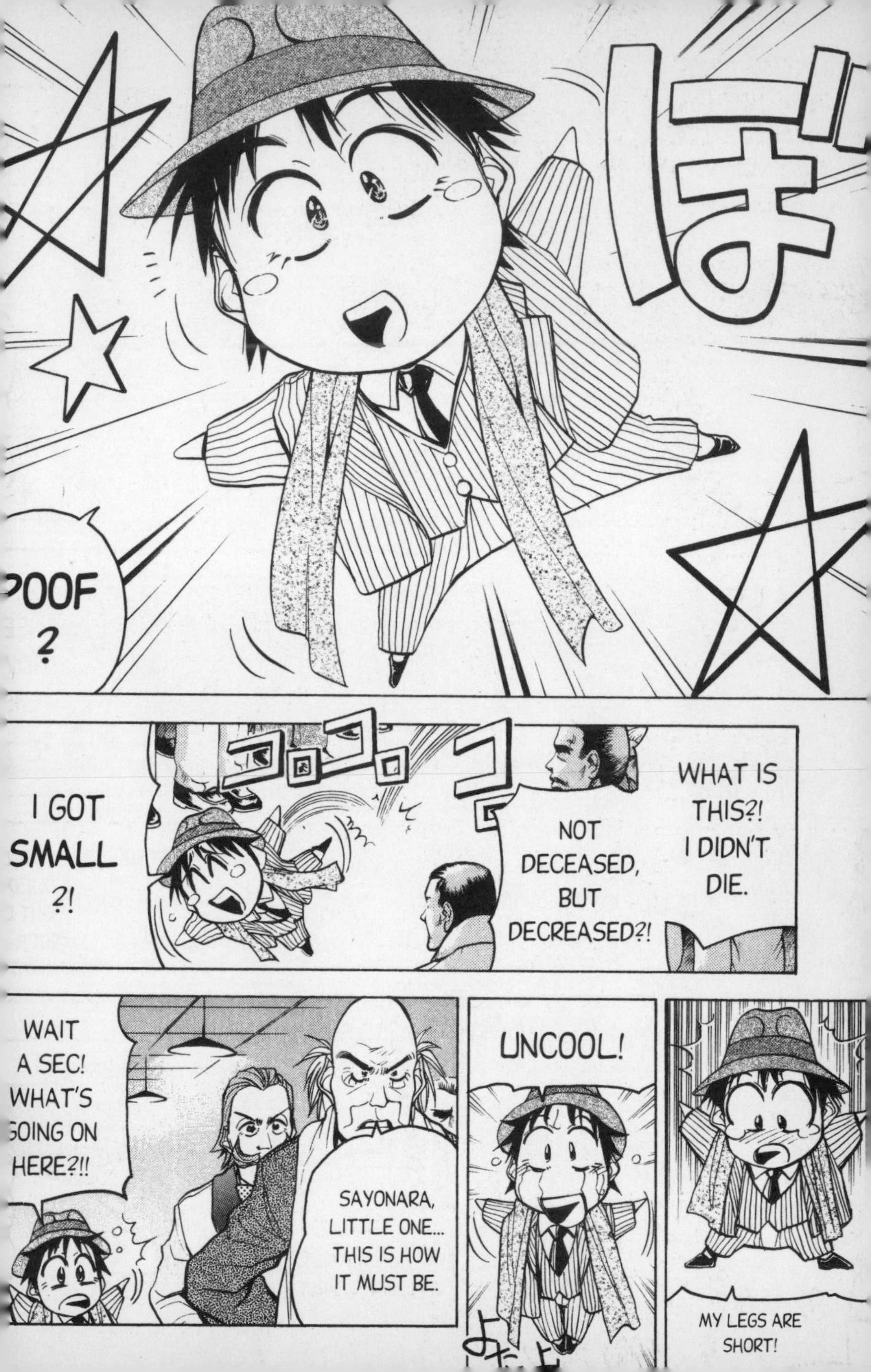
ぼ
POOF ?
WHAT IS THIS?! I DIDN'T DIE.
NOT DECEASED, BUT DECREASED?!
I GOT SMALL ?!
MY LEGS ARE SHORT!
UNCOOL!
WAIT A SEC! WHAT'S GOING ON HERE?!!
SAYONARA, LITTLE ONE... THIS IS HOW IT MUST BE.

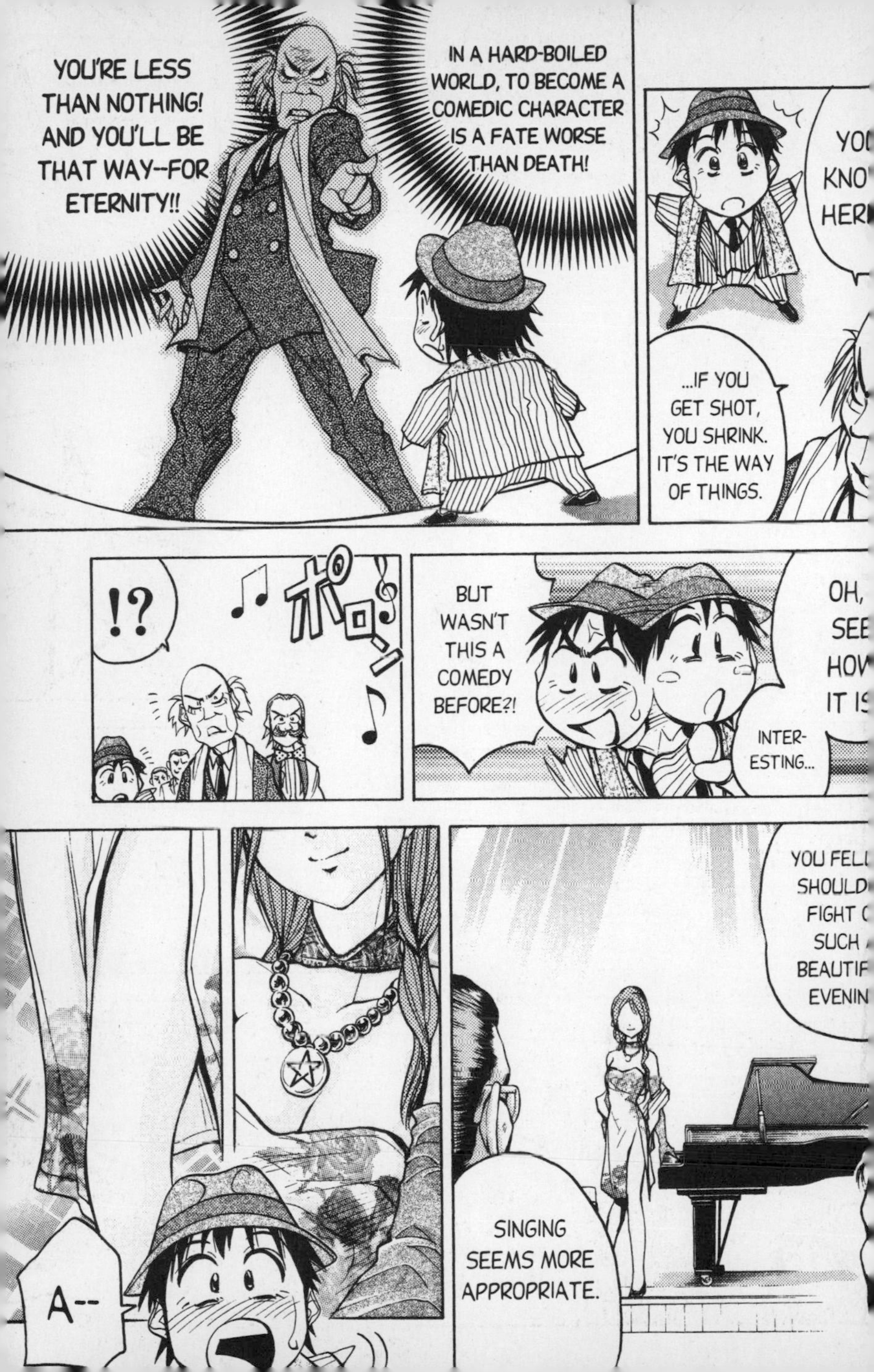
...IF YOU GET SHOT, YOU SHRINK. IT'S THE WAY OF THINGS.
IN A HARD-BOILED WORLD, TO BECOME A COMEDIC CHARACTER IS A FATE WORSE THAN DEATH!
YOU'RE LESS THAN NOTHING! AND YOU'LL BE THAT WAY--FOR ETERNITY!!
INTER-ESTING...
BUT WASN'T THIS A COMEDY BEFORE?!
!?
ポロ〜ン
SINGING SEEMS MORE APPROPRIATE.
A--

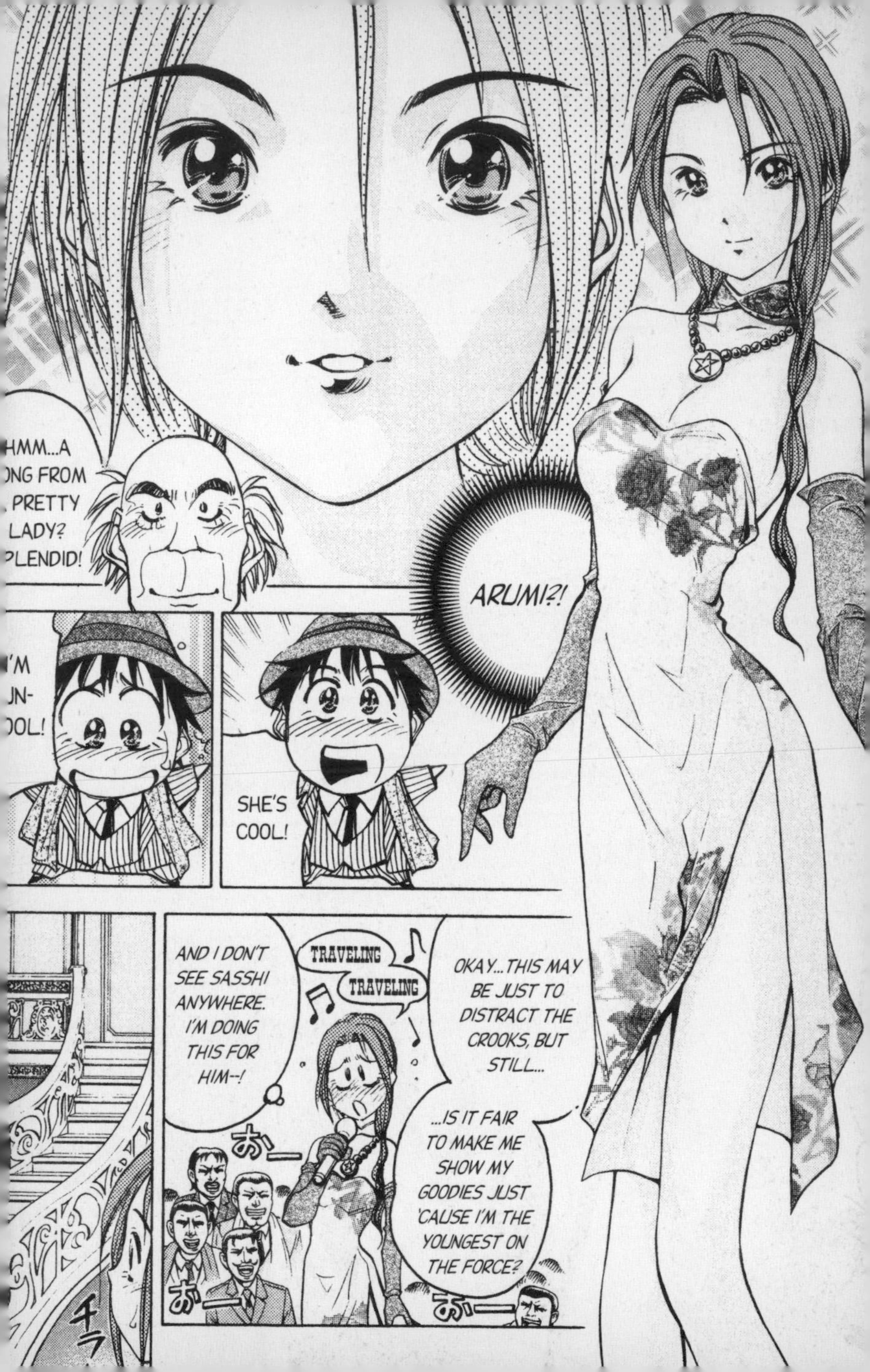
ARUMI?!
HMM...A ONG FROM PRETTY LADY? PLENDID!
SHE'S COOL!
I'M UN-OOL!
OKAY...THIS MAY BE JUST TO DISTRACT THE CROOKS, BUT STILL...
...IS IT FAIR TO MAKE ME SHOW MY GOODIES JUST 'CAUSE I'M THE YOUNGEST ON THE FORCE?
TRAVELING
TRAVELING
AND I DON'T SEE SASSHI ANYWHERE. I'M DOING THIS FOR HIM--!
おー
おー
おー
チラ

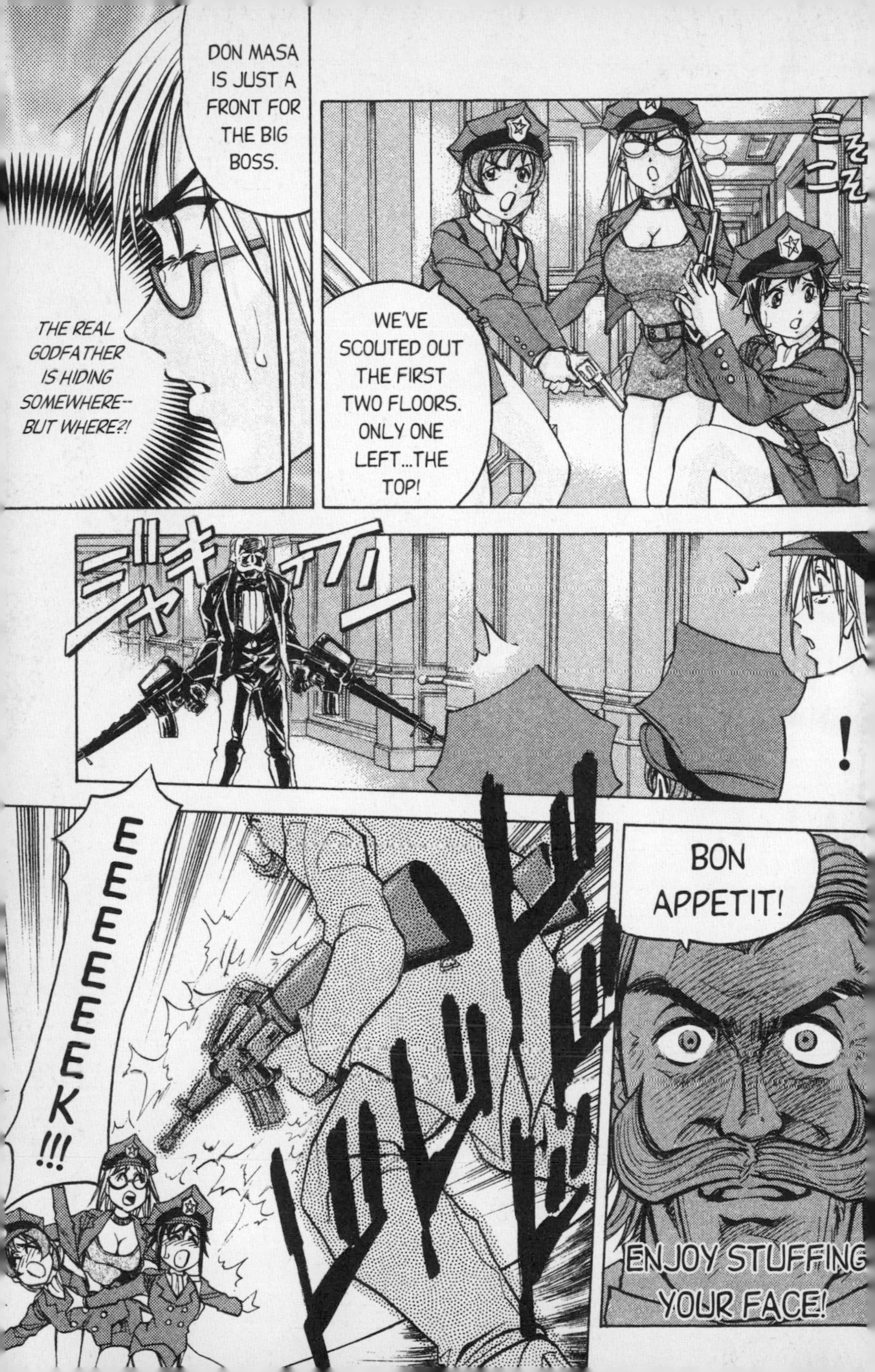
WE'VE SCOUTED OUT THE FIRST TWO FLOORS. ONLY ONE LEFT...THE TOP!
こそこそ
DON MASA IS JUST A FRONT FOR THE BIG BOSS.
THE REAL GODFATHER IS HIDING SOMEWHERE-- BUT WHERE?!
!
BON APPETIT!
ENJOY STUFFING YOUR FACE!
EEEEEEK!!!

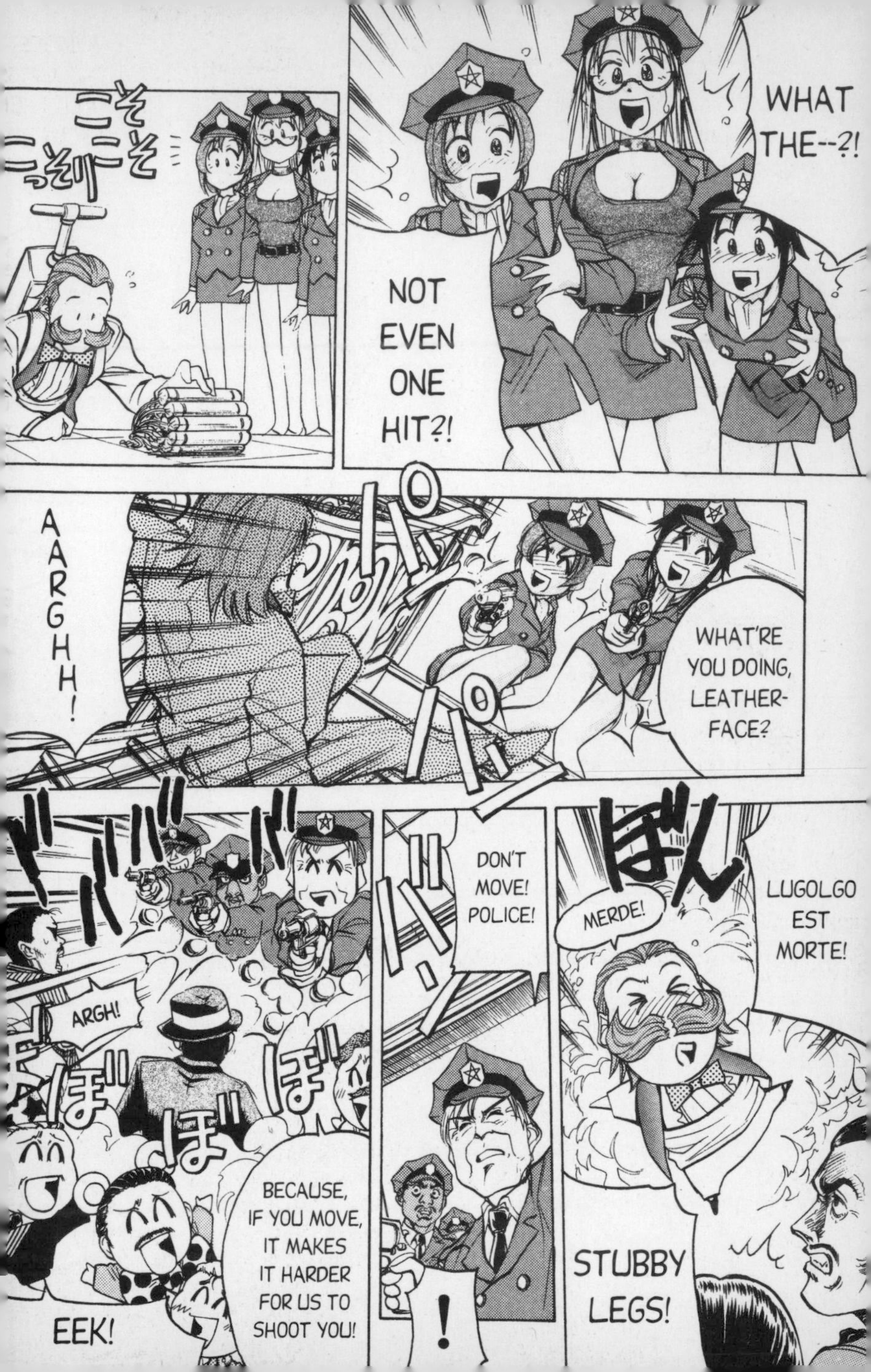
WHAT THE--?!
NOT EVEN ONE HIT?!
こそこそ
こっそり
パ
パ
WHAT'RE YOU DOING, LEATHER-FACE?
AARGHH!
ぼん
LUGOLGO EST MORTE!
MERDE!
STUBBY LEGS!
DON'T MOVE! POLICE!
パ
!
ババババ
ARGH!
ぼぼぼ
BECAUSE, IF YOU MOVE, IT MAKES IT HARDER FOR US TO SHOOT YOU!
EEK!

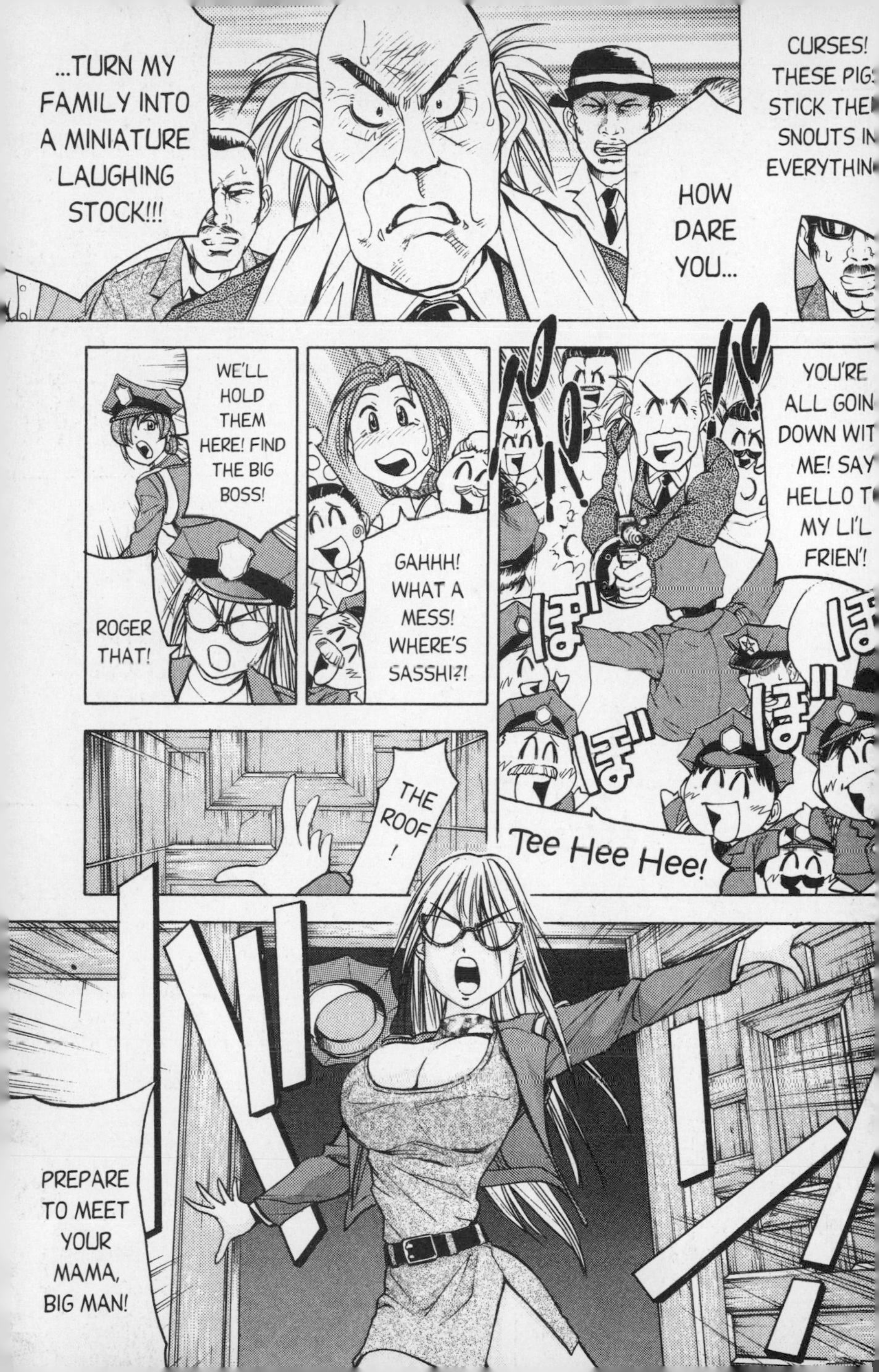
CURSES! THESE PIG STICK THE SNOUTS IN EVERYTHIN
HOW DARE YOU...
...TURN MY FAMILY INTO A MINIATURE LAUGHING STOCK!!!
パパパ
YOU'RE ALL GOIN DOWN WIT ME! SAY HELLO T MY LI'L FRIEN'!
ぼ ぼ ぼ ぼ
Tee Hee Hee!
GAHHH! WHAT A MESS! WHERE'S SASSHI!?!
WE'LL HOLD THEM HERE! FIND THE BIG BOSS!
ROGER THAT!
THE ROOF!
PREPARE TO MEET YOUR MAMA, BIG MAN!

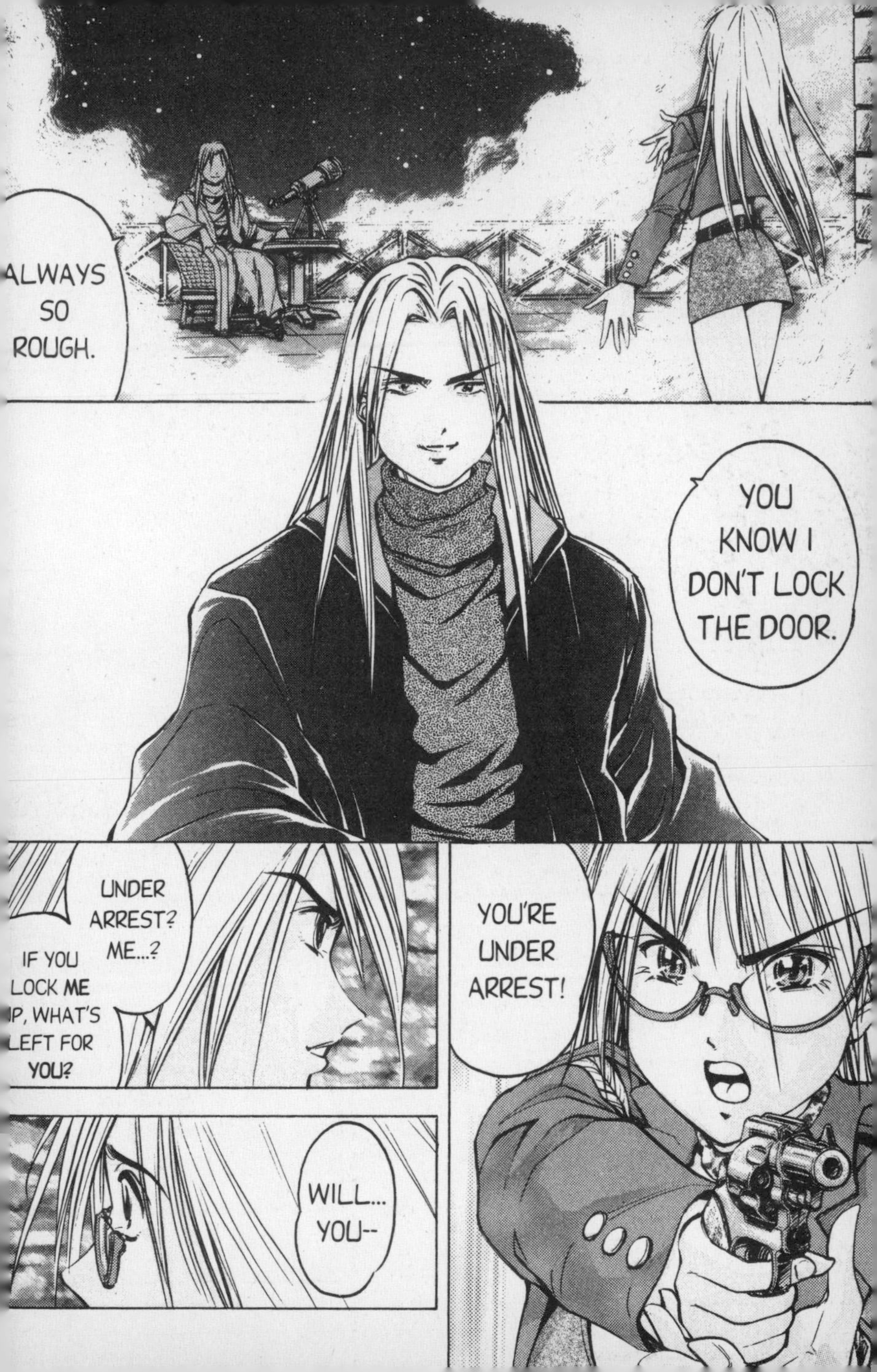
ALWAYS SO ROUGH.
YOU KNOW I DON'T LOCK THE DOOR.
YOU'RE UNDER ARREST!
UNDER ARREST? ME...?
IF YOU LOCK ME UP, WHAT'S LEFT FOR YOU?
WILL... YOU--

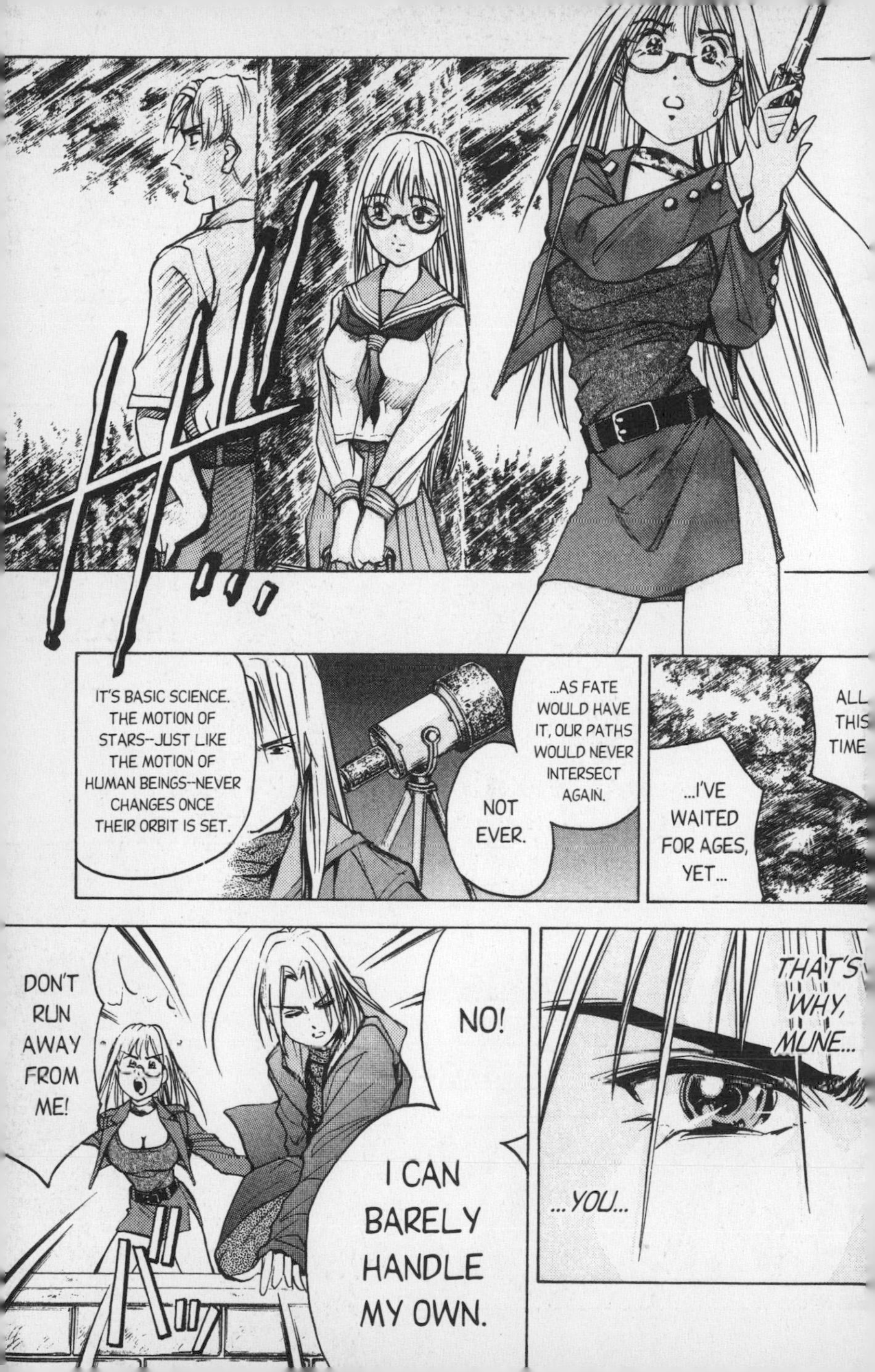
ALL THIS TIME
...I'VE WAITED FOR AGES, YET...
...AS FATE WOULD HAVE IT, OUR PATHS WOULD NEVER INTERSECT AGAIN.
NOT EVER.
IT'S BASIC SCIENCE. THE MOTION OF STARS--JUST LIKE THE MOTION OF HUMAN BEINGS--NEVER CHANGES ONCE THEIR ORBIT IS SET.
THAT'S WHY, MUNE...
...YOU...
DON'T RUN AWAY FROM ME!
NO!
I CAN BARELY HANDLE MY OWN.

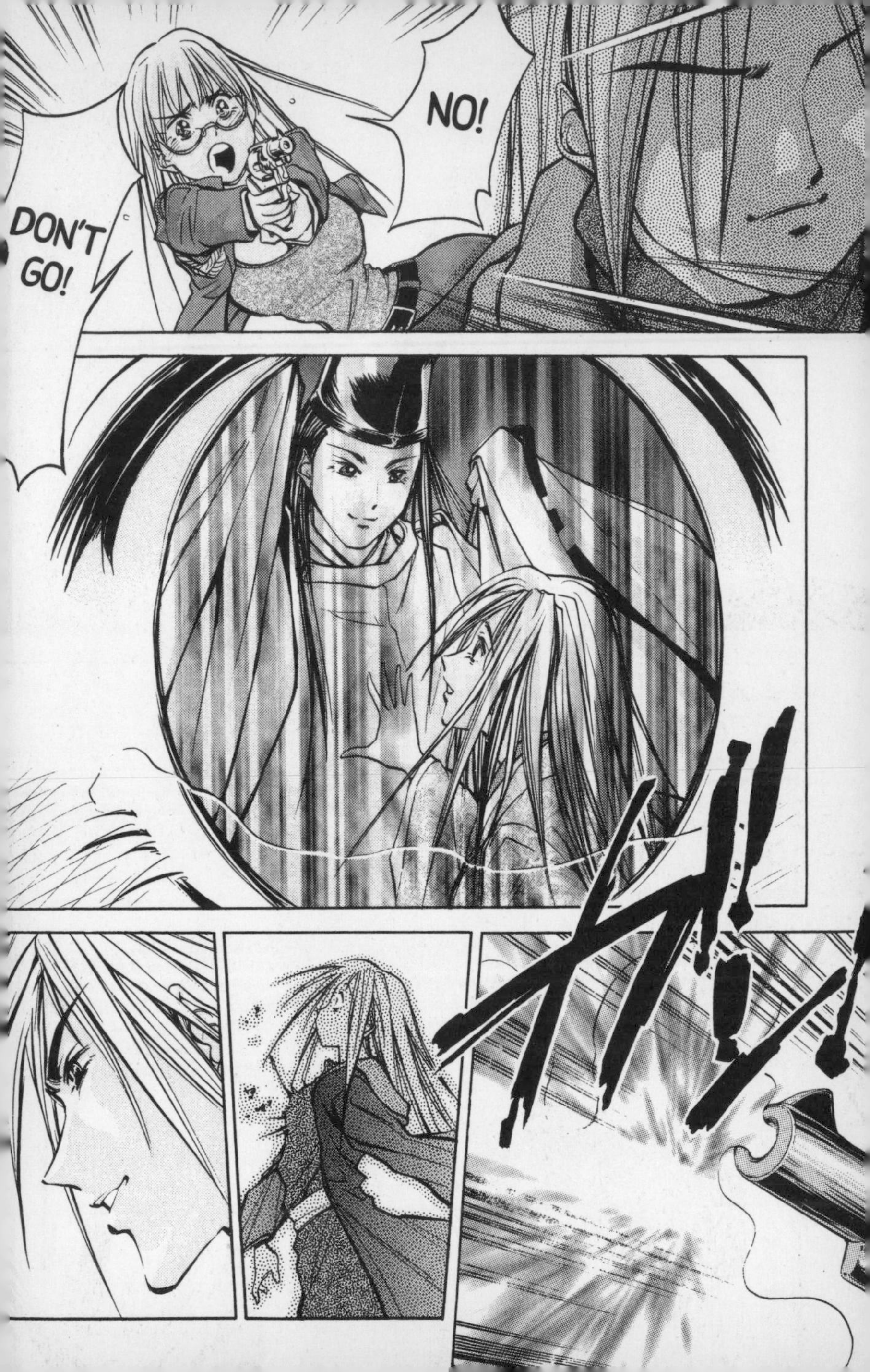
NO!
DON'T GO!

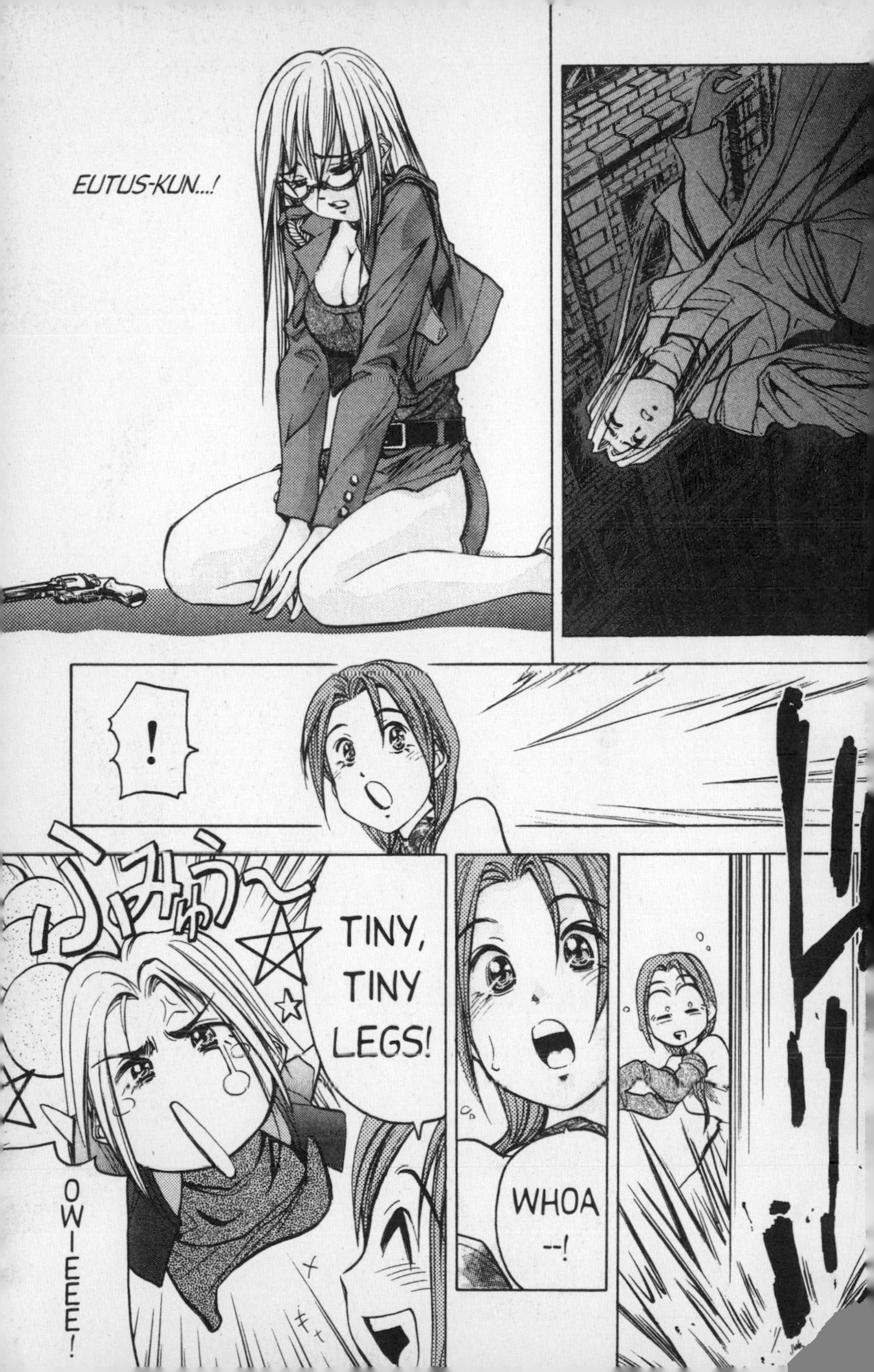
EUTUS-KUN...!
!
WHOA --!
ふみゅう〜
TINY, TINY LEGS!
OWIEEE!

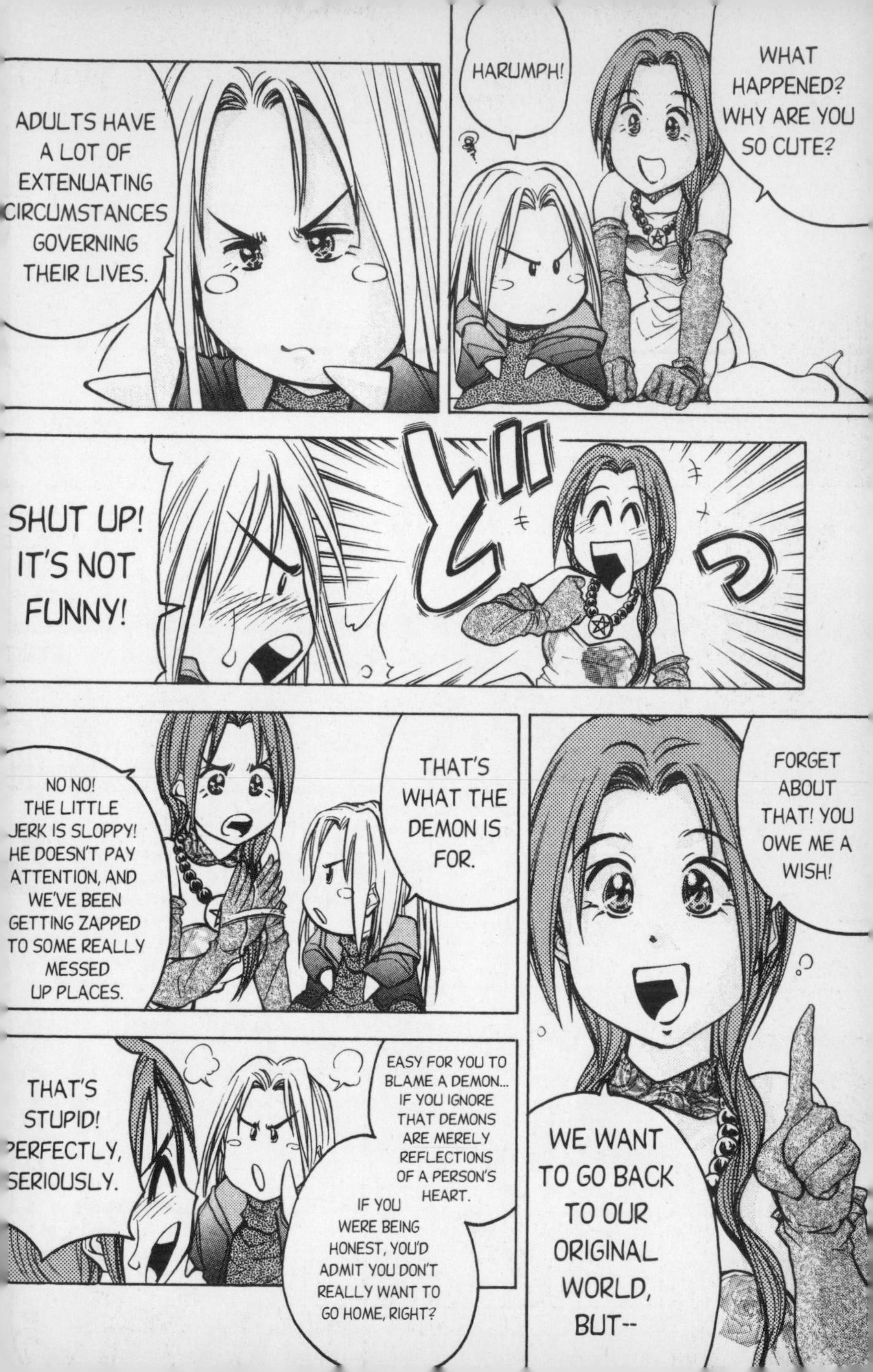
WHAT HAPPENED? WHY ARE YOU SO CUTE?
HARUMPH!
ADULTS HAVE A LOT OF EXTENUATING CIRCUMSTANCES GOVERNING THEIR LIVES.
どっ
SHUT UP! IT'S NOT FUNNY!
FORGET ABOUT THAT! YOU OWE ME A WISH!
WE WANT TO GO BACK TO OUR ORIGINAL WORLD, BUT--
THAT'S WHAT THE DEMON IS FOR.
NO NO! THE LITTLE JERK IS SLOPPY! HE DOESN'T PAY ATTENTION, AND WE'VE BEEN GETTING ZAPPED TO SOME REALLY MESSED UP PLACES.
EASY FOR YOU TO BLAME A DEMON... IF YOU IGNORE THAT DEMONS ARE MERELY REFLECTIONS OF A PERSON'S HEART.
IF YOU WERE BEING HONEST, YOU'D ADMIT YOU DON'T REALLY WANT TO GO HOME, RIGHT?
THAT'S STUPID! PERFECTLY, SERIOUSLY.

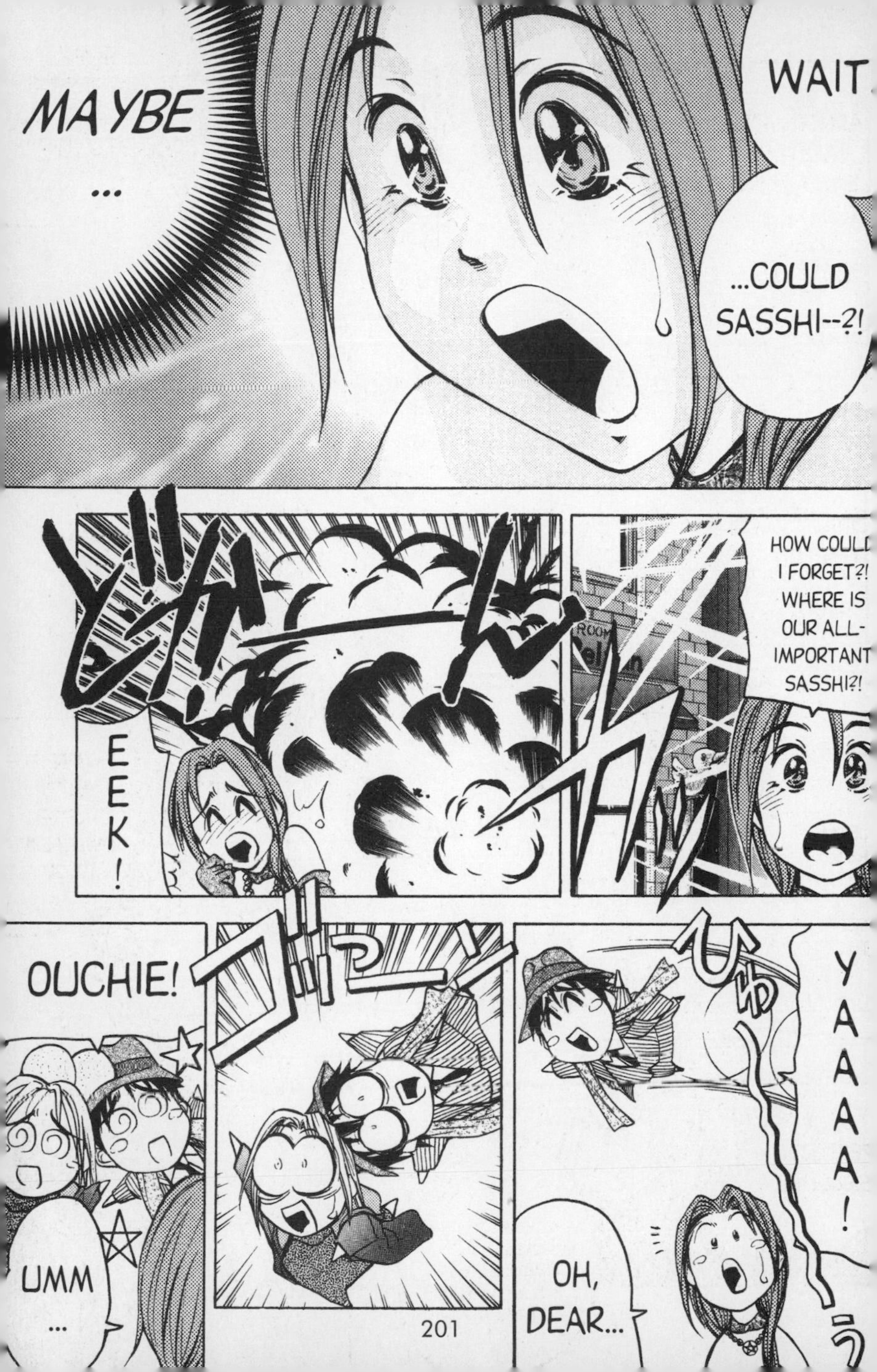
WAIT
MAYBE ...
...COULD SASSHI--?!
HOW COULD I FORGET?! WHERE IS OUR ALL-IMPORTANT SASSHI?!
EEK!
YAAAAA!
OH, DEAR...
OUCHIE!
UMM ...

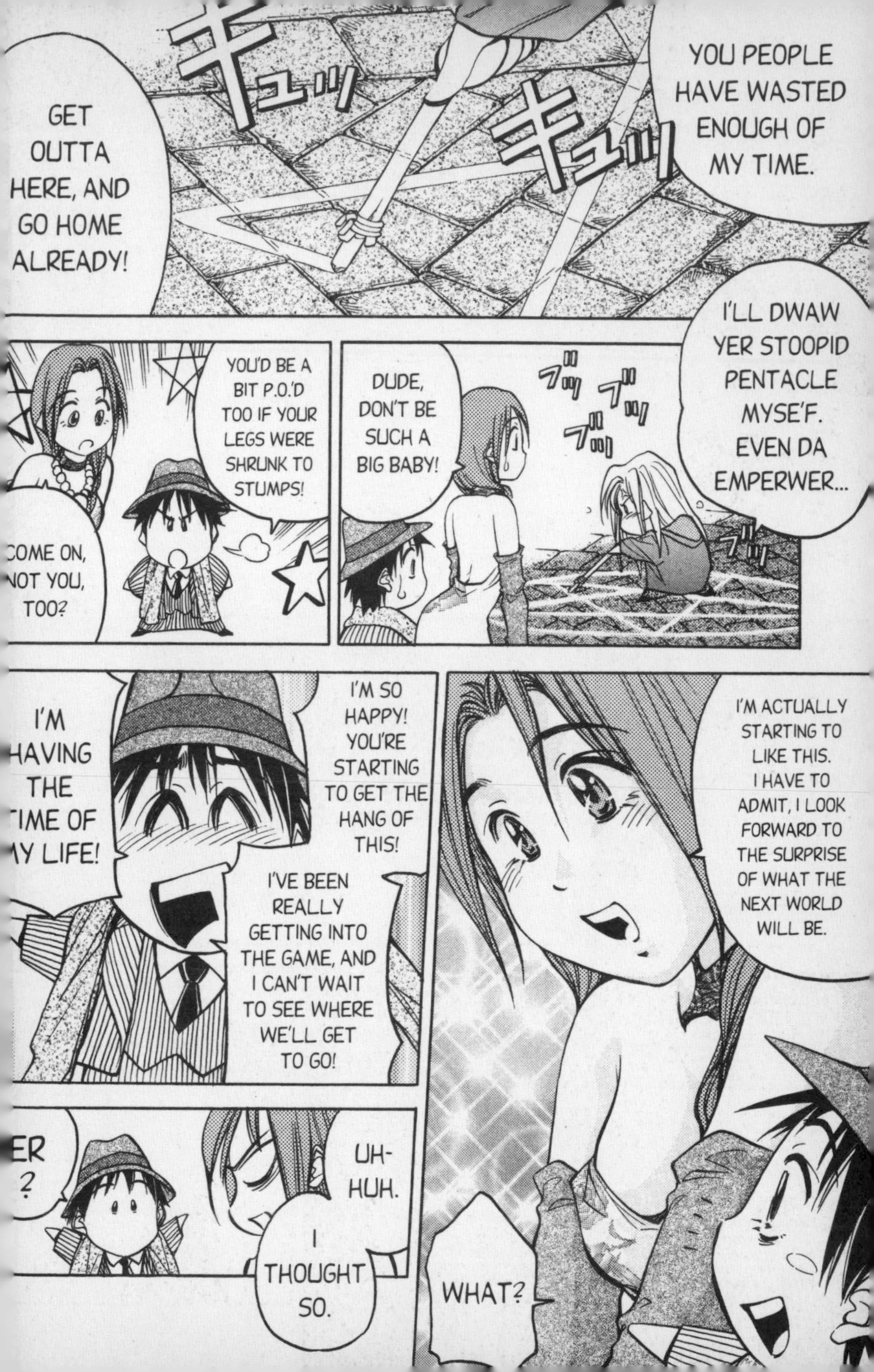

YOU PEOPLE HAVE WASTED ENOUGH OF MY TIME.
キュッ
キュッ
GET OUTTA HERE, AND GO HOME ALREADY!
I'LL DWAW YER STOOPID PENTACLE MYSE'F. EVEN DA EMPERWER...
ブツ ブツ ブツ ブツ
DUDE, DON'T BE SUCH A BIG BABY!
YOU'D BE A BIT P.O.'D TOO IF YOUR LEGS WERE SHRUNK TO STUMPS!
COME ON, NOT YOU, TOO?
I'M ACTUALLY STARTING TO LIKE THIS. I HAVE TO ADMIT, I LOOK FORWARD TO THE SURPRISE OF WHAT THE NEXT WORLD WILL BE.
WHAT?
I'M SO HAPPY! YOU'RE STARTING TO GET THE HANG OF THIS!
I'VE BEEN REALLY GETTING INTO THE GAME, AND I CAN'T WAIT TO SEE WHERE WE'LL GET TO GO!
I'M HAVING THE TIME OF MY LIFE!
UH-HUH.
I THOUGHT SO.
ER ?

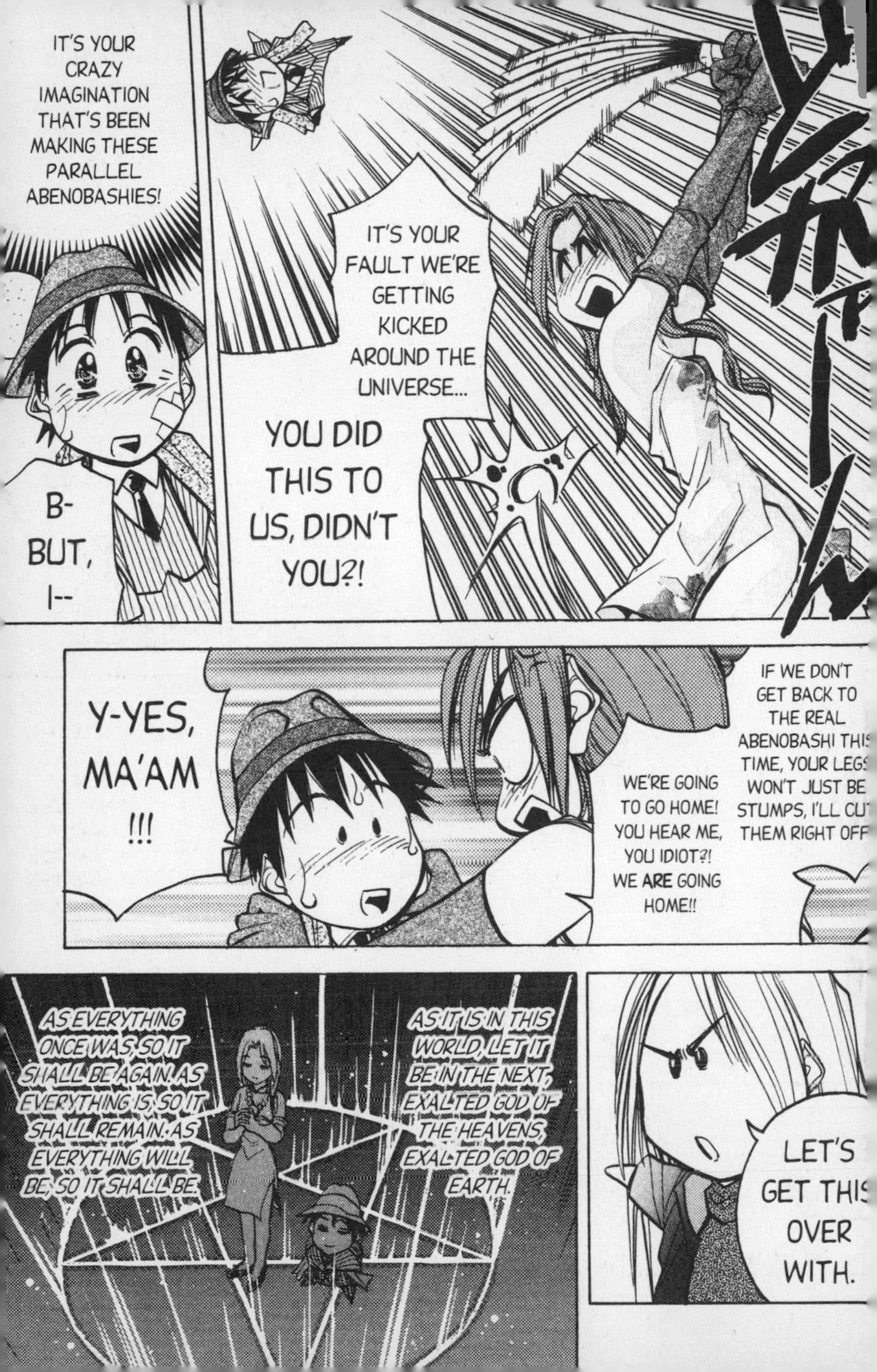
IT'S YOUR FAULT WE'RE GETTING KICKED AROUND THE UNIVERSE...
YOU DID THIS TO US, DIDN'T YOU?!
IT'S YOUR CRAZY IMAGINATION THAT'S BEEN MAKING THESE PARALLEL ABENOBASHIES!
B- BUT, I--
IF WE DON'T GET BACK TO THE REAL ABENOBASHI THIS TIME, YOUR LEGS WON'T JUST BE STUMPS, I'LL CUT THEM RIGHT OFF
WE'RE GOING TO GO HOME! YOU HEAR ME, YOU IDIOT?! WE **ARE** GOING HOME!!
Y-YES, MA'AM !!!
LET'S GET THIS OVER WITH.
AS IT IS IN THIS WORLD, LET IT BE IN THE NEXT, EXALTED GOD OF THE HEAVENS, EXALTED GOD OF EARTH.
AS EVERYTHING ONCE WAS, SO IT SHALL BE AGAIN. AS EVERYTHING IS, SO IT SHALL REMAIN. AS EVERYTHING WILL BE, SO IT SHALL BE.

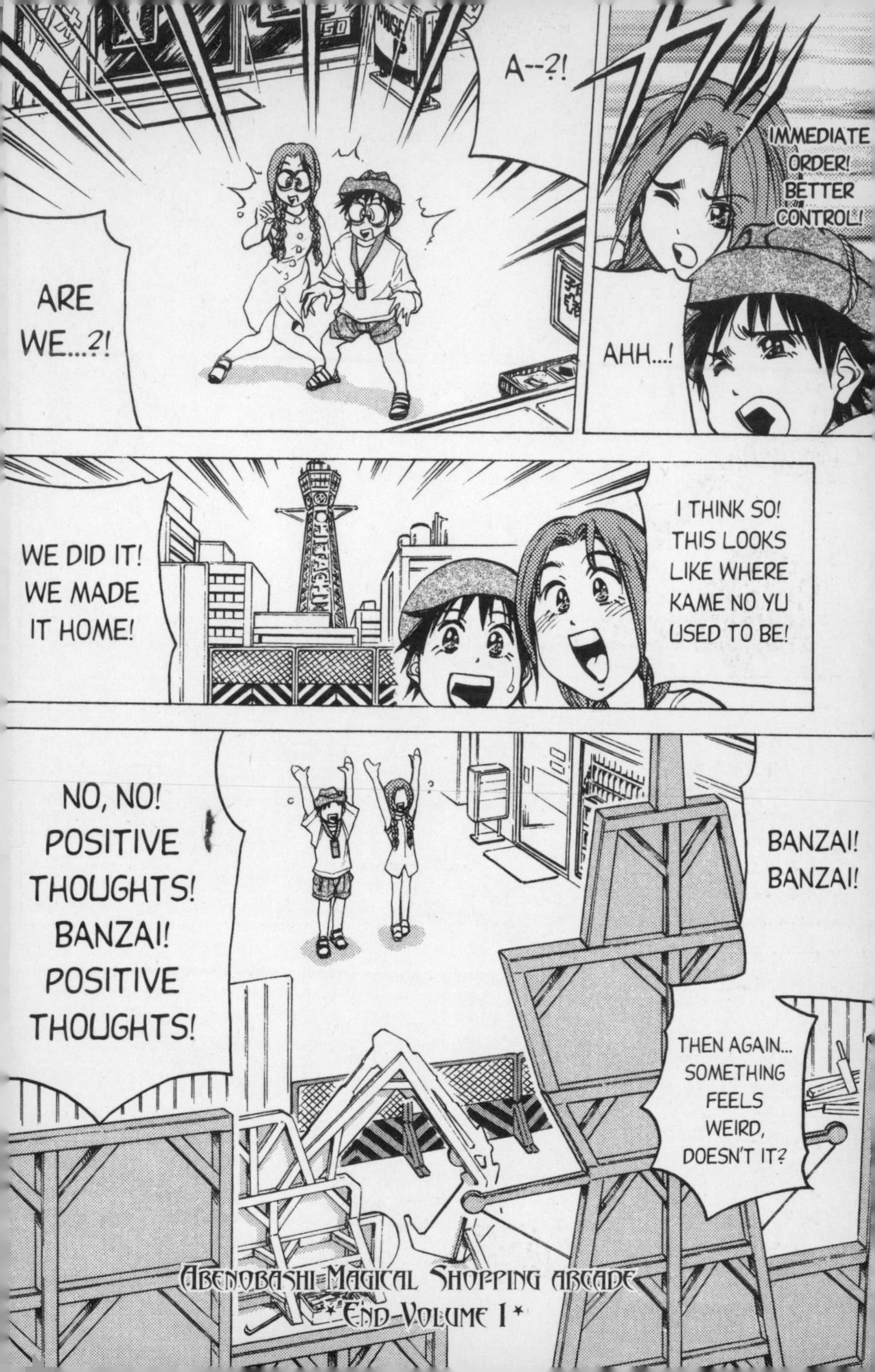
IMMEDIATE ORDER! BETTER CONTROL!
AHH...!
A--?!
ARE WE...?!
I THINK SO! THIS LOOKS LIKE WHERE KAME NO YU USED TO BE!
WE DID IT! WE MADE IT HOME!
BANZAI! BANZAI!
NO, NO! POSITIVE THOUGHTS! BANZAI! POSITIVE THOUGHTS!
THEN AGAIN... SOMETHING FEELS WEIRD, DOESN'T IT?
ABENOBASHI MAGICAL SHOPPING ARCADE
END-VOLUME 1

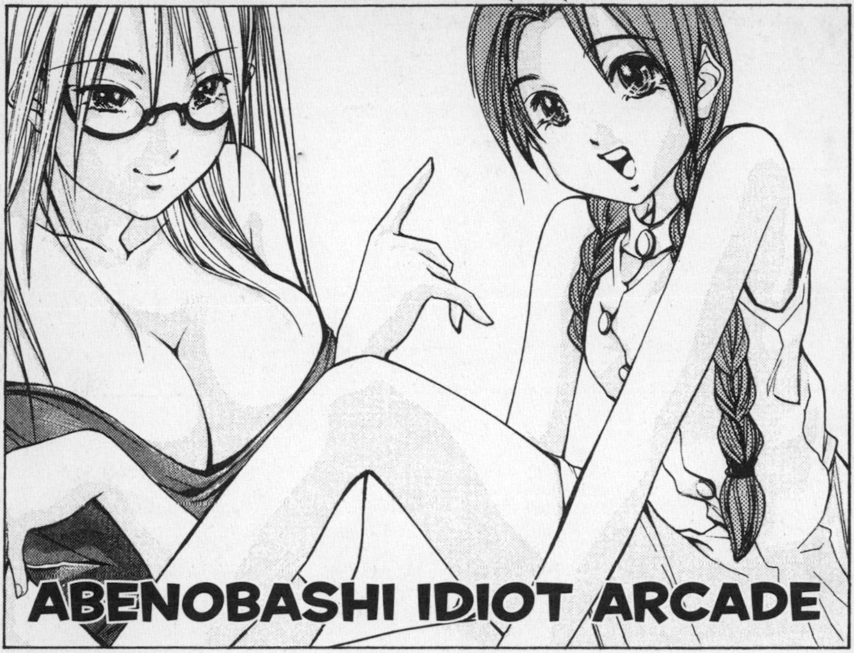
ABENOBASHI IDIOT ARCADE

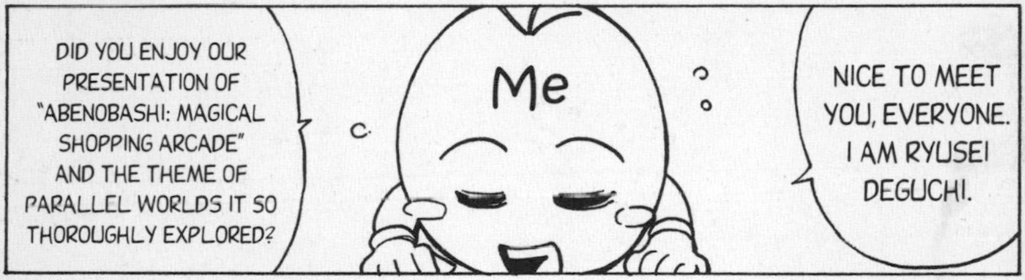
NICE TO MEET YOU, EVERYONE. I AM RYUSEI DEGUCHI.
Me
DID YOU ENJOY OUR PRESENTATION OF "ABENOBASHI: MAGICAL SHOPPING ARCADE" AND THE THEME OF PARALLEL WORLDS IT SO THOROUGHLY EXPLORED?

SOME PEOPLE BELIEVE THAT ART ITSELF SPINS OUT OF A PARALLEL WORLD AND INTO THE ARTISTS' BRAINS, GUIDING THEM THROUGH THE CREATION OF ANIME, NOVELS, AND MANGA STORIES, ALL VARYING ON THE SAME THEME. THOUGH SOME MAY SEEM TO HAVE DIFFERENT APPROACHES, THEY INITIALLY SPRING FROM THE SAME CREATIVE WELL.

THAT WOULD MAKE THIS SCENARIO REAL, DOWN TO THE SMALLEST DETAIL.

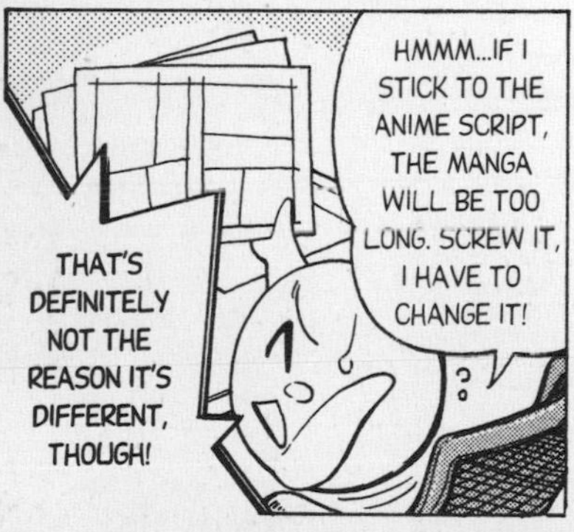
HMMM...IF I STICK TO THE ANIME SCRIPT, THE MANGA WILL BE TOO LONG. SCREW IT, I HAVE TO CHANGE IT!
THAT'S DEFINITELY NOT THE REASON IT'S DIFFERENT, THOUGH!

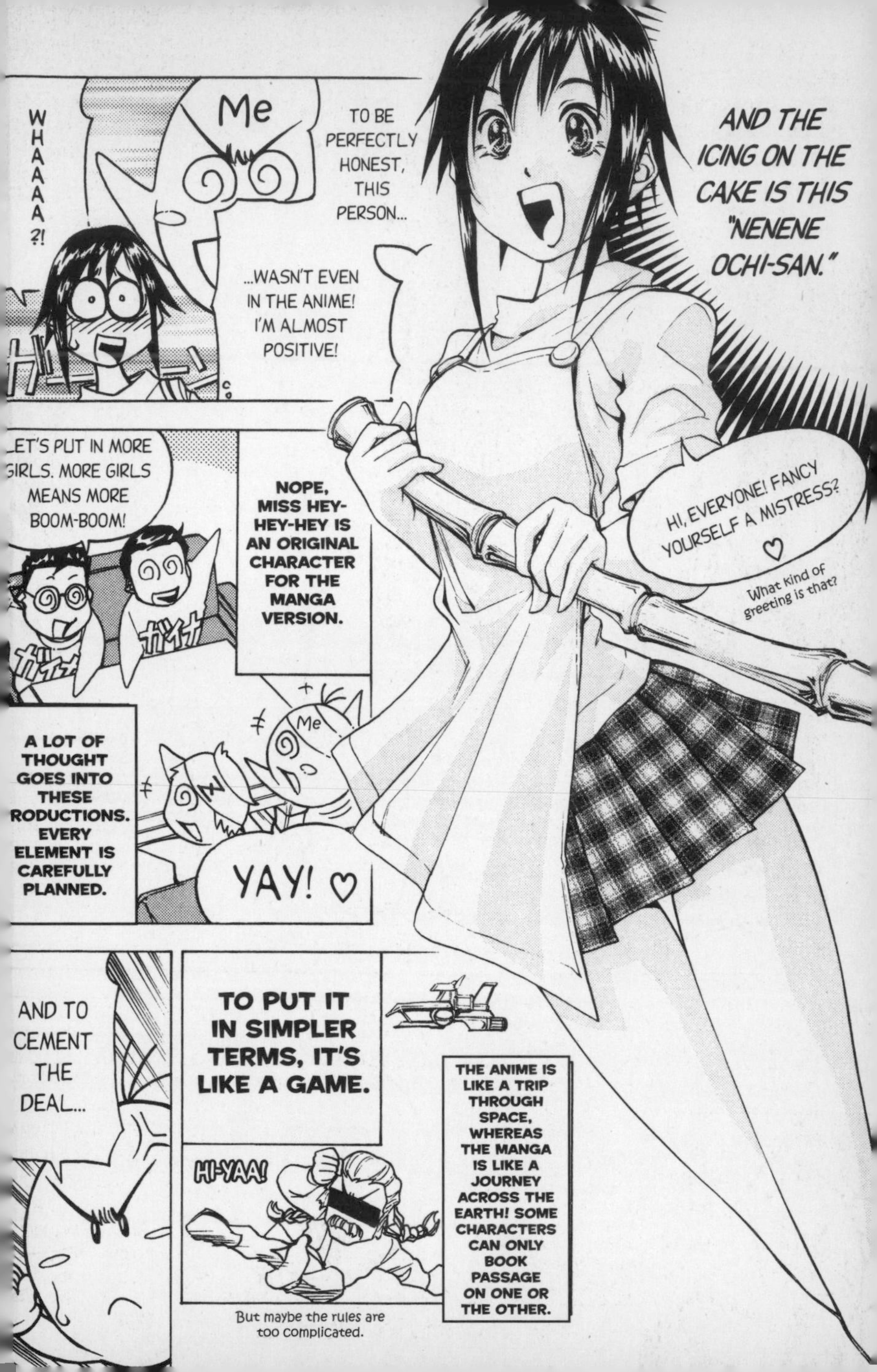
AND THE ICING ON THE CAKE IS THIS "NENENE OCHI-SAN."
HI, EVERYONE! FANCY YOURSELF A MISTRESS? ♡
What kind of greeting is that?
Me
TO BE PERFECTLY HONEST, THIS PERSON...
...WASN'T EVEN IN THE ANIME! I'M ALMOST POSITIVE!
WHAAAAA?!
NOPE, MISS HEY-HEY-HEY IS AN ORIGINAL CHARACTER FOR THE MANGA VERSION.
Me
YAY! ♡
LET'S PUT IN MORE GIRLS. MORE GIRLS MEANS MORE BOOM-BOOM!
A LOT OF THOUGHT GOES INTO THESE RODUCTIONS. EVERY ELEMENT IS CAREFULLY PLANNED.
THE ANIME IS LIKE A TRIP THROUGH SPACE, WHEREAS THE MANGA IS LIKE A JOURNEY ACROSS THE EARTH! SOME CHARACTERS CAN ONLY BOOK PASSAGE ON ONE OR THE OTHER.
TO PUT IT IN SIMPLER TERMS, IT'S LIKE A GAME.
HI-YAA!
But maybe the rules are too complicated.
AND TO CEMENT THE DEAL...

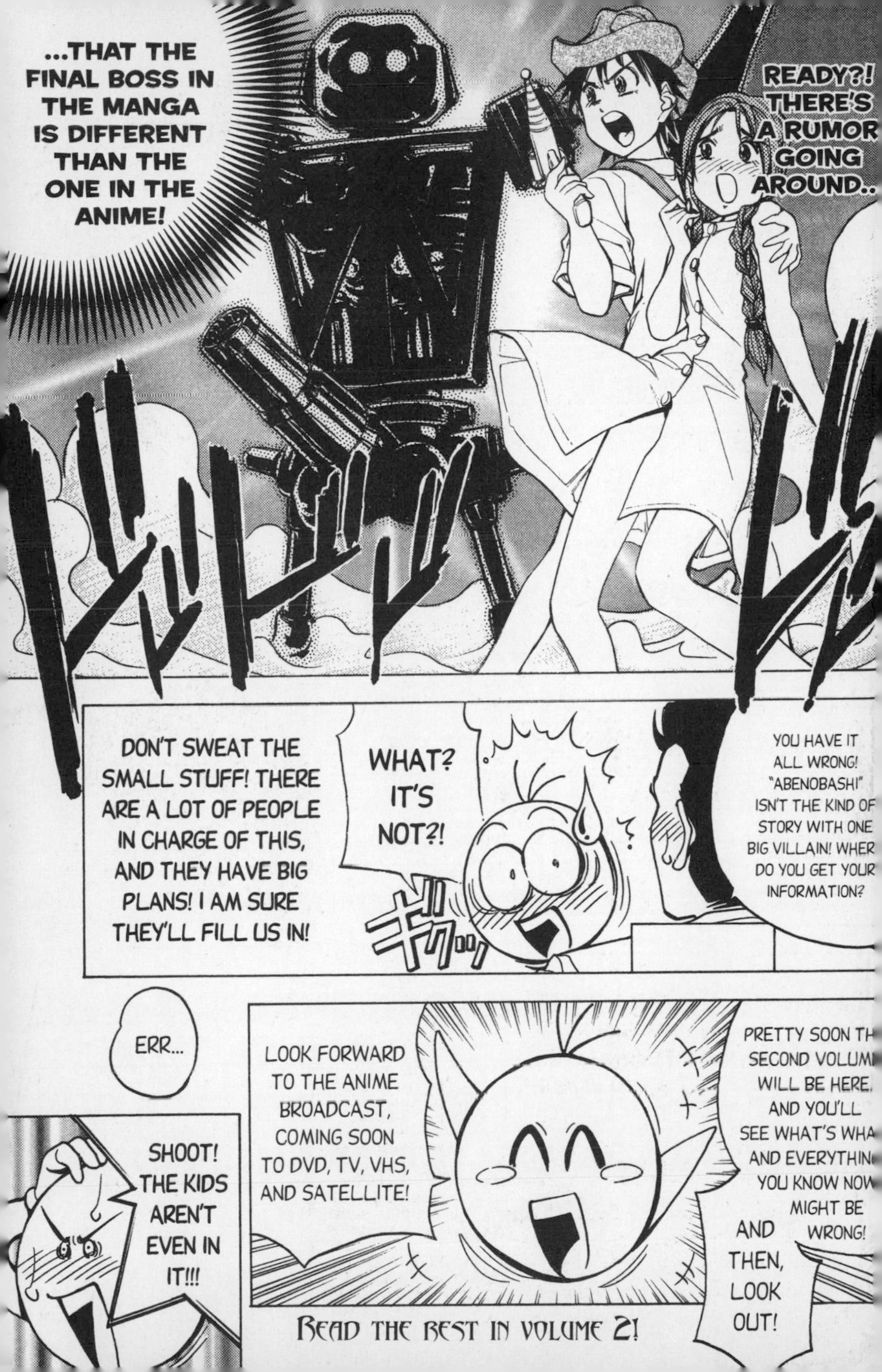
READY?! THERE'S A RUMOR GOING AROUND...
...THAT THE FINAL BOSS IN THE MANGA IS DIFFERENT THAN THE ONE IN THE ANIME!
YOU HAVE IT ALL WRONG! "ABENOBASHI" ISN'T THE KIND OF STORY WITH ONE BIG VILLAIN! WHER DO YOU GET YOUR INFORMATION?
WHAT? IT'S NOT?!
DON'T SWEAT THE SMALL STUFF! THERE ARE A LOT OF PEOPLE IN CHARGE OF THIS, AND THEY HAVE BIG PLANS! I AM SURE THEY'LL FILL US IN!
PRETTY SOON TH SECOND VOLUM WILL BE HERE. AND YOU'LL SEE WHAT'S WHA AND EVERYTHIN YOU KNOW NOW MIGHT BE WRONG!
AND THEN, LOOK OUT!
LOOK FORWARD TO THE ANIME BROADCAST, COMING SOON TO DVD, TV, VHS, AND SATELLITE!
ERR...
SHOOT! THE KIDS AREN'T EVEN IN IT!!!
READ THE REST IN VOLUME 2!

THE DELIRIOUS ADVENTURES OF SASSHI AND ARUMI REACH A FEVER PITCH IN VOLUME 2 AS OUR TWO HEROES TRY TO ESCAPE ABENOBASHI'S FANTASY WORLDS. BUT SASSHI'S IMAGINATION HAS GONE AMUCK, SPIRALING HIM AND THE EVER-VEXED ARUMI FROM ONE ODDBALL FANTASY ADVENTURE TO ANOTHER... INCLUDING A HAIR-RAISING THEME PARK ROLLER-COASTER RIDE, A BIZARRE WORLD OF FORGOTTEN MANGA CHARACTERS, AND A PARALLEL UNIVERSE WHERE THE KIDS FACE MULTIPLE VERSIONS OF THEMSELVES! THIS CONCLUDING VOLUME OF *ABENOBASHI* IS CHOCK-FULL OF HILARIOUS HIJINKS, EYE-POPPING FANTASY AND EVEN *MORE* EYE-POPPING GIRLS AS THE FATE OF OUR FAVORITE MAGICAL SHOPPING ARCADE RESTS IN SASSHI'S RESTLESS IMAGINATION!

POINT YER PEEPERS AT THESE PROVOCATIVE PANELS AND PARTAKE IN SOME PROGNOSTICATED PIECEMEAL PERILS!

B-BUNNY ARCADE?!!

WELCOME, CUSTOMER-SAN.

AKI-NEE! THIS PLACE AIN'T NO GOOD!

DON'T FORGET, SASSHI-CHAN, I'M HERE, TOO! TWO FOR THE PRICE OF ONE!

OKAY, SERIOUSLY, THIS SUCKS!

EEEK! CLAWS!

IT'S A WHOLE UNIVERSE OF MUNE-MUNES?!!

WH-HOOAA!

ABENOBASHI
MAGICAL SHOPPING ARCADE

VOL. 2
AVAILABLE NOVEMBER 2004!

ALSO AVAILABLE FROM TOKYOPOP®

ALSO AVAILABLE FROM  TOKYOPOP®

MANGA

.HACK//LEGEND OF THE TWILIGHT
@LARGE
ABENOBASHI: MAGICAL SHOPPING ARCADE
A.I. LOVE YOU
AI YORI AOSHI
ANGELIC LAYER
ARM OF KANNON
BABY BIRTH
BATTLE ROYALE
BATTLE VIXENS
BRAIN POWERED
BRIGADOON
B'TX
CANDIDATE FOR GODDESS, THE
CARDCAPTOR SAKURA
CARDCAPTOR SAKURA - MASTER OF THE CLOW
CHOBITS
CHRONICLES OF THE CURSED SWORD
CLAMP SCHOOL DETECTIVES
CLOVER
COMIC PARTY
CONFIDENTIAL CONFESSIONS
CORRECTOR YUI
COWBOY BEBOP
COWBOY BEBOP: SHOOTING STAR
CRAZY LOVE STORY
CRESCENT MOON
CROSS
CULDCEPT
CYBORG 009
D•N•ANGEL
DEMON DIARY
DEMON ORORON, THE
DEUS VITAE
DIABOLO
DIGIMON
DIGIMON TAMERS
DIGIMON ZERO TWO
DOLL
DRAGON HUNTER
DRAGON KNIGHTS
DRAGON VOICE
DREAM SAGA
DUKLYON: CLAMP SCHOOL DEFENDERS
EERIE QUEERIE!
ERICA SAKURAZAWA: COLLECTED WORKS
ET CETERA
ETERNITY
EVIL'S RETURN
FAERIES' LANDING
FAKE
FLCL
FLOWER OF THE DEEP SLEEP
FORBIDDEN DANCE
FRUITS BASKET
G GUNDAM

GATEKEEPERS
GETBACKERS
GIRL GOT GAME
GIRLS' EDUCATIONAL CHARTER
GRAVITATION
GTO
GUNDAM BLUE DESTINY
GUNDAM SEED ASTRAY
GUNDAM WING
GUNDAM WING: BATTLEFIELD OF PACIFISTS
GUNDAM WING: ENDLESS WALTZ
GUNDAM WING: THE LAST OUTPOST (G-UNIT)
GUYS' GUIDE TO GIRLS
HANDS OFF!
HAPPY MANIA
HARLEM BEAT
I.N.V.U.
IMMORTAL RAIN
INITIAL D
INSTANT TEEN: JUST ADD NUTS
ISLAND
JING: KING OF BANDITS
JING: KING OF BANDITS - TWILIGHT TALES
JULINE
KARE KANO
KILL ME, KISS ME
KINDAICHI CASE FILES, THE
KING OF HELL
KODOCHA: SANA'S STAGE
LAMENT OF THE LAMB
LEGAL DRUG
LEGEND OF CHUN HYANG, THE
LES BIJOUX
LOVE HINA
LUPIN III
LUPIN III: WORLD'S MOST WANTED
MAGIC KNIGHT RAYEARTH I
MAGIC KNIGHT RAYEARTH II
MAHOROMATIC: AUTOMATIC MAIDEN
MAN OF MANY FACES
MARMALADE BOY
MARS
MARS: HORSE WITH NO NAME
MINK
MIRACLE GIRLS
MIYUKI-CHAN IN WONDERLAND
MODEL
MY LOVE
NECK AND NECK
ONE
ONE I LOVE, THE
PARADISE KISS
PARASYTE
PASSION FRUIT
PEACH GIRL
PEACH GIRL: CHANGE OF HEART
PET SHOP OF HORRORS
PITA-TEN

05.11.04T

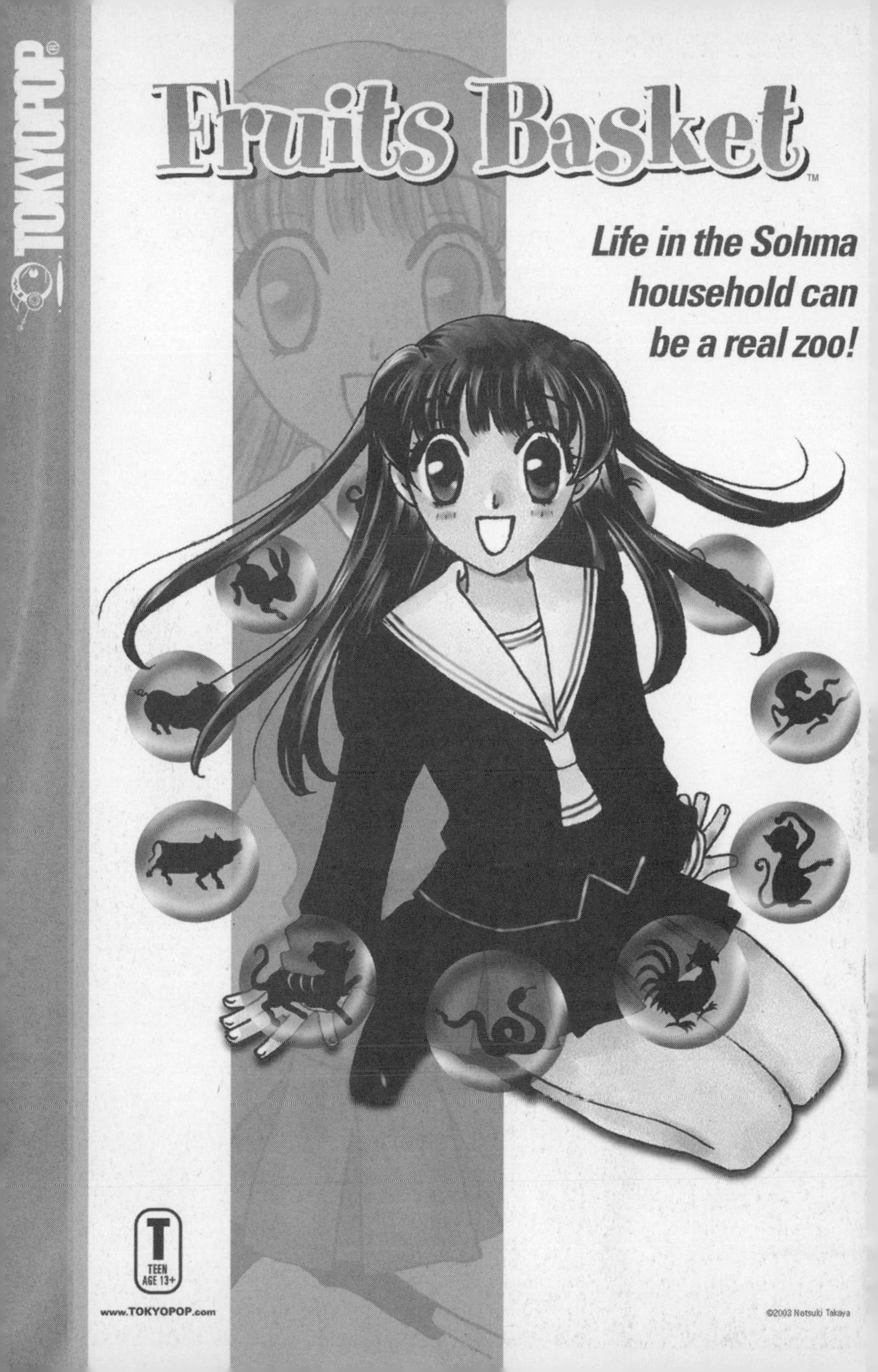
TOKYOPOP
Fruits Basket™
Life in the Sohma household can be a real zoo!
T
TEEN AGE 13+
www.TOKYOPOP.com
©2003 Natsuki Takaya

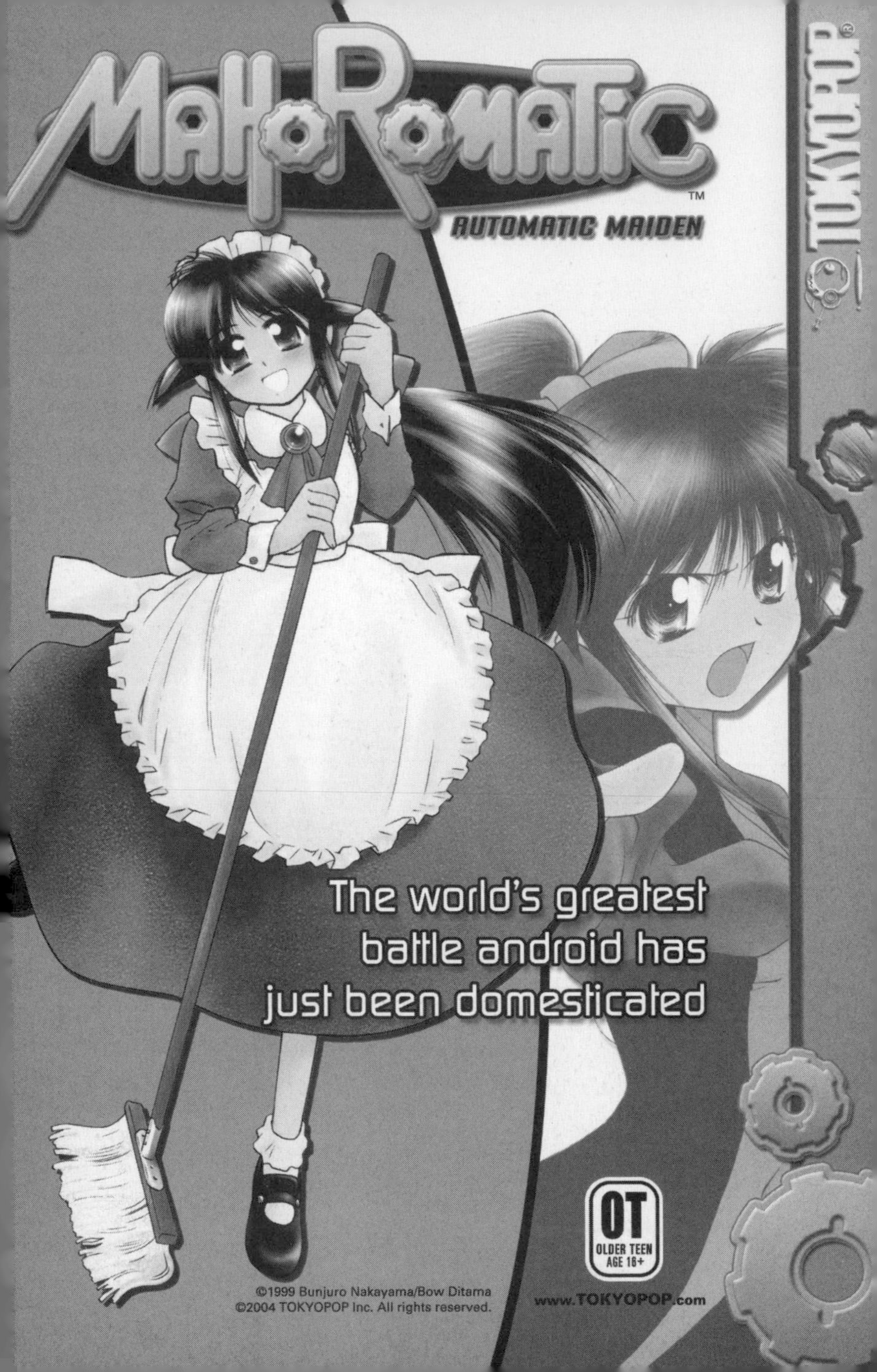
MAHOROMATIC™
AUTOMATIC MAIDEN
TOKYOPOP®
The world's greatest battle android has just been domesticated
OT OLDER TEEN AGE 16+
©1999 Bunjuro Nakayama/Bow Ditama
©2004 TOKYOPOP Inc. All rights reserved.
www.TOKYOPOP.com

STOP!

This is the back of the book.
You wouldn't want to spoil a great ending!

This book is printed "manga-style," in the authentic Japanese right-to-left format. Since none of the artwork has been flipped or altered, readers get to experience the story just as the creator intended. You've been asking for it, so TOKYOPOP® delivered: authentic, hot-off-the-press, and far more fun!

DIRECTIONS

If this is your first time reading manga-style, here's a quick guide to help you understand how it works.

It's easy... just start in the top right panel and follow the numbers. Have fun, and look for more 100% authentic manga from TOKYOPOP®!